CASEBOOK IN CHILD AND ADOLESCENT TREATMENT

Cultural and Familial Contexts

CASEBOOK IN CHILD AND ADOLESCENT TREATMENT

Cultural and Familial Contexts

FAITH McCLURE
*California State University,
San Bernadino*

EDWARD TEYBER
*California State University,
San Bernadino*

THOMSON

BROOKS/COLE

AUSTRALIA • CANADA • MEXICO • SINGAPORE • SPAIN • UNITED KINGDOM • UNITED STATES

THOMSON

BROOKS/COLE

Sponsoring Editor: *Marianne Taflinger, Julie Martinez*
Marketing Team: *Caroline Concilla, Margaret Parks*
Editorial Assistant: *Mike Taylor*
Production Service: *Shepherd Incorporated*
Manuscript Editor: *Francine Banwarth*

Permissions Editor: *Sue Ewing*
Cover Design: *Roger Knox*
Print Buyer: *Vena Dyer*
Typesetting: *Shepherd Incorporated*
Printing and Binding: *Transcontinental, Ltd.*

Library of Congress Cataloging-in-Publication Data

McClure, Faith H.
  Casebook in Child and Adolescent Treatment : Cultural
and Familial Contexts / Faith H. McClure and Edward Teyber.
     p.   cm.
  Includes bibliographical references (p. 280) and index.
  ISBN 0-534-52940-2
    1. Problem children—Counseling of—Case studies.
2. Problem youth—Counseling of—Case studies. 3. Child
psychotherapy—Case studies. 4. Adolescent
psychotherapy—Case studies. 5. Cross-cultural
counseling—Case studies. I. Teyber, Edward. II. Title.
HV713 .M36 2003
362.74'86—dc21

                                            2001056843

For those committed to helping children

Also by Edward Teyber

Interpersonal Process in Psychotherapy: A Relational Approach, 4/e
and
Helping Children Cope with Divorce

CONTENTS

CHAPTER 8

**Elizabeth: An Asian American Adolescent Resolving
Rape Trauma**   157

CHAPTER 9

**Sam: Developing Resilience in Group Therapy as He Copes
with Abandonment by Drug Abusing Parents**   180

CHAPTER 10

Brian: Recovering From the Foster Parent System with Conduct Disorder   210

CHAPTER 11

Linda: A Depressed Third-Culture Kid Clarifying Spiritual Values   241

PREFACE

This casebook is written for counselors-in-training in an effort to increase their understanding of the complex problems young people often face and ways in which they can best be helped. The problems addressed here are ones that are regularly presented by the children and adolescents in schools, day-care settings, outpatient treatment centers, medical facilities, and group homes. These problems include attention deficit/ hyperactivity disorder, a range of anxiety disorders, depression, and aggressive, antisocial behaviors. In addition, many children and adolescents are faced with parental divorce, violence or drugs in their families or neighborhoods, sexual abuse, or may be struggling with eating disorders.

In this casebook we address:

1. the etiology or causes of the most common problems or disorders seen in children and adolescents;
2. their defining symptoms and characteristics; and most importantly
3. how these problems can be addressed and resolved in treatment.

Rather than just defining and describing child and adolescent problems, we try to teach about them by illustrating them and bringing them to life. Each chapter provides an indepth case study with extensive client information and counselor-client dialogues in an effort to help the reader "make sense" of each child or adolescent. We want to bring the reader in on the counseling process in the hope that the reader will feel as though he/she is in the room with the counselor and the client. Although the first part of each case study describes the symptoms and characteristics of the disorder, this book is not about diagnostic entities or categories—it is about the person. Our first goal is to help each reader see the child or adolescent within the disorder—rather than just learning about treatment approaches for young people with bulimia or borderline personality disorder.

Our second goal is to highlight how the issues of race, class, religion, and other cultural factors shape both the symptoms and strengths that young people develop. In each chapter, the case study presented highlights the central role of culture in shaping the child or adolescent's experiences. We believe that cultural experiences (race, religion, socioeconomic status, etc.) are *significant* dimensions of people's lives that must be incorporated into the treatment process. Individual and familial experiences are embedded within a cultural context. To fail to recognize culture's role in contributing to each child's uniqueness would be failing to honor *all* that each child is. In this book, we highlight how culture shapes each child's experience and emphasize the importance of responding to children and adolescents within their cultural context.

The third goal of this casebook is to address the ambiguity that often surrounds the treatment process and help readers see how counseling works and understand how change occurs. In each of the case studies that follow, a different counselor is working with a child or adolescent who is coping with a common psychological symptom or disorder. The central role of culture in shaping the child's experiences is highlighted. The counselor in each case utilizes techniques and interventions from different theoretical orientations: cognitive-behavioral, interpersonal/dynamic, family systems, behavior modification, parent education, and other approaches. In addition, the cases include interventions with parents (e.g., working on parent-child communication, strengthening the couple's marital relationship, clarifying intergenerational boundaries), group counseling, and the use of community resources such as sports and church. Although counselors are drawing flexibly from each of these treatment approaches, you will see that there is a unifying theme throughout each case study: *the relationship between the counselor and the client.* In every case, the different counselors share the same three treatment goals. First, they are trying to establish trust and create interpersonal safety for the client. Second, they are highly empathic and repeatedly try to understand the client's personal experience and make sense of the issues *from the client's point of view.* Third, they are trying to recognize interpersonal patterns cognitive schemas and relational templates in order to understand how the client has been treated by important people in his/her life and how the client views the world. In treatment, the counselor tries to create a relationship with the child that is different from the problematic patterns the child has been experiencing with others, so the child can be empowered to:

1. let go of the faulty beliefs that have grown out of their negative life experiences;
2. develop more flexible coping styles; and
3. become better able to make healthier choices for their lives.

Finally, each chapter follows the same format and is divided into three parts. In the first part, the symptom or problem (e.g., depression) is described and the reader learns about the multiple causes and defining symptoms of the disorder. Next, a comprehensive and indepth case study is provided that brings the reader in on the counselors' thinking so the counselors' questions, concerns, and why they chose to respond the way they did can be understood. Following each case study, two study aids are provided: (1) Suggestions for Further Reading and (2) Questions for Thought and Discussion. At the end of the book are two appendices: (1) to help counselors-in-training begin to understand their own interpersonal style when interacting with clients; and (2) to help counselors-in-training become alert to their own countertransference propensities when interacting with clients.

We hope our readers will take from these cases useful information that can be applied to their lives and their work.

Faith McClure
Edward Teyber

ACKNOWLEDGMENTS

Writing and producing a book is a team effort and we have had the privilege of working with a wonderful group of professionals. Most importantly, we were very fortunate to have Marianne Taflinger as our guide throughout the writing, reviewing, editing, and production process. Her practical manner and patience were highly reassuring, and her good friendship always prized. We are also grateful to other members of our team including Julie Martinez, Mike Taylor, Caroline Concilla, Margaret Parks, Roger Knox, Mary Anne Shahidi, Peggy Francomb, Vernon Boes, Samantha Cabaluna, Sue Ewing, and Kathleen Morgan for their assistance. Their thoroughness and attention to detail made completing and launching this book so much more manageable.

We are also indebted to the many reviewers of this book, whose insightful comments and suggestions greatly enriched the final product: Susan Anzivino, University of Maine at Farmington; Gordon Atlas, Alfred University; Debora Bell-Dolan, University of Missouri–Columbia; Rebecca Bigler, University of Texas at Austin; Michael J. Bologna, College of Saint Rose; Irene R. Bush, Monmouth University; Connie Callahan, East Kentucky University; Brecky Church, Northeastern Illinois University; June Clausen, University of San Francisco; Jon Ellis, East Tennessee University; Robert Hampson, Southern Methodist University; Norma Jones, Howard University; Kathleen Minke, University of Delaware; Fred Stickle, Western Kentucky University; Mary Stinson, Jacksonville State University; Denise Worth, California State University–Chico.

Our colleague and friend, Margaret Doods-Schumaker, graciously filled the role of "unofficial" reviewer and editor and made significant contributions to our thinking and writing of this book. We also appreciate Dr. Stanley Sue's support for this work.

The quality of this book was greatly enhanced by the generous contributions of the counselors in the cases presented: David Chavez, Barbara Graf, Cassandra Nichols, John Powell, Dawn Terrell, Sandy Tsuneyoshi, Nancy Wolfe, and Anthony Zamudio.

Finally, and most importantly, we are grateful to our families for their patience and consistent support. They inspire and challenge us to live in the authentic and emotionally responsive ways we write about.

ABOUT THE AUTHORS

Faith H. McClure, Ph.D.

Dr. McClure is a Professor in the Psychology Department at California State University, San Bernardino. She grew up in South Africa during apartheid. Dr. McClure received her Ph.D. in Clinical Psychology from the University of California, Los Angeles. Her counseling and research work focuses on children, families, and adults, with a particular focus on factors that promote resilience in those who have experienced trauma. She has provided consultation and training to organizations serving the mental health needs of children and their families both in the United States and overseas. Her publications are in the areas of sexual abuse, substance abuse, and variables that affect treatment outcome. She is co-producer with Dr. Teyber of *Challenging Therapeutic Interventions: A Student Training Video.*

Edward Teyber, Ph.D.

Dr. Teyber is a Professor of Psychology and Director of the Psychology Clinic at California State University, San Bernardino. He is also the author of *Helping Children Cope with Divorce* and of *Interpersonal Process in Psychotherapy: A Relational Approach.* He is co-producer with Dr. McClure of *Challenging Therapeutic Interventions: A Student Training Video.* He has published research articles on the effects of marital and family relations on child adjustment, and contributed popular press articles on parenting and post-divorce family relations to newspapers and magazines. Dr. Teyber is interested in supervision and training and maintains a clinical practice.

HELPING OUR CHILDREN AND ADOLESCENTS

CHAPTER 1

INTRODUCTION AND OVERVIEW

We wrote this casebook to teach you as you begin your counseling career how you can better help young people with their problems. As practicum and intern students many of you are just beginning to see your first clients in schools, clinics, and community agency settings—embarking on the deeply rewarding enterprise of clinical practice. However, as graduate student counselors you are likely finding how challenging it can be to help with the complex problems that children and adolescents present. Maybe some of you have asked your instructors, "How do I deal with these difficult cases I'm seeing?" We realize that most of you are highly motivated to learn how to better understand and intervene with the serious problems you often face when working with children and adolescents and need practical guidelines that can provide help for the clients you are treating right now. We wrote this book to help you become more effective in your efforts to improve the lives of young people. We want to increase your understanding of the problems children and adolescents face and ways they can best be helped. The case studies in this book outline an effective, integrated, and practical approach for reaching troubled young people and their families and assisting them to make positive changes. Regardless of the clinical setting where you are training, the problems described here are ones you will likely see. These problems include attention deficit/hyperactivity disorder, a range of anxiety disorders, depression, and aggressive, antisocial behaviors. In addition, most of you will be working with children or adolescents who are coping with parental divorce, with violence in their families or neighborhoods, are struggling with eating disorders, or have been victims of sexual abuse.

How do these problems develop? Are there defining features or characteristics that children and adolescents exhibit that we should be alert for? What can counselors do to help children and adolescents cope better with these problems? What is the course of treatment and how does change come about?

This casebook will address these questions and help you understand the following:

1. the etiology or cause of the most common problems or disorders seen in children and adolescents;
2. their defining symptoms and characteristics; and
3. most importantly, how these problems can be addressed and resolved in treatment.

Rather than just defining and describing child and adolescent problems, we will try to teach you about the problems by illustrating them and bringing the treatment process to life for you. Each chapter provides an in-depth case study that highlights the most commonly occurring symptoms or problems that children and adolescents bring to social workers, school counselors, and psychologists. Our hope is that each case study will illuminate how problems develop and how they can be addressed. We want you to be able to "make sense" of each child or adolescent problem, understand why and how it developed, and grasp more fully how children and adolescents can be helped. Through extensive case vignettes and counselor-client dialogues, we want you to see what the counseling process is really like. As you read each of the 10 case studies that follow, our hope is that you will feel as though you are in the room with the counselor and the client. Although the first part of each case study describes the symptoms and characteristics of the disorder, this book is not about diagnostic entities or categories—it is about the person. Our first goal is to help each of you see the child or adolescent within the disorder—rather than just learn about young people with bulimia, borderline personality disorder, or separation anxiety disorder.

Our second goal is to highlight how the issues of race, class, religion, and other cultural factors shape both the symptoms and the strengths that young people develop. In each chapter, the case study presented highlights how culture influences the child's or adolescent's experiences. Some would argue that, since we are all human beings, we are basically all the same and cultural influences don't really matter. We disagree, however, and believe this description, which characterized the field of psychology for decades, fails to capture the richness of each person—a richness that is influenced in significant ways by their familial and cultural history. To illustrate, consider *fabric*. Fabric comes in varying colors, textures, and sizes. While silk, rayon, cotton, and corduroy are all fabric, they are also all different from each other. Their weave, texture, and colors make each piece of fabric unique. The term fabric, while accurate, fails to capture the distinctive magnificence of each piece. In much the same way, to say we are all basically human and therefore the same is only partially accurate. It fails to capture the richness and variation seen in children and adolescents based on their familial and cultural experiences (e.g., gender, geographic origins, race, religion, socioeconomic status). It is important to recognize that culture provides the context in which individual and familial experiences are embedded, shaping the individual's experiences and presentation. Thus, in the same way that different types of fabric have richly varying features yet are still fabric, children of different cultural backgrounds are both similar to and different from each other. To fail to recognize culture's role in contributing to each child's uniqueness would be failing to honor *all* that each child is.

In this book, we highlight how culture shapes each child's experience and we emphasize the importance of responding to children and adolescents within their cultural and familial context.

Working with their first clients, beginning counselors experience firsthand the serious problems that many young people are coping with and often are deeply touched by the pain children are suffering. At the same time, many feel painfully inadequate to help as they are faced with the complexity of many clients' problems, the ambiguities of the treatment process, and the uncertainty of how to help ("What do I do?"). Thus the third goal of this casebook is to clarify the treatment process and help readers understand or "see" how counseling works and change occurs. We will do this by clarifying how the client-counselor relationship can be used to assess clients' problems, formulate treatment plans, and guide intervention strategies. Each of these diverse case studies will illustrate how counselors can systematically utilize the client-counselor relationship as the focal point for effecting change.

In each of the comprehensive case studies that follow, a different counselor is working with a child or adolescent who is coping with a common psychological problem or disorder. The central role of culture and family both in shaping the child's experiences, and in solving the child's problems, is highlighted. The counselor in each case utilizes techniques and interventions from different theoretical orientations: cognitive behavioral, interpersonal/dynamic, family systems, narrative, behavior modification, parent education, and other approaches. The counselor operates using an "assimilative integration" model in which (1) the belief is that the client and counselor relationship, and the interaction or process that transpires between them, is the foundation on which change is built; (2) treatment goals and interventions take into account the clients' personal, familial, and cultural history so that values arising from that history are treated with respect; and (3) techniques from all theoretical orientations may be incorporated provided they support the specific process or relational experiences the counselor is trying to provide for this particular client. In many cases you will see that counselors are conceptualizing their young clients' problems from a family systems or attachment theory perspective—for example, while intervening with behavioral, cognitive, or educational techniques (see Stricker & Gold, 1996; Wachtel, 1991, for excellent models of this integrative approach).

Although counselors are drawing flexibly from each of these theories, *the relationship between the counselor and the client provides the unifying theme for this treatment approach* (see Blatt, Sanislow, Zuroff, & Pilkonis, 1996; Gelso & Carter, 1994; Sexton & Whiston, 1994 for informative research reviews). Throughout each case study, the counselors are systematically using the relationships they establish with their young clients to facilitate change. More specifically, the different counselors share the same three treatment goals in every case. First, they are trying to establish trust and create interpersonal safety for the client (Kahn, 1997; Weiss, 1993). Second, counselors are striving to be accurately empathic. To provide this, they must have the personal flexibility to de-center from their own perspective, enter the client's subjective worldview, and make sense of the issues from the client's point of view. The counselors repeatedly invite the client to engage in a process of *mutual exploration* that is characterized by active negotiation between counselor and client. This type of collaborative effort is needed in order to give clients the crucial experience of being understood (Barkham & Shapiro, 1986). Third, counselors are trying to recognize *interpersonal patterns* (Strupp & Binder, 1984) and understand how clients are being treated by important people in their lives (e.g., have others been overly controlling or demanding, been emotionally unavailable, provided too little discipline or predictability, and so forth?). These interpersonal themes, which recur throughout the client's life, are central to her problems and provide an organizing focus for treatment.

In this treatment approach, *the counselor's overarching goal is to create a relationship with the child that is different from the problematic patterns the child has been experiencing with others* (Alexander & French, 1980). For beginning and experienced counselors alike, this cardinal concept is far easier to say or comprehend intellectually than it is to enact or actually provide with clients. In the case studies that follow, the counselor is trying to find the most effective way to communicate to this child that he or she is worth being cared about (when this child has not felt cared about before by the significant others in his or her life); that mistakes can be made and recovered from (when this child has learned in other important relationships that he or she has to be perfect in order to win affection, earn approval, or feel safe); or that discipline can be enforced in a fair and caring way (when it has been arbitrary or discriminatory in other significant relationships). This new response from the counselor, which is different from what the client expects and has been experiencing with others, is an *experiential relearning* that is often a pivotal step in the change process. Breaking the unwanted or problematic interpersonal pattern with the counselor is an "in-vivo" experience of change (Bandura, 1997). Following this experiential relearning in the relationship with the counselor, the counselors can then begin helping clients to generalize this experience to other relationships. That is, the client can learn that at least sometimes relationships can be different and better. The reparative relationship with the counselor becomes a springboard from which clients can begin to make related changes with others in their current lives. Let's talk through what this process of change looks like. In the case studies ahead, you will see that clients change when counselors and clients collaboratively:

1. identify the pathogenic beliefs, faulty expectations, and disruptive interpersonal patterns that have been occurring for the client with others;
2. change these problematic beliefs, expectations, and interactional patterns in the counselor-client relationship and ensure they are not reoccurring between them;
3. generalize the client's new and more effective way of relating so that it occurs with classmates, parents, teachers, siblings, and others in their current lives.

How do clients develop this new and more effective way of relating? Based on the more affirming experiences with their counselors, clients are more able to:

1. let go of the faulty beliefs that have grown out of their previous negative life experiences (e.g., I don't matter, it's my fault, others will betray me or leave if I risk getting close);
2. develop more flexible coping styles (e.g., use words rather than act or hit, seek others who will listen or can be affirming, listen to music, hit a tennis ball); and
3. become empowered to make better choices for their lives (e.g., I can set limits and say no, make friends and ask others for help when I have problems and need them, or succeed even though my parent cannot).

In sum, many different theories and techniques will be utilized in these case studies. Rather than drawing on just one counseling theory, such as cognitive-behavioral or psychodynamic, this approach uses the counseling relationship as an integrating focus for treatment. Further, the cases include interventions with parents (e.g., working on parent-child communication, strengthening the couple's marital relationship), group counseling, and the use of community resources such as sports and the Church. In each case, however, you will see that it is the corrective or reparative relationship between the counselor and client that is central to change—not just techniques or theories. This orienting concept that, across differing theoretical orientations, the client-counselor relationship is central in facilitating treatment effectiveness, is supported by a large and growing body of literature (see Horvath & Symonds, 1991; Marziali & Alexander, 1991; Teyber & McClure, 2000). The cases that follow illustrate that it is in the context of a strong therapeutic alliance between client and counselor, built on empathic understanding, that the client will:

1. experience increasing hope for change;
2. be more willing to confront rather than avoid his problems;
3. begin to reappraise the faulty beliefs and problematic expectations that are contributing to his symptoms and problems;
4. begin to change maladaptive interpersonal patterns and to try out more effective coping strategies with others in his life; and, as a result,
5. begin to develop a greater sense of self-efficacy.

In this way, the relationship between client and counselor is the central fulcrum that helps clients change. Contemporary researchers are increasingly documenting the significance of these factors in accounting for change in treatment with all treatment approaches (Frank & Frank, 1991; Snyder et al., 2000; Weinberger, 1995). Counseling theories are sometimes polarized into two competing theories of change. Whereas dynamically oriented theories posit that insight leads to behavior change, behaviorally oriented theories argue that self-awareness and insight often follow from behavior change. Although we find that both of these mechanisms of change occur, a third or additional process of change is emphasized here. Across the differing theoretical orientations of the counselor, we find that behavior change usually occurs first in the relationship with the counselor—as they begin to enact new and more adaptive interpersonal patterns in their relationship. Following this real-life experience of change with the counselor, effective counselors working within varying theoretical orientations, can then help the client generalize these more effective ways of relating to others in the client's life (Teyber, 2000).

As you see the counselors in the cases that follow illustrate these same treatment goals and processes with diverse children and problems, you will gradually find that you are able to frame children's problems in these helpful ways. Not at first, perhaps, because these can be personally challenging and complex concepts to apply. However, with a little time and patience, you will see that you can make these concepts work for you in your own counseling. As authors, helping you understand and translate these constructs into practice is our primary goal.

Finally, each chapter follows the same format and is divided into three parts. In the first part, the syndrome or problem (e.g., depression) is described and the reader learns about the multiple causes and defining symptoms of each disorder. Next, a thorough case study is provided that brings you, the reader, in on the counselors' thinking so that the counselors' questions, concerns, and rationale for why they chose to respond the way they did can be understood. Following each of these ten intensive case studies, two study aids are provided. First, "Suggestions for Further Reading" provide interesting articles and books that readers can explore to learn more about treating each disorder. The second study aid for each chapter is "Questions for Thought and Discussion." We hope you take the time to look over these questions, consider how they might apply to your life and your work, and even write out answers to the questions posed. Finally, for those of you seeking further learning experiences, we have also provided two appendices with the following learning tools:

- A questionnaire that will help you clarify your own personal reactions (counter-transference) to clients you work with, reactions that may sometimes get in the way of being an effective helper and, at other times, may help you understand your client and how others in your client's life may react to or feel about them
- A self-assessment questionnaire that will help you evaluate your own interpersonal process skills, the same intervention skills which the counselors will be illustrating in each case study

CORE CONCEPTS

As you read the case studies that follow, the interventions and treatment may seem easy for the counselor sometimes, but you may find that they are not so easy for you at this early stage in your training. It is important to keep in mind that these counselors are experts who have worked for years with many clients with similar problems. It also helps to be able to understand the guiding principles that these counselors are applying over and over again in their work with clients. We want to take the mystery out of the treatment process and help you learn how to work in these ways too. Thus, throughout the case studies that follow, you will see how each counselor repeatedly applies three core concepts in order to provide an integrating focus for treatment. In each of the case studies that follow, the counselors' interventions and responses to their clients are based on three orienting constructs: (1) subjective worldview; (2) client response specificity; and (3) reparative relational experiences. Let's examine each so that you will be able to recognize them in the case studies ahead and understand what the counselor is doing and why.

Subjective Worldview

The first core construct is *subjective worldview*—how the client views something and what is salient or holds meaning for him or her (see Sue & Sue, 1999, for a discussion of some of the factors that contribute to worldviews). Existential therapists have called this notion "existential reality" (King & Citrenbaum, 1993), further highlighting that this refers to *the client's reality, the client's perspective or point of view, and the client's subjective experience.* Within this construct, the counselor's ability to be flexible enough to cognitively de-center and emotionally enter the client's highly personal, uniquely subjective experience, which often differs greatly from the counselor's, is a core intervention skill for effective counselors. Authors from many different theoretical orientations have written elegantly about this construct, which involves having accurate empathy for the client's perspective and experience (Jordan, 1991; Kahn, 1997; Rogers, 1951; Stolorow, 2000; and others). Although it is easy to talk about accurate empathy, we have found that few counseling trainees are able to provide this to clients *consistently*. While emotional presence and empathic understanding can be deceptively easy to describe, it is a highly challenging, complex skill that takes years of focused training to develop and a great deal of supervisory feedback to provide with a wide range of diverse clients.

When the counselor can consistently enter the client's subjective worldview and distill the core meaning or grasp the emotional message in what the client has just said, the counselor has achieved credibility. Sue and Zane (1987) have suggested the concept of *credibility* as an organizing construct for providing meaningful and culturally sensitive interventions. According to their description, *ascribed credibility* is assigned by clients, to their counselor, based on counselor characteristics such as title, educational qualifications, age, race, gender, and so forth. For example, being an African American counseling psychologist is an ascribed role based on external, identifiable criteria. Ascribed credibility seems to be more important to clients in the initial phase of counseling. That is, some clients may be more willing to come to counseling initially because the counselor possesses specific characteristics that are important to them (e.g., the counselor is mixed race and female, as is the client). Thus, it is at this initial phase of treatment that cultural match or fit (e.g., similarity in race, gender, religious affiliation, age, sexual orientation, and so forth) may be highly valued.

In contrast, *achieved credibility* results more directly from the counselors' skills and the effectiveness of their interventions. It becomes more salient or significant beyond the initial phase and impacts whether the client continues in treatment and ultimately makes progress (Sue & Zane, 1987). Thus, achieved credibility is an outcome of the counselors' sensitivity and skill. More specifically, it is related to the manner in which (1) the counselor and client *jointly* formulate with the client a meaningful conceptualization of the problems to be addressed that is congruent with the client's subjective worldview and sociocultural context; (2) the client feels *ownership* of (and thus is committed to) clearly defined treatment goals that are compatible with the client's familial and cultural value system; and (3) the process or interaction that transpires between counselor and client *resolves rather than reenacts* (subtly or thematically repeats) the client's maladaptive relational patterns in a manner that is culturally acceptable and compatible. For example, when the interaction between counselor and client conveys respect, and this adolescent client often has not felt respected by authority figures in the past, the counselor's respect takes on additional meaning. That is, the experience of being respected may empower the client to feel better about himself, be more assertive, and interact in more meaningful and appropriate ways with others.

With the construct of achieved credibility the focus is not on culture or culturally specific techniques per se. Instead, it is on the counselor's ability to achieve credibility by consistently entering the client's subjective worldview with accuracy, empathy, and affirmation. In order to accurately enter the client's subjective worldview, however, counselors often need to attend to cultural factors more systematically than they have in the past (e.g., culture-bound beliefs, values, lifestyle) since these will substantially impact symptom presentation, therapeutic process, and treatment outcome.

To illustrate, an adolescent, African American male who is "paranoid" around authority figures is often accurately discerning a persecutory or hostile environment given his life experiences. A counselor who diagnoses him as paranoid (which frequently occurs) and focuses on helping him see "reality" (i.e., the *counselor's* subjective worldview) would quickly lose credibility. Similarly, encouraging a young adult from a traditional Asian family to emancipate and become more autonomous from her family may only engender increased distress. If the young adult sees this intervention as incongruent within her family and culture, the counselor's credibility as a potential helper would be impaired.

Faced with ambiguous guidelines for how to become more culturally sensitive counselors, trainees often try to learn lists of culture-specific characteristics and associated interventions. Given the complexity of culture, however, *and the wide differences that exist between individuals within subcultures,* this culture-specific model often fails to capture the reality of each individual's unique experience. Instead, we are proposing a multicultural approach that emphasizes *the counselor's ability to articulate and enter into each individual's subjective worldview.* This multicultural approach is more comprehensive in that it acknowledges the contributions of individual uniqueness, cultural variables, and universal human principles. The counselor's sensitivity to the client's subjective worldview, and responsiveness to each individual client's varying needs, becomes the essential skill that differentiates the most effective counselors working within dynamic, cognitive-behavioral, or humanistic-existential frameworks (see Stricker & Gold, 1996). That is, the counselor attends to the client's subjective worldview, which has been shaped by their individual, familial, and cultural experiences. Using this approach, which is based on attachment theory's "empathic attunement" (Karen, 1994), the counselor (1) creates a secure environment by being emotionally present and affectively attuned; (2) affirms the client's own subjective worldview by validating his subjective experiences or personal perspectives; and (3) facilitates the client's connectedness to his own voice and expression of his own authenticity in relationships. The counselor does this by helping the client clarify her own thoughts, feelings, and preferences, which empowers the client to exercise more choice in her life and experience greater self-efficacy (Bandura, 1997; Gilligan, 1982; Pipher, 1995).

To conclude, sensitivity to cultural factors gives counselors one more layer of understanding to help them respond more effectively to their clients. We believe that effective counselors recognize the relevance of cultural diversity, appreciate the unique experiences of each individual, and strive to provide clients with the specific relational experiences they need in order to change. This approach challenges counselors to be flexible enough to cognitively de-center and empathically enter the subjective worldviews of each individual client. Thus, following closely from the work of Ibrahim (1985, 1991), Pedersen (1991), Wrenn (1985), and others, we define culturally sensitive counselors as follows:

1. they recognize that many cultural factors and social influences contribute to each individual's subjective worldview. That is, they accept that reality is not defined according to one set of cultural assumptions or stereotypes.
2. having considered the cultural/religious/economic and other factors that have contributed to their own worldviews, they respect and genuinely appreciate the client's differing realities.
3. they are sensitive to variations among individuals and understand their own worldview sufficiently to have the security or capacity to be able to relinquish it and enter the client's differing worldview.

4. they focus on the counseling process—the interaction that is transpiring between the counselor and the client—which frees them to draw flexibly from a range of techniques rather than being wedded to one theoretical point of view (i.e., incorporate techniques from varying orientations that this particular client can utilize to make progress in treatment).

5. they are able to validate their client's experiences, even when these experiences differ vastly from their own. In doing so, they support the client's own initiative and sense of efficacy, which we believe is at the heart of effective counseling.

Client Response Specificity

The second core construct is *client response specificity*. This means that counselors must tailor their responses to fit the specific needs of each individual child—one size does not fit all! There are no cookbook formulas or generic techniques for responding to the complex problems, diverse developmental experiences, and multicultural backgrounds that children and adolescents present. In this regard, *the same therapeutic response that helps one client progress may only serve to hinder another.* In play therapy, for example, children are often encouraged to find an appropriate expression for their anger by hitting a punching bag. This may reduce an inhibited child's anxiety over expressing his anger, especially if his parents are themselves emotionally inhibited. Alternatively, this may intensify anxiety in a child for whom it is culturally unacceptable to resolve conflict via overt aggression. Further, the same technique may have a different outcome for a child who is living in a disorganized and unpredictable home, does not sleep in the same bed every night, and receives little adult supervision. For this child, hitting the punching bag is likely to foster further, unwanted acting-out and aggression. As can be seen from this example, an intervention that might free one child may increase anxiety in another or unhinge a child whose control is fragile.

Let's use a different example to look more closely at client response specificity. Suppose a counselor has just self-disclosed to an early adolescent client how the counselor felt when his own parents divorced many years ago. If this client's parents are too preoccupied with their own marital distress to be able to "see" or communicate with their son, the counselor's disclosure may be helpful and foster further sharing and investment in the relationship.

In contrast, the same disclosure from the counselor may have very different effects on another client. For example, if the second client has a parent who is depressed and leans on the adolescent for emotional support, the counselor's well-intended self-disclosure is likely to be unwanted and burdensome to the client. Or, if the divorcing parents argue with each other through the client and embroil their daughter in their ongoing wrangling, the counselor's self-disclosure may be counterproductive. It would be likely to raise the client's anxiety about having to meet the needs of yet another adult, thereby fostering discouragement or depression about the hopelessness of having her own needs met.

In still another circumstance, it is possible that this counselor's credibility could be jeopardized by the nature of the disclosure and how the counselor managed to resolve the problem in his own life. For example, self-disclosure of an issue that the counselor had great difficulty resolving could be viewed as unprofessional by some Asian clients and raise doubt about the counselor's ability to be helpful to them. This would be especially true if the counselor is looked on as a teacher who is being consulted for her knowledge and wisdom.

However, the same disclosure with some African American clients may be welcome and convey that the counselor is human and less likely to be judgmental. That is, since many African Americans have experienced discrimination in which they were portrayed as inferior (note views from slavery to the more recent "intelligence" debates), they will experience the counselor's sharing on a personal parallel level. Thus, when counselors portray themselves as human, fallible, faced with challenges, and in no way superior to the client, this provides an experience for the client that differs from the sociopolitical experiences the client has previously faced. The client-specific response facilitates a therapeutic alliance between the client and counselor, which is essential for effective treatment (Horvath & Greenberg, 1994). In the case studies that follow, you will see how the counselors go through this kind of thought process with each client and try to assess the different types of responses or interventions that this particular client can utilize best in order to change.

Reparative Relational Experiences

The third core construct is *reparative relational experiences*. As you read the following case studies, you will see how each counselor tries to *identify the problematic relational patterns* that children are repetitively enacting in their play, living out with family members and others, and starting to re-create or reexperience in their relationship with their counselor. The counselor wants to (1) identify the hurtful or problematic interpersonal patterns that repeatedly occur for the client with parents, siblings, friends, and classmates; (2) clarify how aspects of the problematic interpersonal style that occurs with others may be occurring between the client and counselor; (3) engage the client in exploring and understanding this relational theme or interaction pattern; and (4) work together to change this problematic pattern—first in their relationship and then with others. As emphasized earlier, this change begins in the counseling relationship and then is generalized, with counselor support, to the rest of the client's life.

So we ask: What spells the differences between re-enacting versus resolving the client's problematic relational patterns as they emerge in the therapeutic exchange? First, counselors do not literally respond in the same hurtful ways that others have, ways that have caused the child's problems. More importantly, as familiar but problematic interaction patterns or themes emerge in the client's relationship with the counselor, the counselor has the opportunity to address these in a helpful way. In counseling, that is, clients often begin to evoke in the counselor the same type of interactions or responses that have been causing problems for them in other relationships. For example, without being fully aware of it, the counselor may be pulled to engage in a control battle with the client or become overly protective. In listening to the client, the counselor realizes that "control" or "overprotection" are the very same issues the client is struggling with at home, issues that have kept the client from functioning effectively. The counselor, realizing that responding similarly would not be in the client's best interest, decides to respond in a new or different and more helpful way that does not repeat the old relational pattern. In this instance, the counselor would identify what is happening so the client can recognize how this pattern, which has been disruptive at home, is being repeated in her interaction with the counselor. From this, the client becomes empowered to *choose* how she relates to others. This issue of subtly reenacting in the counseling relationship the same types of interpersonal problems that the client is struggling with in other relationships is a foreign concept to most beginning counselors. Usually, it does not hold much meaning until trainees start seeing their own clients and begin to experience this in their interactions with their clients. Let's explore more closely how young clients do not just talk about their problems in the abstract but begin to re-create or enact them in their relationship with the counselor.

Effective counselors from every theoretical orientation are emotionally attuned, "understand" the client's distress from the client's perspective, discern what this particular client views as problematic and needs from the counselor, and provides a response that is corrective. When clients *experience* this new or reparative response, a response that differs from previous relationships and that does not fit the client's negative expectations or relational schemas, it is a powerful type of experiential relearning that readily can be generalized to other relationships (Bandura, 1997). Through this in-vivo relearning with the counselor, clients become freed from using their old maladaptive coping strategies (e.g., excessive attention seeking, self-deprecation, compliance with everyone, being inflexibly demanding), behaviors that have been creating symptoms and problems in their lives. This behavioral experience of change with the counselor is far more compelling than words alone can provide.

What can the counselor do to help clients initially recognize, and then change, these faulty coping styles or maladaptive relational patterns? The counselor may provide the client with interpersonal feedback that highlights, clarifies, questions, or fails to reinforce the old unwanted relational scenario. The counselor first acknowledges that the client's coping strategies or interaction patterns made sense given the client's personal, familial, and cultural history, but that these patterns have ceased to be useful. For example, excessive compliance might have been life saving in an abusive family. In session, the counselor does not permit the same problematic but familiar interpersonal patterns and consequences to occur in their relationship. For example, the child or adolescent learns that, at least in this relationship, she does not have to comply excessively, take care of or meet the adult's needs, take sides in parental conflict, experience unclear boundaries or lack of limits, and so forth. Instead, the counselor (1) offers a safer and more affirming solution to the child's problems in their relationship; and (2) helps the child generalize this experiential relearning to others. The case studies that follow will provide many concrete illustrations of this orienting construct, which can be utilized by counselors working within any theoretical orientation.

Long ago, Frieda Fromm-Reichman (1950) captured this relational focus succinctly by stating that clients need an *experience* not an *explanation.* In other words, clients do not change just from explanations about how their problems developed, interpretations about what their behavior means, nondirective support, or advice about what they should do. Although each of these responses may be helpful at times, change is facilitated when clients have a real-life experience of change in how they are treated in their interaction with their counselor, and when this relearning with the counselor is bridged to other important relationships in the client's life.

Clinicians from diverse theoretical frameworks have highlighted the *interpersonal process dimension* and noted that clients do not merely talk with counselors about their problems. Clients, in fact, bring critical aspects of their problems with others into their current interaction with the counselor. That is, clients convey their conflicts in *how* they interact with the counselor (the process), or, with children, in how they play. When this happens, the counselor's job is to respond in a way that is different from the problematic relational experiences they have had in the past. This new experience allows the client to see that relationships can be different. The client is then empowered to challenge the old beliefs, schemas, expectations, and/or ways of relating that have been disrupting her life. She now has the opportunity to think, feel, and behave in ways that are more effective. The following example illustrates this core construct.

Suppose you are treating a 6-year-old boy whose parents are recently divorced. During your first session, your client begins to kick you. You intervene and tell him firmly that his behavior is unacceptable. Johnny begins to cry and runs out of the playroom. Thinking in terms of "client response specificity" and "reparative relational experiences," how can you discern the best way for you to respond at this particular moment? Per client response specificity, different responses will be appropriate for different children. To begin structuring your thinking, however, *it is useful to hypothesize that Johnny is probably beginning to reenact with you a problematic and repetitive relational pattern with which he has also been struggling with others.* For example, if you surmise from what you have already been told or from observations you have already made about Johnny and his family that Johnny has an intrusive parent who does not give him space, he may need a cooling-off period. In this case, the counselor would need to let Johnny know that she recognizes his need for some space (e.g., Counselor: Looks like you need some time alone. When you're ready, come back to the playroom.). The counselor then sits quietly several yards away and maintains sufficient physical distance from Johnny so he does not feel intruded upon.

In contrast, however, if your initial observations have led you to hypothesize that Johnny has a rejecting or uninvolved parent, he may need to know that you are not going to reject him for acting out. That is, that disapproval of his behavior and firm consequences for violating rules is not the same as rejecting him. In this case, the counselor would convey continued engagement with Johnny by being close to where Johnny is during his cooling-off period. While following Johnny out of the playroom and staying next to him, the counselor might say: "You may be wondering if I'm angry and won't want to be with you. I don't like being kicked but I would like to get to know you better and would like to continue playing with you. Let me know when you are ready to go back to the playroom." By providing the "intruded" Johnny with a cooling-off period alone, or the "rejected" Johnny with an invitation for continuing contact, the counselor is providing an experiential resolution of Johnny's conflict (e.g., intrusion or rejection) in the counseling relationship, a corrective or reparative relational experience.

If the counselor can continue to respond in many other big and small ways that enact a solution to his problems in the counseling relationship, Johnny will have the experience that at least some relationships can be different. This knowledge and experience can increase the likelihood that Johnny (and other clients in similar situations) will seek out more affirming relationships in the future and, with the counselor's help, begin to discern relationships which are intrusive or rejecting from others that can be better. In this and many other ways that we will explore, counselors can help clients generalize the experience of change to other real-life relationships beyond the counseling setting via encouragement, role playing, conjoint sessions to facilitate communication between parent and child, and so forth.

Thus, the process-oriented counselor tries to:

1. identify the faulty beliefs and expectations, problematic relational scenarios, or ineffective interpersonal coping styles that may be reoccurring with others in the child's life;
2. anticipate how these interpersonal patterns are most likely to be evoked in the counseling relationship;

3. provide new and more satisfying responses in the counseling relationship that help to resolve rather than repeat this familiar but problematic relational scenario; and
4. help the client generalize this new way of interacting with the counselor and begin to respond in more effective ways with others.

A reparative relational experience is not usually sufficient for sustained change, but it is often the pivotal experience that initiates change. Based on the interpersonal safety arising from the affirming client-counselor relationship, the client becomes more willing to try out interventions from educational, behavioral, cognitive, and other theoretical approaches. The collaborative alliance between them also facilitates clients' commitment to follow through on mutually set goals and interventions, which results in greater effectiveness. In other words, when clients *experience* a different type of relationship with the counselor that does not go down the familiar but problematic pathways they have come to expect from others, the counselor is seen as someone who can help. Clients invest further in the treatment process and become more willing to try out new coping strategies and ways of responding with others. In contrast, when clients successfully elicit the same type of reactions from the counselor that they tend to find with others (e.g., the counselor begins to feel frustrated, controlled, discouraged, or disappointed, as significant others in the client's life feel), intervention techniques from every theoretical perspective will falter. Thus the interaction between the counselor and the client provides a "meta" perspective for understanding what is occurring and what to do in counseling relationships, and can readily be integrated with other therapeutic modalities. Because these interpersonal-process concepts may seem too vague to apply at first, the following example further illustrates the process dimension and how the counselor can either resolve or reenact the client's problems in the counseling relationship.

Suppose an inhibited, worried, and depressed 8–year-old child has learned from repeated interactions with a depressed, lonely, or alcoholic parent, "If I grow up, become stronger, and act more independently, I'm hurting my mother and she'll withdraw emotionally and stop paying attention. In treatment, this child will repeatedly "test" the counselor to verify or disconfirm her problematic belief. For example, this child will test her expectation by *acting* independently with the counselor (e.g., being insightful, disagreeing with the counselor's observations, asserting the direction of play). Immediately after acting stronger or more independent in one of these ways, this child will carefully evaluate how the counselor responds to this new, anxiety-arousing behavior. If the counselor needs to be "right" or the authority and takes issue with the child's observations, disagreement, or new initiative, the counseling relationship behaviorally confirms the child's expectations of others and reinforces her problematic relational pattern. That is, regardless of what the counselor *says* (e.g., "I'd like to know how you see things, even when you might disagree with me."), it is the counselor's *behavior* that will be more important and have all the impact. If the counselor is uncomfortable with her assertiveness or independence, as is her mother, the child will continue to be inhibited and anxious about asserting herself. Even if the counselor has been accurate in talking with the client about the *content* of the child's problem (e.g., Counselor: Your mother seems to need you to need her . . . ; When you succeed at something, it seems to make your mother sad rather than happy . . . ; or Is that guilty feeling coming up again now as we talk about how well you did in the spelling contest?), this child cannot make progress as long as their interpersonal process is awry. That is, if the counselor is reenacting the child's problem by behaving in a nonaffirming way when the child succeeds, is assertive, or shows her independence in some way, the child cannot benefit from the counselor's interventions. This reenactment of the child's conflict with the counselor along the process dimension is a regular occurrence in counseling relationships—and one of the greatest impediments to client change.

In contrast, if the counselor is attending to the process (i.e., the way they are interacting) as well as the content (i.e., what they are talking about), he may disconfirm the child's problematic belief by welcoming the child's independent expressions. That is, the counselor disconfirms the child's problematic belief by being interested in the child's insight even when it differs from the counselor's. By being receptive to the child's disagreement, nondefensive about her criticisms, and responsive to the child's initiative or new direction, the counselor gives the child a real-life experience of change in the counseling relationship that helps resolve rather than reenact the child's problems with others. Here, as in all relationships, it is what the counselor *does,* not what she *says,* that counts.

Further, if the child is a member of a group that has been consistently discriminated against or treated as inferior, the counselor's acceptance and validation of the child's point of view may begin to diminish the impact of the damaging socio-political messages the child has had to contend with. Over time, the child may be empowered to become increasingly self-affirming and begin to advocate for him or herself within the context of the child's cultural and familial values. The culturally sensitive counselor can help the child find ways to have a voice and discern where self-assertion and independence are appropriate, while still continuing to maintain family/cultural values such as respect for elders, loyalty to family, and so forth.

Thus, we suggest that the underlying vehicle for change in counseling relationships is in-vivo or experiential relearning with the counselor that does not repeat the client's maladaptive relational patterns or confirm their problematic beliefs and expectations about others. On their own, however, counseling trainees do not usually see how aspects of the client's maladaptive relational patterns are being reenacted between them along the process dimension. This is because they are often focused exclusively on the *content* of what they are discussing rather than attending to the *process* or how the issues are being presented and responded to as well. How do you know when some aspect of the client's problems are being reenacted in the therapeutic relationship and counseling is failing? Oftentimes you know when the treatment process becomes intellectualized, repetitive, or "stuck," and when the client is missing sessions, coming late, or about to terminate prematurely. Or, the client repeatedly elicits advice from the counselor, which does not prove useful and the client rejects, evoking the same irritation, feelings of inadequacy, or emotional disengagement in the counselor that this depressed adolescent client elicits in others. Or, the client tells stories without any focus or theme, evoking boredom or disinterest in the counselor that leaves the client and counselor emotionally disconnected, reenacting the loneliness or cynicism that originally brought this client to treatment. In sum, it is the reparative experience in the here-and-now, real-life interaction with the counselor that is the primary vehicle for facilitating change.

In the case studies that follow, you will often see that change occurs in a predictable sequence. First, clients have a reparative experience of change with the counselor when their old relational patterns and problematic expectations do not reoccur along the process dimension. Second, the counselor helps clients generalize this experience of change that has occurred between them to other relationships. The counselor does this by (1) identifying and clarifying how these same relational patterns are disrupting other relationships; (2) formulating and rehearsing new, more adaptive client responses that alter the client's contribution to current interpersonal problems; and (3) helping clients anticipate future situations that are likely to evoke their old problematic response patterns so they can more actively *choose* how they wish to respond instead. In this way, clients are empowered to act on their own behalf in more flexible ways, rather than rigidly repeating old familiar response patterns which are not succeeding in many current relationships.

CASE ILLUSTRATION

To illustrate our three core concepts of subjective worldview, client response specificity, and reparative relational experience, let's examine a case vignette. This vignette also highlights how the *content* of what the counselor and client discuss is different than the *process* or way in which they interact together. Usually, counselors do not literally reenact with clients the same hurtful responses they have received from others (in this case, the problem is sexual abuse). Unwittingly, however, the *way* in which they interact often thematically evokes the same issues that the client is struggling with in other relationships (in this case, compliance and having to go along with the counselor and others).

Suppose a counseling trainee and her 17-year-old client, Teresa, are talking for the first time about Teresa's sexual contact with her stepfather. The content of what they are talking about is sexual molestation. Depending on the process they enact, however, the effectiveness of this discussion will vary greatly. On the one hand, suppose the counselor is initiating this discussion and pressing Teresa for disclosure about what occurred. The counselor is a graduate student who is genuinely concerned about Teresa's safety. However, her "need to know" is intensified by her concerns about her legal responsibilities as a mandated reporter, and her concern that her supervisor will want to know more details or facts about Teresa's molestation.

In response to the counselor's continuing press for disclosure, Teresa complies with the counselor's authority and reluctantly speaks. Although useful information may be gained under these circumstances, the opportunity for therapeutic progress is lost because aspects of Teresa's basic problem are being reenacted with the counselor in the way they are interacting. How is this a problematic reenactment along the process dimension? Teresa is again being pressured to obey an adult, comply with authority, and do something she doesn't want to do. Of course, being pressured to talk about something she doesn't want to disclose in no way retraumatizes her as the original abuse did. However, their interpersonal process of demand/comply is awry and will reevoke in Teresa the same type of feelings and concerns that the abuse initially engendered. That is, her helplessness will lead to depression and her compliance to feelings of shame. Because the therapeutic process is (thematically or metaphorically) reevoking the original problem, her disclosure is likely to hinder her progress in treatment and slow the process of reempowerment.

The situation may be further complicated if Teresa belongs to an ethnic group where family loyalty is highly prized, or if she is a member of a religious community where obedience to authority and hierarchical relationships are emphasized. In this situation,

Teresa is being asked to violate rules sanctioned by her family's cultural group (i.e., religious, ethnic). Other family members and friends may not approve of the stepfather's behavior. Even so, they may not provide Teresa with the support she needs because she took this information to someone outside the family (the counselor), or because she violated their religious proscriptions that emphasize obedience and forgiveness. Thus, although disclosure violates family rules and loyalties for most victims, this may take on additional significance and add much more distress for Teresa if she were a Hispanic adolescent who belonged to a conservative religious community.

What should the counselor in this example do instead? Wait nondirectively for Teresa to volunteer this information—while she may continue to suffer ongoing abuse at home? Of course not. But by attending to the process dimension, the counselor may be able to begin providing Teresa with a reparative therapeutic experience while gathering the same information. That is, instead of pressing for disclosure, what if the counselor *honored* Teresa's "resistance" or cultural prescriptions. For example, instead of pressing for more disclosure, the counselor could "metacommunicate" and make a process comment (Cashdan, 1988; Teyber, 2000) by inquiring supportively about Teresa's reluctance to speak:

COUNSELOR: You seem reluctant to talk with me about this right now. Something doesn't feel safe. I'm wondering if you are concerned about what might happen at home if you talk with me about this.

OR: Perhaps talking about this violates family rules and you are concerned what your mother or stepfather might think or do? Would you feel OK talking about your family's rules and what's OK or not OK to talk about outside your family?

OR: Would you get more support and would it feel safer if we discussed this together with your minister or another family member?

Only if the counselor can help Teresa identify and resolve her potential concerns about disclosing can she find it relieving. This reparative relational experience (in which Teresa's expectations of having to comply with authorities is not reenacted, and new respect for her limits and compassion for her experience is provided) is essential. Only then will Teresa feel safe enough to engage with the counselor in discussing what happened and begin to make progress in treatment. Given her previous experience and expectations, there may certainly be "reality" to the concerns she presents. However, her contextual concerns (cultural, familial, personal) typically need to be addressed *before* Teresa can find the safety she needs to act on her own behalf, rather than continuing to comply as she has been doing in other problematic relationships. For example, in response to the questions suggested previously, Teresa might reply that:

- her mother won't believe her;
- her stepfather will be sent away;
- she will be told it is all her fault;
- she will be chastised for not keeping it in the family and trying to resolve it there;
- the counselor may take her parents' side;
- the counselor may want to remove her from her home immediately;
- the counselor may see her as shame-worthy or "defective" in some way; or
- the counselor may feel anxious talking about this sensitive material and will not want to explore it fully.

Although this process difference may seem subtle, its effect is powerful and will have far-reaching impact on the course and outcome of treatment. In the second illustration, Teresa is already beginning the empowerment process just by the way in which she shares her trauma. For the first time in her life, she is able to participate in the decision process with an authority figure, have her concerns expressed and taken seriously, and, to the extent possible, accommodated as best they can. In a way that is new and different, Teresa can at least have some shared control over what she says and to whom, yet still remain emotionally connected and supported. This reparative interpersonal process with the counselor is a prerequisite for the client to be able to begin acting in similarly empowered, authentic, and self-affirming ways in some of her other relationships. The counselor can then help Teresa to systematically begin discerning other people in her life with whom it is safe to be similarly assertive, and those who will punish this or demand that she merely comply again.

But what if the counselor's efforts fail and Teresa still does not want to speak or disclose the secret? The counselor is a mandated reporter, and still will need to contact Child Protective Services. In some cases, the counselor's attempts to empower the client by giving her more choice or participation in the reporting/treatment process clearly will have helped, and other times it will seem as if it hasn't. Even if not, however, Teresa has seen that the counselor is sincerely trying to find ways to include and empower her rather than merely demand that she comply. In this way, a small but significant difference is occurring that is likely to facilitate her recovery, as Teresa sees that the counselor's intentions are different than what she has come to expect from others.

In sum, concepts and techniques from all theoretical approaches can be helpful, but they are not likely to be effective unless the interaction or process that transpires between the counselor and client is enacting a solution to the client's problems. In the case studies that follow, you will see a variety of counselor techniques, behaviors, and goals. These might range from providing empathy and a sense of being valued, to helping the client recognize thought processes or behavior patterns that are maladaptive, to role-playing new behaviors. In all instances, the underlying philosophy is that all techniques are acceptable and will be incorporated provided they are appropriate for the client-therapist *process*. We believe further that counselors of every theoretical orientation will be less effective when the client's conflicts are metaphorically reenacted along the process dimension. That is, if the process is incongruent with or asks clients to violate strongly held cultural values, the counselor will lose credibility and the client may not stay in treatment. In this regard, effectiveness in counseling is not necessarily predicated on the degree of religious or ethnic similarity between counselor and client, gender and age matching, or even personality characteristics or theoretical orientation of the counselor. Client matching will certainly facilitate some clients entering counseling, and it will be essential for others. Over the course of treatment, however, the counselor's achieved credibility (i.e., the effectiveness of the process that transpires between counselor and client) will largely determine the outcome of treatment (Teyber & McClure, 2000).

In closing, we welcome you as you journey with us through these young lives. We hope you will take from these cases useful information that you can apply to your life and the work that lies ahead for you.

Questions for Thought and Discussion

1. Think about the concept of privilege. In what ways is your life more privileged than others, and how is it less privileged? In what ways do cultural dimensions such as gender, age, race, socioeconomic status, religion, and so forth impact your response?

2. Recall an experience in which you were treated unfairly (e.g., discriminated against, misjudged, etc.). What happened and how did you feel? What factors contributed to the unfair treatment? Looking back, what would you like to have changed about your response in that situation?

Suggestions for Further Reading

Brems, C. (2002). *A comprehensive guide to child psychotherapy.* Boston, MA: Allyn & Bacon. Provides a practical, comprehensive, and sensitive guide to interventions with children.

Gibbs, J. T., & Huang, L. (1997). *Children of color: Psychological interventions with minority youth.* San Francisco: Jossey-Bass. Provides useful guidelines for assessing and treating minority children.

Sue, D. W., & Sue, D. (1999). *Counseling the culturally different: Theory and Practice* (3rd ed.). New York: Wiley. Aimed at helping mental health professionals develop cultural competence. Stresses the importance of being open to alternative worldviews as well as the importance of developing culturally appropriate intervention strategies.

Teyber, E. (2000). *Interpersonal process in psychotherapy: A relational approach* (4th ed.). Pacific Grove: Brooks/Cole. Shows beginning counselors how they can use themselves and the relationships they establish with their clients to facilitate change.

ALLIE: RESOLVING HER BULIMIA AND FINDING A POSITIVE BIRACIAL IDENTITY

It seems like I spend every waking hour consumed with thoughts about food, wanting it but feeling I shouldn't have it, or not wanting it but knowing I'll have it anyway. I even dream about food! I feel like I'm fighting this battle to control food and my weight and everything related to it, but really it all controls me. The thing that's really scary, though, is that when I manage not to think about food or my weight for just a little while, sometimes I feel even crazier. I feel more scared . . . or even worse, totally empty. So I end up going back to obsessing about food.

This quote came from Allie, an 18-year-old multiracial woman who came to the university's counseling center, concerned about her destructive eating habits. Allie's words portray the painful struggle experienced by many with eating disorders. Why do people, especially young women, develop eating disorders? What needs arc they trying to meet by their behavior? What might Allie have in common with celebrities like Princess Diana and Jane Fonda, who have also struggled with destructive eating behavior?

Although there are several types of eating disorders, this chapter will focus only on *anorexia nervosa* and *bulimia nervosa,* disorders that typically emerge during adolescence and young adulthood. For those who suffer from eating disorders, food represents many things. Their lives feel out of control (e.g., they experience uncontrollable changes in hormones and body shape) and food becomes one of the few things they feel they can "control." They desperately wish to be nurtured and loved, and food helps them cope with the anxiety and depression of those unmet needs. They also feel the need to be admired, valued, affirmed, "fit in" and be accepted by others, and regulation of food intake becomes salient to these needs. Indeed, because of society's emphasis on, and valuing of, thin bodies, a "culture of thinness" has developed (Gilbert & Thompson, 1996), which has led young women to believe that being thin will bring them the admiration and esteem they so deeply desire.

Thus, it seems that a struggle with unmet needs is at the core of destructive eating behavior. Growing children's needs for a nurturing, secure attachment is central because that is the basis on which feelings of self-worth, developing a positive identity, and the ability to be intimate with others develops (Zraly & Swift, 1990). As a result, many young women feel the need to be "perfect," and desperately seek the regard and admiration of others. In the struggle to win approval from others, these young people stifle their own views, comply with others, try to please, and become overly focused on appearance, qualities defined by the culture as "feminine" and "pleasing." (Note: Since more than 90% of those with eating disorders are female this chapter will focus primarily on women.)

This chapter describes the work Allie did in counseling to understand and overcome her struggle with food, and to resolve the underlying issues that gave rise to that struggle. Although young, White women from middle- to upper-class backgrounds have been reported to be at greatest risk for these disorders (Connors, 1996), other authors have disagreed. These authors have suggested that the risk may, in fact, be higher for those who come from different cultures and must adapt to the mainstream culture while still maintaining their own cultural identity (Kuba & Harris, 1992; Root, 1990). In the case that follows, Allie's struggle with bulimia was deeply connected to her identity as a person of mixed ethno cultural heritage. For Allie, fitting in, belonging, and being valued were intensified because of her cultural identity, an identity that was not valued by some of the people in her life whose opinions she held in esteem. In the following sections, we will discuss the clinical aspects of these disorders, briefly review the literature on anorexia and bulimia, then present Allie's case.

CLINICAL FEATURES

The major features of anorexia nervosa include weighing less than 85% of expected weight and being terrified of gaining weight. Individuals diagnosed with anorexia nervosa see their body shape and weight in a distorted way (i.e., as significantly larger than reality), and frequently stop menstruating. While body image distortion and actual weight levels are part of the DSM-IV-TR diagnosis, it is important to note that there are cultural differences in preferred body type and using the strict weight criterion can contribute to underestimation of this disorder in minority groups (Kuba & Harris, 1992). Some individuals with anorexia, while still having a strong appetite, remain painfully thin by reducing food intake (referred to as anorexia nervosa: restricting type). Others, in contrast, binge (eat large amounts of food at one sitting) and then use laxatives, vomiting, or other methods to purge (anorexia nervosa: binge-purging type).

One of the major ways those diagnosed with bulimia nervosa differ from those who are diagnosed with anorexia nervosa, is that those with bulimia may be normal weight, slightly underweight, or even overweight. However, they binge (eat large amounts of food at one sitting twice a week or more) then try to "compensate" to keep from gaining weight. Some compensate by purging through use of laxatives, vomiting, diuretics, and so forth (bulimia nervosa: purging type) while others don't purge but compensate by going on fasts or engaging in excessive exercise (bulimia nervosa: non-purging type). Like those with anorexia, they too are concerned with body shape and weight, and use this to determine self-esteem. A major differentiating criterion between anorexia and bulimia is that individuals with bulimia do not meet the severe underweight criterion necessary for the anorexia diagnosis.

Anorexia typically arises during the transition to adolescence while bulimia is more likely to arise during the transition to young adulthood (Attie & Brooks-Gunn, 1995). These disorders often follow a period of weight gain followed by dieting, usually in connection with a major life disruption (e.g., a move to new school, a change in a relationship, or a remark from someone that they are putting on weight). The adolescent's intense sensitivity to how they are perceived by others, the developmental challenges they are facing (e.g., identity formation, negotiation of relationships with parents and peers), combined with the physical changes that adolescence generally triggers, all contribute to development of these eating problems.

As noted earlier, eating disorders reflect (at least in part) underlying struggles with identity, self-worth, and intimacy, which help to explain their emergence during adolescence. Adolescence and young adulthood are periods in which the chief developmental tasks are to forge a positive sense of identity and be able to develop close relationships with peers (Erickson, 1959). For some people, these developmental challenges are frightening. They feel overwhelmed at the prospect of growing up and don't feel able to cope with the demands of adolescence and young adulthood. Their eating behavior becomes one of the ways in which they try to ward off or manage their feelings of inadequacy. Sadly, these feelings of inadequacy are in turn made worse by the feelings of shame and guilt that come about as a result of their destructive eating behavior. Thus begins an often painful spiraling cycle of behaviors where attempts to control food represent a means of coping with difficult feelings. As Bruch (1984) noted, bingeing and purging, or the anorexic person's restricted eating, become a habitual means of coping, "a psuedosolution for . . . problems of living" (p. 10). Indeed, Hilda Bruch's (1973) suggestion that young girls suffering from anorexia are unable to distinguish between various internal states such as hunger, anger, and sadness, has been supported by the literature (Lyon et al., 1997).

Compared to adolescents with anorexia, those with bulimia tend to be more extroverted, more likely to use alcohol, and to be emotionally unstable. They tend to be more sexually active, come from families with psychological problems and overt hostility or discord, and have a family and personal history of maternal obesity. In contrast, those with anorexia tend to be socially isolated, rigid, highly controlled, and disinterested in sex. Compared to those with bulimia, those with anorexia tend to come from families who are enmeshed, overprotective, resistant to change, and have poor conflict resolution skills. Both those with anorexia and those with bulimia are sensitive to rejection, tend to be high achievers, and have high rates of comorbidity with mood disorders, personality disorders, and anxiety disorders. Excellent reviews of these disorders can be found in Foreyt and Mikhail (1997), and Wilson, Heffernan, and Black (1996).

Disordered eating is frequently associated with depression and low self-esteem (APA, 2000). Biochemical changes brought on by the disordered eating may account in part for the mood disturbances, though mood disturbances may have been present at the onset of the eating symptoms. Suicidal thoughts and impulses are also common clinical features and need to be carefully assessed and worked with in treatment. Counselors can address suicidal concerns by asking about them directly, and by establishing a contract in which the client agrees to seek specific help (e.g., contact the counselor or a crisis line) should suicidal feelings increase.

For individuals with eating disorders, physical complications such as fatigue, sore throats, potassium loss, dehydration, dental problems, heart problems, and even death, occur. Studies suggest that fatality rates for anorexia may be as high as 10% and somewhat lower for bulimia (APA, 2000; Foreyt & Mikhail, 1997; Mizes, 1993; Pike, 1998; Wilson et al., 1996).

PREVALENCE AND ETIOLOGY OF EATING DISORDERS

Until recently anorexia and bulimia were considered rare. However, reports of the number of people who suffer from these disorders have increased dramatically in recent years (Lucas & Holub, 1995). Although DSM-IV-TR indicates that approximately 1% of women have had anorexia and 1 to 3% have had bulimia, "subclinical" levels (e.g., *episodic* or occasional bingeing and purging, fear of fatness, dieting, fasting, excessive exercise) occur significantly more often. For example, Mellin, Irwin, and Scully (1992) found that 38% of 11-year-olds had a distorted body image and 58% saw themselves as overweight even though only 15% were objectively overweight. Similar reports of feeling fat, fearing weight gain, dieting, fasting, bingeing, vomiting, and using diuretics have been reported in young children and adolescents (Childress, Brewerton, Hodges, & Jarrell, 1993).

Sociocultural Factors

Anorexia occurs primarily in females, with only 4 to 8% of those with the disorder being male; however, for bulimia, estimates are that 10 to 15% are male (Carlat, Camargo, & Herzog, 1997). The greater prevalence of anorexia and bulimia among females has been explained (in part) by sociocultural factors. Some theorists argue that eating disorders have increased largely as a result of cultural trends in society that set thinness as a standard of beauty, power, and status for women. Certainly, social pressures to be thin have led to widespread dissatisfaction with body size among women, resulting in what has been termed "a normative discontent" with weight and appearance (Rodin, Striegel-Moore, & Silberstein, 1990). Research has shown that men are less concerned about, and more satisfied with, their weight and body size and hence may be less at risk for developing eating disorders.

Until recently, anorexia and bulimia were thought to be disorders experienced only by young, affluent, White females. However, Root (1990) notes that the stereotype that eating disorders occur only in this population has meant that relatively few studies of the prevalence or frequency of eating disorders have included people of color in their samples. Those studies which have been more inclusive indicate that eating disorders not only occur in people of color, but also suggest that ethno cultural factors may play an important role in the development of eating disorders (Kuba & Harris, 1992; Root, 1990). In fact, when young people from other cultures are exposed to Western ideals of weight and appearance, their rates of eating disorders increase significantly (Fairburn & Beglin, 1990; Pate et al., 1992).

It is important to recognize that many ethno cultural groups hold values concerning body size that differ from those of the mainstream culture. This difference can present a source of acculturation (adaptation) stress for some young people of color struggling to achieve a sense of identity, particularly where the mainstream values demean or devalue characteristics of people from their cultures. As Allie's case will illustrate, conflicts concerning body size, negative racial/ethnic stereotypes, and the adolescent task of developing a positive identity may thus place those who are ethno culturally diverse at greater risk for developing these disorders. That is, resolving a bi- or multicultural identity, and coping with the stress of "fitting in" with the mainstream culture, can lead to a "double oppression" (i.e., oppression based on both race and gender) for young women of color (Root, 1990). Similarly, Yates (1989) suggests that minority youth from upper-middle-class families may be particularly at risk for eating disorders as they negotiate acceptance or adjustment to the dominant White culture.

Psychodynamic and Family Systems Views

In addition to the role of sociocultural stereotypes and acculturation conflicts in the development of eating disorders, most theories emphasize early psychological experiences as primary contributors to developing these disorders. Psychodynamic theorists focus on the mother-child relationship, particularly the child's difficulties in successfully separating from the mother and developing her own identity. Family systems theorists look more broadly at the nature of family alliances (i.e., how loyalties are defined), the families' difficulties managing conflict, and the families' difficulties communicating their needs directly, as contributors.

Hilde Bruch (1973, 1984) developed one of the most widely cited psychodynamic formulations of the etiology of eating disorders. It is helpful to remember that in normal development, parents respond to their children's cries in ways that help them differentiate between their various needs—hunger, fatigue, wanting playful attention, and so forth. According to Bruch, mothers of individuals who develop eating disorders fail to respond appropriately to their young child's varying needs. For example, an infant's hunger cries might or might not elicit feeding. A young toddler's wishes to play may go unheeded by the mother who is not attentive or responsive to the signals her child is giving. The child therefore, has little opportunity to recognize her own needs, identify the internal cues that signal those needs, or differentiate between the various needs that may exist. For example, the baby is crying because she is wet and the mother consistently misreads this signal and quiets the child by feeding her. Bruch argued that as a consequence of such repeated "empathic failures" (i.e., responses that did not accurately address the need), the child is unable to form a stable and positive sense of self that honors their true or authentic needs. Instead, the child experiences strong feelings of inadequacy and cannot effectively confront or cope with normal developmental tasks. This sense of inadequacy reaches a crisis point as the child approaches adolescence. The emergence of disordered eating at this time represents an attempt to defend against feelings of inadequacy by attempting to exert control over one's body.

The nature of the mother-child relationship, and how it leads to disordered eating, appears to differ for those with anorexia versus bulimia. Johnson (1991) suggests that for those with anorexia, the primary caretaker was overprotective and controlling. The child experienced subtle or even overt punishment for any attempts to master *self-regulation*. That is, all initiative and attempts to move toward autonomy (e.g., identify their own needs, have their own views and express their own opinions) were discouraged. Instead, the child was expected to comply with parental expectations. Children who have this history then grow up striving to be "model" children who do all they can to please the parent and fit the expected mold. While children seem able to manage this adaptation during childhood, the pressures of puberty and adolescence make this unmanageable. The refusal to eat seen in young adolescents with anorexia may represent an attempt at separating from their overinvolved parent and exerting some control over their own lives.

The adolescent with bulimia, conversely, often has an underinvolved parent (Johnson, 1991). Instead of rigidly controlling the child's movement toward autonomy, the child is "propelled" or pushed toward self-sufficiency before she is ready for it. That is, the child is expected to meet her own needs early on, and often those of the parent as well. Expressing the need to be nurtured is discouraged. Although the child may appear to be more independent and comfortable with separation as a result, this comes at the expense of feeling safe, nurtured, loved, and taken care of. These individuals, pushed too soon to be independent, will also feel overwhelmed when confronted with developmental challenges. Although they may be better able to cope with some early developmental tasks, their difficulties emerge when the need to develop intimate relationships arises, which generally occurs in late adolescence. For these individuals, their experience of unmet dependency needs makes it difficult for them to show their vulnerability and to negotiate the mutual nurturing and emotional interdependence that is part of intimate relationships.

While achievement of separation and autonomy has been presented as the foundation of psychological health, this view has been challenged because it is based largely on a Eurocentric (i.e., Western or European) and Androcentric (i.e., male dominated) model of mental health. Steiner-Adair (1991), for example, notes that this model may not be adequate in discussing the development of young girls, which is also shaped by the core value of relatedness. Steiner-Adair argues that young girls are caught in a difficult bind precisely because they are expected to conform to both the "masculine" values of separation and autonomy and the "feminine" value of relatedness. This bind, she notes, causes confusion and internal distress and is a significant contributor to the development of eating disorders. It is only in recent years that some writers have come to dispute the old "mainstream" notion of autonomy, which implied that autonomy is being separate and not needing others (Jordan et al., 1991). Instead, these writers describe autonomy as an awareness of one's own values, needs, and wishes, while still remaining connected to others.

Young women from ethno culturally diverse backgrounds face further complications in their development. For many young girls of color, the values of interdependence, belongingness, and family loyalty clash with the mainstream view and value of separation and autonomy (Kuba & Harris, 1992). Thus, forging a positive identity in the face of racial and gender oppression, and coming to terms with the cultural values of one's own ethnic group and those of the mainstream culture, creates heightened vulnerability for eating problems (Root, 1990; Yates, 1989).

Discussions by family theorists help shed light on how socialization experiences within the family and the larger culture may impact the development of eating disorders (e.g., Minuchin, Rosman, & Baker, 1978; Schwartz, Barrett, & Saba, 1984). They describe eating disorders as a symptom of family dysfunction. They note that enmeshed (overinvolved) families typically have strong family rules, whether overt or covert, that prohibit expression of conflict or any intense, negative emotion such as anger, sadness, or fear. Compliance with family norms is enforced through withdrawal of affection or other means. The child in such a family grows up unable to express strong emotions, and lacks a firm sense of personal identity. Who is she? What are her likes/dislikes? What are her needs? Will she be able to develop friendships and negotiate the developmental tasks of adolescence? For this child, the family system has not equipped her to launch into adolescence. Becoming "sick" may be a way of coping with the conflicts that arise as she moves toward further individuation. Though not all families of eating disordered individuals are enmeshed, they all fail in some way to provide an appropriate environment for supporting the child's development of an autonomous identity, which is the foundation for genuine or authentic relating.

It has also been observed that families of eating disordered individuals tend to be particularly preoccupied with food and appearance (Bruch, 1984; Schwartz et al., 1984). Parents may make intrusive comments about the developing child's size and weight, or otherwise evoke anxiety in the growing child about her appearance and food intake. These early, extreme weight concerns then contribute to later development of eating disorders (Killen et al., 1996).

All families have their own values and rituals concerning food and weight, and these may become important in the child's risk for developing an eating disorder. For example, some families may use food as a reward for children or as a symbol of nurturance. Others may see eating together as a sign of family closeness, while still other families will promote a feeling of deprivation and secrecy around food and eating. Some families value thinness as an ideal body type, while other families see plumpness as pleasing.

Family values, rituals concerning food, and views about body size are shaped by the family's cultural milieu. These characteristics are often important in the development of eating disorders among people of color (Kuba & Harris, 1992; Root, 1990). For example, some children of immigrants develop eating problems because they experience great distress at being caught in the middle of two competing family messages. One message is to "fit in" with the dominant culture and thus strive to be thin; the other message is to maintain allegiance to the culture of origin, which may value a non-thin body type. Faced with competing messages, developing a positive personal identity becomes a far bigger challenge.

Despite the increased information we have regarding anorexia and bulimia, it is important to note that we still have much to learn. Indeed, the high comorbidity of these disorders with other psychiatric disorders such as depression, and the significant medical complications that arise from these disorders, make treatment highly challenging. Often, physicians, nutritionists, and other medical personnel need to be included in the treatment process. Even then, these disorders tend to be chronic with low recovery rates. According to some studies, full recovery may be as low as 10% for anorexia, although about half will show partial recovery (Herzog et al., 1993). In general, the recovery rates are more optimistic for bulimia, and range from 50 to 90% (Herzog et al., 1993; Lewandowski et al., 1997). However, as noted by many researchers, periods of recovery are often interrupted by episodes of relapse.

In sum, the nature of the child's cultural and interpersonal world are central factors in the development of eating disorders and are especially important issues in the unfolding relationship between client and counselor. Further, recovering from an eating disorder will require the development of new, flexible ways of coping with feelings and of relating to others. Treatment is aimed at helping the client discover who she is rather than focusing on who or what others want her to be. It also aims to empower her to stop complying with others and help her make choices about the values she wishes to adopt and how she wants to live her life. The chief vehicle for the client's stronger sense of self is the counselor-client relationship. In counseling, clients are provided with an affirming relationship where they can identify their own authentic feelings and make choices for their own lives with a caring adult.

CASE ILLUSTRATION
Presenting Problem

Allie sought treatment because of an upsurge of episodic bingeing and purging following the breakup of her first serious romantic relationship. This made sense given the issues surrounding intimacy and unmet dependency needs often seen in individuals with bulimia. Allie reported bingeing and vomiting as many as five times a day in the two months since the breakup, a significant increase over the two to three episodes she had averaged each week since the age of 15. Current triggers for bingeing were her acute feelings of rejection, sadness related to the breakup, and her anxiety about being able to continue to live up to her own high standards for academic performance. She was having difficulty carrying out daily activities such as studying and attending classes, and had also begun to avoid socializing with friends. Fear that her increased bingeing would lead to weight gain was the primary reason she sought treatment. She also hoped that being able to talk about her feelings about the breakup would help her reduce the episodes of bingeing.

Client Description

Allie was a short, well-groomed, 18-year-old. Though I readily recognized that she was of mixed racial/ethnic heritage (my own biracial background perhaps heightening my awareness of telltale signs), Allie seemed to obscure any signs that she was not White. She straightened her long, dark, and naturally curly hair to heighten her resemblance to a well-known musical celebrity (who ironically also identifies as White though of mixed heritage). Allie's careful makeup was not effective in covering up the dark circles under her eyes, a feature that frequently occurs in those with bulimia. Although thin, she also had the puffiness along the jaw line that is characteristic of individuals who are actively bulimic (due to swelling of the parotid glands from purging). She was dressed in a baggy sweatshirt and fashionable jeans.

Allie seemed to experience a great deal of shame initially in talking about herself, making only sporadic eye contact and sinking into her chair as if to hide. While her discomfort in talking could have reflected cultural constrictions on drawing attention to self and seeking help for psychological problems, Allie was at that time highly identified with mainstream cultural values. Her reticence seemed to reflect instead her feelings of self-disgust about her eating patterns. She also remarked that she had little experience talking about her feelings to anyone, particularly feelings of sadness or anxiety, her primary emotions at the beginning of treatment.

Allie met all of the diagnostic criteria for bulimia nervosa. Initially, her inability to carry out her normal daily activities, her low energy level, sadness, and low self-esteem made me suspect an underlying depression. However, her sadness and low energy diminished with the reduction of her bulimic episodes making her depressive symptoms seem secondary to her bulimia.

Social Context

Allie's parents, Gloria and E.J. (Earl Jr.), were teenagers when they married just a few months before Allie was born. Their families strongly disapproved of the marriage and the pregnancy that prompted it. Gloria's parents, Rafael and Alicia (Allie had been named

Alicia, in honor of her grandmother) were immigrants from Mexico who had worked hard to secure a middle-class lifestyle for their only child, and they were bitterly disappointed that Gloria postponed going to college to care for Allie. They also disapproved of the marriage because E.J. was of a different ethnicity and religion. E.J. was biracial, himself the product of a brief teenage romance between his African American father, Earl Sr., and a young Dutch woman studying in the United States. Raised by his paternal grandparents, Earlene and James, E.J. was well aware that his birth had disrupted his father's educational and athletic aspirations and he was determined that marriage would not derail his own ambitions to become a professional athlete. Because they were well off, Earlene and James were able to assist the young couple financially, and E.J. finished college while married to Gloria.

During the four years of their marriage, the couple lived for some time with Earlene and James, and Allie developed an especially close bond to her great-grandparents. Gloria, however, did not get along with her in-laws and frequently clashed with them about child-rearing practices. Earlene and James, consistent with African American cultural norms, encouraged Allie to play actively with other children even as a young toddler. Gloria tended to be more restrictive with Allie and felt her play should be limited to "lady-like" activities like doll play. Increasing tension between Gloria and her in-laws, and resentment that E.J. was able to pursue his goals while she was not, contributed to the ending of the marriage.

Following the divorce, Gloria moved in with her parents for five years. Alicia and Rafael were primary caretakers for Allie from the ages of 4 to 9. Allie remembers them being warm and affectionate with her, as her father's family had been. This was in sharp contrast to her mother, who tended to be a strict disciplinarian with high expectations. Gloria's parenting style was at odds both with her parents' and her culture's values. Gloria's goal as a parent was to help her child achieve upward mobility and also to help Allie assimilate into mainstream culture, something her parents had never sought to do, remaining tied to the close-knit Mexican and Mexican American community in the city in which they lived. Gloria herself felt a strong need to assimilate to "get ahead." She worked a series of jobs during this time, while attending and completing college part-time.

At age 9, Allie abruptly moved with Gloria across town from Alicia and Rafael, and Gloria cut off all communication with them. Allie later learned that this was because they had disapproved of a romantic relationship between Gloria and a then married White politician, Greg. Gloria remained cut off from her parents, but allowed Allie to visit for holidays and special occasions. Allie found these visits increasingly painful because her grandparents were quite critical of Gloria, especially after Gloria's marriage to Greg when Allie was 11.

Following her mother's remarriage, Allie once more made a major move, this time to a very exclusive, predominantly White suburb about an hour from the working-class, ethnically diverse city where she had grown up. The move was difficult for Allie, who missed family and friends. She found it difficult to make new friends at first, and felt out of place. Nevertheless, she worked very hard to get good grades and to fit in so that her family would think of her as a model student and daughter.

Because of Allie's very light complexion, most of her new classmates and neighbors assumed that she too was White. Allie never corrected their impression or said anything when they would make racist jokes or engage in racial stereotyping. From 11 on, all of Allie's classmates and friends were White.

When Allie was 13, her mother and Greg had a daughter, Jennifer. It was decided that Greg would adopt Allie so that she would have the same last name as her mother and half-sister. It was at this point that Allie officially changed her first name from Alicia to Allie, a name that sounded less Mexican American than Alicia, though she'd had the nickname of Allie for many years. Her grandmother does not know about the name change.

Allie entered high school with a new name and a new family. She got along well with her stepfather, who left all parenting decisions concerning Allie to Gloria. Allie was at first thrilled with the birth of Jennifer, but found frequent requests that she look after the baby burdensome once she became more active at school. Allie began to have frequent arguments with her mother while Gloria complained that Allie had become selfish. Allie felt that her mother was too demanding. She resented the long-established expectation that she be "mother's little helper." The arguments reached a peak when Allie became a cheerleader in her sophomore year of high school. Allie also started dating and was spending more and more time away from home.

The arguments with Gloria diminished after the sudden heart attack death of Earlene the spring of Allie's sophomore year. Though never close to her former mother-in-law, Gloria was nevertheless deeply affected by Earlene's death and began telling Allie that it was important to live as if death could come at any moment. She continued, however, to focus on Allie's looks and school achievement and was critical if Allie did not look and act like a model daughter (e.g., Gloria would suggest she dress in certain ways or would comment on her weight especially if she was beginning to put some on). Allie was devastated by her great-grandmother's death, and felt guilty about not having visited Earlene as much since she'd become more popular at school. Allie cherished the relationship with Earlene in part because this was her primary link to her father, who had become a well-known professional athlete. Gloria's continuing hostility toward her ex-husband, and his own preoccupation with his career, meant that Allie had had virtually no contact with her father since the divorce. Thus, Allie's attachment to her parents was insecure, making the loss of Earlene, her primary secure relationship, all the more painful. Following Earlene's death, Allie redoubled her efforts to be a model child—this was her only way to try to have more of a relationship with her mother.

At the start of her junior year of high school, Allie began dating John, a 17-year-old, White senior. Allie was attracted to John because he was "smart, ambitious, and gorgeous." They began dating seriously midyear, after John learned he had been accepted by a prestigious college back east, and they became sexually intimate shortly thereafter. Gloria and Greg approved of Allie's relationship with John, though Gloria constantly hinted that Allie should be taking precautions to avoid pregnancy. Allie's maternal grandparents, Rafael and Alicia, whom she saw only occasionally, were less impressed with John, though they assured Allie that they just wanted her to be happy.

Wanting to "look good for John," Allie began to purge after large meals. She had first heard of the tactic from a fellow cheerleader. Although she did not initially see this as a problem, she was very secretive about purging from the beginning. It was not until she also found herself seeking opportunities to eat secretly that she became concerned about her behavior, especially since she would force herself to throw up after these binges. Allie was terrified that John would find out, and was actually relieved when their relationship switched to being long distance after John left for college. Concern about her eating problem was a factor in her decision to attend the large, public university near the city she had grown up in rather than go to a more prestigious college nearer to John's school. She was aware that her bingeing and purging were worse during periods of stress and felt that she could not handle the stress of another big move or of a rigorous academic program.

Allie's immediate and extended family were pleased that she chose to stay close to home for college, though the decision caused tension in her relationship with John, who felt Allie had limited her options. Other differences began to emerge between John and Allie, particularly John's discomfort with Allie's relationship with her father's family. After several arguments about his reluctance to spend any time with them, John admitted that he had some prejudices against African Americans and that he probably would not have begun dating Allie had he known she was part African American. Allie stopped asking him to spend time with her father's family, and again cut down the time she spent with them as she had before Earlene's death. This devaluing of her identity, and her efforts to please John, meant denying her own needs and forsaking her own family, adding further compliance and shame for Allie. Just before the beginning of Allie's sophomore year in college, John decided he wanted to date other people.

Initial Sessions

Individuals with eating disorders, like substance abusers, often enter treatment denying the extent of their problems and are hesitant to give up their primary means of coping. They usually enter therapy because friends or family members have asked them to. They are generally reluctant to commit themselves to the treatment process and hope for a quick (and preferably spontaneous) recovery. Although they may have many "friends," I have found that these clients have rarely had deep, enduring relationships in which their emotional needs and authentic feelings were fully and honestly expressed.

Although the counseling relationship is initially anxiety provoking because it is a forthright and authentic relationship, clients with eating disorders manage to stay in treatment because they are in acute distress and want help controlling the crises. The challenge for counselors is to balance responding to the client's fear, pain, and other unmet needs while avoiding gratifying the client's wishes for easy solutions. These challenges were apparent in my work with Allie, and I sought to address them in our first meeting.

First Contact

I knew before meeting Allie that she was coming in because she had concerns related to food and eating. In addition to gathering personal information, I obtained a thorough history of her experiences with dieting, weight fluctuations, bingeing and purging, and her family history (including attitudes about food and eating). This fact-finding approach may seem to overemphasize food and weight. However, I have found it helpful to convey from the very beginning of treatment that *anything* related to eating can be discussed openly and honestly. Most individuals with eating disorders expect to receive judgment or criticism. To ward off this shame, eating becomes a secret that dominates their lives. I knew that Allie's problem would not be resolved until this shame was no longer evoked in our relationship. This open and honest approach also helps to reduce denial and clarify that their behavior is an ineffective coping strategy that exerts great emotional and physical toll. A sample of our discussion of Allie's eating history follows. It illustrates how a fact-finding approach may help discover relationships between disordered eating and problematic feelings, and identify the meanings the client attaches to food and weight.

TH: It sounds like the episodes of eating and then throwing up become more frequent when you're under a lot of stress or when you're dealing with difficult and painful experiences.

CL: Yeah. It's always been like that, since I started. In the beginning, though, I just wanted to keep my weight down.

TH: How often were you having these episodes?

CL: At first once or twice a week, then two or three times, sometimes more.

TH: So you found yourself bingeing and then purging more and more over time, just to keep your weight down?

CL: (pauses, then in a softer voice) I guess so.

TH: Is this something you've thought about before?

CL: Well, yeah, I guess I knew I was doing it more and more, even before the breakup, but it just was a way to not get fat.

TH: Tell me more about your concerns about not getting fat.

CL: Well, you know, guys are so into their girlfriends looking just right, and I have some family members who are kind of heavy. I'm short and I can't afford to gain any weight . . . and my mother really gets on me about my weight . . . so I've just really always had to watch it to not get fat.

TH: What would it mean to you to be fat?

CL: I'd be a failure, and no one would love me.

    Allie's painful association of fat and failure and her concern about "image" and "love-worthiness" came to the surface readily with this fact-finding approach. I have found that this approach also brings to the surface the client's fear that the counselor will try to control her eating behavior or force her to gain weight, a fear having its roots in an often overcontrolling mother-child relationship. The fear needs to be addressed explicitly in the initial contact, as it was with Allie:

CL: My ideal weight is 100, anything over that and I feel fat.

TH: Why 100?

CL: That's what I weighed when I looked my best, was happiest, when I started dating John.

TH: Sometimes there are fluctuations in a person's base weight—by this I mean the weight a person can naturally maintain without needing to diet or to use excessive methods to control weight. If you think about the period of time since puberty when you've been able to maintain a certain weight without resorting to dieting or purging, what would that weight be?

CL: Well, maybe 110 or even 115.

TH: So 110 or 115 might be a weight it would be more possible for you to maintain than 100.

CL: I don't want to weigh 115, and I don't want to be fat. If I have to get fat to get better, then I'm not sure it's worth it.

TH: I can hear that you have real concerns about getting fat. I'm sure there are lots of reasons why this issue is so important to you, and I hope we can talk about those reasons. I want to assure you that my goal is *not* to make you get fat. Instead, if we were to work together, I would want to help you find healthier ways to achieve your goals, including not getting fat. It seems like it would be important to help you find a way to really like yourself as you are, and not feel like you have to throw up to be a certain weight.

CL: Yeah, well, that would be good, if it could happen.

Common in most individuals with eating disorders, Allie had been excessively controlled in earlier relationships. In line with this, she expected me to try to control her as well. To change this core problem, it was important to emphasize that our work would be *collaborative*. I pointed out that her wishes and goals would be addressed in a mutually respectful and caring relationship. I also wanted to convey to Allie my belief that she could get better, especially given her feelings of helplessness in overcoming her problems.

CL: I've tried everything to stop, and I just can't.

TH: Well, it's not easy and it may take some time, but my sense from all you've told me is that you really do want to get a handle on this. I'd like to be able to help. Everybody's experience is unique, and we'd have to really get to the bottom of understanding how eating got to be such a problem, but I do think that it's possible to get to the place where eating is not the problem it is for you now.

CL: I guess you know a lot about these kinds of problems.

TH: Some, yes, but like I said, everybody's unique. If we were to work together I would want to get to know *you*. We'd have to find solutions that work for you. What do you think?

CL: (silently starts to weep) Yeah . . . yeah . . . (seems unable to speak for a moment or two). If we could, you know, find a way for me to get a handle on this. If I could get better . . . I mean, I really want to. I'd really like to do this. I'm willing to try.

TH: OK. That's a good place for us to start.

This was an intense interaction for Allie. I was later to learn that the intensity of her response was because I had emphasized that I would help her—that this time she was not alone with her problems and that it was okay to ask others for help. I also emphasized that we would not be following my agenda but that she would have choice and control in our relationship. My goal was to empower her by providing support for her interests, encouraging her initiative, affirming her stronger stance when she risked expressing her own ideas and feelings, and taking pleasure in the things she did well. Given the expectations she had learned in other important relationships, each of these responses from me were likely to be new and reparative for her.

Establish the Working Alliance

One of the issues relatively neglected in the literature on eating disorders concerns the strong initial reaction clients and counselors often have toward each other. The counselor, particularly if a woman, must confront personal feelings about her own appearance and body size. The client, in turn, will be attentive to both the counselor's appearance and to the counselor's attitude *toward* her own physical appearance. The client will likely also be curious about the meanings food holds for the counselor, how the counselor manages shame, and deals with personal appearance and self-esteem. Cultural similarities and differences, including beliefs about food, appearance, and personal relationships, will also be attended to. For both client and counselor, a major question is whether they will be able to identify with each other sufficiently to form a strong working alliance.

When I met Allie, I had been working with women with eating disorders for only a few years, yet I had had an almost lifelong history of weight problems. A key issue for me, therefore, was to separate my own experiences from Allie's while at the same time using these experiences where appropriate to gain insight into what Allie might be feeling.

In our initial sessions I found it more difficult to maintain my objectivity with Allie than with other clients with eating disorders with whom I had worked. I was more than usually aware of how I looked to Allie, and wondered what she thought of me. The source of the extra self-consciousness became clear as we began to discuss Allie's perceptions of me. Allie and I had both immediately recognized that we were both racially mixed and she was curious about me and wanted to know how I saw myself.

CL: Well, I was wondering what your background is . . . I mean, how you got started working with people with eating disorders.

(I thought that Allie was asking about my cultural background, as well as expressing curiosity about my interest in eating disorders. I felt it was important to explore why these questions were important to her before answering them directly.)

TH: Seems like there are two questions here—what my background is, and how I came to do work in this area. I'll be glad to answer both questions, but I'm curious too. I'm wondering why you might want to know about me and my experience, and what my answers might mean to you.

CL: I was just wondering if you were mixed, you know, um, racially mixed. 'Cause I am. I mean some of my family is not White.

TH: Yes . . .

CL: So I thought maybe if you were mixed too maybe, you know, you might understand about that.

TH: About what it means to be of mixed heritage?

CL: Yeah.

TH: Well, it's something we could certainly talk about. Especially if you have some feelings about it, or questions.

CL: So are you?

TH: Yes. My mother is White and my father was Black.

CL: So what does that make you?

TH: I see myself as Black.

CL: Oh. (Pauses, looks directly at me for one of the first times in our work together.) My grandparents—actually they're my great-grandparents—on my father's side are Black.

I have thought a good deal about whether I handled this interaction appropriately, and I would undoubtedly handle it differently if I had it to do over. I was aware that we had left her other question unanswered, and that we had not fully explored why she wanted to know about my background or experience. I also felt that by declaring a monocultural identity, I might have made it difficult for Allie to explore her own experience of being ethnically mixed. My response was prompted by my own solution to the question of identity, which had little relevance for Allie's current ethno cultural identity. However, this is one instance where a therapeutic mistake provided an opening for productive work.

When we talked later about how my answer affected her, Allie said that I had given her the idea that I felt good about myself and my ethnicity. She thought then that perhaps I might really be able to help her learn to feel good about herself after all. She also said that she thought of how proud her great-grandmother, Earlene, had always been of being Black. Unknowingly, I had tapped into an early experience Allie had had of being cared for by Earlene, and this was to become significant in the transference (feelings toward me) that Allie developed. I thus gained a certain amount of credibility with Allie by addressing the issue of cultural identity directly, and this proved important in establishing our working alliance. Allie became more open in our work together, and she also gradually became more comfortable exploring how she felt about our relationship as it unfolded.

In addition to the issue of cultural identity, Allie quickly raised the issue of my weight and appearance. She made several efforts to broach the topic and eventually said, ". . . uhhh, . . . mmm, I was just wondering if you have ever worried about your weight. I mean, have you been overweight? Have you ever thrown up to keep your weight down?" Although this question about my weight was not entirely unexpected, I found myself wrestling with what the appropriate response for Allie would be. What did Allie really need at this moment? What response would be most helpful to her? What would my response mean to her? Was this a question about my ability or credibility as a helper? Was the issue a need to identify more closely with me? So we explored these issues together. As we did this, it became clear that Allie was ashamed of her eating disorder. She was also concerned that if I had never struggled with a similar problem that I might be judgmental or critical. She also wanted reassurance that she was not "crazy" and that she could get better. As I responded to these underlying issues, Allie's "need to know" about my weight history dissipated.

CASE CONCEPTUALIZATION

Client Conceptualization

The emergence of Allie's disordered eating was associated with her first serious romantic relationship. The upsurge in bingeing and purging that led her to seek treatment was triggered by the breakup of that relationship. It thus appeared that intimacy issues were important in understanding Allie's bulimia. I speculated that Allie's many early disruptions in relationships were central in explaining her apparent difficulty with intimacy. It seemed likely that the disruptions, particularly the divorce and the abrupt partings from both sets of grandparents, had seriously impacted Allie's sense of self and her ability to trust that she would be cared for. She had experienced little continuity in being cared for. Though her early experiences with her extended family were warm and affirming, she soon learned that responding to her grandparents' warmth meant possibly incurring the wrath of her mother, the only figure consistently present in her life. I imagined that like many young children, Allie had blamed herself for any conflicts her mother had with others and for her parents' divorce, and that she had come to feel she was therefore unworthy of love and affection. Neither parent had provided Allie with the opportunity to disconfirm her beliefs about her unworthiness. Indeed, her father's absence and mother's criticism exacerbated her feelings. Allie's attempts to be a "model" child may well have been a response to her self-blame and sense of unworthiness and represented an attempt to prove herself "love-worthy" to her mother.

I hypothesized that low self-worth and self-blame were underlying Allie's self-destructive bulimic behavior. My experience in working with individuals with eating disorders led me to believe that Allie, like other clients I had seen, did not believe she deserved to be loved and cared for. The bulimic episodes were at least partly an expression of this inner sense of unworthiness. As long as she binged and threw up, Allie had "evidence" of her defectiveness. Allie was thus acting out an inner conviction, but in doing so she was holding on to a faulty assumption. A major focus of treatment was to help her understand the underlying feelings of unworthiness that were being acted out in bulimic episodes. More specifically, I knew that Allie would need to be able to recognize that the feelings of unworthiness were tied to her past. They were based on a child's valiant but unsuccessful attempts to understand the attitudes and behaviors of the significant adults in her life.

I also hypothesized that the bulimic episodes expressed a good deal of ambivalence on Allie's part: she both wanted and feared the food. This paralleled her fear of intimacy: she yearned for closeness yet it carried great emotional costs, so she feared it. For Allie, intimacy costs included having to suppress her own needs to gain her mother's approval. The costs were also evident in her relationship with John: she felt she had to look a certain way to be loved by John; she also cut herself off from her father's family because of John's dislike of African Americans.

It is perhaps not surprising that Allie's symptoms emerged in the relationship with John, since the symptoms themselves have to do with living inauthentically: denying one's real self, true feelings, and personal needs. The bingeing and purging help maintain a fiction that one is normal—at least normal weight. The symptoms also serve to keep out of awareness the ways in which basic needs for appropriate care and affection are not being met.

I speculated that the feelings of sadness and rejection Allie was experiencing when she began counseling had to do not only with her current loss of the relationship with John, but might also reflect unresolved issues associated with earlier losses. Allie had never had the opportunity to discuss, let alone fully work through, her feelings about her parents' divorce, the loss of her relationship with her father, and the repeated emotional loss of her mother who kept withdrawing. As discussed in the chapter on counseling children of divorce, young children often respond to divorce and the disengagement of a parent following divorce with acute feelings of abandonment. Children need to be helped work through these feelings. Allie was not helped because of bitterness about the marriage and divorce on both sides of her extended family. I hypothesized that Allie's feelings following the divorce were so painful that she had to cover them over, only to have them stirred up again by the breakup with John. Adding to this vulnerability to loss, Allie had grown up experiencing repeatedly her mother's disapproval and disengagement whenever she failed to meet Gloria's demanding expectations.

While Allie's bulimia indicated to me that she had serious psychological problems, I was also aware that Allie had much strength. She was a very bright young woman who had maintained an excellent academic record while engaged in a variety of extracurricular activities in high school and college. She had warm feelings for her immediate and extended family, and was well liked by her peers though she tended to keep her friendships superficial. I believed that Allie possessed a solid set of coping skills to manage many aspects of her life. Her coping skills seemed deficient primarily when it came to handling intimacy and strong emotions such as sadness. I hoped that her more general coping ability would be an asset in our work together, and it did prove critical to the success of her work to gain control of her bulimic symptoms.

Orienting Constructs

My understanding of Allie's difficulties fit with the literature on the etiology of eating disorders discussed earlier. It was clear from Allie's early history that her mother had failed in many ways to respond appropriately to her needs or support her development of a firm sense of self. Gloria's high expectations of Allie and insistence that she assimilate to mainstream cultural values (even to the point of denying her mixed ethno cultural heritage) all served to foster in Allie a sense that she must deny her real self and her own needs to be loved and cared for. Allie's lack of comfort with intimacy, feelings of unworthiness, and unresolved sadness, were readily understandable in light of her early experiences. I could see how disordered eating became a means of coping with unmet needs, intimacy conflicts, and other painful feelings.

Allie had also been caught in another bind: she was expected to be independent and excel academically *and* be able to form romantic relationships with males. Unfortunately, for many adolescent females, these expectations are experienced as contradictory, believing that to be attractive (and nonthreatening) to men, they must deny their own academic and independence strivings. The issue of *denial*—denial of strengths, of needs, of feelings—seems to underlie much bulimic behavior.

For Allie, the situation was further complicated by pressure to deny her ethnic heritage and to adopt cultural values that denigrated her family background. Indeed, as treatment progressed, it became clear how much mainstream cultural messages about appearance and attractiveness confused and distressed Allie. The following discussion illustrates this confusion and its role in her disordered eating:

CL: At school it was really hard to be with people when they would make these totally racist comments, talking about how ugly Black people were, or how lazy Mexicans were.

TH: What would you be feeling when you were with people making these comments?

CL: These people were my friends, and I'd be thinking to myself that must be what they really think of me, or it's what they would think of me if they knew that members of my family were Black and Mexican. So, of course, I didn't want them to know.

TH: So you were feeling like you couldn't let your friends know who you really were.

CL: I knew that the things they were saying weren't true, at least not about the people in my family that I loved, but it was hard to fight back. I felt that if I told them I'm part Black and part Mexican and I'm not ugly or lazy, they would just totally reject me instead of changing their views. And, in a way, maybe I was agreeing with them by trying so hard to be White. Because I never wanted anyone to think of me as ugly, and I guess I did believe you had to be White to be pretty.

TH: You talked a lot about needing to be seen as pretty, and how that tied in to your starting to purge. How do you think your need to be seen as attractive ties in with the racist comments your friends would make?

CL: Well, I guess I really believed the things they said at some level, 'cause you know I would hear it so often, and see it too in the way people get portrayed, and I guess I *felt* unattractive. So I would obsess about it and then try to make myself more attractive. That meant being thin, and it also meant being White. I was terrified they would find out I wasn't all White, so maybe I focused on trying to be thin.

Kuba and Harris (1992) discuss the concept of *internalized oppression* to describe the experience of young women of color who adopt mainstream values concerning appearance and feel themselves to be unattractive as a consequence. These authors believe that internalized oppression is a central factor in the development of eating disorders among women of color. Though conflicts in her ethno cultural identity were apparent from the beginning of our work together, it was not until counseling was well underway that Allie was able to see how they contributed to her pattern of disordered eating and how they related to her deeper feelings of being unworthy.

Children are helped to develop positive ethno cultural identities by affirming experiences with others and by the opportunities to interact with role models who themselves have positive identities. Allie's extended family provided her with experiences that helped to offset some of society's stereotypes about African Americans and Mexican Americans, but she had only sporadic contact with them from age 11. Since her parents' families did not get along with each other, they were not able to help Allie develop an identity that integrated their separate cultural traditions. More significantly, Allie's mother had herself not been able to forge a positive ethno cultural identity. Gloria remained strongly identified with mainstream cultural values and had in fact cut herself off entirely from her parents and from her cultural heritage. Allie's primary role model, and the environment she was in from age 11 on, thus could not help her move beyond viewing herself in terms of the values and stereotypes of the dominant culture. I began to suspect that Allie's inability to forge a positive ethno cultural identity contributed to her disordered eating. Had she been able to see herself more positively as a person of mixed ethno cultural heritage, she might not have felt the need to make herself over into a thin, mainstream cultural ideal.

TREATMENT PLANS AND INTERVENTION STRATEGY
Initial Treatment Plans

My goals for the first stage of treatment with Allie were to:

1. establish a collaborative relationship of trust and cooperation;
2. help Allie gain mastery over her bulimic symptoms; and
3. help Allie begin to make connections between her symptoms and underlying feelings and conflicts (i.e., struggles with personal identity and ability to be authentic in close relationships).

I hoped that achieving these short-term goals would make it possible for us to do more in-depth work in the second stage. My goal for the second stage was to trace Allie's problems with intimacy to her early experiences of disruptions and to help her understand where her feelings of unworthiness and sadness came from. Since relational themes are typically replayed in the therapeutic relationship before they are fully understood by clients (Teyber, 2000), I assumed that this second stage would involve Allie and me exploring the nature of our relationship. My goals for the third and final stage were initially quite simple: I hoped that Allie would be able to forge a positive sense of self so that she would no longer feel the need to resort to bingeing and purging to make herself into a lovable person. I knew this new sense of self could emerge from having an affirming or healing/reparative experience in treatment. I believed this meant giving Allie the experience of being truly understood and accepted as she was, rather than for how she looked or how hard she worked.

The first stage of counseling with eating disordered individuals, like work with substance abusers, is typically focused on helping the individual to stop the disordered or addictive behavior. Many clinicians believe that real progress can only come about after the individual has given up reliance on disordered eating or substances. This belief is based on the fact that disordered eating and substance abuse are used defensively to avoid experiencing painful feelings. As a result, these feelings are not available to explore in treatment as long as the client continues the symptoms. My own experience bears out the importance of focusing on strategies for reducing and eliminating symptomatic eating at the beginning of counseling. I do believe, however, that clients are able to gain insight into the role of the disordered eating from the beginning of counseling, and that care and attention must be given to helping the individual maintain their recovery *throughout* treatment. Exploration of particularly painful material during the course of therapy may prompt relapses and these must be addressed immediately to ensure continued progress. I believe further that the therapeutic relationship forged in the initial stage of treatment is what makes possible the later work in therapy.

A good deal of the work Allie and I undertook during the initial stage of treatment, which lasted about four months, was aimed explicitly at eliminating Allie's reliance on bingeing and purging as a means of coping with stress and conflicts. This involved providing information: Allie needed to learn facts about the consequences of bulimia, the need for proper nutrition, and healthy strategies for weight management and stress reduction. I was able to refer Allie to a time-limited support group run by the university health center as a supplement to our work. The group's psycho-educational format provided Allie with the information she needed and a forum to ask questions about diet, and so forth. When groups such as this one are unavailable, I usually make suggestions about reading materials and provide a referral to a nutritionist.

It is also important during this stage to have the client carefully monitor the emotions and events that trigger episodes of disordered eating. For most clients, being able to identify the triggers of their disordered eating is an empowering step. They are surprised to learn that the episodes that once seemed completely out of their control actually follow a certain pattern. Identifying the pattern is a first step in gaining control over the disordered eating. The next step is to develop a range of new coping strategies for handling the emotions and events that trigger the episodes. Although clients may ask the counselor for suggestions about new strategies, their fear of being controlled means any suggestions from the therapist are likely to be resisted. I have found that, with encouragement, clients are able to list ways of coping that have worked for them in the past, or that seem to work for people they admire. The workability of the strategies should also be explored. Following is an example of the kind of work Allie and I did to explore one possible trigger for a binge and to help Allie discover other ways of handling the situation:

CL: I was noticing that whenever I get angry with Margi (her roommate), I want to eat lots of candy.

TH: Do you have the urge to binge whenever you're angry, or just when you're angry with Margi?

CL: I haven't really noticed it with anyone else, but now that you mention it, I don't get angry much. When I was angry with John, I wouldn't say anything, but I would try to sneak away and eat. It was a way of getting back at him, behind his back.

TH: Seems like anger is hard for you. What else could you do when you find yourself feeling angry, say with Margi?

CL: I could avoid her.

TH: Hmmn. Isn't that what you're doing by bingeing?

CL: I could ask her for some space.

TH: How would that be for you?

CL: Hard.

TH: Any thoughts about why it might be hard? Why anger is hard for you to express?

CL: I hate it when people get angry you know, when they yell and scream.

TH: Do you yell and scream when you get angry?

CL: No. I just eat (laughs). I guess I'm afraid people will yell and scream at me if I tell them I'm angry at them, like my mom does if I let on I'm not 100% happy with her.

TH: Is Margi like your mother?

CL: No.

TH: Will she yell and scream if you ask for some space?

CL: No.

TH: Or tell you that she's not 100% happy with you?

CL: (laughs at my using her terminology) No, I guess not.

TH: And if she did?

CL: I guess I could leave *then.*

TH: Would you binge then?

CL: Probably. What else could I do?

TH: You tell me. We've talked about some of the things you find helpful when you're stressed—like running, going for a drive, seeing a movie, reading a magazine. Would any of those things satisfy rather than a binge?

CL: Maybe going for a drive, though I might run over someone!

TH: Yeah, seems like you've got to find a way to get some of the anger out without attacking a candy bar or a poor pedestrian.

CL: I could always go downstairs and play video games.

TH: I think it will be important for us to look at why anger is hard for you, but in the meantime playing video games sounds better than bingeing and then wanting to purge. Maybe you could try this the next time you're feeling angry with Margi.

In this interaction, Allie found a short-term solution to handling an interpersonal trigger rather than bingeing. Gradually, Allie was able to build a repertoire of these short-term solutions. The longer-term goal of also understanding what keeps her from expressing her anger is alluded to, though exploring the roots of Allie's conflicts with anger in more depth was a second stage goal. Although Allie had developed some ease in the therapeutic relationship, I did not feel that we had established a solid enough alliance at this stage to explore her anger fully or to work on ways of communicating her anger more directly.

Although it is generally a very positive experience for clients to begin to respond differently to events that formerly triggered disordered eating, they may also experience a sense of loss as they give up their symptoms. They may also begin to experience, for the first time, the unwanted or threatening emotions they have been warding off with the disordered eating. Finally, they will likely experience relapses in their attempts to eliminate disordered eating. The counselor must attend to the shifting moods accompanying the early stage of recovery and help the client to hold onto gains, while working through temporary setbacks and/or the exploration of more intense material. Alerting the client to the possibility of relapses and helping her see these as *temporary* setbacks will facilitate progress.

When Allie began to gain some mastery over her bingeing and purging (reducing her bulimic episodes to two times a week and eventually being able to go without purging even after a binge), we moved to exploring more charged material. During the second stage, Allie's core conflicts emerged in the context of our relationship. Anger at my being away for vacation, disappointment following a misinterpretation, and feelings of warmth following an empathic connection were all explored as they arose in our relationship. Addressing Allie's feelings toward me often led us to the roots of the feelings in earlier experiences. In this way, our relationship became a vehicle for understanding how Allie had originally come to feel that her own needs did not matter.

There was no discrete turning point between the second and third stages of therapy with Allie. Instead, as Allie began to examine her early relationships in the safety of our relationship, her attitude toward her family and herself began to change. This was most immediately discernible in her shifting ethno cultural identity. As Allie's and my relationship strengthened, Allie began to talk about her close bond to her great-grandmother, Earlene. Allie's admiration of Earlene's efforts to reach out to Gloria and to her father's Dutch mother, while continuing to be strongly identified as African American, helped Allie begin to embrace the different ethnicities represented in her parentage.

Less immediately, but no less significantly, Allie came to understand how her feelings of being unlovable were linked to her parents' divorce. Giving voice at last to the feelings of loss, anger, and bewilderment freed Allie from the pervasive sense that she had been to blame and helped her see that her parents, like herself, were imperfect people who had not been able to cope with a difficult situation. Her need to be the model child/adult also abated, though the skills she had developed in pursuing perfection in schoolwork still stood her in good stead.

Balancing Goals

The chief task in the early stage of treatment was to balance the goal of helping Allie gain mastery of her eating behavior while exploring the core conflicts that were being masked by the disordered eating. Although Allie could readily talk about a specific binge episode, she had more difficulty relating it to her feelings and to past experiences. As Allie gained information about bulimia through the psycho-educational group, and also developed strategies for coping with situations that triggered bulimic episodes, her narrow focus on specific binge episodes shifted to a focus on understanding the underlying causes of her disordered eating.

Revised Treatment Goals

The treatment goals did not shift significantly during the 12 months of therapy, though my understanding of the specific issues and emotions needing focus did. One factor underlying Allie's eating behavior, that I had missed in my original conceptualization, was her difficulty with anger. As we explored the roots of this difficulty, it became clear that Allie had a great deal of unresolved anger toward her mother because Gloria had taken her away from the two family situations in which Allie had felt most loved and affirmed. I thus began to pay special attention to how Allie defended against her anger in our relationship and found this exploration a key part of our progress in the later phases of treatment.

THERAPEUTIC PROCESS

Replay of Relational Patterns

Clients' interpersonal styles of relating often get replayed in their interaction with the counselor. These "replays" and how they are managed become crucial in contributing to the client's progress. With Allie, separations or breaks in our work together (e.g., due to vacations) evoked replays of Allie's typical ways of thinking and interacting. One episode, about four months into the therapy, led us to deeper exploration of Allie's difficulties with anger. This session followed a three-week holiday break. Allie, for the first time, was able to express anger directly:

CL: It was the trip from hell from the beginning. When I got back up here no one was around to talk to about it. My first night back I went straight to Taco Bell, and just totally pigged out. It's been really hard since. All those things we talked about doing, well, I haven't done any of them. There doesn't seem to be any point.

TH: I'm sorry it's been such a hard time for you Allie. Do you want to talk about what made the trip hard? Was it the things we talked about before you went home?

CL: I don't remember what we talked about; I only know it was bad, and I've been eating like a pig ever since.

TH: I imagine my being away didn't help any.

CL: You have to take your vacation, right?

TH: Right, but it seems like it was a hard time for you, and maybe you're feeling upset about my being away.

CL: What makes you think that?

TH: I notice today you're not looking at me much, and you sound like you're not happy with me, to use your phrase. And also, I know *I* would probably be angry if I needed to talk to someone and my therapist was away.

CL: That's crazy, therapists have the right to take vacations.

TH: They have the right, but that wouldn't stop me from feeling mad, or at least disappointed. How do *you* feel about my being away?

CL: I don't know. Maybe I am disappointed a little; I don't know, like you make it seem like things are going to get better, and then you disappear just when they get worse . . . So maybe I am a little pissed. Mostly, I just wonder if this is really going to do any good.

TH: Well, I'm really glad you could tell me you're pissed at me. Seems like now that I've let you down, you're wondering if it's safe to trust me again, trust that the therapy can be helpful.

CL: It's not that *you* let me down.

TH: Well, you needed me and I wasn't here.

CL: I know it's not your fault. I mean, I should know how to handle things by now without having to eat like a pig.

TH: Allie, do you see how you went from being able to acknowledge that you were mad at me to blaming yourself for feeling bad that I was away? Why do you think that happened?

In this interaction, Allie directly expressed her anger and also replayed her tendency to quickly try to "placate" the person she was angry with. I had to explicitly invite Allie to express the anger. Although I typically refrain from naming feelings with clients (to avoid imposing my assumptions of what a client is feeling), I have found that some clients need help being able to recognize and give voice to their feelings. This has been particularly the case with my clients who have eating disorders. I felt that Allie would be able to express her anger directly only with some prompting. My invitation to Allie to express her disappointment with me was a very new experience for her and she clearly expected me to invalidate or minimize her anger—"After all, therapists need vacations." Instead, I tried to show Allie that her feelings were understandable and that I cared about what she felt. In addition, I let her know that I was sorry that I had not been there for her—which was different from the love-withdrawal she expected for expressing her anger. My apology came later rather than earlier because I did not want to cut Allie's anger off prematurely. Instead, we talked about how she herself tried to cut it off. We went on to explore the many interactions with others, especially John and her mother, that had taught her that it was not okay to be angry. We had already discussed how her unexpressed anger was a trigger for bingeing. A significant drop in her disordered eating accompanied this direct expression of anger toward me. Following this healing experience, Allie began to express her anger and disappointment more directly with me and with others. She also became more comfortable expressing other feelings, including sadness and happiness.

It may seem strange that Allie would have had difficulty expressing pleasure, yet it became clear that Allie experienced feeling happy or good as threatening. She feared, in particular, that she would lose the source of her pleasure because of retaliation from a jealous other. This issue was played out in our interaction during the tenth month of therapy as Allie was preparing for a summer study course abroad. By this time, Allie had made real progress in recovering from her bulimic episodes and she was much more insightful about some of the factors that had contributed to her problematic eating. She was, at this point, talking about terminating counseling. The episode arose, in part, because of my feelings toward Allie, her upcoming trip, and termination of therapy.

In one session, as Allie talked about taking a side trip to Paris, I asked her if she thought it was really a good idea to go off on her own, away from her travel companions. She then began to look away from me and, with diminished enthusiasm, began to identify reasons why the side trip might not be such a good idea after all. In that moment she reminded me of the shy, reticent young woman I had begun working with and I realized that there was a part of me that missed the old Allie—the one who needed my help. I was proud of the work she had done, aware that I would miss her, and apparently was not yet ready to let her go. I realized then that I, like her mother, was having a hard time recognizing Allie, as a person in her own right, capable of succeeding without me. It became critical that I address this and give Allie a different experience from the ones she had had with her mother. It was important that I affirm her growing independence:

TH: You know, Allie, it's just hit me that I've kind of poured cold water on your idea about Paris when I should be celebrating with you the opportunity to go.

CL: What do you mean?

TH: Just that the very fact that you're looking forward to doing something on your own, for yourself, is something to celebrate, and instead I seem to be trying to discourage you.

CL: I did think you were being kind of negative, but then I thought maybe you know something about Paris that I don't know.

TH: No, I'm sure you know more about Paris than I do. Maybe that's the problem. You're going somewhere I've never been. And I'm happy for you. This is a big step for you.

CL: I don't know. Maybe it's too big a step.

Here Allie was ready to talk herself out of the pleasure of independent travel in her effort to keep her overprotective therapist from feeling bad. When I pointed this out to Allie, she immediately related it to a relationship pattern with her mother. Allie had learned not to relish her steps toward independence because Gloria would respond by finding fault with those steps. When this pattern was repeated in our relationship, I responded in a different way than Gloria had. I acknowledged the feelings behind my response, and also supported Allie's right to experience pleasure in her approaching independence:

TH: When I think of your trip to Paris, I realize that I'm a little envious, and even more, that I'm going to miss you. But I'll enjoy thinking of you in Paris. I *am* really glad for you, Allie. It seems like you're on your way in more ways than one.

CL: Yeah, it does, and I guess deep down I'm really happy about it too.

Recognizing and sharing my feelings toward Allie with her was an important part of our work, particularly as we drew closer to termination. I was able to do this because we had developed a strong working relationship, a relationship characterized by warm, positive feelings, and honesty. I knew that Allie had transferred to me the warm feelings she had had to her African American great-grandmother, whom she saw as wise and affirming. I was honored that she saw me as this wise woman role model, a role model that she needed at that stage in her development. I believe that this, combined with my mixed ethno cultural heritage, a heritage I was comfortable with, helped Allie achieve a more positive sense of her own ethno cultural identity.

Impediments to Treatment

The chief impediment to treatment was Allie's initial discomfort with the idea of giving up her bulimic behavior. Purging was a strategy Allie employed to ward off unwanted weight gain. Even though she developed new, healthier strategies to manage her weight (e.g., healthy eating, exercise, stress management techniques), Allie still struggled with her unrecognized motives for purging: to ward off painful, difficult feelings. At first she resisted exploring these feelings by, for example, coming late or missing a session, or by talking only about superficial things. We acknowledged how important it was for her to feel safe with me before being able to explore these feelings directly. Sometimes we went in circles as she would move closer to core conflicts and painful feelings, then feel the need to defend against these by resorting to distancing and being more superficial. Allie herself became very aware of the "cycles" and of how she defended against painful feelings. She was able to recognize how she avoided being close to others because she was afraid others would find the "real" Allie unlovable.

Allie had particular difficulty allowing herself to experience anger and sadness. In time, in the safety of our relationship, she learned to understand and accept her feelings. Allie's reluctance to experience anger and sadness in counseling made sense in light of her history. She had, for example, avoided facing the pain and bewilderment evoked by the ending of her relationship with her father following her parents' divorce. How could her father have abandoned her so completely? How could her mother have allowed the abandonment to happen? It was only after Allie finally asked these and other questions out loud, and experienced the resulting anger and profound sadness they evoked, that she realized that she had falsely believed that she was somehow to blame for her parents' failure to appropriately nurture her. Engel and Ferguson (1990) have used the term *imaginary crimes* to describe how individuals sometimes assume guilt or blame themselves for parental inadequacies. They discuss the many ways in which the self-blame for imaginary crimes gives rise to self-punishing psychological problems. As Allie began to mourn her early losses, and to experience the confusion they evoked, she realized that her feelings of unworthiness were rooted in situations she had had little control over. Instead of protecting herself from the feelings through purging, or protecting her parents from her anger through her self-blame, Allie was able to finally gain some sense of mastery over the feelings by experiencing them fully in the relative safety of the counseling relationship.

TERMINATION AND SUMMARY THOUGHTS

Counseling ended almost 12 months after it began when Allie left to go abroad. Although the timing for ending was prompted by an external event, both Allie and I felt that she had made sufficient progress to end treatment. While part of me wanted to hold on to Allie, and she was a little apprehensive about ending treatment altogether, we were both delighted to have come so far. Allie had gained real mastery over the bulimia and was no longer plagued by the secret shame that marked her entry into therapy. Instead, she was able to experience a range of feelings, none of which was disabling. Significantly, she had moved through experiencing and expressing some of her anger toward her mother, and had come to have a fuller appreciation of who Gloria was—her deficiencies as a mother, but also her strengths. Allie was able to see that Gloria had struggled to raise a child without the help of a partner. She also saw that Gloria had been overprotective on the one hand and unresponsive on the other because of the

issues she (Gloria) was struggling with rather than because Allie was a defective child. Resolving these faulty beliefs helped Allie forge a more open relationship with Gloria. Although their relationship was still marked by high expectations, criticism, and guilt-inducing withdrawal from Gloria, Allie had successfully changed her response to all of this. Allie no longer responded to the expectations with efforts to be the model child, but with clearer assertion of her own goals and wishes. Perhaps most importantly, she was able to maintain this sense of identity even under pressure from Gloria to be, once again, a "model" child.

While Allie's sense of self had also undergone marked changes, she still had not fully integrated a sense of identity as a worthy, deserving young woman. She was still, for example, consolidating her ethno cultural identity that integrated her mixed ethnic background. This process was further helped by the relationships she was forming with mixed-race friends. Allie also still experienced anxiety when beginning relationships with men, fearing that they would not care for her once they really knew her. I fully expected that Allie would be able to take these further steps toward a positive sense of self as she entered new relationships and continued the work we had begun in counseling.

Questions for Thought and Discussion

1. What did your mother tell you about your appearance? What did your father tell you? How did these messages affect you? Were any of these messages based on their cultural backgrounds? Which messages have continued to affect you into the present and which have changed?

2. Think for a moment about your feelings toward food and your body image. Imagine you are a counselor helping an eating disordered adolescent. Identify one way your own issues with food might facilitate treatment and one way they might hamper or impede treatment. Which of your cultural features (e.g., gender, race, age) seem to be most salient as you respond to this exercise?

3. List some cultural or familial factors that you think are important contributors to the development of an eating disorder. Thinking of someone you know with an eating disorder, which of these factors played a role?

Suggestions for Further Reading

Garner, D. M., & Garfinkel, P. E. (Eds.). (1997). *Handbook of treatment for eating disorders* (2nd ed.). New York: Guilford. Provides a comprehensive presentation of the main approaches to the treatment of eating disorders. Practical, detailed, provides instructive case illustrations.

Foreyt, J. P., & Mikhail, C. (1997). Anorexia nervosa and bulimia nervosa. In E. J. Mash & L. G. Terdal (Eds.), *Assessment of childhood disorders* (pp. 683–716). New York: Guilford. Excellent review of the literature.

Root, M. P. P. (1990). Disordered eating in women of color. *Sex Roles, 22,* 525–536. Provides an illuminating discussion of the cultural and familial dynamics that underlie the emergence of eating disorders in women of color.

Wilson, G. T., Heffernan, K., & Black, C. M. (1996). Eating disorders. In E. J. Mash & R. A. Barkley (Eds.), *Child psychopathology* (pp. 541–571). New York: Guilford. Excellent review of the literature.

SHEILA: AN AFRICAN AMERICAN ADOLESCENT COMING TO TERMS WITH SEXUAL ABUSE AND DEPRESSION

CHAPTER 3

INTRODUCTION

Sexual abuse of children is a major public health problem. In the United States alone, there were more than 120,000 child sexual abuse reports in 1996 (U.S. DHHS, 1998). While these are the reported cases, actual numbers may be significantly higher. In fact, other studies evaluating lifetime prevalence rates of childhood sexual victimization report that 6 to 62% of women and 3 to 31% of men have experienced this violation (see Damon & Card, 1992; Finkelhor, 1990; Finkelhor et al., 1990; Gorey & Leslie, 1997; Peters et al., 1986). These rates vary so dramatically because people define sexual abuse differently and collect the information differently (e.g., by phone, in-person interviews, paper-pencil surveys). The issue of definition is a very challenging one. For example, is it sexual abuse when a 10-year-old forces his 8-year-old sister to touch him sexually? Would it still be abuse if his sister were older than him or if she initiated the contact? Which dimension is most critical in the definition: The use of force or threat, their ages and difference in age, power differences between them, the lack of mutual consent, or some other dimension? In addition, at what age should children be considered competent to "consent" to sexual activity? As can be seen from this example, the issue of definition is not as straightforward as one might think and profoundly influences all of the information we collect about sexual abuse.

In the first section of this chapter we will discuss some general information about sexual abuse and its impact. We will then present a case study illustrating treatment of "Sheila," an African American adolescent who was sexually molested by her stepfather.

Research Findings on Sexual Abuse

As mentioned earlier, there is no universal agreement on how to define childhood sexual abuse. However, most researchers and clinicians agree that sexual contact between a child or adolescent and someone who is older (some suggest a five-year difference) and/or someone who has more power and control (such as a teacher, youth group leader, or older sibling) is abusive. The National Research Council (1993) includes, in their definition of sexual maltreatment, incest, sexual assault, exposure to sexual acts, and involvement in pornography.

Many children who are abused suffer long-term negative consequences (Kendall-Tackett et al., 1993; Wekerle & Wolfe, 1996). According to Kendall-Tackett et al. (1993), the impact of the abuse on the child will be shaped by many factors. For example, the child's age, the child's psychological adjustment before the abuse, the type of assault (e.g., use of violence, threats, bodily penetration), how many times it happened, how many offenders were involved, and the relationship between the victim and the perpetrator (e.g., a known and trusted neighbor or a parent versus a stranger), are all significant moderators of the impact of the abuse. Kendall-Tackett et al. (1993) suggest that one of the *most* important factors determining how well the child copes with this violation is how the important people in the child's life (e.g., parental figures) react to discovery of the abuse. You will see in the following case illustration that Sheila's intense emotional response was in part because her stepfather (someone known and trusted) had molested Sheila. The abuse had begun at a very early age (age 7), had included intercourse, and had occurred frequently over a long period of time (until Sheila was 15). In addition, Sheila feared loss of support from her mother and others if she rejected her stepfather's advances or reported him.

The consequences of childhood sexual abuse are multiple (Beitchman et al., 1992; Briere, 1996; Kendall-Tackett et al., 1993; Neumann et al., 1996; Taussig & Litrownik, 1997; Wekerle & Wolfe, 1996). According to these researchers, children who are sexually abused often end up with emotional problems (e.g., become anxious, afraid, angry, depressed), develop cognitive difficulties (e.g., have trouble concentrating, difficulty remembering things), don't feel good about themselves, and find it difficult to be close to or trust others. Sometimes they become promiscuous (i.e., have sex with many partners) or go to the other extreme where they have difficulty being sexual at all. Further, sleep problems such as insomnia or nightmares are common. Some also become self-destructive (e.g., abuse alcohol and drugs). Perhaps the biggest problem in studying or diagnosing sexual abuse stems from the finding that these survivors end up suffering from a wide range of symptoms, rather than one specific or unique set of symptoms.

Boys and girls seem to show similar emotional responses to being sexually abused. However, children do tend to show different symptoms based on their age (Downs, 1993; Kendall-Tackett et al., 1993; McClellan et al., 1996; Wekerle & Wolfe, 1996). For example, anxiety, nightmares, regression (e.g., clinging, bedwetting, having tantrums), and sexually inappropriate behaviors (e.g., excessive masturbation, seductive behavior toward adults, compulsive sexual play) tend to be common in sexually abused preschoolers. In contrast, school-age children are usually fearful, depressed, and have difficulty coping with their schoolwork. And, consistent with their age, adolescents are more likely to hurt themselves by abusing substances, developing eating disorders, being sexually promiscuous, running away, or being suicidal or self-mutilating. Useful resources for further understanding the impact of sexual abuse can be found in Berliner and Elliott (1996), and Trickett and McBride-Chang (1995). It is very important that clinicians working with children and adolescents familiarize themselves with the developmental impact of sexual abuse, as well as with the laws regarding child abuse reporting in their state.

We think it is important to understand what helps children cope with and successfully recover from sexual abuse and other potentially disruptive life experiences. Researchers have suggested that there are several factors that promote good coping or "resilience" despite exposure to risk or trauma in children. For example, having an easy-going disposition, athletic, artistic, academic, or other skills valued by society, and social and emotional support from one's family or other caring adults are among the identified resiliency factors (Masten & Coatsworth, 1998; Rutter, 1990). In addition, being economically secure, and being involved in prosocial institutions such as church have also been identified as factors that can serve "protective" functions and promote or maintain healthy development (Masten & Coatsworth, 1998).

As mentioned before, children who are sexually abused can show a wide range of symptoms. DSM-IV-TR does not have a category that adequately captures or describes this trauma. As a result, sexual abuse survivors receive many different diagnoses such as posttraumatic stress disorder, major depression or dysthymia, an adjustment disorder, or a "V-code" (i.e., sexual abuse of child). Finkelhor and Browne (1985) have provided a more useful way of understanding the effects of sexual abuse. They suggest that we focus on how the abuse impacts the children's views of themselves, others, the world, and their overall emotional adjustment. They identified four traumagenic (trauma-creating) effects of sexual abuse: traumatic sexualization, betrayal, powerlessness, and stigmatization. According to Finkelhor and Browne, *traumatic sexualization* is the process in which children's sexual attitudes and feelings are "shaped in a developmentally inappropriate and interpersonally dysfunctional fashion as a result of the sexual abuse" (Finkelhor & Browne, 1985, p. 531). What this means is that these children may exhibit inappropriate sexual behavior (e.g., masturbate in public, be sexually promiscuous), may have difficulty accepting and/or understanding their own sexuality (e.g., reject age-appropriate sexual behavior or interest), and/or may develop inaccurate or incorrect emotional associations with sexual activities (e.g., associate affection with sexual activity regardless of the context or setting). For some, sex becomes a mechanism by which to manipulate others to meet their needs.

Betrayal results from the recognition that an important person in their life has manipulated them, caused them injury, and shown little regard for their well-being. This betrayal can result in the inability to trust others or the inability to judge the honesty or integrity of others. In addition to feeling betrayed by the perpetrator, they also feel betrayed by those who failed to protect or believe them. For example, incest survivors often feel more betrayed by the nonoffending, sometimes called "nonprotective," parent. Children who are not believed ("Your father would never do anything like that.") or are asked to deny the reality of their distress ("It's over so just forget it happened.") feel even more betrayed. We will see this heartbreaking situation in the case study of Sheila.

Powerlessness, which can result from being assaulted, coerced, manipulated, misunderstood, or trapped, robs children of their self-efficacy and sense of control. This brings about a sense of helplessness, makes the children feel hopeless about the future, and often leads to depression.

Finally, *stigmatization,* which becomes part of the children's view of themselves, results from blaming messages given by the abusers and others who shame them. Sadly, these children come to believe that they are indeed shamefully marred, guilty, and lacking in honor. Sheila's case aptly demonstrates all four of these long-term effects.

It is important to note that while many children report or exhibit problems resulting from sexual abuse, up to one-third may exhibit few or no symptoms (Kendall-Tackett et al., 1993). These are more likely to be individuals where the abuse was less intrusive (i.e., no bodily penetration), the perpetrator was a stranger, and the family responded to the report of the abuse with support for the victim. Nevertheless, the possibility of a "sleeper effect," in which symptoms related to the abuse emerge at a later time, has been suggested (Williams, 1994). For example, symptoms may only emerge for some victims when they enter adolescence or young adulthood where sexuality and intimacy become more important. In fact, retrospective research with adults abused as children does indicate higher rates of depression, anxiety, substance abuse, conduct problems, posttraumatic stress disorder, and suicide in this population compared to those who were not abused as children (Duncan et al., 1996; Fergusson & Horwood, 1996). Whether these findings include children who showed no early symptoms following sexual abuse is unclear. Nevertheless, the field will benefit from continued attention to factors that promote good short-term and long-term adjustment following sexual victimization.

What causes child maltreatment? Many factors contribute: cultural, community, familial, and individual (See Araji & Finkelhor, 1986; Finkelhor et al., 1986, 1990; Vizard et al., 1995). For example, some say cultural and community attitudes toward children, such as viewing them as property, are involved. Others have noted that there are more male than female perpetrators because our patriarchal society gives men most of the power, control, and "property rights." In one study with families where father-daughter incest had occurred, the researchers noted characteristics such as a weak coalition between the parents, enmeshment and discouragement of autonomy, adherence to rigid family belief systems, and parental inability to have empathy for the child's needs (Vizard et al., 1995).

In terms of family factors, other conditions prevail such as the prolonged absence of one or both parents from the home, maternal employment outside the home, an unhappy family life, parental discord, having a stepfather, and being socially and geographically isolated. In addition, intergenerational patterns of incest have been suggested. It is important to remember that although most who are abused *do not* reenact and molest others, those who do molest others often report their own experiences of having been molested (see Araji & Finkelhor, 1986; Finkelhor et al., 1986, 1990).

Finally, although no specific psychological profile has been identified for molesters, several common features have been noted. Some abusers have antisocial features and abuse alcohol; others are timid, unassertive, and have poor coping skills (e.g., are unable to find age-appropriate adult friends); while others yet are authoritarian and rationalize their behavior. Finkelhor and colleagues (1984, 1986, 1990) have suggested that adults who offend often find the behavior emotionally congruent (i.e., they are emotionally immature, controlling, and feel the need for power). Sometimes, they have been affected by the modeling of sexual behavior and interest in children as a result of their own abuse in childhood. They may reenact their own abuse as they narcissistically identify with the child and/or misattribute arousal to the child. The likelihood of molesting children is higher when disinhibition (due to factors such as low impulse control and use of alcohol) and access to children with no external constraints (such as having a physically ill or emotionally unavailable (e.g. depressed) mother) are present. Sadly, a substantial proportion (27 to 36%) of perpetrators are juveniles (Vizard et al., 1995). Characteristics frequently seen in juvenile perpetrators include being socially isolated, having poor social skills, a history of alienation from their families, a history of having been sexually abused, learning difficulties, and depression.

Sociocultural Considerations in the Prevalence of Sexual Abuse

Sexual abuse and abuse in general are reported to be higher in (1) poor families and (2) families with many children (U.S. Department of Health & Human Services, 1998). However, research findings with regard to ethnicity vary. For example, some report no differences in sexual abuse rates based on ethnicity (Wyatt & Peters, 1986); others report higher rates among Latinos (Kercher & McShane, 1984), lower rates among Asian females (Russell, 1986), and higher rates in White and Latino compared to Black children (Lindholm & Willey, 1986). It is unclear why these studies report discrepant findings. However, it is likely that there are many contributors. For example, how the information is gathered (social service reports versus community surveys), differing cultural beliefs about family functioning (e.g., keeping things within the family), and socioeconomic status (affecting resources for child supervision, number of people living in the house, and degree of contact with social services).

In most studies, the majority of the perpetrators are found to be male and the majority of victims are female. For example, Finkelhor et al. (1990) in a national survey reported that of those who abused girls, 98% were male, and of those who abused boys, 83% were male. They also reported that by adolescence, girls were six times more likely to be victims than were boys. Some researchers have suggested that the socialization of males to dominance and the erotic portrayal of children and women in the media are among the contributors to these findings.

Do people from different ethnic groups experience similar abusive experiences? The data are limited, but in one study, intercourse was found to occur more often in Latinos and Blacks, fondling more often in Latinos and Whites, and oral copulation more often in Whites. Sodomy was rare but occurred more often in Latino boys (Lindholm & Willey, 1986).

Do people from different ethnic groups respond similarly or differently to sexual abuse? While some studies report higher levels of psychiatric symptoms in minority compared to White women (Morrow & Sorell, 1989), others find few differences in symptoms based on ethnicity (Wyatt, 1990). The effects of ethnicity are probably mediated by factors such as age at time of abuse; by specific characteristics of the abuse such as whether it included oral copulation, sodomy, or intercourse; and by religious and cultural attitudes regarding sexuality. Mennen (1995) noted, for example, that penetration was especially traumatizing for Latina women. This may be related, in part, to traditional Latino cultural roles and values (see Arroya & Cervantes, 1997; Diaz-Guerrero & Szalay, 1991; and Ho, 1992 for a discussion of these values). For example, respect and obedience to authority may make it harder for these women to fend off the male sexual perpetrators. In addition, sexual penetration outside marriage may violate important ethnic and religious values such as maintaining sexual "purity" and sustaining family image and honor. This situation puts the women in a bind wherein they are expected to obey authority but doing so violates other important family and religious expectations. Given these cultural parameters, it makes sense that Latina women whose sexual abuse involves penetration experience even more significant distress.

Finally, the precise role of child-rearing practices on the prevalence of sexual abuse is not well understood. However, family composition (e.g., having a stepfather), family size (e.g., having a large family of more than four children), and the quality and quantity of parental supervision (e.g., insufficient nurturance, insufficient monitoring of children's activities) all seem to play a role (Finkelhor et al., 1986, 1990; U.S. Department of Health & Human Services, 1998).

CASE ILLUSTRATION

Presenting Problem

Sheila, a 15-year-old African American female, was brought to therapy by her foster mother. Sheila had just been released from a psychiatric hospital following an attempted suicide (she had ingested pills). Her hospital diagnosis was "Major Depression with Psychotic Features." Shortly before her hospital stay, Sheila had told a friend that her stepfather had sexually abused her since age 7. With her friend's help, the abuse was reported to Child Protective Services and to the police. Her stepfather was then removed from the home. Because Sheila's stepfather was a church elder, the pastor of the church was contacted. Many church members asked what had happened and soon many knew about the sexual abuse report. Sheila's mother denied knowing that the abuse was occurring. Of great significance, however, she was not supportive of Sheila when the report was made, nor did she protect Sheila from family acquaintances who asked her to withdraw the abuse charges against her stepfather. Shortly after the report had been made, Sheila found her mother's lack of support intolerable and ran away from home. It was at this time that her sense of hopelessness became overwhelming and she made the suicide attempt. Fortunately, she called her friend who contacted the social worker assigned to the case. Sheila was hospitalized, and, on release, placed in foster care. It was at this point that I saw her in counseling. Most of her initial history was obtained from a Child Protective Services report and from the social worker assigned to her.

Client Description

Sheila was a tall, overweight, taciturn 15-year-old at intake. She had short hair and her hazel eyes were very sad and often filled with tears. During the initial session she shuffled into my office, slouched on the couch, made occasional eye contact, and barely said a word. Her low energy level was an indicator of how severely depressed she was.

Counselor-Client Engagement Process   I wanted to convey to Sheila that I knew she was here for counseling rather than for an evaluation and that we therefore did not have to focus on obtaining a detailed history of the abuse. My initial attempts to engage Sheila were almost painful. We sat together in long silences as I tried to let her know that I was available, interested, and supportive. Knowing that she had been forced to comply with adult demands in her home, it seemed really important that she not feel forced to engage with me. So I remained attentive and responded to even slight nonverbal behavior from her. Although I considered using drawings, sand-tray, and other indirect expressive techniques, it seemed as though Sheila's depression at intake was so severe that she would have responded very little to all intervention approaches. At times during these initial, painful sessions, I found myself questioning my competence.

TH: Sheila, I know from the CPS report and from the hospital's report that you have had to deal with a very difficult situation at home and that it has been hard for you to talk about it.

CL: (barely nods but turns her eyes toward me)

TH: I would like to know more about you. I would like to be as helpful as I can be. We don't have to talk about what happened with your stepfather right now unless you want to.

CL: (tears in her eyes . . . shakes her head to indicate that she does not want to talk)

TH: Perhaps later when we get to know each other better we can talk about that. Would it be okay with you if I asked a few questions about your school, friends, and things you like to do?

CL: (slight affirmative nod)

The session continued in this manner with Sheila responding with brief statements, nods, and shrugs. At the end of this session, I asked Sheila if she would be willing to return and she nodded affirmatively. It is very important that adolescents, especially those who have been sexually abused, feel they have a choice, since they have often been forced to obey other people's demands. Choice seemed even more important given Sheila's status as a minority woman.

Although Sheila had suicidal thoughts, she had no plan. However, I did ask her to sign a short-term "no suicide" agreement with me. This was done because of her severe depression, her suicidal thoughts, and her history of suicide attempts.

Sheila met the DSM-IV-TR criteria for both major depression and post-traumatic stress disorder. She had been severely traumatized by the incest, was hypervigilant, and experienced frequent nightmares. She reported often being afraid to sleep, of waking up with choking sensations, and of sometimes having difficulty breathing. She said that she heard "voices" that told her she was bad and a "sinner." It was unclear if these voices were actually hallucinations or whether they were negative thoughts that kept on repeating in her head. She described the voices as being critical, similar to criticisms she had heard from her family and their friends. At school, Sheila found it difficult to concentrate. She was sure all the kids at school knew that she was "damaged." She saw no hope for the future and often thought she would be better off dead. In addition to being in treatment with me, Sheila was taking antidepressants (Prozac) prescribed by the agency's psychiatrist.

Social Context

Information about Sheila's family background and early life experiences was sparse. She had never known her biological father and had very little contact with her maternal grandparents. She was raised by a single mother until age 7, when her mother met and married Mr. B. Sheila had two younger half-siblings, a brother age 7 and a sister age 5. As a young child, Sheila was obedient and often looked for ways to please her mother. Unfortunately, Sheila's mother was often depressed and had difficulty providing Sheila with consistent attention (e.g., responding to her questions, playing with her, and initiating activities they could do together). According to Sheila, she was happy when her mother met Mr. B. at their church—he seemed kind and attentive and she imagined him being the father she had always wanted.

Shortly after Mr. and Mrs. B. were married, Mrs. B. became pregnant and had a very difficult pregnancy. Mr. B. then took over several caretaking tasks including putting Sheila to bed at night. Although never physically abusive, Mr. B. was "short-tempered" and yelled a lot. Sheila quickly learned to be obedient and do whatever her stepfather asked.

In the following years, Sheila continued her attempts at being an "ideal" and obedient daughter. However, as often happens in incestuous families, a role reversal emerged. For example, Sheila began to take on more of her mother's household responsibilities and became the person her father interacted with more often.

Sheila's family went to church regularly. Her stepfather was a respected elder at the church and was often described as a "fine" Christian father. Sheila heard these praises, never contradicted them, and did not believe that she would be believed if she told anyone in that setting that she was being abused. Further, family loyalty and obeying one's elders, which was prized both in her family and church, made her hesitant to tell anyone about the abuse.

While no culture condones abuse, cultural and family values can impact reporting of abuse (Heras, 1992). Many children, like Sheila, come from families where the survival of the family as a group is so highly valued that the child's individual molestation experience can take on a secondary role. Thus, reporting the abuse, especially to nonfamily members, would be viewed as disloyal and culturally unacceptable. It becomes critical that counselors honor the child's cultural context. They might do this by acknowledging the role of family values, especially loyalty, and by looking for ways to help the child cope given that context.

Initial Sessions

The teen years are often challenging because of the many social, psychological, and physiological changes that emerge. It is even more difficult for teens who have experienced betrayal and violation within their families. For African American females, feelings of powerlessness and pessimism are fueled by the sociopolitical climate. Sheila had been violated by her stepfather, felt betrayed by her mother's lack of support, discounted by family friends who asked her to drop the charges against her stepfather, and let down by society's treatment of African American women. Under these circumstances, it made sense that Sheila felt worthless, powerless, and hopeless about her life and her future. It was clear early on that Sheila needed experiences that would help her develop trust and a sense of control over her life.

My initial treatment goals were to establish a relationship with Sheila in which she would feel safe, cared about, and could begin to develop hope that her future was not as bleak as she thought. Although there were many silences in the first few sessions, I felt it was important to let Sheila know I cared about her, since the issue of worthiness is one that frequently arises for sexually abused children. My efforts to accomplish this included always facing her, listening attentively, and responding to all her behavior including shrugs and brief statements as they occurred. As is the case with most sexual abuse survivors, issues were approached cautiously so that she would know that she had a choice regarding what to focus on. It was significant that she know we did not have to talk about things she was not ready to deal with yet. I think Sheila began to see that I was supportive, nonjudgmental, and empathic, and it was not too long before Sheila began to open up to me.

CASE CONCEPTUALIZATION
Understanding Sheila

Sheila had been sexually molested by her stepfather for almost eight years and had not, until now, directly told anyone about the molestation. There were, of course, many symptoms and behaviors related to the abuse, such as depression, overeating, expressions of anxiety about staying home alone with her stepfather, and several suicide gestures (which included taking over-the-counter pills and leaving the empty bottles on her parents' bathroom counter). However, it was only as she entered the teen years, with the boys teasing about how she was "developing," combined with her first really close friendship, that Sheila directly told someone about the abuse. Sadly, it was Sheila's desperate wish to be loved that made her vulnerable to the abuse.

Sheila believed that her mother knew she was being molested. She felt that her mother's silence meant she was expected to continue to obey her stepfather's demands. Her suicide gestures (with the pills) usually followed nights when her stepfather had intercourse with her. Neither her mother, nor her stepfather, ever commented on the empty pill bottles. Sheila's mother later stated that she had never seen these empty bottles. These disturbing incidents of denial were often followed by increased tension in the home. Sheila often then felt responsible for finding ways to please her family and reduce the tension.

Sexual abuse is abhorred in Sheila's cultural and religious community. However, Sheila's understanding of some of the values held within this community, such as family loyalty and obedience, unintentionally contributed to her continued submission to her stepfather. Sheila believed that saying "no" to her stepfather would have been disobedient and telling someone outside the family disloyal. Part of my intervention included helping Sheila connect to supportive Christian African Americans through a new church where she was able to sort through these issues.

In addition to Sheila's sexual abuse, her early life experiences played an important role in her development. Sheila's mother was a single parent with little personal, social, or financial support. Although she did her best to provide a home and stability for Sheila, she also suffered from recurrent depression. Sheila felt it was up to her to make her mother happy so she worked hard at school, was always obedient, and was always looking for ways to please. This obedient, people-pleasing attitude became Sheila's way of relating to most adults in her life, and her own needs and wishes frequently went unmet. Sadly, this scenario leaves many children like Sheila more vulnerable to exploitive adults.

Religion was important in Sheila's life. She felt that God wanted her to be humble and obedient. Her "hallucinations" in the early phases of treatment were moral and religious in nature, with the "voices" telling her she was not a good Christian. Like many abuse victims, Sheila felt caught in an excruciating bind—she believed she was a "sinner" for having premarital intercourse but also a "sinner" for being disobedient and disloyal in reporting her stepfather.

My Ideas About Sheila's Psychological Development

I believe that children's relationships with early caregivers influence how they see themselves and serve as templates or patterns for future relationships. Based on Sheila's early relationships, she saw herself as "good" only when she was taking care of others and responding to their needs. She believed her own needs were not as important as other people's needs. She also thought it very important to avoid anger and disapproval at all costs, both with her parents and with other adults in her life.

Sheila's experience of being violated, betrayed, and disregarded made her feel unworthy, powerless, and hopeless about the future. Out of these experiences Sheila developed *cognitive schemas* (ways of viewing the world, herself, others, and the future) that were highly pessimistic. Consistent with Beck et al.'s (1979) "cognitive triad," Sheila came to view herself as negative (worthless, defective, and inadequate); the world as difficult, demanding, unmanageable, and uncontrollable; and the future as bleak, with goals unattainable and failure likely. Sheila's family experiences and her status as an African American woman in a culture that was often not affirming of African American women made these feelings all the more poignant.

Consistent with the people-pleasing attitude she had developed, Sheila struggled in therapy to be a "good client." It was hard for her to trust me and believe that I would be consistently supportive and caring, even when she behaved in ways I did not think were in her best interest. We had to work on our relationship so Sheila did not feel that she had to take care of me (as she had taken care of her mother) or that I would betray her and force her to act in ways that she did not feel good about. It was important that Sheila have an experience with me that differed from her past so she could see that the past did not have to repeat itself. Children like Sheila who have been sexually abused also benefit from knowing that their needs *do* matter and that they have the ability to make different choices in the future. One of the goals here was to provide an environment for Sheila that was stable, consistent, safe, and supportive, so she could express all her feelings, identify her needs, and allow herself to develop to her full potential.

TREATMENT PLANS

Initial Treatment Plan

In addition to establishing a relationship with Sheila where she would feel safe, valued, and develop hope about the future, helping to reduce her depression, suicidal thoughts, and auditory hallucinations were important early goals. I anticipated that as counseling progressed, Sheila and I would explore her childhood experiences, especially her relationship with her mother and with her stepfather, and that in doing so we would together try to understand how her symptoms and coping patterns had developed. I felt that if these goals were met, Sheila would be more able to choose how she wanted to relate to others in the future. My goals for the final phase of treatment were to help her find activities that would further increase her self-esteem, and help her develop new, supportive relationships.

The goals in the first phase were to:

1. establish a safe and trusting relationship; and
2. help reduce her depression, suicidal thoughts, feelings of hopelessness, and self-condemnations.

In the second phase, the goals were to:

1. help her explore her childhood history and sort through her range of emotions and needs;
2. work with her feelings of guilt, shame, and grief; and
3. help her tolerate and accept the various thoughts and emotions that she struggled with.

In the third phase, the goals were to:

1. help increase her self-esteem and self-acceptance; and
2. help her develop new, meaningful, gratifying relationships.

Phase 1   In this initial phase, I tried to engage Sheila in counseling by closely tracking or following her words, gestures, and tones. The goal included working with her to clarify the underlying beliefs and core affective messages she conveyed. Sheila was understandably wary of discussing certain topics, so I approached these with care and respect. It was important that she control the pace of counseling.

Sheila felt that the reason bad things had happened to her was because she was "flawed." In time she came to see that bad and damaging things had *happened* to her but that *she* was not bad. It meant a lot to see Sheila begin to resolve these deep feelings of shame. Sheila and I also explored together her interpretations of the moral and religious messages she had heard. I frequently asked questions such as, "Is that what you think (or believe or expect)?" "What makes you think that way?" "Are there other ways of thinking about it (or Are there any other possible explanations)?" "Whose rule (or demand or should) is that?" "Is that what you choose (or want) to believe?" My questions were intended to let Sheila know that I valued *her* thoughts, feelings, and beliefs and that therapy was a safe place to explore *all* her feelings and beliefs. This process was further helped by Sheila's involvement with a warm, caring church, where the focus was on love and understanding rather than on criticism and judgment.

Sheila approached most situations with great pessimism. She had few positive expectations and held many negative assumptions (i.e., "there's something wrong with me," "I can never do anything right," "nothing I do is ever good enough and I guess it will always be that way so there's no use trying"). In time she began to understand that she saw herself in these negative ways because she had not had many positive or affirming life experiences. Few people in her life had ever acknowledged what she did right or celebrated her achievements. She also began to understand that her pessimism had been her way of making sense of the past. As Sheila evaluated the "reality" base of the negative messages, her negative self-perceptions that she was flawed (i.e., unworthy of being cared about) became less automatic.

Sheila struggled with the idea of dropping the charges against her stepfather because she worried about how her family would manage with her father being jailed. In the end, she did not drop the charges, feeling that to do so would be "a lie" and would be further evidence that she was not "worth" being punished for. It was critical that Sheila, and not me as counselor, make this decision. My job was to help her voice all her feelings and fears.

Sheila had a history of complying with others. It thus made it necessary for me to be careful about the extent to which I gave her a directive or told her what to do. However, her level of depression during the initial phase made it important that I be active (e.g., provide information, ask questions, and validate her feelings). I often checked with her to see if she experienced me as demanding or controlling. It was important that Sheila know that her needs, feelings, and choices were the important ones.

As previously mentioned, Sheila was also taking antidepressant medications prescribed by the agency's psychiatrist that were especially helpful in assisting her with sleep. Her suicidal thoughts were dealt with directly by establishing a "no suicide" agreement. As Sheila's depression lessened, so did her suicidal thoughts. In addition, her self-condemnations, which were impacted greatly by her religious beliefs, diminished as she began to explore her views of God and began to think of him as more compassionate and less judgmental. Her involvement in a new church group that was affirming of her was very important to this process.

I also referred Sheila to a group for adolescent incest survivors. She was at first hesitant about this but reluctantly agreed to attend at least one session. The group experience became a significant part of Sheila's recovery. In the group, Sheila learned that she was not the only African-American to have been molested by a family member. She also learned that others had similar feelings and struggles as she had, which helped reduce her feelings of being different, flawed, and unworthy of being cared about.

Phase 2   During this phase we explored past relationships in order to understand how they contributed to who she was and how she coped. This process was often distressing and Sheila would then feel self-destructive. During one counseling session, for example, Sheila talked about her closeness to her mother as a young child. She described how alone and unloved she felt when her mother did not stop the abuse. The following day, Sheila was caught stealing food at the school's cafeteria. She anticipated being caught but did not care—she did not know how else to make her pain visible (seen or heard).

Knowing that this episode followed a painful counseling session, I questioned myself: Had we moved too fast in treatment? Were there other things I ought to have said or done during that counseling session? Were there things Sheila was trying to communicate to me that I was not hearing? Sheila's stealing had occurred right after we had talked about how desperately she had *wanted her mother to take care of her.* Since food is often thought of as a symbol of nurturance (it nourishes or nurtures the body and clients often report eating when emotionally distressed), I hypothesized that Sheila's stealing the food probably symbolized her wish to be nurtured. I also hypothesized that the overt, blatant nature of the event indicated that she wanted me to be aware of her deep distress, as she had done when she left empty pill bottles in her parents' bathroom during her suicide gestures. It seemed that Sheila needed me to respond definitively and protectively and not minimize the event—something her mother had failed to do when Sheila had cried out for help. We scheduled an emergency session that day to underscore that I had heard her cry for help and would not minimize her suffering. For the first time in our time together, Sheila allowed herself to sob freely. She talked about having learned in her family not to share her feelings or communicate her needs because they usually were minimized or ignored. We agreed to try and deal with issues more directly and overtly in our relationship. Sheila was encouraged to "talk out" rather than "act out" her feelings. We were also able to talk about the potential that she might be self-injurious following painful disclosures and that we needed to identify together, in advance, better ways to cope when these difficult feelings came up.

During this phase Sheila and I also talked a lot about her stepfather's abuse of her. She recalled him coming home during times when he knew she was alone or coming to her room at night when the others were asleep. As we focused on this, Sheila's negative thoughts increased (e.g., "maybe this happened to me because there's something wrong with me," "maybe it was my fault that this happened") and she was overwhelmed with feelings of shame and of rage. I explained to her that she had become depressed, in part, because she was alone with these intolerable feelings. Now that she had me to see and understand her, these feelings could be tolerated or "lived through." Sheila's depression began to lift as she continued this deep sharing with me.

Secrecy and deep shame (e.g., seeing one's self as disgusting, repulsive, loathsome, unworthy, and undeserving of good things) often accompany sexual abuse. Encouraging Sheila to talk about her experiences in a supportive, nonjudgmental setting broke the secrecy and reduced her profound shame. One of the things I often do when I work with sexual abuse survivors is to encourage them to journal their thoughts and feelings. Sheila was quite hesitant about this—she was concerned about whether she could trust that what she wrote might be safe and remain private. I understood her fears and we agreed that this was a tool she might choose to use at some later point in her life. However, in the following session, Sheila was rather withdrawn and quiet—a distinct change from previous sessions. As we explored this, Sheila began to cry and stated that she "knew" I would be mad at her.

TH: Mad?

CL: Well, I didn't start a journal.

TH: Yes?

CL: I was supposed to.

TH: Only if you wanted to.

CL: But you wouldn't have brought it up if it hadn't been something you wanted me to do. I'm sure you wanted me to do it. (tears in her eyes)

TH: Sheila, you are crying. Can you tell me about it?

CL: I've been afraid all week that you might be mad at me. I tried to do it once but just couldn't.

TH: I'm not angry with you Sheila. I appreciate you bringing it up and talking about it. (In most situations I would have explored the expectation of anger more fully before reassuring her that I was not angry. However, I felt that Sheila had taken a great risk in expressing her concern and that the reassurance had to precede further exploration.) But I do think it would be helpful if we talk about your expectation that I might be angry.

CL: So I can still come and see you even if I don't do the journal?

TH: Absolutely. (Again I felt it important to let her know right away that we were still connected.) Can we talk about your concern that I might not want to see you?

CL: I worry that if I don't do what you want you might not want to see me anymore. At home if I didn't do what they wanted, they stopped talking to me. I hated the silences so I always did it their way in the end.

TH: And you are concerned that I might act in the same way?

CL: Yes.

TH: Sheila, I'm really glad that you brought this up with me. You don't have to do things my way or please me for me to be here for you. I think it is terrific that you decided for yourself what you wanted to do. I appreciate it when you let me know how you feel and I welcome you letting me know when you don't agree with me. From what you have said about your family your concerns make sense. (We then went on to talk about her history of compliance, how it had developed, and how it affected her and her relationships with others including me. Even though I had not given her a directive about journaling, that reality was not important. What seemed most important here was her fear of being abandoned if she did not comply. This incident highlighted again how powerful early templates or cognitive schemas are and how these ways of thinking impact other relationships, including the counseling relationship.)

Sheila's religious faith also served a positive role. She found that talking to God helped her feel calm, especially as she came to see Him in a more loving and nonjudgmental light. She also developed friendships in her new church with people who genuinely cared about her.

Sheila's deep sense of hurt for the violation she had experienced emerged during one particularly poignant session. Sheila began pounding a pillow as she questioned why her stepfather had molested her. As she talked, her ambivalent feelings toward him emerged. On the one hand she felt hurt and anger toward him but also remembered some of his characteristics that she had valued. She remembered him helping her make breakfast and praising her for an accomplishment. She struggled to understand how he could be so kind at times and then be so hurtful at other times. Sheila's ability to acknowledge both the positive and negative aspects of her stepfather was crucial in helping her develop empathy for herself. Sheila was learning that people had good and bad parts to them. Further, that people, including Sheila, could be loved despite their flaws. Grasping this helped Sheila to not remain stuck in her anger toward her stepfather.

Sheila's case highlights how important it is for counselors to be careful of expressing their own feelings toward the perpetrator. Many incest survivors have ambivalent or mixed feelings toward their perpetrators. If counselors express their own negative feelings, they make it hard for the survivor to deal with his/her full range of feelings, which often include genuinely positive feelings as well.

The day after Sheila expressed her mixed feelings toward her stepfather, I returned from running an errand during the lunch hour to find Sheila in my office, curled on the couch in a fetal position.

TH: Hi Sheila.

CL: (opens her eyes and in a barely audible voice): I needed to come to a safe place.

TH: Something has frightened you?

CL: I couldn't sleep last night, I could smell him (stepfather), I could see his shoulder, and it was just hard . . .

TH: You have been having more memories of your stepfather and his abuse?

CL: Yes. I couldn't sleep. I went to school this morning but couldn't think. At lunch I told the nurse I was sick and came here. I slept a little here.

TH: I'm glad you found a safe place. How can I help?

CL: Can I stay for a while longer?

TH: Yes. I will wake you in 15 minutes so we can decide where we go from here. (At this point it seemed to me that her need to feel cared for and responded to overrode any potential "boundary" issues.)

(15 minutes later)

TH: Sheila, we have about 15 minutes to talk before my next client. I know we have been talking more about your stepfather and from what you said earlier it sounds like you are having bad dreams and frightening memories.

CL: (crying) I've been remembering things. I can't go to sleep and the medicine isn't helping.

TH: OK Sheila. We have a few options. I want you to feel safe. I also realize that we do need to talk about what happened with your stepfather—in time it will make the memories more manageable. And talking to me will also mean you won't be alone with the memories.

CL: (interrupts) I don't want to go back to the hospital. I think I could manage if I saw you more.

TH: OK. I do need an agreement that you won't hurt yourself.

CL: I promise to talk to you first when things feel really bad.

TH: How many times a week do you think you would like to come in?

CL: How many times can I come?

TH: What do you think you need?

CL: I'd like to come every day but I know you have other people to see. Can I come twice a week?

We then scheduled the additional appointment and agreed to review the need for the additional session after one month. This was an especially difficult period for Sheila and the additional session helped sustain her through this crisis period. She also saw the psychiatrist who increased her medications slightly. This episode represented a balancing dilemma for me. I felt it important that we explore this highly charged, painful material that Sheila had had to manage alone. It seemed crucial to help her through it and I believed that talking about it would diffuse its powerful impact and make it more manageable. However, I was concerned for her safety, especially since she had made suicide attempts before. So I balanced our move into this painful material by being more physically available to her, knowing that in time she would need me less. Over the following months Sheila began to tell me more explicit details of what had occurred in the abuse. As she entered this material more fully, this disrupted her and her nightmares increased. However, with frequent contact with me, her deeply painful recollections and feelings became more manageable and her nightmares decreased. As this happened, Sheila became more open to people and began to develop new friendships. She also started to get involved in other social activities such as joining the school chorus and church choir. As this happened, her need to see me more often decreased and we cut back to sessions once a week.

Sheila also had ambivalent/mixed feelings to deal with toward her mother. On the one hand she felt angry and betrayed by her mother who had not protected her. This rage was fueled by her conviction that she would have done anything in the world for her mother. As she explored this, her profound sadness emerged. She had always fantasized that if she was a "good enough" daughter her mother would love her and protect her. Her hurt and anger were mixed with a deep love for her mother, which was important for her to acknowledge and embrace.

Sheila's incest survivor's group was extremely useful in helping her deal with the issue of "good enough." Sheila was able to see that the other incest survivors had also not been protected and she did not see them as lacking in goodness. This made it possible for Sheila to stop blaming herself and consider explanations other than her unworthiness for what had happened to her.

I was aware of my own feelings (my countertransference) at this point. I felt angry that Sheila's mother had not protected her, sad for all she had suffered, and wished I could somehow make her pain go away. Yet I knew that Sheila was resilient and that she needed to be in control and in charge of her life—empowered. As she began to heal, she was able to see that she had more options in her life.

During this phase Sheila grieved the loss of her fantasized mother. She talked a great deal about their relationship, her wishes, and her disappointments. She also, at this time, tested our relationship. She seemed to be exploring whether I would become her substitute mother. Given my feelings of sadness for the lack of protection and lack of consistent affirmation she had experienced, I had to work hard to keep my feelings in check and always asked myself if my responses were in Sheila's best interest.

CL: Would you give me a ride home today?

TH: Sheila, I'm not completely sure what brought this request up today. Do you have any thoughts about this?

CL: I just want you to give me a ride home, that's all.

TH: I would like to check something out with you. I could be wrong and if I am, tell me. One thought I have is that we have been talking about your mother and how much you wanted her to protect you, to take care of you. Does your request for me to drive you home have anything to do with wishing to be taken care of, by me?

CL: (silent, begins to tear up)

TH: (after several minutes) How are you feeling?

Sheila acknowledged being hurt and disappointed that I had not granted her request. As we explored this, her anger that I was available to her on "my terms" (i.e., in the counseling relationship) emerged. She wanted more of my time and attention. Given her childhood deprivation, I understood this and let her know I appreciated her honest expression of feelings. Yet, Sheila's childhood had also contained boundary violations where appropriate roles were not maintained. I tried to let her know that I valued her and our relationship *and* that I would not violate the boundaries or appropriate roles in our relationship. I said, "I value you and your point of view but will not change the rules of our relationship. In the past, when the rules of your relationship with your parents changed, it hurt and confused you. Driving you home would begin to change our relationship and I think it is important that that not happen. I want you to always know what you can expect with me."

This became a very rich phase in our work together. Sheila's struggles often emerged in the context of our relationship. For example, her need to be mothered would come in a request for me to call her teacher to excuse her from a particular class period. I considered it healthy that Sheila was, in our relationship, trying out the child role by asking to be taken care of rather than being the caretaker. I helped her find appropriate people and appropriate ways to ask for caretaking in her everyday life. This was helpful in reducing Sheila's self-isolation in her foster home and she became much more integrated in the family and their activities.

There were times when Sheila struggled with her old family role of being the caretaker. For example, I had injured my knee and came to work in a knee brace. She immediately offered to reschedule the session so I could go home and rest. Knowing how often she had looked for opportunities to meet her mother's needs, and how the mother/daughter roles had often been reversed, it seemed important that Sheila know our roles would not be reversed and that she did not have to be my caretaker. I did not want Sheila to think that taking care of others was a bad thing, but felt that it would be inappropriate for me to be taken care of by her, which I said to her in a caring and respectful way. By this time Sheila was able to see the connection between this and other relationships (e.g., with mother and stepfather) that she had struggled with. This gave us an opportunity to sort through when it was appropriate to ask to be taken care of and when to take care of others.

At the beginning of counseling Sheila had a people-pleasing stance. As time progressed, however, Sheila tested this problematic coping strategy in our relationship. For example, she began to call and ask to change appointment times. On one occasion she missed a session without canceling. I believed she needed to test and see if I would abandon her (i.e., stop seeing her) if she were not the "perfect" client. These were opportunities for me to let her know that although certain things were important to me, such as calling to cancel an appointment, violating my rules or expectations was not going to end our relationship. Knowing that we would remain connected, even when she acted out, helped her further accept the idea that she was worthy and that I cared about her, regardless of her "flaws."

As so often happens with children who have been traumatized in this way, Sheila dissociated (spaced out) at times. Although this had been a helpful coping strategy while she was being molested, it now had the potential of limiting her recovery and her ability to accept and cope with all parts of herself. Together we discussed how this had been a useful coping strategy that was no longer needed or useful. Sheila learned to recognize the early signs of detaching and to ground herself in her physical environment. For example, she would stop the tendency to dissociate and ground herself by touching her chair, noticing that she was wearing shoes of a particular color, and so forth. In time, Sheila was more able to be present with me, and then with herself, by learning other ways to cope with difficult thoughts and feelings.

Phase 3   As we moved into the third phase of counseling, we focused more on Sheila's strengths and on developing meaningful and gratifying relationships. We also began to deal with her hopes and dreams, and tried to make practical goals for her immediate future.

As Sheila's depression lifted, she began to acknowledge her interest in music and joined the choirs at church and at school. In addition, her ability to concentrate improved and she began to receive outstanding reports from school. These changes increased Sheila's sense of competence and her old views of herself as worthless, helpless, and hopeless were now visibly challenged.

Although Sheila began to establish new relationships with people at her church and at her school, her old interpersonal "script" or style of responding sometimes emerged and interfered. For example, she sometimes engaged in activities or responded in ways that she thought would please her friends and would then feel resentful. Together we worked on identifying her wishes and how to express these more effectively, role-playing frequently together problematic situations that might come up.

Sheila also began to think about the future more positively. An interest in her future goals was that she thought she might like to become a nurse arena in which to be a caretaker!

Revised Treatment Plan

Although the overall goals did not change, the relative importance of the various issues shifted. For example, as my relationship with Sheila strengthened, her great sadness at the loss of her relationship with her mother became a major focus. Sheila did invite her mother to several counseling sessions. Mrs. B. was at first quite hesitant about this because she expected to be "blamed." As she realized that the sessions focused on understanding how the problems had developed rather than blaming her for the abuse, she became more comfortable with attending. This process was extremely useful in helping them develop empathy for each other and slowly begin the process of reestablishing a relationship. These sessions occurred in the later part of Sheila's counseling, when she was further along in her individual work. This was important because Sheila was able to be more realistic in her expectations of her mother. However, she sometimes still had high expectations. For example, she wished that her mother would unquestionably acknowledge that the abuse had occurred and that she had not protected Sheila. Although Mrs. B. was able to concede that Sheila had been "hurt" by "things" that happened, she was unable to be more explicit or acknowledge that she had not responded to Sheila's cries for help. In treatment Sheila was able to talk about her feelings of disappointment at her mother's vague support and try to come to terms with the limits of their relationship. Contact with her mother allowed Sheila increased access to her siblings, which was especially meaningful for her. Unfortunately, I left the agency soon after this (about 15 months into counseling). However, the counselor who took over with Sheila planned to meet with both Sheila and her mother on an occasional basis.

Balancing Goals

As noted earlier, the issue of being an active but not a directive counselor had to be balanced. Sheila needed to make choices for herself given her history of having to comply with the demands of others in her own home. Further, in a society where she was faced with restricted options by virtue of her gender and race, empowerment was an essential counseling goal. Sheila's developing self-esteem, her increased involvement in rewarding activities, establishment of affirming relationships, and recognition of those aspects of her life in which she could make choices were all significant in this respect.

Meyer (1993) writes compellingly about the need for survivors of abuse to have a "holding environment" with a therapist who can allow and tolerate "phase appropriate dependence" while also looking for opportunities to encourage growth and maturation. This is a critical balance, especially with children and adolescents who have had inadequate nurturance. I often found myself looking for the most appropriate balance between Sheila's requests for more contact, advice, and so forth and my wish for her to feel empowered and self-directing.

Another balancing issue involved confronting memories of the abuse. Addressing these sexual experiences explicitly intensified her symptoms, in the short run, yet relieved them as she found that I could tolerate them and remain compassionately connected to her. It was important that I be careful not to panic or overreact to an increase in symptoms since she needed to know that I could be with her in her pain and know that I believed she had the strength and resilience to cope with it. At the same time, it was important that I not minimize the significance and intensity of her pain, especially in light of the fact that she had not felt heard by her parents when she had been suicidal earlier. Thus, I had to simultaneously communicate my understanding that she had been greatly hurt, but also my belief that she had the strength and personal resources to change and find more adaptive ways of coping.

TERMINATION AND SUMMARY THOUGHTS

This relationship had been a significant one for both of us. My own issues with caretaking emerged as I contemplated a job offer elsewhere. Sheila and I had made great progress together. However, I knew that she would have to repeatedly rework many of the issues that we had addressed. Other issues, which had not been addressed in our work together, would also need to be focused on. For example, although many adolescents with histories of sexual abuse act out sexually, Sheila was very uncomfortable and awkward in dealing with young men who showed sexual interest in her. Although she had begun to develop some platonic male friendships, one of her "crises" toward the end of counseling followed an occasion during which one of her male friends told her he was sexually attracted to her. She reported being attracted to men (in the abstract), but felt very awkward and uncertain about developing an intimate sexual relationship. This was clearly an area that was going to need greater attention, especially as she approached young adulthood. I realized, however, that Sheila was a truly resilient young woman who had survived tremendous loss and betrayal. She was doing well in school, was involved in extracurricular activities, and had developed new support systems. Sheila had been attending an incest survivors group and had an excellent relationship with the counselor running the group as well as several friends in the group. She would also be able to continue individual treatment with a new counselor.

Sheila's response to my announcement that I was leaving the agency included alarm, a sense of being abandoned, and anger. She began by acknowledging how important our relationship had become to her and how afraid she was of getting as depressed as she had been. I, in turn, conveyed that this had been an important relationship for me and that it had been a privilege for me to work with her. I also invited her to share the range of feelings she might be experiencing:

TH: I appreciate you telling me how important this relationship has been for you. I wonder if my leaving raises any other feelings for you?

CL: What do you mean?

TH: Over the past year we have found it helpful to talk about both the good and the bad feelings that come up in different situations, as well as the good and bad feelings we have about people. I want to check and see if you feel you could talk with me about all the different feelings that my leaving raises for you.

CL: (tears in her eyes) I'm frightened, and sad, and mad.

TH: Yes. There are lots of different feelings . . .

CL: I'm afraid I might get depressed again and I won't have you to come to. And part of me is mad because I have come to trust you and told you lots of things and now you are leaving me.

TH: Part of you is angry with me because it feels as though I am abandoning you and makes you wonder if it was a good thing to trust and share yourself with me?

CL: I know you've helped me a lot and talking about my anger makes it seem as though I don't appreciate it.

TH: I know you appreciate me. However, your anger at me also makes a lot of sense. I appreciate it when you can share both the good and bad feelings you might have about me. It makes me feel that we can be honest and genuine with each other, that our relationship is not phony.

We spent much of the remaining eight weeks talking about her relationships with others and with me, underscoring her strengths and the gains she had made, and discussing the potential "mine-fields" (i.e., her pleasing, caretaking, dissociating, unassertiveness, and other tendencies that sometimes got in the way of developing fulfilling relationships). We also began to look forward and Sheila spoke hopefully of going on to college. What a contrast from the despondent, hopeless young woman I had first seen at intake! I could see that Sheila was now responding to herself with the same caring attitude that I held toward her and I felt that she was taking a part of me with her that might prove helpful as she encountered new challenges. I felt certain that her intelligence, her increased awareness of her strengths and weaknesses and of her patterns of relating to others would serve her well in the future.

Questions for Thought and Discussion

1. Think of what it means to trust someone deeply. Create a list of the developmental experiences that (1) made you feel safe (where you could trust); and (2) made you feel that your trust had been broken or betrayed. How have these good and bad experiences shaped your current relationships?

2. Do you know someone who has experienced sexual abuse? How might you react if you learned that a close relative had been a victim of this crime? What would you be likely to say and do?

Suggestions for Further Reading

Briere, J. (1996). *Therapy for adults molested as children: Beyond survival* (2nd ed.). New York: Springer. Well-written, instructive textbook that highlights how early sexual abuse trauma can interfere with normal development. Provides a very thoughtful, sensitive approach to interventions with clients.

Ciottone, R., & Madonna, J. (1996). *Play therapy with sexually abused children: A synergistic-developmental approach.* Northvale: Jason Aronson Publishers. Useful for work with children. Highlights developmentally relevant issues that may emerge.

MARY: A NATIVE AMERICAN CHILD FINDING HER PARENTS IN THE AFTERMATH OF DIVORCE

CHAPTER 4

INTRODUCTION

Marital disruption and post-divorce family relationships may be the most common problem that child and family counselors work with. Fortunately, there is a rich body of research on the effects of divorce on children that we can use to help children adjust more securely. In the first section, I will summarize the research findings on the factors that shape children's adjustment to their parents' breakup. In the second section, I will present the case of 11-year-old Mary and her family to illustrate an educational, short-term counseling approach for helping children cope with divorce.

Social Context and Prevalence of Divorce

The divorce rate escalated rapidly in the late 1960s and 1970s and stabilized at a high rate in the 1980s and 1990s. Nearly half of all first marriages end in divorce within 10 years (U.S. Bureau of the Census, 1992), and an additional 17% separate but do not divorce (Castro-Martin & Bumpass, 1989). As a result, more than 1 million children in America experience parental divorce yearly. Why are there so many divorces? Could it be that "People just don't care anymore"? Although such a simple assignment of blame is often heard, it is not very accurate. There were many complicated and far-reaching social changes during the 20th century that led to great modifications in family roles and relationships (Cherlin, 1992). With industrialization in the early 1900s, for example, people began moving to cities where jobs were being concentrated. During and after World War II, women began entering the workforce in large numbers. And, in the 1960s, regulation of fertility through birth control became widespread. These sweeping social changes brought about profound shifts in traditional roles, responsibilities, and decision-making power in families. In addition to these changes, new public policies such as the adoption of no-fault divorce resulted in the divorce rate doubling between 1960 and 1975. As a result, it is projected that 40 to 50% of children born in the 1990s will live in a single-parent family, usually headed by a mother (85%), and most of these children will also experience life in a stepfamily (U.S. Bureau of the Census, 1992; Glick & Lin, 1986). Next, we will look closely at the outlook for these children, and consider the factors that predict successful versus problematic adjustment.

The escalating divorce rate in the 1960s and 1970s led researchers to begin studying the effects of divorce on children more carefully. They were interested in learning about children's immediate reactions to the breakup and, more importantly, the factors that predicted successful versus problematic long-term adjustment. It is important to note that while large differences in the patterns of divorce and remarriage across racial and ethnic communities exist (Orbuch et al., 1999), most of the research conducted on the effects of divorce has used Caucasian, middle-class samples. We know, for example, that divorce rates are higher for African American families compared to White families, and that African Americans are less likely to remarry than Whites (Castro-Martin & Bumpass, 1989). Unfortunately, we know little about how ethnic and racial factors influence the way families cope in the aftermath of divorce. In particular, Native Americans living near or in reservations have their own divorce laws, separate from those utilized by individual states in the rest of the country. There is no empirical research available on how the values in these codes might influence Native Americans' reactions to divorce. We will summarize the findings we do have regarding divorce, keeping in mind that the summary is primarily from a Caucasian sample and does not consider how social and economic factors will influence Native Americans differently than Whites. This summary is drawn from several comprehensive review articles, and interested readers are encouraged to explore these informative research reviews in more detail (Amato & Keith, 1991b; Hetherington, 1998; Simons, 1996; Zill et al., 1993; Cherlin et al., 1991).

Children's Reactions to Divorce

Marital disruption is profoundly painful for most children. Initially, almost all children will be very upset by the breakup and may show anger, fear, depression, and guilt during the first year. Most will not understand what is happening and will be shocked and surprised by the separation, even though it did not happen suddenly. In general, children do not welcome the parental breakup or find relief in it unless they have been witnessing physical violence. Fortunately, the troubled reactions that many children initially experience in response to the marital disruption usually lessen during the second year. However, their long-term reactions will vary greatly, depending on how parents and significant others respond to the child during and after the separation. The most important factors that shape long-term adjustment are (1) the degree of parental conflict children are exposed to; and (2) the quality of parenting they receive after the breakup (Amato & Keith, 1991b; Hetherington, 1993). We will see the impact of these two cardinal factors in the case study that follows.

In addition to these two factors, children are also affected by the broader social context in which they live. Children will fare more poorly in neighborhoods with high crime and violence. The outcomes may also be more problematic when they lack access to the social supports that can be found by participating in sports, music, theatre, and other group activities. Further, if their now single parent has increased economic stress and decreased ability to provide adequate supervision or attention due to increased work demands (which commonly occurs), the children's adjustment is negatively affected (Forgatch, Patterson, & Ray, 1995). Unfortunately, economic stress after the divorce often leads to increased family mobility (i.e., having to move more often to find better paying jobs or lower cost-of-living neighborhoods). This mobility then results in decreased kinship networks and family support systems, which deprives the families of grandparents and other surrogate parents who could have provided the essential buffers needed to cope effectively in the aftermath of the divorce (Emery & Forehand, 1994). It is easy to see how these multiple stressors of poverty, family disruption, and decreased familial support can tax the family's coping abilities and increase the children's risk for personal, social, and academic problems. The adjustment faced by divorced families can be even more challenging in cultures where marital disruption is atypical or less accepted, such as among Catholic Latinos. With these considerations in mind, let's see how age and gender affect children's initial reactions to their parents' breakup.

Preschoolers   In response to the initial shock of their parents' breakup, preschool children will feel sad, cry more often, and become more demanding. Many will also regress (e.g., they may resume thumb sucking or need help feeding themselves). Compared to girls, boys tend to become noisier, angrier, and more restless (e.g., disrupt group activities at nursery school and lose the ability to play cooperatively with other children). Girls, in contrast, tend to become "perfect"—for example, overly concerned with being neat and well behaved. In addition to these behaviors, most children this age will be anxious, have more nightmares, wet the bed more, masturbate more, and express fear of separating from the custodial parent.

Six to Eight Years of Age   This is perhaps the most difficult age in which to cope with divorce. Both boys and girls will often feel sad, cry, and express longing for the out-of-home parent, usually the father. Boys, however, show more distress than girls, and experience more negative consequences in the absence of their father as a role model, as a disciplinarian, and as an adult with whom to engage in sports or other activities. Because children at this age are egocentric in their thinking, they routinely believe that they are to blame for the divorce or for an irresponsible parent's lack of involvement. Especially when one parent drifts out of the child's life, many children come to feel that they are basically unlovable and show significant signs of depression. The consequences of lowered self-esteem, loss of initiative, and difficulty concentrating lead to a sharp decline in school performance, which further fuels their symptoms of depression. Finally, parents and counselors often underestimate how worried these children are about their parents' well-being (many children see their parents' distress and how worried, anxious, and angry they are), and how invested children may be in trying to prevent the divorce or in restoring their original intact family.

Nine to Twelve Years of Age   In contrast to 6- to 8-year-olds who tend to be sad, 9- to 12-year-olds are usually angry. They may be intensely angry with both parents for the breakup or at the parent who initiated the separation (or at least the one who is blamed for the breakup). Unfortunately, children at this age are highly prone to taking sides with one parent against the other (aligning) and to assigning blame. As a result, they are especially vulnerable to becoming involved in destructive parental battles, in which one parent seeks to blame, harass, or get revenge on the other. These children also express their anger in other ways, such as abruptly rejecting their out-of-home parent's attempts to spend time with them. Of particular concern are the frequent reports by single-parent mothers that their 9- to 12-year-old sons are "impossible" to discipline.

As we will see in the following case study with Mary, anger is not the only reaction experienced by these children. Under the anger there often are feelings of loneliness, sadness about the breakup, concern about their parents' well-being, and anxiety about what is going to happen to them. Their anger often arises in response to feeling powerless: They do not want the divorce, they want their family intact, they long for the out-of-home parent, and they feel helpless to alter the enormous changes occurring in their lives. These feelings of anger and helplessness often result in the children no longer trying to do well at school, getting into fights with peers, and developing somatic complaints like headaches and stomachaches. While these experiences are problematic for many children, they are even more challenging for children belonging to minority groups or those from economically disadvantaged families. For these families, these experiences represent another arena in which they have no control. Given that control over many aspects of life is typically exerted by those who are in the majority or who are economically advantaged, feelings of powerlessness or unfairness are often compounded for minority children experiencing divorce. We will see that there are many things families can do to help their children successfully adjust. In particular, if the extended families of both parents can remain positively engaged with the children, let them know that they are cared about, and stay away from blaming one or the other parent, this will buffer the children against the negative consequences of the divorce. This approach will also promote resiliency or effective coping in the children.

Adolescence   Fewer adolescents experience parental divorce because most divorces occur when children are younger (i.e., divorce is most common when children are 4 to 7 years of age). When divorce does occur, however, the responses of adolescents tend to vary greatly (Buchanan, Maccoby, & Dornbusch, 1992). On the one hand, adolescents may adjust to the family disruption better than younger children can, partly because they are already becoming more independent, are needing less parental nurturance or guidance, and are distancing somewhat from the family as they become more involved in their own plans and future. Refreshingly, researchers find that some adolescents (usually girls) show a positive developmental spurt in response to the marital disruption and become helpful to their parents and younger siblings during this family crisis. Their own maturity and compassion can be seen as they participate constructively in family decisions, help with household responsibilities, and provide stable, nurturing relation-ships to their younger siblings.

On the other hand, many adolescents feel betrayed by the divorce. Some will angrily disengage from the family and may begin acting-out sexually, especially if they see their own parents becoming readily involved in other sexual relationships. Some adolescents become depressed, withdraw from peers and family involvement, and lose their plans and ambitions for their own futures. Like older school-aged children, adolescents also have problems when they are pulled into loyalty conflicts and feel they have to take sides in parental arguments or choose one parent over the other. For most adolescents, however, the main concern is about their own future. In particular, they often worry about how the marital failure will influence their own future ability to have a good marriage or their ability to go to college. Sadly, research supports their concern. One of the long-term effects of divorce for some adolescents is a decreased ability to succeed academically and to achieve occupationally during their early adult years (Chase-Lansdale et al., 1995).

Gender Differences   In addition to the age differences just discussed, researchers have found marked gender differences for children in the years following divorce (Clarke-Stewart & Hayward, 1996). Although there has been increasing attention to joint custody and father-headed families, almost 90% of all children of divorce still reside with a custodial mother. Studies find that the problems caused by marital conflict, divorce, and life in the care of a single mother is more pervasive for young boys than for young girls. Boys in single-mother families, in contrast to girls in single-mother families and children in intact homes, tend to have more adjustment problems. Younger boys tend to be more dependent and help seeking, whereas older boys tend to be more aggressive and disobedient. In the two years following divorce, for example, boys from divorced homes are far more likely to be in conflict with their custodial mothers and to disobey them than boys from intact homes. In contrast, school-aged girls from divorced families are likely to function as well as girls in intact two-parent homes. Usually, they get along well with their custodial mothers—at least until adolescence when the level of mother-daughter conflict often increases substantially. In sum, compared to girls, boys in single-mother-headed homes exhibit more behavior problems at school and at home, have more trouble getting along with friends at school, and have poorer school achievement. This occurs because boys tend to lose their primary identification figure and source of discipline when the father moves out. They also tend to receive more anger and criticism from their custodial mothers than do girls. The evidence of greater difficulty in raising boys after divorce is also noted in sibling relationships. Researchers report that parents have greater difficulty in handling sons after divorce and find more anger and conflict between sons, and between sons and daughters, than between sisters. Perhaps for these or for other reasons, the U.S. Census Bureau reports that parents with sons are 9% less likely to divorce than are parents with daughters (1992).

These gender differences change as children grow into adolescence, however. As noted earlier, studies suggest that divorce is harder for young boys than for young girls. When girls reach adolescence, however, conflict often escalates between single mothers and their daughters to match the level of conflict between young sons and their mothers. In addition to the increasing mother-daughter conflict, adolescent girls are more likely to develop problems in dating and heterosexual relationships. This is especially true if their father has not been actively involved in their lives, if their mother has not been able to parent authoritatively, and if caregivers have not supervised or monitored them closely. Poignantly, these adolescents tend to have sex at an earlier age and with more partners than do adolescent daughters from intact families. Sadly, these adolescents also are likely to marry at a younger age and eventually become divorced themselves. These problems in heterosexual relationships, and in greater academic and occupational under-achievement for adolescent girls compared to boys, tend to continue on into early adulthood (Hetherington, 1993). These gender differences become even more complex as the families transition from single-parent divorced families to stepfamilies. For example, while boys tend to adjust positively to the introduction of a responsible stepfather, girls are more likely to struggle with this new addition.

In sum, these research findings refer only to the effects of marital disruption on children. They do not generalize to other family changes such as parental death or other family forms such as never-married single-parent families. Marital disruption does pose significant developmental challenges as substantial psychological and behavioral problems are two to three times more prevalent in children from divorced and remarried families than from nondivorced families. However, the large majority of children (70 to 80%) do not show severe or enduring problems and emerge in the long run as well-adjusted individuals (Hetherington, 1993; Zill et al., 1993). Let's turn now from this overview of children's reactions to divorce and move closer to the feelings and experiences that divorce can engender. The following case study of "Mary" will help us see what counselors can do in a short period of time to help children of divorce cope more successfully.

CASE ILLUSTRATION

Developmental History

Presenting Problem   When 11-year-old Mary entered treatment, she was both anxious and depressed. In the months following the stormy breakup of her parents' marriage, Mary had changed from being polite, obedient, and overly responsible, to being sullen and withdrawn in her new home with her mother. Mary had begun to quarrel with friends, and, for the first time, had become unresponsive and disobedient toward her teacher. Her school performance, which had been predominantly A's and B's, had fallen off to C's and D's since the breakup. Upon the advice of Mary's teacher, Mary's mother reluctantly telephoned for counseling for Mary because she seemed so "unhappy."

Client Description   Mary's mother (Mrs. A.) and father (Mr. A.) were both racially mixed (Caucasian and Native American Indian). Mary (pseudonym) had an Anglo first name and a traditional Native American surname. Her facial features reflected her mixed heritage: she had straight black hair, reddish brown skin, and dark brown eyes. Mary was quiet and reserved although she could be engaging with both peers and adults. She was physically inactive and was about 20 pounds overweight. Like many children of divorce, Mary was both sad and mad. At school and with friends Mary seemed angry in response to the breakup, but it was clear in counseling that Mary's primary feeling was sadness. Diagnostically, Mary presented with an adjustment disorder with mixed anxiety and depression in response to the divorce. However, her history of low self-esteem and long-standing dysphoric or unhappy mood suggested that she also suffered from dysthymia, a long-term, low-level depressive disorder.

Social and Community Context   Mary's family lived in a small rural southwestern community. Mary felt safe and known by her classmates and neighbors in their ethnically mixed neighborhood and school. This stable but economically pressed area consisted primarily of working-poor and blue-collar families. In the broader community, a conservative Country Western ethos was prevalent and traditional sex roles were emphasized: men were expected to wear boots and cowboy hats and many carried rifles in their pickup trucks. In contrast, women were expected to remain in nonachieving work roles and assume nonassertive caretaking duties.

Although conformity to these traditional sex roles became a primary source of marital conflict for Mrs. A., both parents were highly acculturated and shared middle-class values of upward economic mobility and achievement through education. Both parents attended college at night, sought advancement at work, and actively supported educational achievement for Mary. However, they had conflict around achieving role flexibility in this "macho" environment, particularly within their home. They were, however, successful in integrating their biracial identities. Both Mr. and Mrs. A. had the interpersonal range and cultural flexibility to succeed in predominantly Caucasian business settings (computer sales and office manager). They both chose to retain their Native American surnames and valued their Native American heritage. Mrs. A., in particular, lived by the Native American ideology of respect and reverence for the earth, honoring nature's role in fulfilling basic survival needs, and understanding nature's role in one's life and in one's relationship with a higher being and with other human beings (Axelson, 1999). Mrs. A. shared this worldview with me and this sharing became an important part of our relationship and the working alliance we were able to create.

The family's social network included Caucasians, Mexican Americans, and Native Americans from a range of blue-collar and middle-class families. Although the couple was successful in achieving identity integration outside the home (i.e., in their work and educational spheres), they were unable to establish shared values and mutually acceptable roles within their marriage and home.

Family Relationships   As we will see subsequently, Mary's functioning was greatly affected by her parents' conflicting views of marital values and roles, and by their unstable family structure. The family was rigidly hierarchical. Mary's father was highly authoritarian, demanded strict obedience, and never explained or gave reasons for his directives. There was no room for compromise with him. Although corporal punishment was condoned in this family, it was not necessary since Mary both feared her father *and* eagerly sought his approval. She would not even consider disobeying him—even after the breakup when so many children no longer obey noncustodial fathers. Thus, although intimidated by and submissive to her stern father, Mary also admired him and looked forward to their shared activities such as horseback riding, target shooting, and watching sports together on television.

Mary grew up watching her mother comply with her domineering husband. In this family, there was no parental coalition or alliance—Mr. A. ruled. However, as Mrs. A. became successful at school and work, earned more money, and gained the respect of her colleagues, her sense of confidence increased and she tried to become more equal within the marriage. Her attempts to redefine the marriage on more equal terms with more shared power failed repeatedly and ultimately precipitated the divorce, but only after several years of escalating marital conflict. Sadly, Mary was exposed to a great deal of yelling, degrading insults, and angry threats between her parents.

Whereas Mary was obedient and overly compliant with her authoritarian father, she had more of a sister-like relationship with her mother during the marriage, and acted like a parent to her mother after the breakup. Thus, the rigid and emotionally distant relationship with her father contrasted starkly with her overinvolved, caretaking relationship with her mother. For example, Mary was sometimes a close confidant and "best friend" to her mother; at other times, Mary acted more like a concerned parent who was worried about her mother's unhappiness and loneliness. Still, at other times, Mary and Mrs. A. acted like bickering sisters or competitive peers. Fortunately, there were also times when Mrs. A. was able to assume an effective parenting role. That is, amidst these confusing role disturbances, Mrs. A. was able to sometimes discipline Mary effectively and be a source of nurturance and understanding. These shifting family roles contributed to Mary's complex blend of healthy and symptomatic features.

Initial Sessions

In treating children of divorce, critical events sometimes occur in the initial telephone contact. For example, one parent may subtly but successfully enlist the counselor's allegiance in the parental battle. That is, the referring parent may successfully define the other parent as "bad," *reconstituting in treatment the same loyalty conflicts that may be central to the child's symptoms and distress.* Or, as occurred in this case, Mrs. A.'s initial resistance to treatment was immediately evident. Had I not responded to her initial reluctance on the telephone, she may not have brought Mary to the first session. Later I will discuss some of the important issues that arose in this initial telephone contact with Mrs. A. and how I tried to establish a working alliance with Mrs. A., and with Mary.

Initial Telephone Contact   As is often the case, cultural and gender differences between the family and me were most significant during the initial sessions. For example, during the initial telephone contact, Mrs. A. was flat, distant, and skeptical about whether and how counseling would help. It seemed that she called primarily to comply with Mary's teacher's request. She did not really want to be speaking with me even though she knew that Mary was struggling and needed help. I assumed that, based on her life experience, there were probably many good reasons why she felt this way. I began to try formulating tentative possibilities/hypotheses about Mrs. A.'s worldview that might help me understand and respond to her more effectively. I wanted to join with her in some way, convey empathy, and let her know that her feelings mattered. I invited her to express any questions, concerns, or reservations she might have about treatment or about me. I also tried to reach her by making an empathic connection. (Counselor: Divorce is harder than most parents expect it to be. Often, after working all day, coming home to more demands and problems can seem overwhelming. It really is hard to be a single parent.) When Mrs. A. brushed off these empathic attempts, I looked for other supportive ways to try and engage with her. (Counselor: Well, it does sound like things have not been going well for Mary, and I can see how hard you've been trying to help her.) Mrs. A. was not responsive to my attempt to affirm her in this way either, and I wondered if she was feeling that even having to bring Mary to treatment was not under her control. She became more responsive only after I suggested a limited commitment that gave her more choice or control. (Counselor: Let's just agree to meet for one session. I would like to meet with you for about 20 minutes, Mary alone for about 20 minutes, and you and Mary together for about 20 minutes. After that, you and Mary will be able to decide for yourselves whether I can be of help or not, and we can decide together how to proceed from there.)

Why was this invitation more effective when other attempts had failed? Based on what I had already heard on the phone about the marital relationship, I hypothesized that Mrs. A. needed to feel more control over the decision to enter treatment, and to shape the direction of treatment. In particular, this response held out the promise of getting the help she needed without having to comply with the teacher or with me, as she may have had to do in other relationships. This initial hypothesis about compliance, which emerged in her initial reluctance to enter treatment, turned out to be important. As I later learned, many relationships with authority figures, and with males in particular, had fueled her expectations of submission and compliance. Later in treatment, for example, Mrs. A. told me that asking for help from anybody was "unacceptable" for her, and that it was "stupid" to even think of asking a male for help. Thus, in the simple act of having to ask for help for her daughter, multiple layers of interlocking conflict were painfully evoked. These included (1) expectations based on her own childhood experience of never having her emotional needs met; (2) humiliating compliance from 12 years of marriage to her domineering husband; and (3) culturally based experiences that led her to distrust Caucasian authority. In sum, much was occurring in this initial telephone contact. Here, Mrs. A. was behaviorally teaching me what the issues were that had caused difficulty in her life and how I needed to respond in order to help.

Initial Child Contact   Following the initial session with Mary and her mother, I began seeing Mary individually to talk about her parents' divorce. It was clear from Mary's wary manner that she was anxious about seeing me. I hypothesized that being in treatment conflicted with cultural sanctions against drawing attention to one's self and seeking help for problems from outsiders. So I chose not to pressure her for personal self-disclosure or obtain any specific history. Instead, my interaction focused on how I could establish some sense of safety for her in our relationship, "join" with her, and begin a more collaborative relationship.

Perhaps in line with cultural norms, Mary was controlled and somber when she entered my office. She folded her hands in her lap and looked at the floor. She was an intimidated and inhibited child. I was aware that as a male, Caucasian, authority figure— with whom she had probably not felt much safety in the past—it was essential that I try to *differentiate* our relationship from problematic past experiences right from the beginning. That is, I did not want to be perceived as dominating or directive as I was learning that her father was, but as friendlier and more egalitarian, someone she could respectfully question and with whom she could express all her feelings (mad, sad, happy, etc.). Thus, rather than go right to work on divorce-related issues, I tried to help her be with me in a different way:

TH: Have you ever seen a counselor before?

MARY: (nonverbally shrugs no)

TH: What have you been told about why you're here and what we're going to do?

MARY: (shrugs shoulders again, suggesting "I don't know")

I made a big to-do about pulling an imaginary pocket watch and long chain out of my pocket and pretended to begin hypnotizing her. Mary liked my joke, smiled, and looked into my eyes for the first time. It was a friendly moment, and allowed me to begin explaining what counseling was and what we would be doing together. After that, it was much easier to take the next step and begin approaching her divorce-related concerns:

TH: I've heard your mom and dad are getting a divorce. What's happening?

Mary accepted my open-ended invitation and began telling me about the big events that had shaken her life. I followed her lead and introduced a series of exploratory topics as they followed naturally from the material she was presenting (these topic areas will be detailed later). Like most children of divorce, she had observed much, had many worries and concerns, and had much to say:

MARY: My dad doesn't live with us anymore. My mom and I live in a new apartment by ourselves.

TH: That's such a big change. How is it going for you?

MARY: I don't know.

TH: What's the best thing about living in your new apartment with your mother?

MARY: Well, my mom and dad don't argue as much.

TH: That must be a big relief. It can be really upsetting to see your mom and dad fight.

MARY: Yeah, it's better now . . .
(Later in the same session)

TH: Why did your mom and dad break up? What have you been told about all of this?

MARY: I don't know, they just don't get along I guess.

TH: Have your mom or dad ever talked to you about the divorce or why they broke up?

MARY: My dad and I don't talk together much, and my mom just starts crying.

TH: So you have had to figure out all of this on your own and handle everything yourself.

MARY: Yeah.

TH: Well I'm glad you're here with me now so you can have somebody to talk to about all of this. Are there any questions I can answer for you right now?

In this way, I explored a series of divorce-related issues in order to assess what was troubling Mary the most. In addition to assessment, I used this discussion to begin intervening and correcting some important misconceptions she had about the divorce. For example:

TH: Sometimes children tell me that they think they caused their parents to divorce. Have you ever felt like you were to blame?

MARY: Maybe.

TH: What did you do that might have caused your parents to break up?

MARY: Well, they argued about me a lot, you know.

TH: How so?

MARY: My dad would get mad at my mom for being too easy on me. And I think my mom disagreed with my dad because he was too strict with me. I would listen to them arguing about me like that a lot.

TH: So you think you caused your parents to divorce because they argued over how to discipline you?

MARY: Mm hmm.

TH: Well, yes, Mary, they were arguing with each other over how to raise you, but that doesn't mean that you caused them to break up. Lots of kids tell me they feel this way, but children are never responsible for their parents' divorce. You know how some things are child business and other things are adult business? Well, deciding to get married, having a baby, or getting a divorce are all adult decisions that children really have no control over.

Thus by being friendly, interested, and giving her open-ended bids, this intimidated girl was able to begin talking to me in important ways about her parents' divorce. By conveying understanding for the difficult feelings that the divorce aroused for her, and articulating more fully the dilemmas she was coping with, I began to establish credibility with her. (Counselor: It's really hard when you feel like you have to take sides between them because you want to be close to both of your parents at the same time.) Over the course of our first few individual sessions, Mary became increasingly more animated and forthcoming with me. That she could be so stiff or frozen initially, and later respond so well, informed me that there were healthy aspects of her family life that coexisted with the problems that were also evident.

Case Formulation and Treatment Planning

Mary's family belonged to an HMO insurance plan that allowed 16 counseling sessions. With these limitations in mind, I thought about Mary's treatment in three phases. As we have seen, Mary initially presented as anxious, compliant, and overweight. Her parents had recently separated, she had moved to a new apartment with her mother within the past month, and she had been exposed to much parental wrangling during the breakup. I hypothesized that her compliance and obesity reflected longer-term developmental conflicts, but I did not yet know much about the potential causes and meaning of these symptoms. However, because of her parents stormy breakup, I knew it was likely that she was highly anxious as a result of being exposed to ongoing parental conflict. To address her anxiety, and because this was the initial mandate I had been given for treatment, I began to assess and help her resolve a series of generic divorce-related issues. During the first phase of treatment I worked individually with Mary for six sessions in an active, educational, and problem-solving approach. Phase 2 lasted for two sessions and provided parent education or "coaching" sessions for each parent separately. Phase 3 consisted of eight parent-child sessions with Mary and her mother. These three treatment phases are discussed next.

Phase 1   As we saw in the Introduction, there has been a great deal of empirical research on the effects of divorce on children and the type of family interactions that predict how children will adjust. Guided by these research findings, I wanted to explore with Mary five topic areas that often shape how children adjust (Teyber, 2001). Thus, the first few sessions focused on her parent's breakup and exploring the following five content areas.

Parental Conflict   Divorce engenders significant and enduring problems for children when they are exposed to ongoing parental conflict. That is, although most children will be initially anxious in response to marital disruption, children are almost certain to suffer intense anxiety and long-term adjustment problems when they are exposed to chronic or ongoing parental wrangling such as arguing, verbal or physical fighting, yelling, threatening, and so forth. In contrast, parents of children who make a secure and successful adjustment (even if they may not like or trust each other), have the good sense to shield their children from their parental conflicts. Further, they don't undermine the other parent to the child (e.g., "Your mother's an idiot, you don't have to listen to her." Or, "Your father's a liar, why do you want to see him?"). In particular, they don't embroil children in adult conflicts (e.g., "Tell your father the next time he's late with the support check . . .").

I asked Mary directly about this all-important aspect of the breakup:

TH: How did your parents get along these past few months? Did they argue or fight a lot?

MARY: (nods, tears)

TH: They fought a lot; were you scared?"

MARY: (looks down): Yeah.

TH: What was the scariest thing about their fights?

MARY: I was afraid that maybe my dad was going to hurt my mom.

TH: Yes, you were scared that it wasn't safe for her and she might get hurt. Tell me what happened.

MARY: Well, my dad would get real mad and start yelling at her and my mom would start crying and stuff.

TH: What kind of stuff would happen next?

By helping Mary discuss her fears, I was able to help her make sense of the events and, as we will see, come up with better ways to cope with future parental conflicts that were likely to arise.

Continuity of Parent-Child Relationships   By two years after the divorce, over one-half of all divorced fathers have no regularly scheduled contact with their children. When one parent disengages and fails to fulfill an active (even if part-time) parenting role, children often absorb responsibility for the parent's lack of involvement and blame themselves. Many of these children begin to feel that they are lacking in some way and are not love-worthy. They often become depressed, suffer a loss of initiative, show declines in school performance, and seem unable to make realistic long-term plans for their future. Children who are better adjusted, in contrast, have usually maintained physical and emotional access to both parents following the breakup. That is, they do not lose either of their parents through the divorce. This issue quickly emerged in my explorations with Mary:

TH: What is the hardest thing about living in your new apartment with your mother?

MARY: I miss my dad.

TH: How often do you get to see him?

MARY: On weekends.

TH: You wish you could see him more.

MARY: Yeah.

TH: Sure you do, you don't get to see him every day like you used to. What could we do to help with that feeling?

MARY: I don't know.

TH: Does your dad know you miss him? Do you tell him?

MARY: Uh uh.

TH: What might happen if you told him how you feel?

MARY: I don't know. We never really talk together like that.

TH: What do you think he would do if you told him that you missed him, or if you asked him if you could talk together on the phone every Wednesday night at eight o'clock?

In these ways, I was able to help Mary find a way to maintain more frequent, ongoing contact with her dad.

Loyalty Conflicts   Virtually all children who have long-term problems adjusting to divorce feel they have to take sides and choose between their parents. These children do not have permission to love and be close to both parents at the same time. Instead, parents give children the message (often nonverbally or in subtle and covert ways) that they have to choose to be close to one parent at the expense of closeness to the other. For example, the mother may look sad or hurt when the son expresses how eager he is to visit his dad, or the father may feel mad when the daughter expresses how much she misses her mother. Almost every child wants to be close to both parents—no matter how limited or superficial that relationship may seem to the other parent. Children feel torn apart inside (i.e., stomachaches, headaches, and peptic ulcers) when they are pressured to take sides. These already difficult circumstances are often exacerbated for biracial children such as Mary. Mary not only had to cope with the challenging developmental task of establishing a biracial identity, but she had to do this in the strained context of not being able to experience a relationship with both parents simultaneously. Feeling how immobilizing these loyalty issues were for her, I tried to help by asking directly about them.

TH: Your parents argue a lot and haven't been getting along very well. Do you ever feel like you have to take sides between them?

MARY: What do you mean?

TH: Do you ever feel like you get pulled into their fights or have to be on your mom's side or your dad's side?

MARY: Oh yeah, my dad gets mad sometimes and says, "You always take her side."

TH: That wouldn't feel very good to hear. Does your mom feel okay if you miss your dad or want to be with him?

MARY: Uh uh. I think it makes her kind of sad.

TH: This must be hard for you because you love them both. It's unfair when kids feel they have to take sides and choose between their parents. Children should be allowed to be close to both of their parents at the same time.

MARY: Yeah, it is unfair.

Acknowledging that Mary could indeed love *both* parents and didn't need to take sides, even though both parents sometimes had difficulty with this, visibly reduced her anxiety.

Parenting Competence   Divorce seems commonplace because it occurs so frequently, but it is still an earth-shaking crisis for every family member when it occurs. Most separating parents do not anticipate how stressful the divorce will be both for themselves and their children, and underestimate how much time and effort it will take to recover emotionally. Researchers find that it often takes parents two to three years to fully regain their equilibrium, and that parents often reach a psychological low point one year after the separation. As a result of their severe and prolonged personal distress, most adults' parenting competence declines markedly following the breakup. That is, most parents are not able to nurture, discipline, or provide an organized household with predictable daily routines as effectively as they did before the divorce. This is especially unfortunate because the children are distressed by the breakup and have heightened needs for structure, routine, and parental attention at this time. For example, children feel more secure when their parents can be in charge and discipline effectively by providing clear limits and regularly enforced rules. When so many other things in their lives are changing, children are also reassured by predictable daily routines. Thus, a negative interaction can occur as the parent's diminished child-rearing capabilities coincide with the child's escalating needs for parental responsiveness. This negative interaction is one of the most important causes of children's problematic adjustment to divorce.

I tried to assess this issue with Mary throughout the initial phase of treatment and wanted to determine if her parents were still parenting her effectively. More specifically, I wanted to know three things: (1) if and how she got her emotional needs met; (2) how discipline was handled in both households; and (3) how much structure, organization, and predictability she experienced in her daily life. To answer these, I asked questions such as the following:

1. What do you do when you're sad? Who do you talk to when you're lonely? What would your mom/dad do if you asked him/her to hug you for a minute?
2. Are the rules the same or different at your mom's and your dad's house? What happens if you break the rules at your mom's/dad's house? Now that your parents are separated, is it easier for you to get out of doing the chores you used to have to do?
3. Tell me about dinnertime. Who decides what you're going to eat? Who prepares dinner? Who sits together—do you sit at the table or eat in front of the TV? Who cleans up afterwards? What do you do every morning to get ready for school? Tell me what happens in a typical day. When do you wake up?

Like most children, Mary had clear perceptions about these issues and could explain in detail how her mother and father handled each of them. Exploring these three areas confirmed my initial hypothesis that Mary was struggling with long-standing problems beyond the immediate divorce crisis, and clarified further problems that needed to be addressed in treatment. In particular, these explorations revealed how Mary was (1) lacking in emotional support from her father and (2) serving as a *parentified* caretaker for her mother. These two issues became the basis for the second and the third phases of treatment and will be discussed later.

Explanation for the Divorce   Almost all parents feel painfully guilty about the divorce. Most parents want to do the best they can for their children and worry that their marital failure will hurt their children in some unknown but irreparable way. One of the many problems with excessive parental guilt is that it serves to keep parents from talking to their children about the divorce in general, as well as from giving children a basic explanation for the divorce and what is going to happen. In the absence of effective parental explanations, children fill the void with their own egocentric and problematic explanations in which they typically blame themselves for the divorce.

Especially for children under 6 years of age, the principal concern that divorce arouses is separation anxiety and abandonment fears. Indeed, from children's eyes, their worst fear often comes true. If dad can suddenly pack up and move out on Saturday morning without any forewarning, and without telling the children specifically when and where they will see him next, it is understandable that children worry, "Won't mom go away too?" Children need to be prepared in advance for departures and reassured repeatedly of the continuity of parent-child relationships. For example, parents can say:

> Mom and Dad have decided we are not going to be married anymore. We are going to get a divorce. We are going to live in different houses from now on, but we will still always be your mom and dad. That is never going to change. Dad is going to move to a new apartment on Saturday, and you will be with him at his house on . . . Even though we are not going to be married anymore, you will always live with one of us. We will both always love you and work together to take care of you until you are grown up. We are going to need to talk together a lot about all of this. What questions can we answer for you right now?

Young children are egocentric in their thinking and place themselves at the causal fulcrum of family changes. If you ask preschool and school-aged children if they ever feel responsible or to blame for their parents' divorce, the majority of them will say "yes." These children carry an unnecessary burden of blame and guilt for the divorce. As we saw earlier, Mary did indeed feel responsible for her parents' divorce because they frequently argued over how to discipline her.

Finally, children also need an explanation for the divorce that does not assign blame. Parents often give ineffective explanations for the divorce that demand children see only one parent's reality as "truth," embroil children in parental conflicts, or draw children into adult conflicts and concerns that are beyond their understanding. This occurs, for example, when one parent explains the divorce by saying, "Your father is leaving us for another woman!" or "Your mother is ruining our family because she wants to meet her own selfish needs."

Such explanations undermine the parenting authority of the other parent to the child and take away that parent as a role model or identification figure. In effect, such explanations cause the child to lose that parent through the divorce. Similar to the explanation suggested earlier, Mary's mother had provided an effective explanation for the divorce that avoided blame and was reassuring to Mary. She explained that over the years she and Mr. A. had grown apart, that their differences in values, in needs, and their ongoing arguments had grown so large that the relationship had become too hurtful. As a couple, they had become angry and unkind to each other, and were both unhappy. She tried to emphasize that no one was to blame and acknowledged that perhaps if they had gotten counseling when the problems began things might have turned out differently. To make this explanation concrete, Mrs. A. suggested that a relationship is somewhat like a quilt. When a tear or hole appears in the quilt, it needs to be fixed fairly quickly or the quilt will continue to tear and eventually it will have many holes and end up in shreds. When that happens, the quilt becomes almost impossible to fix. She told Mary that all couples face problems in their relationship. However, if these difficulties keep adding up, and if the couple doesn't get help to resolve them, eventually the relationship has so many tears in it that it is difficult to fix. In the end, the couple's differences and their ongoing problems couldn't be resolved and resulted in divorce. She repeated that both partners are responsible for the success or failure of the marriage, that no one person is to blame. It was important for Mary to receive this explanation from her mother since her father continued to insist that the divorce was her mother's fault and wouldn't have occurred if her mother wasn't so "selfish."

In sum, phase 1 of treatment lasted six sessions and was successful in reaching limited but important goals. First, I was able to convey that our relationship was going to differ from what Mary had usually experienced with other males, authority figures, and Caucasians. I did this by finding a balance between establishing a friendly working relationship in which Mary received permission to initiate and lead, but still maintain the role of counselor and authority that was consonant with my role and did not clash with what was expected culturally. Second, I was able to assess her current functioning and identify other non-divorce-related issues that had been problematic throughout her development and contributed to her longer-term depression. Third, I was able to begin the relearning process and help her come to terms with the central worries and concerns precipitated by the divorce.

This brief, focused intervention was successful in reducing Mary's presenting anxiety and in improving her depressed mood. Mary had many important questions about the divorce answered, certain misconceptions clarified, and her emotional reactions to the breakup affirmed. Through discussions and role-play techniques she also gained some new strategies for coping more effectively with ongoing problems. For example, leaving the room when her parents' argued, and telling her parents that she felt uncomfortable carrying messages back and forth to the other parent when they asked her to do that, were especially helpful.

A brief, educationally oriented intervention such as this is often sufficient to help many children of divorce. Working within this structured/educational modality would not have succeeded, however, without sensitivity to how familial patterns and cultural differences could play out between us. For example, it was evident in our initial contact that Mary was anxious and distrustful with me—but also compliant. Her experience with males, authorities, and Caucasians had sometimes been dominating, demanding, and intimidating. I believe that Mary would not have been able to utilize the divorce-related information, problem-solving strategies, and emotional support I offered had I not (1) differentiated myself from her past relational experiences and provided a corrective (more affirming, supportive, nondirective) relational experience; and (2) balanced permission to stop complying and begin responding to her own needs with the realities of her cultural context (i.e., do this respectfully).

Specifically, Mary needed a relationship with me that did not reenact the problematic interpersonal patterns that she was experiencing with her parents. For example, Mary was enmeshed with her mother, and saw her mother as needy, vulnerable, and not effectively in control of her own adult life. In contrast, by being interested in and accessible to Mary, while remaining a professional who was capable and in charge, Mary could see that I did not need her in the way she had learned to expect from her mother. Clear therapeutic limits and boundaries were reassuring to Mary. She was able to feel close to me and let me help her without worrying about being responsible for me or for taking care of me, as she had to do with her mother. This would not have occurred if I had relinquished my professional role, tried to be more of a "friend," or offered much self-disclosure. On the other hand, if I was too formal, demanding, or distant, I risked being experienced as her authoritarian father, thereby activating the expectations that she also had to capitulate and comply with me. Providing this new middle ground or more "authoritative" relationship was an important task for me if I was to help Mary.

Maintaining my credibility as an effective helper in the ways described earlier also was consonant with her cultural expectations. It was important that I balanced giving permission to initiate, lead, and be more assertive with me with the reality of needing to comply, be quiet, and go along under certain circumstances within her familial and cultural context. That is, I needed to help Mary distinguish situations/relationships where it was safer to be compliant and situations/relationships when this was not necessary. Within her cultural context, I also needed to affirm that following or being quiet and deferential were valuable and appropriate ways to behave at times toward some of the people in her life. We will see subsequently how I had to balance Mary's cultural prescription to respect and honor her parents, with permission to stop taking care of her mother and to begin attending to her own needs as well. Without working with the cultural meanings that these changes held for her or helping her to make these important discriminations and find a new balance, I would have lost my "credibility" and been ineffective in helping Mary resolve her problems within the parameters of her life situation. Thus, assessing and providing the specific relational experiences that each client needs is a central, orienting construct for me, but I cannot do this effectively without appreciating the familial and cultural context that shapes the client's worldview.

Phase 2   Clearer treatment goals emerged out of my initial work with Mary. In phase 1, I simply wanted to engage this reluctant mother and daughter in treatment and establish a working alliance. Beyond this general aim, my goals in phase 1 were to (1) identify Mary's principal divorce-related concerns via exploring the five topic areas presented earlier and (2) begin diminishing these concerns wherever possible.

During the second phase of treatment, my goals were to enlist both parents in a brief educational or "coaching" intervention to help them change certain parental interactions that were creating problems for Mary. Specifically, I wanted to (1) reduce her exposure to interparental warfare and (2) alleviate her loyalty conflicts—giving her greater freedom to be close and involved with both of her parents.

As we will explore later, my longer-term goals in phase 3 were to engage both parents in treatment with Mary and to try to ameliorate two long-standing conflicts that were being generated by ongoing patterns of family interaction. Specifically, I hoped to help Mary's father respond to her in a less authoritarian manner so that she wouldn't be so anxious, compliant, and inhibited. I also wanted to facilitate clearer intergenerational boundaries between Mary and her mother and help them assume more appropriate parent-child roles.

The first goal in the second phase of treatment was to reduce interparental conflict and shield Mary from her parents' ongoing battles. Mary and I had already made some progress on this goal in our initial phase of treatment by (1) affirming how "scary" it was to see her parents fight; (2) clarifying that she was not responsible either for causing or stopping their battles; (3) acknowledging that it is unfair when children are pulled into parental battles or pressured to take sides; and (4) rehearsing and role-playing what she could say and do to remove herself from her parents' wrangling.

Although each of these interventions offered some help, I believed that Mary would remain anxious and unable to achieve a secure post-divorce adjustment as long as the parental battles continued. To reach this goal of greater security, I began the second phase of treatment by asking each parent to meet with me individually for one session.

As often occurs, mother was ready to participate but assured me that father would not be willing to meet with me. In general, many fathers will not participate in treatment if the mother asks them. However, most fathers will participate in treatment when the counselor reaches out and helps them feel included. Counselors can do this by (1) speaking directly to the father rather than triangulating through the mother; (2) explicitly validating the continuing importance of his role in the child's life; and (3) asking him to share his understanding of what can be done to make things better for his child.

Mary's father accepted my invitation to meet for one session and attended this appointment. He began the session by announcing that he didn't believe in therapy and didn't like therapists. I accepted his point of view without challenge, clarified our common goal of helping Mary, and emphasized his good intentions and sincere wish to help his daughter. This affirmation defused his combativeness and we began to talk constructively about Mary and her problems. During the course of this session, I was able to help him recognize that Mary's anxiety (nail biting, overeating, nightmares, losing homework) followed closely on the heels of parental arguments. He could see that parental arguments upset Mary and ultimately he agreed to "conduct business" with his ex-wife only when Mary was not present, and to use me as a mediator with the mother to resolve parenting disputes that would otherwise embroil Mary. This complex issue was not resolved in one meeting, of course, but Mary was exposed to less interparental conflict after this frank discussion. *This reduction in exposure to parental wrangling was probably the single most important change that could have occurred for Mary.*

Success in this cardinal arena was not matched by significant improvement in other areas, however. Regarding loyalty conflicts, for example, Mr. A. was rigid in his belief that his ex-wife was "selfish" and to blame for breaking up the family and that "Mary should know the truth" about her mother. Although he could acknowledge that this might put Mary in a strained position between her parents, he would not consider the possibility that both parents had contributed something to the marital breakup. Further, even if he did believe that his wife was completely to blame, he was unable to accept that it wasn't in Mary's best interest to hear this. Similarly, Mr. A. was unwilling to discuss or consider relaxing his authoritarian parenting style and offer Mary more approval, affection, or allow her greater self-expression.

In many cases, counselors will be able to continue working with parents on child-rearing issues such as these. In this case, however, Mary's father declined further involvement on these issues of parenting and loyalty conflicts. Several factors contributed to this reluctance. He was angry about the breakup, but broken-hearted too. He had grown up in a brutally authoritarian family and the marital rupture evoked his own long-standing separation anxieties, the shame of being left, and of having unmet needs exposed. Like most of the men he knew and worked with, Mr. A. coped with these unacceptable feelings in rigid and externalizing ways—through anger, emotional withdrawal, and alcohol. I was afraid that if I pressed for more, which a part of me wanted to do, I would rupture the fragile alliance I had with him and threaten the limited but important gains we had made. Cultural prescriptions against a man seeing a counselor and appearing "weak" also made it harder for him to become further involved in treatment. Thus, I supported the changes we had agreed upon, validated his important contributions to Mary's development, and invited further contact at any time he wished in order to help with any future concerns that may arise.

Mrs. A. was also wary in our session together but she could see that counseling was helping Mary. As a result, she also joined me in the principal goal of shielding Mary from further parental conflicts. Although I spoke in terms of helping Mary, Mrs. A. was visibly relieved to have my support in finding ways to reduce the personal distress for her of ongoing parental battles.

Mrs. A. was able to enter into these discussions more freely than Mr. A. and we evolved a joint plan of action. First, whenever parental conflicts were escalating in Mary's presence, Mrs. A. would terminate the conversation with a specific statement ("I do not want to talk about this anymore right now. We will continue this adult conversation later when we are alone."). If that did not stop the escalating tension, she would announce that she would not continue with this conversation at this time and she would then physically depart without further comment. Ultimately, Mr. and Mrs. A. agreed to discuss issues only in a public restaurant where neither one would be likely to lose their temper or escalate the conflict.

Although significant improvement occurred with the primary goal of shielding Mary from exposure to parental conflict, Mrs. A. was as unable as Mr. A. to work on the issue of reducing loyalty conflicts. Mrs. A. believed that a girl "belonged" with her mother—which supported Mr. A.'s view that she had always undermined his relationship with Mary. As with Mr. A., I felt that I had more to lose than gain by pressing my agenda and suspended this goal for now. Mr. A. was unwilling to work on the goal of more effective, *authoritative* parenting (e.g., discipline with warmth, clear guidelines, reasonable consequences, and parental follow-through), but Mrs. A. was willing to participate further. This introduced the third phase of treatment, which focused on the goal of easing mother's parentification of Mary.

Phase 3   The third phase of treatment began as I started working with both Mary and Mrs. A. on reducing Mary's parentification. Mary had become inappropriately concerned about her mother's well-being and felt responsible for shoring up her mother's emotional state. Mary's "parental" concern for her mother stemmed from three realistic concerns. First, Mr. A. was physically intimidating and often yelled and made threats toward Mrs. A. Although these arguments had not erupted into physical violence, Mary accurately sensed that their emotions were out of control and the potential for harm was readily imagined. Mary's worry and concern about her mother's well-being also made sense in terms of their new living status. Following the breakup, Mrs. A. was tired and distressed. She worked full-time and came home to the "second shift" of shopping, cooking, cleaning, and responding to Mary. Mrs. A. felt guilty about the breakup; worried about "hurting" Mary; was sad; missed the good things in the marriage; and felt overwhelmed by the very real demands of a career, running a household, and caring for a child. Mary could see the sadness in her mother's face and the fatigue in her slumped posture. Sadly for both, she often saw or heard her mother crying.

Finally, Mary's preoccupation with her mother's well-being was not based solely on the situational circumstances described. Despite being a hard-working and successful office manager, Mrs. A. had probably been moderately depressed (dysthymic) most of her life with periodic bouts of major depression. Mrs. A.'s own childhood had been grim. Her own single-parent mother had been manic-depressive, and Mrs. A. had repeatedly been sent away to live with relatives when her mother was not functional. Mary was highly sensitized to her mother's pain and hopelessness, and her self-esteem was based largely on taking care of or shoring up her mother. For example, Mary was vigilantly responsive to her mother's unspoken emotional needs, and served as her mother's confidant and "best friend." Mary was much too grown up, helpful, and concerned about her mother's emotional well-being to be able to have her own childhood.

In order to resolve this role reversal, I met once weekly for the remaining eight sessions in varying combinations with mother alone, daughter alone, or mother and daughter together. Many of the sessions in this final phase of treatment were with Mrs. A. individually in order to reduce the parentification by helping Mrs. A. find other sources of support and new ways of coping. As Mrs. A. made gains in understanding how and why she was parentifying Mary, we then scheduled conjoint sessions with Mary so they could address these issues in their relationship more directly. During these conjoint sessions, we would all talk together about this role reversal and, utilizing the personal gains she had made, Mrs. A. would own or make overt to Mary the specific ways she had been placing Mary in this adult role. Mrs. A. also would communicate how she felt stronger now. She let Mary know that although it was generous of Mary to try and offer this support, she did not need Mary to assume this caretaking role anymore. In addition, Mrs. A. began to engage in social activities (e.g., going to the movies and dinner) with some of her co-workers, who provided a new avenue of support.

Sometimes Mary and Mrs. A. would interact in a way that crossed generational boundaries or in a role-reversal mode during our sessions. Whenever this happened, I would observe aloud (make overt) what I was seeing. I would note, for example, how at that moment they seemed to be squabbling like siblings, or interacting more as friends than as mother and daughter, or how Mary was worrying about her mother and trying to take care of her as a parent. Mary and Mrs. A. both became able to recognize and change their individual participation in these familiar but problematic patterns. It was clear, however, that Mary needed directly spoken permission from her mother to relinquish her caretaking role. To understand this problem more fully, let's look at the three issues Mrs. A. and I focused on in our individual sessions that allowed her to reclaim her appropriate parental role.

First, Mrs. A. felt guilty about initiating the divorce and "selfish" for breaking up the family "just because she was unhappy." This guilt, in part, kept her from effectively disciplining Mary and enforcing the rules she set. For example, rather than taking charge and simply telling Mary to wash the dishes, Mrs. A. would complain ineffectively and try to cajole her. Mrs. A. was increasingly able to recognize how her guilt led them to squabble like sisters, with no parent effectively in charge of the family.

Second, Mrs. A. needed to develop a better support network for herself. After the breakup she now had to do many things herself that her husband used to handle. She found that being a single parent was far more demanding than she had imagined. However, Mrs. A. also felt guilty about doing anything for herself and ashamed of having her emotional needs seen or met by others. Over the course of treatment, however, she became more able to let herself "have" our relationship and allow me to help her—which we were then able to begin generalizing to other relationships (e.g., with co-workers). With my encouragement, she began to develop two friendships and reestablished ties with several extended family members in a nearby city. Although it never became easy, Mrs. A. became better at seeking support and sharing her personal concerns in these adult relationships. As these important changes occurred, her depression and loneliness diminished and she stopped turning to Mary as much for her emotional support.

Third, in the course of working on these two issues, the profound deprivations that Mrs. A. had suffered throughout her own life emerged. She had never known her father and her mother suffered from bipolar disorder. As a child, Mrs. A. was shunted back and forth from her mother to various homes of relatives when her mother was incapacitated. For the first time, Mrs. A. risked sharing this painful story and the feelings of shame, helplessness, and loneliness that were engendered.

As Mrs. A. became able to talk about what she had experienced, her lifelong orientation toward depression and compliance improved. Initially, she wanted to use this awareness of her own victimization and chronic depression to further punish herself, which increased her feelings of guilt and helplessness about helping Mary. By emphasizing my own genuine admiration for the way she had been able to survive, and to give so much more to Mary as a parent than she had received as a child, Mrs. A. was gradually able to begin feeling some compassion for herself and her own poignant dilemma. As Mrs. A. allowed me to respond more directly to her own emotional needs she, in turn, became more responsive to Mary. That is, she became more interested in Mary's concerns about school and peers, more responsive to Mary's initiative, and better able to tolerate Mary's negative feelings when Mary was frustrated or angry with her. Mrs. A. knew that she was getting better, and spoke about these changes as a new season in her life, part of nature's way of healing.

As Mrs. A. became stronger in these ways, we began to use conjoint sessions with Mary to try and translate her personal changes into changes in their current interaction as well. During these conjoint sessions, I repeatedly focused Mary and Mrs. A. on talking directly to each other about their relationship, rather than about Mr. A., friends, or other topics. For example, I often gave them cues such as: "What's going on between you two right now?", "What isn't working for you two in your relationship this week?", or "How does this problem with your dad that you are talking about affect your relationship with your mom?" Their communication improved greatly as they spoke more directly with each other.

While exploring their communication and interaction patterns, Mary's preoccupation and worry about her mother's well-being became even more apparent. Significantly, it also became clear to everyone that Mrs. A. no longer needed Mary to fulfill this caretaking role. I was especially gratified when Mrs. A. joined me or initiated on her own: (1) acknowledgment that Mary had indeed been taking care of her as a parent; (2) appreciation of how loving this concern was, while still recognizing how burdensome this was to Mary; (3) validation of the reality that Mrs. A. had been depressed a lot (rather than continuing to deny how sad she often seemed); and (4) indication that Mrs. A. was stronger now and no longer needed Mary to take care of her in these ways.

By responding in these new ways in the sessions, Mrs. A. was behaviorally demonstrating to Mary that she was stronger now and that Mary no longer needed to be taking care of her in the way she had before. Mary soon tested this new strength, of course, by criticizing something her mother had done. Rather than argue defensively, or shrug and look hurt, Mrs. A. simply said, "Okay, let's talk about it" and proceeded to allow Mary to be angry with her. When they finished their discussion, I punctuated the obvious by saying, "Your mother is stronger now than she used to be. I don't think you have to be the parent here anymore."

Significant changes occurred as Mary saw that her mother was becoming stronger and more self-affirming. In particular, Mary's teacher reported that she was showing more initiative at school, doing better in her schoolwork, succeeding as a member of her school volleyball team, and seemed generally more active and involved than she had been in a long time. Although I was sorry to terminate while so much progress was being made, especially since there still remained work to be done, our 16 sessions were over and important changes were clearly underway.

TERMINATION AND SUMMARY THOUGHTS

In conclusion, let's look back over some of the important issues that shaped the treatment process. Initially, Mary was conflicted about letting herself have a relationship with me and allowing me to help her. She feared that I was likely to subjugate her as her father had because I was also a male authority figure; she was afraid of betraying her mother by establishing an alliance or having a meaningful relationship with someone else; and she was violating the family taboo against talking about problems with Whites or others outside the family. These are complex, reality based problems that Mary faced and that occur for other children in similar circumstances. For Mary, as is the case for others, treatment would not have progressed very far until these concerns were addressed.

I tried to help Mary with these concerns by discussing them directly with her, by expressing that it made sense to me that it was sometimes difficult for her to come to see me, and by giving her many opportunities to talk about the good news and the bad news in our relationship (e.g., "What's the best and the worst thing about coming to see me?"). I also tried to differentiate myself from the problematic relational patterns she had with both parents. I did this by being friendlier and more communicative than her father, and by being more authoritative and mindful of not acting in ways that she could readily perceive as tired, needy, depressed, or confused like her mother. As we talked about these concerns, and she experienced me as different than her parents in these specific ways, it gave her the freedom to explore and come to terms with the problems she had with each parent.

When children get stuck on the same problem, separate and distinct conflicts they are having with each parent have often dovetailed or overlapped to create an immobilizing double bind. For example, Mary's core conflict revolved around having her own mind (visà-vis her dominating father), responding to her own needs and interests (vis-à-vis her needy mother), and proceeding with her own developmental task of identity formation. Mary's highly authoritarian father was punitive if Mary freely spoke her own mind, disagreed with him, or acted independently without first seeking his permission. To complicate matters, she could not, with her mother, focus internally and attend to her own feelings, needs, and interests. Instead, she was living outside of herself—vigilantly attuned and highly responsive to the ups and downs in her mother's emotional life. Although this may seem benignly empathic, sensitive, or caring at first, it was not. Mary could not initiate any action on her own behalf without first worrying about the consequences for her mother, or the response from her father. While Mary seemed adaptive in her environment, this outward appearance of competence belied the insecurity, guilt, and worry that prevailed internally. That is, as long as Mary was being "good" and compliant via her father, and responsible, helpful, and loyal via her mother, she was safe—but at the expense of her own development. As a result, whenever Mary was in a situation that called on her to initiate, express her own wishes, or assert herself on her own behalf, she became anxious and immobilized. Although being respectful and caring was culturally sanctioned, of course, the extent of Mary's responses went beyond appropriate cultural norms.

Over the course of treatment, I was able to help Mary recognize and label this bind that was constricting her. By clarifying both sides of her conflict, and being sympathetic to the very real family interactions that engendered it, she was able to act a little freer with others outside her family. More significant gains occurred when the issues were made overt and resolved with her mother, especially when Mrs. A. was able to give Mary permission to stop taking care of her and to begin attending to her own schoolwork and friends instead. Unfortunately, we were not able to attain parallel changes on the issues with her father. However, Mary did make gains in differentiating when she had to comply with others and when she could say "no" and do more of what she wanted.

Of significance was the understanding that cultural factors overlaid these familial conflicts and that changes with mother or father could not have occurred without working within the family's worldview. In this instance, for example, sensitivity to the cultural context meant helping Mary realize that developing her own mind was not the same as being disrespectful to her father, and that responding to her own needs was not being insensitive to her mother. Mary was able to progress in treatment only as we were able to define this new middle ground that preserved cultural prescriptions for respecting and helping parents, while allowing her greater permission to attend to her own needs and her own life. It was a great pleasure for me to be able to help Mary and her family through this family crisis.

Questions for Thought and Discussion

1. Think about your parents' marriage. How did they handle problems in their relationship? Is there anything they could have said or done to make you feel more secure when they were not getting along? If you were a divorcing parent today, what would you want to say and do to help your child?

2. Think about the process of choosing a marital partner. How will (has) your relationship with your parents, and their relationship with each other, both helped and hindered your ability to make a good choice?

Suggestions for Further Reading

Gardner, R. (1991). *The boys and girls book about divorce.* Northvale, NJ: Jason Aronson. A helpful book for counselors to recommend to 4- to 8-year-old children going through a parental divorce.

Hetherington, M., Bridges, M., & Insabella, G. (February 1998). What matters? What does not? *American Psychologist,* 167–184. An informative review article for readers seeking more empirical information about divorce and remarriage.

Sutton, D. & Broken Nose, R., (1996). Native American Families: An Overview. In M. McGoldrick, J. Pearce, & J. Giordano (Eds.), *Ethnicity and family therapy,* 2nd ed. (pp. 31–44). New York: Guilford. Useful guidelines for counseling Native American Indians.

Teyber, E. (2001). *Helping children cope with divorce.* (Rev. Ed.) San Francisco: Jossey Bass. For divorcing parents, helps parents explain the divorce to children, establish custody/visitation arrangements that will benefit children, shield children from parental conflict, and parent more effectively in single-parent and stepfamilies.

5

JONATHAN: FINDING A SENSE OF SELF AS HE COMES TO TERMS WITH HIS GAY IDENTITY AND BORDERLINE PERSONALITY DISORDER

INTRODUCTION

Characteristics of Borderline Personality Disorder

The DSM-IV-TR describes borderline personality disorder (BPD) as a "pervasive pattern of instability of interpersonal relationships, self-image, and affect" (APA, 2000). Individuals who have this disorder express uncertainty about many aspects of their basic identity, including their self-image, sexual orientation, career goals, friends, and values. This inability to achieve a stable self-identity leads to their hallmark characteristic: *highly unstable and problematic interpersonal relationships.* They have intense relationships that are marked by periods of unrealistic idealization of others, which are soon followed by contemptuous devaluation of those who have (inevitably) disappointed them. Similarly, their moods shift from serious depression to irritability, anxiety, and often fury. This low frustration tolerance and intense anger is often expressed in the form of temper outbursts that may include verbal rages and physical fights (Lish, 1996). Another defining feature for these individuals is a chronic feeling of emptiness or boredom. They have difficulty tolerating being alone and make desperate attempts to avoid real or imagined abandonment. They cling to others, demanding constant attention and exaggerated loyalty. This feature of the borderline's relationships is well portrayed by the actress Glenn Close in the film *Fatal Attraction.*

Impulsive behavior is evident in various arenas of their lives. For example, irresponsible spending, unsafe sex, substance abuse, shoplifting and delinquency, reckless driving, and binge eating often occur (Morgenstern et al., 1997). These troubled individuals recurrently make both manipulative suicidal threats and real suicide attempts—Moskovitz (1996) reports a suicide rate of 6 to 9% among patients with BPD. Their impulsive and self-destructive behavior may also lead them to engage in self-mutilating behavior—occurring on a continuum from simple body piercing to blood-letting and far more disturbing acts such as deep razor cuts in hands, arms, and face.

Their inability to moderate their behavior and modulate their emotions results in multiple problems in their own personal lives and for those who become involved with them. Individuals diagnosed as BPD are often appealing to others initially because of their intensity, emotional accessibility, and idealization of others. However, their appealing responsiveness is usually short lived because those engaged in relationships with them soon learn that they cannot fulfill the intense dependency needs and unrealistic devotion that these individuals demand. Others are doomed to fail—and to evoke their contempt and wrath.

Even though the DSM-IV-TR now specifies clearly observable symptoms to diagnose BPD, it is often difficult to differentiate borderline personality disorder from other personality disorders—especially narcissistic and histrionic personality disorders. As noted earlier, individuals with BPD have intense and unstable interpersonal relationships, feel profoundly empty and desperately try to avoid abandonment, and have difficulty modulating their intense anger, mood swings, and impulsive behavior. While disrupted interpersonal relationships are core aspects for the histrionic and narcissistic personality disorders also, these individuals have less identity disturbance. That is, what differentiates those with BPD is their lack of an integrated sense of self, which inhibits their capacity to reflect on their own behavior. This lack of coherence also contributes to their impulsiveness, self-destructive behavior, and mood shifts. This cardinal feature helps clinicians differentiate and accurately diagnose borderline personality disorder.

The prevalence of BPD has been estimated at 2% of the general population. Women with this disorder display more self-destructive behavior and are likely to be depressed as well (they often respond well to the SSRI (selective seretonergic reuptake inhibitors) class of antidepressant medications, such as Prozac and Paxil). Male patients seem more likely to have coexisting conduct disorders, attention deficit, and antisocial personality disorders (Androlunis, 1991). The course of BPD varies greatly from person to person. The most common pattern is for the instability and risk of suicide to peak during young adulthood, then gradually wane with increasing age. Fortunately, many better functioning clients with high intelligence or less severe symptoms seem to stabilize and improve over time (McGlashen, 1992). There is much disagreement among clinicians as to the origins of borderline personality disorder, how to treat it, and when to apply the diagnosis. Let's look more closely at the history and causes of this important disorder that troubles many adolescents and has generated so much interest and controversy in recent years.

Etiology of the Disorder

Borderline personality disorder has multiple causes. Biological predispositions, familial and developmental experiences, and trauma all seem to contribute to the development of this disorder. Historically, the diagnosis of BPD began in the 1940s from clinical observations. Psychiatrists working in inpatient hospital settings observed a certain type of patient who demonstrated intense affect, made very strong dependency demands on the therapist, and became increasingly enraged at the therapist (Hoch & Polatin, 1949). Staff members working in psychiatric hospitals also observed highly destructive behaviors (e.g., self-mutilating, suicide attempts) even within the supportive confines of hospitals, which had proven helpful to most other patients (Gunderson, 1984). Other therapists described intense countertransference reactions—generally reported as feelings of helplessness and/or rage toward the client. In the 1960s and 1970s more systematic studies were undertaken which have broadened our understanding and treatment of BPD. For example, Kernberg (1996) heightened our awareness of how extensively those with BPD rely on "splitting defenses." He described compellingly how these individuals assign either all-good or all-bad attributes to people. Their inability to integrate the range of personal qualities of others into a more realistic middle ground, where both strengths and limits exist, is exhibited in their own behavior and symptoms. This is seen, for example, in their inability to moderate their own anger or dependency needs. This will be demonstrated later in the chapter by Jon's tendency to idealize new acquaintances, followed by his total rejection of them when they demonstrate more human or flawed responses.

Drawing on developmental research by Margaret Mahler et al., (1975), James Masterson highlights how interpersonal factors contribute to development of BPD in adolescents (1985). Observing mother-child interactions during the first three years of life, Mahler identified a developmental phase that she termed "rapprochement." This period, between the 18th and 30th month, involves a complex process whereby the toddler experiences rapidly cycling needs to risk venturing out into the world while continuously returning to "home base" for reassurance. This period encompasses the child's tantrums, power struggles, and mood swings that are unfortunately referred to as the "terrible two's" by some parents but seen as the "terrific two's" by others. This struggle between autonomy and dependency is an important developmental challenge for every young child, and it can be a difficult period for some parents as well. It is common to observe a child climbing in and out of her parent's lap, at one moment pushing away and rejecting the parent ("hate you") and, the next moment, clamoring for the parent ("hold you") and wanting to return to the lap. For some parents, the young child's movement back and forth is a delight. They see it as an opportunity to communicate to the child the total acceptance of who they are at that moment—affectionate, angry, independent, or needy. For other parents, however, this love/hate, need/don't need behavior evokes problems. These parents experience the child's exploration and newfound independence as painful personal rejection at times or, at other times, experience the unyielding physical and emotional needs as overwhelming. Parents of children who develop BPD tend to be unavailable, unresponsive, or overtly rejecting when the child "reapproaches" after wandering off to explore independently (Plakun, 1991). The child learns from this experience that unwavering loyalty to the caregiver and trying to be an ideal or perfect child is the only way to be love-worthy. Of course, this unrealistic course is unattainable and the child is doomed to fail. The child is also likely to experience intense anxiety over being alone and anger over unmet attachment needs.

As an adolescent, and later as an adult, this child may only see extremes in others—they must be perfect, loyal, and have no needs of their own. When these idealized others fail to fulfill their fantasy of the perfect dependency relationship that will end their suffering, the individual with BPD may be filled with fury and contempt and will see these once perfect people as totally reprehensible. For example, their ability to project a charming appearance in the short run enables them to make a credible presentation in court and successfully litigate against well-intended, responsible others who they now view as "bad." As we will see in the following case study of Jonathan, the back and forth pattern where needs are never overtly acknowledged and resolved continues to be a problematic behavior pattern in adolescents with BPD.

In families where BPD develops, the child's attempts at independence are thwarted and his or her own sense of self-efficacy is undermined. Some parents deal with this period by refusing to let go since, "You're just going to want to get right back up anyway, so stay still!" In contrast, other parents refuse to allow the child to return once he or she ventures off, "You think you're so big for your britches, you can just take care of yourself!" In both cases, children's ability to venture out and to explore and master the world on their own is curtailed. Children who experience these interpersonal patterns continuously grow up to have difficulty initiating activity, demonstrate problems with decision making, and have difficulty asking for help. At the same time, however, they feel angry and rejected when their intense needs are not met, and struggle with a confusing, shame-based sense of self, and feelings of emptiness and isolation.

In normal or healthy development, in contrast to these two problematic styles, the child receives encouragement for his or her initiative and exploration away from the security provided by the loved one. This young child is welcomed back for "refueling" when the separation begins to evoke anxiety. In this way the healthy child learns to be both separate from, and related to, all-important caregivers at the same time. We will see later that this developmental model that encourages separation and allows for successful rapprochement provides a basic guideline for helping counselors respond to their adolescents with BPD (Gunderson, 1996).

Many clinicians view the inability to resolve this rapprochement conflict that begins in toddlerhood, but continues throughout their development and escalates in adolescence, to be a cardinal feature in the development of the borderline syndrome. Masterson (1985) emphasized how the frustration and rage seen in adolescents with this disorder developed out of the caregiver's emotional unavailability that began during the rapprochement phase. According to Masterson, two distinct self-images emerge. One self-image consists of the good child who is rewarded for compliant dependency. The other self-image consists of the bad child or bad self who is criticized and rejected for expressing his or her curiosity, initiative, and other normal or expectable movements toward autonomy. In treatment, Masterson has described the client's attempts to "test" the counselor's effectiveness both in setting limits and in remaining emotionally available before taking the risk of trusting the counselor, self-disclosing, and forming a working alliance.

Masterson writes expertly about how to confront acting-out behavior in adolescents with BPD, set and enforce firm and fair limits with them, and work with their feelings of abandonment. He actively encourages patients' moves toward individuation—which they have not received developmentally—while still affirming their need for understanding and support. As we have already seen, this essential balance creates a reparative experience for the adolescent with BPD who is still struggling with these rapprochement conflicts. More specifically, it creates this corrective experience by providing a secure base or holding environment which they have needed but have not experienced before.

Other theorists focus on the experience of isolation as the core feature of borderline personality disorder (Adler & Buie, 1979). They emphasize that a child's sense of self or identity develops through a secure attachment to a parent or caregiver. The healthy child is increasingly able to comfort him/herself and feel secure when the caregiver is not available by developing a mental representation or carrying a cognitive schema of the parent and the parent's loving feelings for the child inside him or her. This allows children to draw upon this internalized parent in order to feel secure and manage their emotional reactions in the absence of actual physical contact with the parent. The child who is developing BPD does not experience the secure attachment that allows an internalized parent, or subsequent self-image, to develop. Without this internal, soothing presence, these children cannot calm themselves when distressed or effectively manage their emotions. Feelings of isolation also result, increasing their feelings of frustration and rage. Thus, the young child who lacks a stable, internal sense of the parent as loving and available fails to develop a corresponding sense of self as love-worthy and emotionally connected. Although these attachment and rapprochement issues often seem overly intellectual and theoretically distant while talking about how BPD develops, they quickly begin to sound relevant and meaningful when you begin working with an adolescent who has this disorder.

Buie and Adler (1982) believe that this fundamental experience of isolation (commonly described by the client as feelings of boredom or emptiness) is defended against by projecting it out onto the world—so that the world then appears empty. The unavailability of a soothing presence or attachment figure in the patient's life frequently results in panicked feelings of desperation and an inability to maintain positive images and memories. It is the soothing internal presence that the borderline client has missed developmentally, and what the counselor must provide in the early stages of treatment. As we will see with Jonathan, however, this calm and consistent responsiveness is much easier to say than to do with provocative and demanding adolescents with BPD.

Cognitive-behavioral conceptualizations are also utilized in understanding and treating borderline personality disorders (Beck & Freeman, 1990; Freeman, Pretzer, Fleming, & Simon, 1990). For example, Beck believes these individuals experience many errors in thinking or "cognitive distortions" that often contribute to their symptoms. One distortion of particular importance that we have already addressed is called *dichotomous thinking*. This is described as the "tendency to evaluate experiences in terms of mutually exclusive categories" (e.g., good or bad, success or failure, trustworthy or deceitful). This dichotomous thinking (or splitting) will be demonstrated later by Jon's shifts from one extreme to the other in his evaluation of his friends. Beck, like other clinicians, emphasizes that it is the collaborative therapeutic relationship that is the key to changing this dichotomous thinking and successfully treating the patient with BPD.

Perhaps the most promising treatment for borderline personality disorder is Marsha Linehan's (1993) "dialectical behavior therapy," which is a form of cognitive behavioral therapy specifically for the treatment of chronically suicidal individuals who meet the criteria for BPD. Linehan suggests that the primary goal of treatment should be to help patients accept their strong negative emotions without engaging in self-destructive or other maladaptive behaviors. Her treatment goals are (1) decreasing suicidal behavior; (2) decreasing behaviors that interfere with therapy, such as missing sessions, lying, and getting hospitalized; (3) decreasing escapist behaviors that interfere with a stable lifestyle, such as substance abuse; (4) increasing behavioral skills in order to regulate emotions, to increase interpersonal skills, and to increase tolerance for distress; and (5) other goals the patient chooses. For Linehan, the development of new skills which will promote more effective interpersonal relationships can only take place in the context of a therapeutic relationship in which the client feels validated. A therapeutic relationship that balances acceptance and reality based confrontation helps clients with BPD to integrate good and bad aspects of their personality and aids them to tolerate ambiguity.

In sum, BPD seems to have multiple causes. There is probably a biological component—these adolescents probably have an inborn, temperamental predisposition to be more active, intense, and impulsive (APA, 2000). Environmentally, many have also experienced highly ineffective child-rearing that has been characterized by parental death and divorce, multiple mother and father substitutes, and parental neglect and rejection (Ludolph et al., 1990). Their active, impulsive temperamental styles have interacted in highly problematic ways with the confusing flux of inappropriate parental intrusiveness on the one hand, coupled with nonrecognition or inconsistent responsiveness toward their actual needs at the same time. Adding to this volatile mix, researchers also find that trauma is an important contributor in many cases of BPD (Spoont, 1996). Increasingly, researchers are finding that physical abuse and especially sexual abuse is often found in the backgrounds of those suffering from BPD (Atlas, 1995). In this regard, some diagnosticians suggest that the chaotic behavior in those with BPD resembles in many ways that of an individual suffering from an extended form of posttraumatic stress disorder precipitated by early trauma (Gunderson & Sabo, 1993). Others also relate the higher incidence of BPD in females (75%) than in males to females' higher rate of sexual abuse (Grilo et al., 1996).

Finally, some sociocultural theorists suggest that BPD is especially likely to emerge when a culture changes rapidly. As traditional family structures come apart and a culture loses it cohesiveness, many of its members may be left with identity problems, emptiness, and anxiety (Paris, 1991). Many suggest that such changes in contemporary society may explain the growing reports of this disorder (Millon, 1987). With all of these contributing factors in mind, let's turn from the symptoms and causes of BPD to the challenging but potentially rewarding work of treating clients with this disorder.

CASE ILLUSTRATION

Developmental History and Presenting Problem

Jonathan initially contacted my office after hearing about me from his friend, Steve, an adolescent client of mine. Both Jon and Steve were part of a close-knit group at a private, all-male, Catholic high school. As gay young men, they had gravitated toward each other mostly due to their sexual orientation. Within the group they found support, acceptance, and some relief from their previous feelings of isolation. They confided in each other and occasionally dated each other. Jonathan phoned me to set up an appointment and told me that Steve had told him that I was a safe and understanding person to talk to about "things."

I had some hesitation about this referral as I was already seeing Steve, a student from this same high school group. I was aware that there were difficulties within the group in setting boundaries and defining relationships. Yet, these difficulties made sense to me. These young men were in an environment that valued traditional, stereotypical views of what a man was supposed to be. Like most young gay and lesbian teenagers, these fellows either received critical judgment from their families or anticipated it—their concerns sufficient enough to make them hide their sexuality. Two of these young men had previously been forced to see a therapist called a "change" therapist, whose practice was based on the belief that their sexual orientation was a mental disorder (or a sin against God), and that therapy could change them into heterosexuals. Thus, when these young men found each other, they quickly became friends, lovers, and each other's families.

I told Jon that my relationship with Steve and familiarity with his friends and peer group might make it more difficult for us. I suggested that it might be easier for Jon to see another counselor where there would be fewer complications but that I would leave that decision up to him. He was clear that he wanted to see me and we made an appointment to meet.

This overlap in the relationships I had with Jonathan and his friends was significant because it highlighted the importance of boundaries and of setting limits in a reasonable, caring, but firm way when working with individuals with BPD. Jon later told me that he and Steve had named me "Babs" among their group of friends and that they enjoyed exchanging appointment information: "Oh, you're Babs on Tuesday? I'm Babs on Friday." "You're Babs at four? I'm Babs at two." As we will see, this overlap became a factor at a critical point in our later work together.

Client Description   Jonathan bounded into our first session with a high level of energy and much to say. He was dressed fairly ivy-league, yet with added touches in shoes and a wild watch that demonstrated his creative style. Jon was a 17-year-old African American high school senior of medium build. He was bright and articulate yet I experienced him as distant and he rarely looked at me. Early in our first session, he shared his desire to be an actor and I often found myself feeling like an audience. Jon told stories—which kept me (and others) at a distance. He talked rapidly and animatedly, gesturing often. He occasionally stood up and moved around my office. When he smiled it was a large smile that often, however, appeared strained. Although understandably nervous at his first therapy session, Jon seemed to be working excessively hard throughout our time together.

Certainly, storytelling is more common in the beginning of treatment, when there is much information to share and the client and counselor do not know each other. Clients' needs to be heard and understood are often frustrated by their perception that all information and details must be given in order for them to be really seen and heard. The client can experience frustration—"racing against the clock"—to impart a great deal of information, yet still leaving the session feeling empty. I will often comment on the difficulty in describing one's life to another, how time consuming it must feel and, at times, frustrating. Being able to acknowledge or articulate the client's experience in this way helps clients feel seen—and it is this empathic understanding that allows a working alliance or connection to begin.

Although this empathic process is important in all counseling relationships, it is essential with these clients. Although I sometimes share the client's frustration, I know from experience that slowing down enough to talk about the feelings underneath the stories helps us know each other better and have more meaningful contact. It is this personal connection that prevents this impulsive client from feeling alone and bolting out of treatment before we've really begun. With Jon, however, all attempts on my part to share feelings or elicit his personal reactions were swiftly rejected. There seemed to be no opportunities for more substantive contact or meaningful connection, and I began wondering to myself why relationships had become so threatening for him.

Social Context   Jonathan was the second child of June and Barry. June and Barry had married in their early twenties and soon found their styles and aspirations to be very different. Barry had a small electrical repair shop and June was a secretary. Both had finished high school but June hoped to go on to college. She was better able to set long-term goals for herself, delay gratification, and work hard toward the promise of a return in the future. Barry had no desire to continue his education and liked to have fun. He enjoyed gambling and drinking, which June did not. These activities, while not yet causing problems in other areas of his life, began to cause great difficulty between Barry and June and their fights began to escalate. Another problem was Barry's continuing search for ways to get rich quickly. There were repeated attempts at investment deals and get-rich-quick schemes that became a constant source of conflict for the couple. As often occurs, these marital tensions increased greatly as they became parents and had their first child, Robert, and then, three years later, their last child, Jonathan.

Jon witnessed intense scenes of volatile marital conflict while growing up. His parents shouted insults, derided and emotionally wounded each other, and sometimes shoved or slapped each other. His mother began to work more overtime hours and also began taking night classes toward her college degree. While this was a distraction from her failing marriage and fit with her push for upward mobility, it made her even more physically and emotionally unavailable to Jon. Jon also lacked a sense of security with his father, with whom he had not bonded and who spent more and more time away from the house. Jon reported being bored and lonely—coming home after school to an empty house, feeling afraid to go out and play in an intimidating neighborhood. Emotionally deprived children are vulnerable to predators and Jon, like many needy children, was exploited. As I learned later in treatment (and reported to Child Protective Services), he was seduced into a sexual relationship with a neighbor "who took a fatherly interest" in him. Tragically, sexual contact became the antidote to Jon's loneliness and insecurity. The only person to express an interest in his well-being was sexually exploitive, resulting in Jon confusing love and sex and developing poor interpersonal boundaries.

Another difficulty for Jon at that time was the feeling of "pressure" from his mother. He describes his brother as having been irresponsible and unmotivated and, according to Jon, his family seemed to easily accept that. Excuses were made for his brother and expectations lowered. For Jon, however, expectations were increased. Obviously bright, Jon became his mother's number-one project. She focused obsessively on his schoolwork and the quality of his work around the house, rarely registering what Jon was feeling, thinking, or actually needing at the moment. He felt she was never satisfied but quick to criticize and demand more. Jon's perception was that his mother's support came only when he met her expectations or performed to her satisfaction—painfully exacerbating his feelings that he was alone, unseen, and not valued. Jon's need to put on an act and entertain an audience made sense to me. Jon had learned inauthenticity well. Unable to express his true needs or feelings, eventually he no longer even knew what he was feeling or experiencing. He could only act a part.

When Jon was 11 years old, his parents divorced. Jon and his brother moved with their mother to a predominately White community in the suburbs. While public school was fine for his brother, Jon was placed in an all-male, college-preparatory, private high school run by the Catholic Church. Jon was one of the few students of color, and again was faced with high expectations in an environment that was critical, filled with judgment, and lacked warmth. Jon was once again in an environment where he felt devalued and rejected if he did not follow the rules totally. Thus, in Jon's home and in his school setting, he had no sense of belonging and felt devalued, exposed to unrealistic expectations that he could not meet, and criticized for not being "perfect." Whereas some children are able to outgrow certain problems, other problems persist and continue causing difficulties over time. Children like Jon cannot resolve their problems on their own when the same type of problem or theme (e.g., feeling different or flawed, being treated unfairly) does not just occur in one relationship or setting, but keeps repeating throughout multiple arenas in their lives. Sadly, a corrective developmental opportunity for Jon was lost in this school setting. If Jon could have established just one good relationship with a responsive teacher or mentor, this highly structured school setting could have been helpful to him.

Jon's memories of this time focused on his mother's intense anger at his father and, frequently, at him. Reflecting their superficial relationship, he does not remember feeling loss about his father. Yet, he felt confused about his intense feelings of both loss and anger toward his nurturing, yet sexually abusive "father figure"—the neighbor who had observed his aloneness and befriended him. Jon's lack of consistent, loving relationships with adults seemed to underlie his highly problematic interpersonal relations and difficulty forming enduring friendships or any type of stable relationship. Although Jon and his brother would visit their father occasionally in their old neighborhood, Jon repeatedly felt "left out." Jonathan reports that his father and brother had always seemed close but, even without his brother present, he felt that he made his father "uncomfortable" and that they had great difficulty talking to each other. To this day, Jon does not know whether this was due to Jon's emerging sexuality or his role in the family as the "one with a future" who would surpass his father and receive his mother's admiration in a way the father had been unable to do. Jon began visiting less often, which he perceived to be fine with his father.

An unfortunate twist of fate left Jon with an even more problematic role model. Jon's father eventually did get rich quickly—the result of a lawsuit against the city in which they lived after being injured in an auto accident with a police car on a high-speed chase. With this money, Barry bought real estate and made investments that allowed him a glamorous lifestyle. Jon became further fixed on appearances and the power of an impressive image.

After Barry's change in financial status, Jon's brother began spending more and more time with his father until, upon completion of high school, he moved in with his father full time. Jon stayed behind with his mother, although he did not feel that he was actually with her. He reported going days at a time without seeing her, only to have her storm into the bathroom while he was taking a shower or using the toilet. She would burst into his room to wake him screaming about dishes he had left in the sink or laundry that had not been done. Thus Jon alternately felt (1) abandoned, unloved, and unimportant; and (2) *deeply shamed* by an intrusive, angry, and bitingly critical mother who violated his privacy. Sadly, she constituted the only consistent figure in Jon's life. Jon's primary relationships thus involved rejection (exemplified by his father's and brother's exits from his life and his mother's frequent unexplained absences) or abuse (his mother's shaming, intrusive, volatile outbursts toward him, and his neighbor's sexual victimization). Jon's clinical presentation with borderline personality disorder thus made sense given his rejecting and abusive life history.

Initial Sessions   Jon had mentioned "things" he wanted to talk to me about. Initially, I had difficulty learning what those "things" were. Jon began by wanting to talk about his career goals.

CL: God! This is GREAT being here. I have a lot of ideas I want to run by someone and get some feedback.

TH: I'm glad you're here, too. You mentioned on the phone that there were some things you wanted to talk to me about.

CL: Oh, yeah, lots of things. I want to get going on my career; I'm an actor. I haven't really done anything yet but I know exactly how I want things to be. I know I can make it and be really successful. I'm gonna start going out on calls and trying out for things. Going into acting will be a field I can really relate to—more creativity, wilder people, I won't be the only gay or the only Black. It'll be great.

TH: How is it now? Do you feel like the only gay or the only Black now?

CL: Well, I have my gay friends so that helps, but the school is really straight and in my family or my neighborhood, I don't know anybody who's gay. And there are no Blacks in my new neighborhood and only a couple at my school—but they wouldn't want anything to do with a homo like me. Being a gay, Black man—that's really impossible! I don't know anyone like me.

TH: Yes. That must be very difficult. How is that for you?

CL: Oh, I'm used to it. That's why if I get into the acting thing, I think it will be much better.

TH: Tell me more about what it means for you to be gay and Black.

CL: Oh, I told you. It's just extra pressure. When I'm acting I can really be special. I have this idea for a casting call I'm going on. They're looking for a Steve Urkel type and I saw a pair of glasses at the store that will be just perfect. Here's what I'm going to do.

With that, Jon hiked his pants high up on his chest and began to demonstrate his audition. I found myself looking for a place to land: some opening from Jon where I could enter and start to form a relationship with him. Occasionally, there would be openings, as in his comments about being Black or being gay, but my approaches were quickly brushed aside. I realized that I would need to proceed slowly with Jon and allow him to set the pace. My plan was to continue to speak to the underlying feelings he was alluding to and attempt a connection with him, while listening carefully to his "Do Not Enter" messages and respecting his limits. This became even more salient as I subsequently learned more fully how Jon's boundaries had been violated so profoundly by his angry mother and abusive neighbor. I found myself thinking about how closed off Jon was and realized that much had happened in his life to make it necessary for him to be so protective of himself. As our sessions continued, I learned that I needed to walk a middle ground with Jon that created greater interpersonal safety for him by ensuring that the way we interacted together did not fit his old relational patterns. That is, I didn't want to intrude or press demands on him as others had done. At the same time, I recognized his deprivation and wanted him to see that I could understand what was important to him and respond nonjudgmentally.

In the initial sessions, this entertaining/distancing pattern continued. In talking about a career, Jon was signaling to me that he was getting ready, like most young adults, to venture into the world. I felt he was keeping me at a distance because, on the one hand, he feared that, like is mother, I would ridicule or try to control him. On the other hand, he was testing me to see if I could become a secure base, someone who would delight in his individuation efforts. To become this base, however, I needed to connect to his feelings. Jon gave me more and more pieces of information as time went on, yet still seemed unable to increase his ability to share feelings.

CL: I can't wait to graduate next month and get out of that school.

TH: It's been hard for you there.

CL: Oh, it's okay, it's almost over. But I think college will be cool. They won't tell you what to do all the time and try to control you.

TH: You've mentioned how much you hate being told what to do, especially with your mom.

CL: Yeah! She really tries to control me. Look at this bracelet, she hates this thing. She threw a fit yesterday when she saw it and wouldn't talk to me until I took it off. What a bitch!

TH: Does she battle with you about your appearance often or was this different?

CL: Well, she gets upset at anything different, like these shoes or this watch. You know, I'm sure she knows I'm gay but she never asks anything, never makes any comment. And then she'll get all bent out of shape about something like this bracelet and I think it's cause she thinks it's a gay thing.

TH: You said you're sure she knows you're gay. What makes you think that?

CL: Well, there's my friends. We're always together, no girls anywhere. And some of them dress pretty wild. And she NEVER asks me about girls or dates, she just knows better. But she asks my brother about his love life.

TH: So, there are ways you can tell that she knows, but she never says anything. Have you thought about or wanted to say something to her?

CL: Not too often. A couple times I thought about it, but I just know how it will go—the bitch will really hate me then!

TH: Ouch! That sounds like the worst of both worlds: You can't talk to her about it or get her help or support, yet it's out enough for you to get attacked about it—and in disguised arenas at that.

CL: Yeah, it sucks.

TH: Can you tell me more about how it sucks for you, how you know it will go badly between the two of you.

CL: Well, she's just a bitch. What can I say? Sometimes she's really great and we're really good friends and then she's after me and acts like I've ruined her life. She'd die if the family knew I was gay. I mean, she thinks she's doing me a favor if she lets me live in her lousy house.

As our sessions continued, Jon was able to share information about experiences that were more difficult for him. There was an increased acknowledgement of feelings, yet he still tended to swat away any attempt to stay with his feelings and talk further about them. He used phrases like "What can I say?", "I'm used to it.", and "I'm okay." to convey a message to stay away. As this pattern emerged, I was able to talk about our interaction together and make "process comments" on how difficult these feelings appeared to be for him. For example:

TH: You know, Jon, you say, "I'm okay" while the look on your face changes and you shake your head that way. It seems like a mixed message to me; I'm wondering what's really going on for you when I get two contradictory messages like that.

CL: Well, I just hate this, my mom I mean. She's always been this way and it's never going to change. And I've had to learn to just put up with it. It makes me mad and I don't want to think about it. But then she can be cool, too. I don't know, fuck it.

TH: So, when you say "I'm okay," that's your way of telling me, and maybe your friends too, that you're angry and uncomfortable—and want to talk about something else?

CL: Yeah, I guess it is.

In this way, we could acknowledge his need to share what was important in his life and feel listened to, yet recognize his anxiety when we named or explored the feelings he was having. This change reflected an important piece of progress. It allowed us to be together in a new and safer way for Jon. He could share his difficult feelings and still feel in control because he could trust that I would respect the boundaries he was setting to limit further exploration.

Case Conceptualization

Jon's difficulty with relationships quickly emerged as the most significant problem area and initial treatment focus. Jon did not know how to be with me or with anyone. Jon had experienced deeply shameful rejection and personal violation within his family. At his Catholic school and in his neighborhood, Jon was one of the few African Americans. This, coupled with being gay, meant he had no role models and truly had little idea of "how to be" with others. His race and sexual orientation greatly exacerbated Jon's sense of isolation and rejection, making his community experience similar to the estrangement he had experienced within his family. Jon's problem connecting with me let me know firsthand how difficult it was for him to form authentic and enduring relationships.

Jon's difficulty with boundaries (distinguishing his own feelings, interests, and values from others'; being able to set limits or say "no" to others when he was uncomfortable with something) alerted me to the likelihood that his boundaries had been invaded and that people were not safe for him. Jon had vaguely alluded to the possibility that he had been sexually violated although he was unwilling to discuss this with me yet. He had also described an inconsistent, boundary-violating pattern with his mother that included excessive control and intrusiveness, alternating with anger, criticism, and even contempt for him. As a result, Jon did not seem able to set appropriate boundaries in his relationships with others. His need to push against the boundaries of others was likely to result in those others feeling overrun or angry. For example, Jon would often show up at his friends' houses late at night without being invited and, at other times, not show up when he was expected. In this way, when Jon's friends felt taken advantage of or became angry or rejecting of him, Jon re-created his own conflict and reinforced his isolation. Relationships repeatedly began in exciting and idealizing ways, and inevitably blew apart in angry and intense breakups.

Although Jon fought for distance from me, I understood his dilemma—getting close carried with it the threat of becoming controlled, which was at the core of his relationship with his mother. Developmentally, Jon's experience with his mother was to accept being controlled and criticized or be cast off. When Jon did everything "perfectly" (good grades, clean the house, etc.), he and his mother had "good" times where they shared a great deal. It was at these times when she described Jon in unrealistic, idealized terms as "brilliant" and so much more intelligent than his "worthless" father. However, her good mood and aggrandizement of Jon could shift in a second if he wasn't "good" and she would then become contemptuous of Jon and say he was going to end up like his worthless father. The two distinct identities available to Jon were the "good child" who was compliant and dependent or the "bad child" who was criticized, rejected, and left—for individuating or "having his own mind." Jon repeatedly attempted to individuate. His attempts at establishing his own identity separate from her included wearing the flashy watch, bracelet, and other items that were not acceptable to his mother. He could not tolerate her angry rejection and emotional withdrawal for long, however, and so he would soon comply again. When he complied, however, her controlling stance suffocated him and he would once again try to find a way to break free and establish his separateness—which he typically did in a flashy, acting-out manner.

Jon was hungry for attention, yet believed that attention came with grave consequences: the risk of criticism (as his mother had criticized him), engulfment (as his mother had attempted to engulf him), rejection (as his father—and ultimately his mother—had rejected him), or exploitation (as he had been molested). Adolescents have a continuing need for parents to be physically and emotionally present, even as parents are allowing them more independence, privacy, and personal responsibility. Jon's anger at his parents' inability to respond affirmingly to him could not be expressed—the risk for further abandonment and the sickening depression that accompanied their criticism and withdrawal was too high. At times, he controlled this anger by splitting it off and re-creating it in his relationships with others. His ability to elicit anger from others was impressive; almost everyone became angry and "fed up" with him. Returning to our theme of conflicts that repeat in multiple spheres, as an African American, Jon also experienced a very real risk of discrimination, anger, and rejection and found the world a threatening place. As an African American man who was gay, Jon's feelings of isolation and threat were reaffirmed on a daily basis in his school and in his neighborhood. The world was not a welcoming place for him. Either his race or his sexual orientation alone were enough to put Jon at risk of assault, let alone both together. In combination, Jon's world was doubly threatening. Additionally, Jon's presence as an African American, gay male at a private Catholic school exacerbated his sense of being different and routinely engendered the feeling that he did not belong and was not wanted.

In adolescence, the developmental tasks of separation and individuation are fraught with difficulty for young people with borderline personality disorder. Their lack of attachment makes it all but impossible to cast off and launch their own adult life. As the old saying goes, it's hard to get up from the table when you're still hungry. Never knowing a secure base, it's almost impossible for these youth to feel the internal resources necessary to emancipate and respond to their own important internal needs. Further, they have generally received comfort when dependent, but have been ignored or attacked when they tried to act more independently. In adolescence, the dependence/ independence balance becomes unmanageable and results in more overt acting-out and borderline symptomotology.

Many individuals with this disorder are also unprepared to succeed on their own. In school and at home, for example, Jon was left to make too many important decisions on his own too early. His mother's frequent disappearances, followed by reentries into his life in which she shamed and tried to control him, left Jon confused. His life, paradoxically, had either no structure or too much structure in the form of demands. As he moved into arenas where even less structure or external organization was provided for him, Jon was not prepared to manage his own life, became anxious, and began to deteriorate. Finding less structure as he progressed through high school, for example, Jon began to cut classes, stopped doing his homework, and his grades began to plunge. This inability to tolerate ambiguity and create a structure or routine for their life is a common feature for individuals with BPD. Thus, high school graduation engendered much stress in Jonathan as it increased the demand for him to provide more of his own structure and begin to establish a meaningful life on his own.

Orienting Constructs

In order to gain a picture of Jon or any client, I often use a "movie" metaphor. I will tell interns I am supervising to see the client in front of you as the end of the movie. The movie begins when this person was born, a brand-new, precious baby coming into the world. Your job, as a clinician, is to see the movie—that is, to be able to enter the world of this client and gain a picture of what the years and experiences of their lives have been like. As you increasingly develop the skills to do this, your clients' symptoms and problems will not only become understandable, but will begin to emerge as the best—and sometimes only—choices this person had.

My initial "pictures" of Jon were of a child who had little opportunity for attention or positive parenting. His mother's rejection of him following her failed attempts to control him, absence from home as she pursued her own dreams, coupled with his father's preference for his brother and his lack of attachment to him left Jon feeling isolated and "different." In parallel, Gunderson and Zanarini (1989) found that patients with BPD described their relationships with their mothers as vacillating unpredictably between intense conflict and underinvolvement. Their relationships with their fathers were too distant or superficial to offer a buffer or alternative to the chaotic relationship they were awash in with their mothers.

The failure of Jon's mother to successfully navigate the separateness/relatedness period of development (rapprochement) and the continuation of these problematic relational patterns throughout his childhood left Jon with the patient's with BPD dilemma: choose between engulfment or isolation. He could be his mother's best friend or confidant, when he met her emotional needs, or become the bad child who is rejected for abandoning her when he pursued his own interests or friendships. Jon's brother had achieved a "favored son" role with his father. Father's indulgent interest in Jon's brother increased Jon's sense of rejection and left him feeling "defective," as if there was something fundamentally flawed or wrong with him. Jon's mother, on the other hand, favored Jon when signs of his intelligence emerged. He was destined to be better than his "shittless father." But when Jon disappointed her, he became the embodiment of all that was bad in his father. He could move close to his mother when he performed according to her demands, but to do so meant sacrificing his own needs and interests. Although the possibility of becoming more authentically connected to others left Jon equally threatened by the potential loss of himself in the other person's identity, Jon's fundamental experience was one of abandonment. The family's moves, changes in schools, and loss of community all compounded his isolation. In particular, his parents' divorce exacerbated his feelings of abandonment and, simultaneously, his fear of engulfment. Now, with the divorce, he further needed to save his mother from her own depression and unsatisfying life, which no child can accomplish.

Jon's experience of being a gay, African American male, coupled with a move to a predominantly White community, and change to a strict private school with little emotional support, left Jon with no sense of belonging. By placing Jon in a mostly Caucasian school, his mother offered no support for Jon's cultural heritage. With no adult males of color, Jon had no role model to affirm his cultural identity. He might have felt a sense of belonging in his high school, but not as a person of color with an alternative lifestyle. Jon was stuck between a rock and a hard place. He felt isolated in gay groups, as there were few African Americans, and he did not feel he could join with other African Americans without being heterosexual. I wondered if his initial desire to seek treatment with me and to share appointment days and times with his friend Steve at school was one way of attempting to belong, this time by joining the "Babs" club.

Treatment Plans and Intervention Strategy

My primary initial goal with Jon was to work to establish a collaborative relationship. This was both the most fundamental and most difficult goal of our work together. Jonathan's injuries were in his relationships, originally in the lack of attention and affection, and in the lack of daily structure and predictability from his parents. Later, they were re-created by him in his problematic ways of relating to people in the present. Jon was unable to let people in and unable to leave his own position of egocentrism in order to understand others.

In the beginning of treatment, the goal to establish a relationship took the form of attempting to take the relationship deeper than the "performance" that Jon was currently giving. By performance, I mean Jon's tendency to tell stories without pause for interaction between us nor affective reactions from him. Although Jon was getting from me the attention he lacked, I felt that this experience would ultimately not fulfill his deeper need to connect with someone. As long as I was an audience for Jon, we were not in real, mutual contact with each other. Additionally, I believe that any healing or growth in counseling takes place within the context of a genuine and reciprocal emotional contact. Therefore, establishing this in our relationship was first and foremost.

Establishing this relationship is an ongoing process throughout the course of treatment. Ideally, it deals with different aspects of the client's problems as the relationship grows and the working alliance becomes stronger. In the beginning, my goal was to make the session safe enough for Jon to risk becoming more vulnerable and supporting that openness—while also recognizing his fears and respecting his need to proceed slowly. This was best accomplished by the use of process comments. As in the previous example of Jon's use of the phrase, "It's okay," instead of pushing for feelings that Jon was not ready to share, we could talk about this difficulty and, in later sessions, what made it so difficult to open up. In this way, we were not at cross purposes but truly collaborating about his difficulties.

A second initial goal was to address Jon's difficulty attending sessions on a regular and timely basis. Again, the use of process comments (talking directly about what was going on between us at that moment) were helpful in changing Jon's belief that my comments or inquiries about his attendance were attacks or judgments against him. We will explore this more fully later in this section.

An intermediate and long-term goal for treatment was to address the deeper conflicts in Jon's relationships based on his personality style. These conflicts took the form of his alternating between idealization and devaluation (new friends quickly went from being "perfect" to being "jerks" who let him down), his mood swings, his poor impulse control (unsafe sex, alcohol use), and his feelings of isolation and engulfment. My goal was to give Jon the "holding environment" that would allow him to experience a connection without losing himself and to experience independence without retaliation.

I hoped that by being a stable, consistent, and caring presence in his life that he could begin to care about himself. I hoped that I could present a new role model to Jon who was not all good nor all bad, but be perceived realistically. Most importantly, I wanted him to see that I could survive his anger and temper outbursts and not punish or abandon him.

My plan for carrying out these goals was to be supportive, attentive, and patient. I intended to clearly define the rules and boundaries for treatment and consistently address them in order to create a safe, predictable environment for Jon. I looked for themes in the topics he addressed and pointed them out to allow him to feel understood and listened to. For example, Jon's relationships in the past consisted of threats to his individuality and threats of abandonment. Jon's unmet needs resulted in a great "hunger" that he took into his current relationships. This hunger overwhelmed his friends and, when Jon's demands were not met, left Jon feeling betrayed and enraged. Addressing these themes allowed us to approach intense material within a framework that Jon could tolerate.

Other long-term goals were to reduce Jon's risk-taking behaviors. While his experimentation with drugs and alcohol was not causing difficulties at this time, he was establishing patterns that were almost certain to cause significant problems in the future. A great deal of his social life took place in bars, and Jon had a low tolerance for hurt, anger, or frustration. Drugs, and especially alcohol, gave Jon a short-term escape from unwanted feelings.

I felt that the best way to carry out this goal was to help Jon find that it was safe to share difficult feelings with me. I knew that if he could begin to talk about his feelings, he wouldn't need to medicate them away. We also shared educational information about the effects and interactions of these drugs (e.g., increasing depression or confusion in Jon—who was already depressed and confused). Clarifying maladaptive relational patterns that kept recurring throughout Jon's life also gave us the opportunity to help anticipate how his drug-induced behavior usually affected others. As our sessions continued, Jon was increasingly able to discuss the interpersonal patterns and scenarios that kept recurring for him—as he repeatedly found that I did not judge or try to control him, as he had expected me to do.

Another example of risk-taking behavior was in the area of his sexuality. Jon's understandable joy at accepting his sexuality and finding a support group of other like-minded peers initiated a period of much sexual activity. This "coming out" euphoria, combined with an adolescent fearlessness toward realistic consequences, equaled a very high risk for HIV/AIDS.

Again, educational information was helpful as there was much misinformation between Jon and his friends. Unfortunately, less successful was my attempt to gain credibility with Jon around my belief in his mortality. He consistently refused to believe that he or his friends would become infected. Claiming to be acting responsibly, closer scrutiny often revealed impulsive actions that avoided personal responsibility. Unlike other aspects of our work together, I found myself returning to this topic again and again without success. Seeing oneself as mortal is difficult for most adolescents, but I felt there was an additional obstacle—a failure to make much progress in working with the sexual abuse that Jon would only allude to briefly. Indeed, Jon's sexual acting-out had a disconnected, compulsive quality to it, something often seen in sexual abuse survivors. Jon's ability to connect, commit, and establish a stable, mutually respectful relationship had been profoundly damaged. He seemed to confuse sex and a loving connection.

Therapeutic Process

As Jon shared more of his history and daily life, I began to realize more fully how devoid of connections his life was. He would gather with his friends but would never mention anything of substance to them. They knew little about his life or family. So he was with them physically but emotionally continued to be distant and isolated. Similarly, there would be many days where he would not see his mother, then she would storm in on him. At these times she would be either verbally abusive or idealizing of him if he were playing by her rules. Thus, even here, he was not authentically connected. Jon had virtually no relationship with his brother or father. I became increasingly aware of how unusual and difficult it was for Jon to spend time with me and let me really "see" him and know his interests and concerns. Although we were progressing at what sometimes seemed to be a slow pace to me, I realized that, for Jon who had never been in an authentic, caring relationship, it was not slow at all.

This lifelong lack of connectedness and inability to sustain consistent boundaries would become most evident when Jon would have difficulty attending sessions, begin to tell stories again, or push for special treatment by asking for extra time at the end of sessions or to see me on weekends. I was clear that it was not in Jon's best interest for me to compromise so readily and try to meet these demands. Trying to provide limits for him without making him feel rejected, I would ask about his difficulty with attendance and comment on his struggle (e.g., "Seems like it was hard for you to get here today. I'm wondering if we could put our heads together and try to understand that better."). I was also trying to link his difficulty attending to the relational themes we were identifying in other aspects of Jon's life. For example, these repetitive scenarios included Jon's unreasonable demands on his friends, his feelings of betrayal when they didn't readily respond to his unrealistic demands, and then the breakdown of the relationship when his intense anger erupted. By coming late, Jon was also testing the consistency of my boundaries (e.g., coming late for appointments and becoming outraged when I didn't extend the session). By sticking to my limits, rather than being more flexible and accommodating his demands, I was trying to provide Jon with the structure and predictability he never had at home. Jon's behavior reassured me that I was on the right track by being firm. I repeatedly observed that Jon became calmer and worked more productively after finding, once again, that I could tolerate his temper outbursts (or accusations that I didn't care about him or was rigid and uptight). It was reparative for him when I would remain calm but firm, without going to either extreme by caving in or rejecting him—as others had done and as he expected me to do.

Increasingly, Jon and I were able to identify these maladaptive relational patterns and clarify what precipitated or caused them to reemerge (e.g., something happening in his life that made him feel lonely, different, or on the outside). Jon's life became less chaotic and his relationships improved as he became increasingly able to slow down internally, observe or reflect upon his own inner experience, and anticipate or think about what may happen for him and others before acting. As before, we focused on how these same problems with others played out between us during our sessions. For example, we began to explore how his requests for extra time or special treatment and his difficulty with attendance were a part of the same pattern that caused problems in other relationships. I find that when I can *clarify how a behavior sequence that is causing problems with others is occurring in our interaction, and change or resolve that pattern right then as it is happening between us, clients begin changing this with others in their lives also.* Let's look at another example of this cardinal principle of in-vivo or experiential relearning.

In terms of our interaction together, Jon's initial need to perform and entertain/distance me by telling stories was another way that he repeated with me what he did with others in his life. I intervened by repeatedly wondering aloud if he felt like he had to entertain me or asking what he might be feeling at moments like this when he needed to perform for me. Sometimes he would fly away from these process comments, while at other times he would join with me and begin to reflect on what was occurring between us right then. As we joined together as partners to figure out what was going on for him right then, or what might be happening between us, I would often feel more connected to Jon and make this overt (e.g., "You know, Jon, I'm not feeling pushed away or distanced as I was before. I like it when we are working together like this—I feel closer to you. What's it like for you to be letting me in like this?"). Following such an interaction, Jon would often make progress and begin our next session by telling me how he was able to say or do something different with someone he knew—like stop entertaining them and instead talk with them about something that felt more meaningful to both of them.

As Jonathan and I moved into the middle stage of treatment, I felt we were becoming closer and that his anxiety was rising as a result. Our more authentic relationship was putting Jonathan into uncharted waters. Historically, relationships brought either the risk of abandonment or the threat of being consumed. It became helpful at this point that Jonathan and I had been able to identify these themes in past relationships and become aware of the coping strategies that Jonathan had used in the past (e.g., distancing, performing, provoking) to reduce these threats—and thereby reduce his anxiety.

Jonathan continued to have difficulty either attending sessions or being on time for them. He would also request additional sessions on days when I was not at the clinic. As before, we would talk about these difficulties as they came up. For example:

CL: Well, I'm late! But wait until you hear what happened to me. I knew you'd be mad, but I couldn't help it.

TH: You thought I'd be mad?

CL: Well, maybe not mad, but I KNEW you'd make something out of it. I KNEW you'd want to talk about it, don't you?

TH: Well, if you're asking if I think it's important, I do. We've been struggling for some time now about how difficult it is for you to be here. But it sounds like you were worried you'd get in trouble with me, and that seems very different than you and I together trying to work out more manageable ways for you to be here.

CL: (tearfully) I WANT to be here. You have no idea how much I busted my ass to get here.

These encounters were difficult for me as well. On a conscious level, Jonathan was working very hard to get to our sessions. It was at this point in the conflict that Jonathan would exhibit the greatest degree of vulnerability I had experienced with him—and the only times when the pain or tears even made it up to his eyes for me to see. For me, the difficulty was in knowing that Jonathan was probably going to misinterpret my comments and questions as criticisms, and not as my awareness that he was in conflict and needed help, which I intended.

However, I had learned that if I did not address these issues, Jonathan would escalate his behavior until I did attend to them. I believed this was because, on an unconscious level, Jonathan was attempting to move me into the only kind of relationship he knew how to have. That is, he would bump up against my boundaries or limits in the hope that I would become angry and reject him. He expected the anger and rejection and heard it even when it wasn't there. He was also very good at creating these feelings in others, and there were times I began to feel angry, too. Luckily, this became a great built-in early warning system that alerted me that we were re-creating an old relationship pattern of Jonathan's.

On the occasions when I did not address (or did not recognize) one of Jonathan's attempts to push against a limit, Jonathan was not hurt and enraged, but became distant and disdaining. I believed this was because he could not trust me and feel safe if he could manipulate me. Internally, Jonathan felt abandoned and knew that I could be of no help to him if I could be moved around.

In line with Jonathan's schemas or expectations for relationships, either he would be in control of me or I was attempting to control him. This is what he had experienced in the past. I was attempting to form a different kind of relationship in several important ways. First, I would be in charge of what I did, and not try to control him or allow myself to be controlled. I would continue to set limits, but do so in a calm or self-contained manner rather than becoming angry or exasperated as he expected. This new middle ground of self-control was an important aspect of the corrective experience or in-vivo relearning that I was trying to provide:

TH: You know, I don't underestimate at all how much you want to be here and how hard you work to make that happen. And here you are! I really do see that, Jonathan. But I can also see how difficult it is for you to be here right now. Let's put our heads together and see if we can understand what may be threatening for you about coming here or seeing me today. Maybe we could start with how you felt or what you were thinking as you were driving over here today.

CL: Well, I do want to be here, but sometimes it's really hard. I was thinking today that I don't really have anybody that I can talk to about stuff. I mean, my friends are okay, but there's all this sexual tension all the time. Friends that used to be lovers, lovers that become friends. A couple of my friends will start to see each other romantically and everything changes. The lines get all screwed up. It's easier sometimes just to party and not think about all this stuff with you.

Over and over again, we would resolve the surface conflict about being late for counseling by trying to name and understand the real threat or anxiety that was being evoked. That discussion would quickly lead us to bigger issues around relationships and personal boundaries. That is, addressing this conflict seemed to give Jon the safety to talk about the difficulty he had with boundaries and connections with his friends. In particular, we began exploring in more detail his fears about getting close to others and his belief that all relationships ultimately were destined to end up being rejecting or abusive. As time went on, being late for counseling was no longer a testing ground, but new testing grounds appeared.

Next, we dealt with the issue of cancellations (similarly, by focusing on the importance of the issue and the conflict or anxiety that was being communicated, rather than blaming or attempting to control him). As that was resolved, we rotated to Jonathan's asking for additional sessions on days I was not available (again, these demands were not met, but instead explored). By repeatedly pushing limits and testing my boundaries in these ways, Jon was holding me away—skirting around the threats evoked in him by investing in a real relationship with me or anyone else. Just as I (naively) believed he was about out of ways to attempt to push the boundaries surrounding our sessions, Jonathan became more creative and produced a bigger conflict to resolve. This proved to be a turning point in our work together.

I was scheduled to see Jonathan at 3:00 P.M. one day. At 1:00 P.M., I walked down the hall to the clinic waiting room to get Steve, a relatively consistent friend of Jonathan's who had originally given Jonathan my name and recommended that he see me. As I opened the door to greet Steve, I was surprised to see Jonathan sitting there instead. He jumped up, walked through the door I was holding, and began to walk to my office. I followed behind him thinking that I might have misread my appointment book and that I would check it when we got to my office. However, Jonathan made sure I did not miss the significance of this by turning his head around as we walked down the hall and saying:

CL: This is Steve's appointment time. I asked him to switch with me.

TH: Yes. I was surprised and thinking I might have misread my schedule.

CL: It's okay though, isn't it?

We were still walking down the hall at this point and I felt uncomfortable with Jonathan's switching of the appointments, but I wasn't sure why. His actions hadn't broken any rule. However, over the years, I had learned to both trust my instincts as well as give myself permission to "not know" right away why something wasn't okay. Jonathan's big grin confirmed the feeling I had that this event was significant.

TH: Actually, it doesn't feel okay, and I'm not sure why. But come on down to my office and let's talk about it.

As we reached my office and sat down, Jonathan began to tell me that he couldn't have made the 3:00 P.M. appointment and how hard he'd worked to solve this problem. He said he knew he couldn't cancel or not show and he knew I'd be mad, so he had come up with this wonderful solution that I couldn't possibly mind, and here he was.

For me, I became aware of why this wasn't okay, but felt initially bound by my concern over both Jonathan's reaction to this as well as my concern for Steve, who had become enmeshed in this as well. If I held Jonathan to his 3:00 P.M. appointment time, he could come back in two hours; but Steve's appointment time was right now and he would miss his session. I proceeded, knowing it was not my task to rescue Steve from this situation or hold back the correct response out of concern for Jonathan's reaction.

TH: Jonathan, I understand now why this is not okay. First of all, this is my schedule and I'm in charge of it. If changes are made, they need to be made through me. It would have been all right for you and Steve to switch appointments if either of you had called me and involved me in the plans. Secondly, this isn't an isolated event. For a long time now, we've talked about how hard it is for you to make your appointments. We've also talked about your pushing limits and people not being there for you. I know this is very difficult, but I am here for you and look forward to seeing you later today at 3:00 P.M.

CL: I knew it!! You're not gonna see me! I can't believe you'd get so nit-picky about this. I tried SO HARD to do the right thing. Nothing I do pleases you! I can't come at three o'clock. I told you, I just can't make it. If you want to see me, you see me now.

Jonathan continued for a few minutes more. He expressed outrage that I wouldn't see him, felt betrayed by me, and demonstrated more emotion than I had ever witnessed from him. A couple of tears rolled down his cheek as he talked. I listened intently as he talked. When he was finished, I said:

TH: Jonathan, I can see how hurtful this is for you and how angry you feel. I also know that your whole life you've felt like your mother would pick at you and that there was nothing you could do to please her. I don't feel that way about you and I don't want to join all the people you carry on your shoulders that you have to try and please. However, your appointment time is in two hours and I'll look forward to seeing you then.

CL: I told you, I can't come later.

TH: Then I'll hope to see you next week at 3:00 P.M.

CL: No way!

As Jonathan slammed the door behind him, my first thoughts were about the degree of pain and rage he was feeling. I felt sad for him. My next thoughts were doubts about the position I had taken and I went over the alternatives in my head. This was very helpful in reaffirming my assessment for no other alternative would have been in Jonathan's best interests. Had I not been able to tolerate his feelings of hurt and anger—and modulated my response to minimize those feelings—I would have sent the message that therapy was not a safe place to have those feelings. My intention was to continue providing secure boundaries but my main concern was his perception of abandonment from me—I wondered if he would come the following week.

I thought about Jonathan during the week. As our appointment time approached, I felt that one way or the other, this would be a turning point. Intellectually, I believed that if he was unable to continue that it was still better to have kept the integrity of our work intact. Maybe that would allow him to return in the future when he was ready. On a personal level, however, I was very worried about Jonathan being back out in the world without the slimmest of connections to anyone.

At 3:00 P.M. the following week, Jonathan was sitting in the waiting room. He quietly walked past me down the hall to my office. As I closed the door and sat down, Jonathan reached out his hand to me and, as I held it, he began to sob. He cried for a long, long time.

When he was able to talk, Jonathan began to speak of his loneliness, of always feeling like there was something "bad" inside of him, and that his badness was "too much" for anyone else to bear. He began to relay his more generalized fear of being "too much" for other people, especially his mother. Jon's mother would attempt to control him and, as her demands became endless, Jonathan would attempt to set limits with her and fight for some of his rights. When mother met with his resistance, she would step back, act hurt like a martyr, and become distant—telling Jonathan to "just do whatever you want then. I don't care." Jonathan felt emotionally abandoned at this point and believed that he deserved to be rejected like this because of his badness. Jon also held this same faulty belief that he was "too much" vis-à-vis his friends. He believed that he "was too much for them and wanted too much from them" and that his needs were shamefully bad and needed to be hidden. At times, he expressed, he would get so frustrated about feeling "bad " inside all the time that he would just go ahead and be bad and tell everyone to go to hell.

With our session last week, Jonathan had scared himself that his demands and anger were now going to be too much for me too. Jon was visibly relieved to find his expectations disconfirmed—that I was intact and still eager to work with him. Upon finding that he wasn't "too much," he said a remarkable thing, "I'm not sure why, but I don't feel so alone." As Masterson (1985) emphasizes, when the counselor can set limits and tolerate their anger, patients with BPD can no longer avoid their difficult feelings by acting-out. That is, when the therapist creates a safe environment by setting these limits, painful feelings from past problematic relationships often emerge. The client often learns much about past problematic relationships from this new experience with the counselor, and usually begins to change his own problematic responses to others in current relationships. Thus, finding a new response from the counselor that does not fit their old expectations often propels far reaching behavior change as clients begin to translate their new experience with the counselor to successful changes in their relationships with others.

One of the major challenges Jon and I faced in our work together was the almost intolerable levels of anxiety that Jonathan experienced whenever he moved toward me by sharing difficult feelings, feeling my support for him, or letting me help him in any way. As I would become more important to Jon in any of these ways, he would act out the anxiety this evoked by pushing away from me or by pushing against my limits and breaking rules. If those maneuvers didn't work, he often escalated this defensiveness by expressing rage toward me or attempting to elicit contempt or rejection from me. As we became better at recognizing this pattern and anticipating it, Jon was able to manage this anxiety more effectively by talking with me about it, rather than acting-out to avoid it.

Despite this progress, however, Jon would still move into a period of distance whenever we became closer or more important to each other in some way. I understood this to be Jon's need to know that, in the same way he had found out he could get closer, he still needed to reassure himself that he could be separate, as well. Thus, this treatment challenge was assuaged as both of us learned more about Jon's need for distance to reduce his anxiety, and recognized that the anxiety would return whenever something happened to make us feel closer.

A second challenge was Jon's difficulty integrating good and bad. Many times, his sessions were dominated by alternating themes of the new, wonderful person he had met and the old, worthless friend who had betrayed him. His view of me, and of himself, alternated in this way as well. Over time, Jon increasingly came to recognize that I was a human being with flaws and failings who still honored and cared for him. My caring for him, while not reinforcing his self-aggrandizing view of himself as special, allowed him to begin to consider a middle ground for himself as well that was no longer all good or all bad.

A third challenge was Jon's lack of a familial or social support system, or any individual for that matter, who was there for him beyond surface friendships. This greatly limited the amount of anxiety and disruption he could tolerate and, I believe, limited the amount of work we could do together. My attempts to involve family members in treatment failed. However, as our working alliance continued, it was clear that Jon's friendships improved and became more substantial. I thought that these changes in his social support network, which paralleled the development of our relationship, would be of great help to Jon in the future.

TERMINATION AND SUMMARY THOUGHTS

I had been seeing Jon at a training clinic on the campus of a large urban university. A low-cost, sliding scale fee had allowed Jon and me the opportunity to work together for nearly a year. As it became clear that college was not something he was ready to pursue at this time, Jonathan began to consider a move out of the area. Although I did not believe that our work together had reached a natural conclusion, I felt it important to not undermine Jon's attempts to become autonomous from me. Jon's childhood attempts at autonomy had only been met with parental attempts to control him, followed by threats of abandonment if he did not comply. Unfortunately, his religious training and high school education had taken place in an environment that reinforced this view. Their rules were clearly defined and not to be debated; participation was total or not at all. As a result, I believed it was important to let Jon know that, while I thought we might learn more together in the

future, I respected his desire to move on now. I reflected aloud on how much he had been held back his entire life from pursuing his independence, and expressed my pleasure in seeing him become more independent. At the same time, I also assured him that I would remain interested in his whereabouts and available to see him at the clinic as long as I remained there if he should recontact me in the future. As he had throughout treatment, Jon rejected my suggestions to help him join a support group in his new community.

We discussed these emancipation issues and both shared what our relationship had meant to us. Jon continued to feel this would be a good time to end and soon terminated. I later came to know that Jon would, several times, return for counseling. Every few years, he returns to the area and sees me for a few months or to get help during a crisis. The stories change but the issues remain the same, the relationship painstakingly grows, and the endings always feel abrupt and premature to me. I have now come to believe that these terminations reflect a symmetry that makes counseling a continual wonder to me; we are re-creating his rapprochement phase and cycling through periods of autonomy followed by periods of reunion.

When people have had poor developmental experiences and experienced long-term stressors, and received few buffers or supports to help them cope, counseling often involves continually re-working the same issues over time in order to resolve them. It was certainly challenging to work with Jon toward such integration, and deeply rewarding to be able to share in such a rich and important relationship.

Questions for Thought and Discussion

1. How do you evaluate yourself in terms of your ability to set limits and say no in close relationships? Under what situations is it most difficult for you to hold to your personal boundaries? How do you typically respond when others push your boundaries?

2. Think of yourself as a parent, teacher, counselor, or social worker. How difficult will it be for you to set limits and be effective in control with children without becoming angry or rejecting? Can you identify role models who were able to do this effectively?

Suggestions for Further Reading

Fraiberg, S. (1959). *The magic years*. New York: Scribner. This classic book compassionately takes you into the mind of a child.

Gunderson, J. (1996). The borderline patient's intolerance of aloneness: Insecure attachments and therapist availability. *American Journal of Psychiatry, 153* (6), 752–758. This important work on attachment disruptions in patients with BPD teaches therapists what they can do to help.

Napier, A., & Whitaker, C. (1978). *The family crucible*. New York: Harper and Row. Demonstrates family systems through the use of a case study and brings family dynamics to life.

6

CHAPTER

TIMMY: A BIRACIAL CHILD DEVELOPING FRIENDSHIPS AND COMPETENCE AS HE LEARNS TO COPE WITH ADHD

INTRODUCTION

The Disorder

Most people have heard of attention deficit/hyperactivity disorder (ADHD) and usually think of it as describing someone who is "hyper." However, many children who have this diagnosis actually have problems with attention (inattentive type), whereas others are hyperactive-impulsive (hyperactive-impulsive type), and yet others are both inattentive and hyperactive-impulsive (combined type). This is one of those disorders where people have disagreed greatly about what causes the problem and how it should be defined or described. Even the Diagnostic and Statistical Manual of Mental Disorders (DSM-IV-TR), the standard diagnostic manual in the field, keeps changing its description and definition of this disorder. In the past, terms such as post-encephalitic disorder, minimal brain disorder or dysfunction, and hyperkinesis were used (see Baren, 1994). In the current DSM, "inattention" and/or "hyperactivity-impulsivity" must be present for at least six months, appear before age 7, and cause problems in two or more settings (APA, 2000). However, some in the field view these criteria as too stringent. They note, for example, that girls exhibit the "inattentive" type more often, a type that may not be observed until age 6 or 7 when they start school. The "inattentive" type seems to cause difficulty primarily in school settings. Thus, age and pervasiveness (multiple rather than one setting) continue to be among the many unresolved issues.

Children who have the inattentive type are often described as having difficulty *focusing* (e.g., listening, organizing, carrying out tasks) or as being unable to *sustain* their attention (e.g., stay on task, avoid distractions, complete their work). These

112

children often do not follow instructions, seem absentminded, often lose things, and are forgetful. In addition, their work is frequently incomplete or careless/messy and they are reluctant to engage in tasks that require sustained attention. These difficulties often lead to failing: in their schoolwork, in developing and sustaining friendships, in their relationships with their families, and so forth. Sadly, many begin to feel ineffective and incompetent, especially as they repeatedly fail in friendships because they do not attend to social cues or listen to their playmates very well. A negative behavior cycle develops as their low self-esteem leads to depression, oppositional behavior, and increases conflict with teachers, family members, and peers. These problems usually do not go away especially for those with the hyperactive-impulsive type. Rather, ADHD continues through adolescence and adulthood where substance abuse and other psychiatric disorders such as depression may emerge (see American Psychiatric Association, 2000; Biederman, 1991; Biederman, Newcorn, & Sprich, 1991; Wenar & Kerig, 2000; Wilens, Biederman, Spencer, & Francis, 1994).

Children who have the hyperactive-impulsive type are more easily identified. These children behave impulsively (i.e., act without thinking). They are talkative, interrupt frequently, and tend to blurt out answers even before the question has been completed. Teachers become frustrated with them and peers reject them because they rarely wait their turn, they grab things (e.g., toys, pencils), and often thoughtlessly engage in reckless behavior, which can lead to accidents and injuries.

In most instances, hyperactivity and impulsivity occur together. These children are often described as driven, always on the go, fidgety or squirmy, not able to sit still, and very talkative. They are also prone to accidents from climbing on furniture and other objects.

Diagnostic Challenges

The three of the core dimensions of *inattention, impulsivity,* and *hyperactivity* vary across settings, making diagnosis difficult. For example, ADHD symptoms generally increase in familiar, structured and task-oriented settings like the classroom. They tend to decrease in informal, open settings such as the playground or other settings considered interesting by the child. Symptoms also are more likely to occur in groups (e.g., classroom) than in one-to-one situations (e.g., counseling). Additionally, some children with ADHD seem to be just *situationally* hyperactive (e.g., in task-oriented settings) whereas others are more *pervasively* hyperactive (i.e., many different settings). Situationally hyperactive children have a much better prognosis than pervasively hyperactive children who are more disruptive, function at a lower level at home and school, and are more likely to continue to have problems over time (Campbell, 1990; Cantwell, 1996; Klein & Mannuzza, 1991).

Complicating diagnosis and treatment, most children with ADHD have more than one diagnosis (i.e., it is co-morbid or co-occurs with another diagnosis). A large percentage (by some estimates over 30%) of children with ADHD also have conduct disorder as a diagnosis, for example. Additionally, more than 30% are diagnosed with oppositional defiant disorder and approximately 15 to 20% with a specific learning disability such as dyslexia (Fletcher et al., 1994; McArdle, O'Brien, & Kolvin, 1995; Wenar & Kerig, 2000). These children are also at increased risk for other disorders such as mood disorders, anxiety disorders, and borderline personality disorder (Biederman et al., 1991; Fine, 1997; Wenar & Kerig, 2000).

More boys than girls are referred for ADHD but there is no clear evidence of race or socioeconomic status effects on the prevalence of the disorder (Arnold, 1996; Barkley, 1996). Although ADHD has its onset in early childhood, it frequently persists into adolescence and adulthood, increasing risk for substance abuse, antisocial behavior, and other forms of psychopathology (Biederman et al., 1991; Wilens et al., 1994). Biederman et al. (1995) conservatively suggest that 10 to 60% of childhood ADHD cases persist into adulthood (others suggest much higher persistence rates), which means that at least .3% to 2% of adults have ADHD. Treatment often includes stimulant medication such as Ritalin and Dexedrine, which helps the children be more focused and on-task. However, use of stimulant medication is complicated by the co-morbid (concurrent) presence of other psychiatric disorders such as substance abuse. Thus, physicians are hesitant to prescribe stimulants for adults with ADHD who are also substance abusers.

Etiology

ADHD is child psychopathology's "problem child." What causes ADHD has been greatly disputed. Since it seems to run in families (based on twin and adoption studies), some researchers suggest that genetic factors are involved (Goodman & Stevenson, 1989; Levy, Hoy, McStephen, Wood, & Waldman, 1997). For example, in a study with 1,938 families, Levy et al. (1997) found heritability rates for ADHD ranging from .75 to .91. However, while ADHD may run in families, this could be due to genetic factors, environmental factors, or most likely, an interaction of both (Teeter, 1998).

Both underarousal and overarousal of central nervous system processing and neurotransmitter imbalances have been suggested as "causes," and a great deal of research has been conducted on the neurological basis of ADHD. However, despite many claims over the years from this and other points of view, *we still have no conclusive proof of what causes ADHD.* This is in part because neurological and physiological findings in ADHD compared to non-ADHD controls are frequently found in children with other disorders such as conduct disorder. For example, physiological responses (e.g., heart rate, skin conductance, EEG) are often lower in ADHD compared to non-ADHD controls. This lowered response is also evident in children with conduct disorder. The high co-morbidity of ADHD with conduct disorder complicates efforts to distinguish between the various contributors to these disorders. Over the years, many other causes of ADHD have been suggested. These include minimal brain dysfunction, diet (e.g., food coloring, additives, sugar), allergies, television, and video games, none of which have received empirical support (Adesman & Wender, 1991; Teeter, 1998; Wenar & Kerig, 2000).

Finally, family stress, disorganization in the homes, and abuse have all been suggested as possible causes. However, anyone who has been around a child whose ADHD symptoms are intense will acknowledge that the direction of cause and effect are hard to determine. Does stress and disorganization cause ADHD or does having a family member with ADHD cause stress and disorganization?

One prospective study (Jacobvitz & Sroufe, 1987) suggests that early child-caregiver relationships may play a significant role in the development of ADHD. These researchers followed children from infancy and assessed the mother's behavior at 6 months, 2 years, and 3 1/2 years to evaluate which behaviors predicted hyperactivity in kindergarten (age

5 to 6). They found higher levels of ADHD in children whose parents were intrusive. These parents were not sensitive to when it was appropriate to intervene and when it was appropriate to back off and let the children make their own choices and direct themselves. As a result, these children did not learn to *self-regulate* or control their own behavior. If you recall the description of ADHD children earlier, their behaviors seemed "out of control" (e.g., talking out of turn, fidgeting, grabbing, and climbing on furniture). It thus seems that learning control is important and affects children's risk for developing the disorder. Sadly, mothers of children with ADHD tend to be less responsive and more negative with their children, perhaps because parenting these children is more challenging. In addition to difficulties at home, children with ADHD routinely experience painful peer rejection and social isolation (see Barkley, 1996; Hinshaw, Zupan, Simmel, Nigg, & Melnick, 1997).

How often does ADHD appear in the population? According to DSM-IV-TR (American Psychiatric Association, 2000), the incidence rates are 3 to 5%, while physicians who treat children with this disorder estimate rates of 6 to 8% (Baren, 1994). However, other studies suggest that situational hyperactivity rates may be as high as 30% (see Baren, 1994; McArdle et al., 1995). This disorder is far more likely to occur in boys than in girls, with reported ratios ranging from 4:1 to 9:1 (American Psychiatric Association, 2000). Usually diagnosed after age 5 in a school setting, ADHD is responsible for nearly 40% of referrals to child health care professionals (Barkley, 1998).

To say the least, ADHD is strenuous on the children and their families. It's heartbreaking to watch these children experience failure, be rejected by peers, come to see themselves as dumb, and end up with other problems such as depression, conduct disorders, and substance abuse. For children who are minorities, racial discrimination can exacerbate the rejection, social isolation, and negative attention that commonly occurs for those with ADHD. That is, these children are at increased risk for being singled out as troubled and for being rejected; they are also frequently more vigilant for negative responses from others because as minorities they have often experienced discrimination.

The families of children with ADHD generally feel overwhelmed and parents almost inevitably report having difficulty disciplining their children. Parents feel criticized by teachers, coaches, and others for their child's inappropriate behavior. Their response to this usually involves either giving up with little or no effort to assist their child or becoming overly controlling and not allowing the child to learn self-control. Unfortunately, both of these options only make the child's symptoms worse or more out of control.

What helps? Having a predictable daily routine, an organized household, and firm but affectionate discipline provides important buffers for children who are beginning to show signs of ADHD. In contrast, lack of family support, poor child-rearing skills, family instability, and ongoing marital conflict will place these children at much greater risk. Feelings of helplessness engendered by poverty and discrimination may interact to exacerbate the sense of helplessness to bring about positive change often experienced by families whose children have ADHD. For example, being poor may mean having to work longer hours and having fewer financial and emotional resources (due to fatigue, juggling multiple demands, etc.) to provide structured supervision for the children. As can be seen, being a member of a minority group and having low socioeconomic status (SES) can make it harder for children at risk for ADHD and their families to cope effectively.

Treatment Guidelines

Let's look more closely at what can be done to help children with ADHD . Stimulant medication (Ritalin, Dexedrine, Cylert) is the predominant pharmacological treatment for ADHD (Pelham, 1993; Schachar & Tannock, 1993). Children are typically given a morning and noon dose and may occasionally be given half the dose in the evening. However, because insomnia and appetite loss are frequent side effects, physicians tend to be concerned about evening doses. Sometimes a slow release version of the medication is given in the morning so that the children do not have to deal with the stigma of taking medication at school. Physicians also try to find the lowest possible effective dose and recommend "drug holidays" (e.g., during school breaks and summer vacation) when children can be taken off the medication(s). In addition to stimulant medication, tricyclic antidepressants (especially imipramine) are sometimes used (Busch, 1993). These antidepressants seem to be especially useful for children who are emotionally intense or reactive and have significant symptoms of depression and anxiety. Although it sounds contradictory, the use of stimulant medications does seem to have a calming effect and is useful in improving the children's problems with inattention and task orientation. Children on medication are often reported to be less impulsive, better able to sustain attention, and more able to monitor and regulate their own behavior. Teachers also tend to rate medicated children as more task-oriented, less disruptive, and more appropriate. Improvement in family and peer relationships is also noted as children become less bossy and less aggressive. Despite these very significant benefits, however, medication is far from a cure-all. Sadly, although effective use of medication can set the stage for better learning, researchers find that *it does not result in improved academic performance.* In order to break the strong pattern of school failure, truancy, conduct disorder, and substance abuse that tend to follow like falling dominoes, teachers and parents must use this opportunity of improved attention and task focus to teach the child new study skills. Also, many professionals are appropriately concerned that stimulants are overprescribed simply to make temperamentally active or acting-out children from disorganized or high-conflict homes more compliant. Finally, there are concerns about the side effects of these medications including nervousness, insomnia, anorexia, and suppression of growth. In addition, some children experience irritability and headaches (see Ouellette, 1991; Pelham, Wheeler, & Chronis, 1998).

Clearly, treatment of children with ADHD requires working on multiple levels. As we will see later, this often includes behavioral, cognitive-behavioral, and family interventions in addition to medications (Barkley, 1998; Pelham et al. 1998; Whalen & Henker, 1991). In these approaches, parents receive training in behavior management and other parenting practices so they are able to discipline more effectively and help their children organize and plan more carefully. They also participate in support groups with other parents of children who have ADHD, where they receive support, exchange ideas, and get help managing their guilty feelings, including feelings of failing as a parent and feelings of resentment toward this child who "demands so much." Thus, the goals of these interventions are to help caregivers provide firm and unambiguous discipline, predictable daily routines, and a structured home life. Parents are also encouraged to become "strategic organizers" in their children's lives by helping their children develop self-monitoring and self-regulation strategies. That is, children are encouraged to slow down and think about the consequences of their behavior before acting and are taught how to develop positive peer relationships (e.g., taking turns, listening). Parents also learn to become advocates for their children in school and other settings (Cousins & Weiss, 1993). Both parents and children seem to benefit from parent-training programs, with parents often reporting reduced parenting stress and increased parenting self-esteem while the children show improvement in the severity of their ADHD symptoms (Anastopoulos, Shelton, DuPaul, & Guevremont, 1993; Pelham et al., 1998).

Cognitive-behavioral self-regulation approaches are used to help children assert some level of control/constraint over their own behavior (Whalen & Henker, 1991). In these procedures, the children learn to "talk" themselves through problem-solving tasks, as will be illustrated in the case study that follows.

Social skills training is also very helpful. Learning to follow rules, take turns, and cultivate hobbies or sports activities helps these children develop positive peer relationships and decreases their social isolation. Success doesn't come easily, however, as coaches and teammates can painfully ostracize or exclude a child who doesn't sit still, follow directions, or stay focused.

Working with school personnel and obtaining academic tutoring are central to an effective treatment approach. Since academic failure, poor school adjustment, and conflicts with teachers are common, academic success or failure has profound effects on the child's self-concept and identity.

Thus, the "team" concept, in which school personnel, physician, counselor, and parent(s) work together is the ideal effective approach. A major goal is to help the child have *success experiences* in any arena. In schoolwork, success experiences will encourage initiative and self-confidence—combating the painful self-concept of being a loser or a failure. In interpersonal relationships, success will lead to greater inclusion and decrease the child's sense of being defective, inferior, or unloved. The treatment guidelines discussed previously are illustrated in the case study of Timmy that follows.

CASE ILLUSTRATION

Presenting Problem

Timmy, an 8-year-old biracial child, came to therapy with his mother at the insistence of his school. Timmy was in the third grade. His classroom teacher felt frustrated by the problems he was exhibiting and requested that he be evaluated for attention-deficit/hyperactivity disorder (ADHD). Timmy was described by his teacher as overly active (hands and feet in constant motion), inattentive (seemingly "spaced out," unresponsive when called on), and failing academically. He rarely completed his assignments, did not follow directions, was untidy in his work, talked out of turn, and wandered aimlessly around the classroom. His low frustration tolerance was evident in his frequent temper tantrums. Although these problems were not new, Timmy's teacher was becoming overwhelmed by his behavior and was concerned about his increasing isolation from his peers, who did not want to be associated with his disruptiveness.

Although Timmy's third grade teacher had begun the school year with firm rules that she insisted Timmy adhere to, she was now feeling "overwhelmed" and was allowing him to spend most of each class day playing computer games (since these seemed to hold his attention and decrease his disruptiveness). This sequence, in which she at first tried to manage Timmy, then grew frustrated, and eventually disengaged from him, is commonly experienced by children who have ADHD in their interactions with parents, teachers, coaches, peers, and others. Realizing that this was not in his best interest, Timmy's teacher had requested an evaluation for ADHD and consideration of an alternative classroom placement.

Timmy's mother (Mrs. J.) reported that he had always been an "active" child and that she too felt overwhelmed and frustrated by his "demands." She said his room was always messy, he did no chores, and he rarely followed directions. She stated that, as a single parent, she worked long hours so that much of the time Timmy was home with his 14-year-old sister (Patty). Like Timmy's teacher, Mrs. J. said she often found herself trying to impose strict rules and then withdrawing and "giving up" (essentially disengaging). Mrs. J., like many parents whose children have ADHD, felt she was failing as a mother. Likewise, Timmy felt as if he was a bad boy.

Thus, Timmy's experiences both at home and at school vacillated between rigid controls and detachment, even rejection. No one was in "sync" with him. That is, no one was involved and providing structure while simultaneously giving him the space and opportunity to learn to self-monitor and self-regulate. The inconsistency in how he was treated at home and at school (i.e., excessive control or detachment) was especially confusing for Timmy who, as a biracial child, also had to negotiate multiple racial and cultural heritages. That is, issues of fitting in and being accepted were more salient for Timmy because he was racially and culturally different from the majority of his peers.

Timmy met the DSM-IV-TR criteria for attention deficit/hyperactivity disorder, combined type. His symptoms of inattention and hyperactivity-impulsivity were apparent in a variety of structured (e.g., classroom) and unstructured (e.g., playground) settings.

In addition to my evaluation, Timmy was seen by the agency's psychiatrist and was placed on the stimulant, Ritalin. This referral involved a great deal of thinking through. Was Timmy simply a normal child in a disorganized family? While the family's lack of consistent structure exacerbated Timmy's problems, Timmy was exhibiting his symptoms in multiple settings, the severity of the symptoms was high, and the impact on his life was quite significant. However, concerns about the overmedication of children and about the side effects of stimulant medications such as appetite suppression, abdominal pain, irritability, sleep disturbances, headaches, and growth suppression made this a referral that had to be carefully discussed with the family and the psychiatrist (Schachar & Tannock, 1993). The psychiatrist was sensitive to the issues and she worked closely with the family to ensure that during vacations from school Timmy would be drug free.

Timmy was also seen by the school psychologist and tested. His IQ was found to be normal but his math achievement scores were below his grade level. This was probably because math performance, in particular, requires the ability to sustain attention during a potentially frustrating task.

Client Description

Timmy, age 8 years old, was thin and wiry, with dark curly hair and large brown eyes. He, and both his parents, were biracial (he had African American and Caucasian grandparents). He came to the initial intake session with me accompanied by his mother and 14-year-old sister, Patty. Timmy seemed restless in the waiting room and appeared to examine fleetingly virtually every book and toy in that room. His mother made several ineffectual attempts to contain him (e.g., saying "sit down" in an exasperated tone but with no follow-through). Eventually his sister took him by the hand and led him to a seat. Observing children with ADHD while they are still in the waiting room can be helpful because it provides the opportunity to see if the symptoms or problems that were described during the phone intake are exhibited there as well.

The intake occurred in three parts. I first met with the whole family (Patty was included since his mother indicated that she was home with Timmy most of the time). I then met separately with Timmy and separately with his mother. From the family, I wanted to find out about Timmy's behavior and the developmental factors that may have contributed to it. I especially wanted to know where and when the problematic behavior was most apparent, how they usually coped, what their daily routines were, and how they disciplined Timmy.

When I saw Timmy separately, I wanted to observe him in free play. I was particularly interested in seeing how he would respond to minimal structure. I also wanted to find out what his thoughts were about why he was coming to counseling and what he expected to happen. I also wanted to know about his friends ("Do you have any friends?" "Do you have a best friend?" "What is his/her name?" "What do you and (friend) like to do together?"), about his hobbies ("What's your favorite thing to do?" What do you usually do after school?" "Do you have a favorite television program/book/ toy?"), and his family life ("What kinds of things do you like to do with your mom and sister?" "Do you guys usually eat dinner together?" "Do you ever play or read books or go places with your mother or sister?"). In my years as a counselor I have found that even very young children are able to communicate their interests, if not verbally, by the toys they choose to play with. It is especially important to let children with ADHD know that you are interested in them and what they enjoy doing, because much of the time it is only their problem behaviors that are focused on.

Social Context

Timmy was the younger of two children. His parents had been divorced since he was 2 (although they had been separated shortly after his birth) and he had very little contact with his father who lived in another state. Timmy's father usually called on special holidays and Timmy saw him only once a year or so. Patty, his sister, was 14 years old and was doing well in school. His mother worked as a beautician and was often gone through the afternoon and early evening. The family was rather isolated, with none of their family members living close by. They knew few of the neighbors in their apartment complex and their social support came almost exclusively from their church.

Mrs. J. had grown up in another state. She married right out of high school to a man 10 years her senior. They moved soon after Patty's birth when her husband had a job transfer. When Patty started preschool, Mrs. J. went to beautician school and has worked at the same salon since completing her training.

The problems in her marriage escalated soon after Timmy was born. When her husband was offered a job promotion that meant transferring to another state, he took it and Mrs. J. stayed behind with the children. Although Mr. J. and Patty had developed a warm relationship, he barely knew Timmy. Timmy, therefore, had never had a nurturing or meaningful relationship with an adult male or father figure.

Since her divorce, Mrs. J. had dated several men, all of whom turned out to be emotionally abusive. Mrs. J. was passive and they were controlling. The relationships were all temporary and unstable and none of the men ever served as positive role models for her children. Mrs. J. also indicated that she had been increasingly depressed in recent months after being sexually assaulted by a former boyfriend.

Mrs. J. decided not to move back to her home state after she and her husband separated. She was embarrassed about the breakup, especially since her parents had disapproved of the relationship in the first place. In addition, her parents held strict religious values and she knew that they disapproved of divorce. She was also quite depressed about the breakup and moving was a task she did not feel she could manage with two young children given her depleted emotional state.

As noted before, Mrs. J. reported that Timmy had always been a "difficult" child. She said that even as an infant Timmy didn't sleep much and was hard to soothe. As in most cases of ADHD, however, it was hard to partial out all of the different factors that contributed to his presenting problems. For example, his parents had separated and divorced soon after his birth, his mother was depressed, she was also frequently irritable and unresponsive to him, and his home environment was poorly structured with no consistent daily routines. Although Timmy's school had suggested counseling in the past several years, his mother had not followed through because she was "embarrassed." She also stated that she did not expect much help from the school or anyone else given her race. She was leary of authority figures and wondered if Timmy had been singled out as a problem child because of his race. In addition, her coping style was to avoid things she considered unpleasant. However, with the school's insistence and with the encouragement of her minister, whom she trusted, she agreed to bring Timmy to counseling.

Initial Sessions

During the intake Timmy was restless with eyes flitting around the room, and hands and feet in constant motion. During our time alone, I asked him to draw a house, a tree, a person, and his family doing something together. He completed this in record time and was soon ready to move on to other activities. After the drawing activity, I told Timmy, "You can decide what you would like to play with now." He darted off quickly and played briefly, in an unfocused way, with most of the toys in the room, rarely stopping to put things away. He seemed scarcely aware that I was present. As I sat on the floor and watched the room as it became littered with toys, I was aware of how overwhelming living with this level of chaos must be for Timmy's family.

In most of my play therapy sessions, I prefer to provide minimal structure so I can see what the children will choose to do. I do, however, have a few rules: it is not acceptable to hit me or throw objects at me, and toys are not to be deliberately broken. For children with ADHD, I let them know that they may play with whatever toy they wish. However, they cannot have more than 10 items out at once, which means that at that point they must put something away before they select another toy. While Timmy continued to play, I asked him about his school, friends, and what he liked to do for fun.

I went to Timmy's school soon after the intake to observe. Timmy's impulsiveness (e.g., blurting out answers), inattention (e.g., eyes flitting around the room), and hyperactivity (e.g., restless movement, tipping his chair backwards, getting out of his seat) were all evident. Even when the teacher moved him to the computer he continued to be restless, but this was less disruptive to the class because the computer was in a corner of the room.

CASE CONCEPTUALIZATION

Client Conceptualization

Mrs. J. had a difficult pregnancy during which she gained a lot of weight, was frequently nauseous, and chronically fatigued. She was also depressed through most of the pregnancy because her marriage was clearly falling apart.

According to Mrs. J., Timmy was a difficult baby with an erratic sleep schedule, "colicky," and often inconsolable. Although his walking, talking, and other developmental milestones were within normal limits, his high activity levels and oppositional behavior made parenting him a chore. Mrs. J. thus felt as if she was failing as a mother. These feelings of failure were made even more intense by the marital separation when Timmy was a few months old, where she had also felt a failure as a wife.

Mrs. J. felt overwhelmed and depleted. As a result, it was even more difficult for her to provide consistent limits, emotional nurturing, and predictable daily routines. By the time he was a toddler, her interaction with Timmy had already solidified into a negative pattern. Mrs. J. would either yell at and reprimand Timmy, or withdraw from him and tell him that she just could not handle him or stand to be around him because he drove her "crazy."

Timmy's experience in preschool, kindergarten, and the early grades was frequently negative—his teachers found him oppositional and difficult to manage. The other kids rejected him because of his tantrums and lack of cooperativeness. Although there had been several requests from his teachers for evaluation for possible ADHD, Mrs. J. had resisted these, experienced them as demands and criticisms of her parenting, and felt that they were in part motivated by racial discrimination.

By the time Timmy was in the third grade and the referral to me was made, both his mother and third grade teacher had "given up" on discipline. At school, Timmy was failing—his class work was rarely completed and often incorrect. At home he had no consistent structure or schedule (e.g., meal times and bath times varied daily). He was socially isolated and experienced frequent rejection and criticism from his mother, peers, and teachers. The only consistent relationship he had was with his sister Patty. Timmy frequently felt frustrated and seemed unable to express his feelings except by screaming and being oppositional. Disengagement, by his mother, peers, and now by his teacher who had given up on him, intensified his experience of the world as unstructured and rejecting. As a biracial child, he had the additional task of negotiating and integrating several cultural identities, making issues of "belonging" and social acceptance more salient (see Gibbs & Huang, 1997). That is, while his disruptive behavior contributed to his isolation, he also felt scapegoated because he looked different from most of his classmates. Further, the lowered expectations reported by his teacher, who allowed him to play on the computer during class, increased his sense of being "different" and not as "good" as other kids are. Thus, Timmy's chances of succeeding at school and of developing a sense of competence and a positive self-concept were low.

Orienting Constructs

It is very helpful to know about my clients' previous relationships with important people in their lives because these relationships form *cognitive schemas*. That is, they became the basis of:

1. how they come to see themselves (e.g., good, helpless, worthwhile);
2. the expectations they have of others (e.g., demanding, rejecting, critical);
3. the primary feelings they have (e.g., sad, ashamed); and
4. the patterns they repeat with or expect from others (e.g., being left, excluded, disappointing others).

Knowing about their clients' relationships helps in understanding clients' problems more deeply, how these problems developed, and how they continue to affect their lives. When working with young children it is also useful to assess the cognitive schemas (sometimes called *templates*) of both the child and the primary caretaker and try to understand how they "fit" or dovetail.

From Mrs. J. I learned that she had grown up in a very strict home where disobedience had not been tolerated and had been swiftly punished by spankings. She coped by withdrawing and reducing her exposure to her parents' anger and criticisms. When she met her ex-husband, she was attracted to his self-confidence and was anxious to leave her parents' home. Her parents wanted her to go to college and "become someone" and they made her feel that she had "failed" them as a daughter. The failure of her marriage and her difficulties parenting Timmy further entrenched this view of herself as a failure. She expected others, including me, to be critical and see only her flaws. Her typical coping response of withdrawal was evident, for example, in not returning calls from Timmy's teacher, socializing very little with people at her church, and in the early stages of Timmy's counseling, she wanted to send him to the sessions with Patty. It was only after repeated attempts to reach her in a noncritical and nonjudgmental way that she became a more involved counseling participant. It was helpful that I could understand and express how difficult it was for her as a biracial woman and parent to deal with the criticisms she heard of Timmy, which she felt were leveled partly because of his behavior and partly because of his race. Mrs. J. felt intimidated by the "school authorities" (who, to her, represented the White establishment), and felt incapable of advocating for her son in that setting. She was visibly relieved when I indicated that I would be happy to attend meetings at the school with her and that we could deal with the school together. My goal was to provide a model for relating to school personnel which included inquiring about the services available there and assertively requesting that Timmy receive those services appropriate to his needs.

Although Timmy may have been born temperamentally an intense, active, and distractible child with low frustration tolerance, his parents' separation and divorce greatly exacerbated these inborn tendencies and made things much worse. Responses to his needs were slow in coming, did not come at all, or came at the expense of his initiative and competence (i.e., the responses were rigid and controlling). Timmy was responded to inconsistently and lacked a nurturing or secure attachment. From this he developed sense of the world as a place he could not trust to meet his needs, a place that was unstable and unpredictable. This, combined with his biracial identity, made succeeding and developing a sense of initiative, efficacy, and positive identity all the more challenging.

Thinking about Timmy's cognitive schemas for relationships, my guess was that Timmy expected others (including me) to find him unmanageable. Further, Timmy expected that I, like others in his life, would be inconsistent in limit setting and would exhibit an all or none controlling style. My guess was that he also expected me to become angry and disgusted with him and, in the end, disengage from him as others had before. It was important that I remain actively engaged or involved, set firm and consistent limits, and help him find ways to begin providing structure for himself. I wanted to provide a "secure base" for Timmy—that is, a relationship characterized by warmth, consistent interest and involvement, and predictable responses. I felt that from this base Timmy would be more willing to try new things, develop a sense of initiative, and become more socially and academically successful.

There is a delicate balance in "tracking" the child—conveying presence, availability, and responsiveness—without imposing the same agenda or demands that he/she would find at home and at school. The goal is to create a safe, welcoming place where the child can control the pace of engagement and be free to choose. This provides the child with a corrective developmental experience that fosters exploration and initiative.

Treatment Plans

Interventions focused on (1) Timmy, (2) the family, and (3) the school.

I wanted to develop a warm and consistent relationship with Timmy while helping him increase his attention span, self-regulation skills, and social skills. Most importantly, my initial treatment goal was to help Timmy develop a positive self-identity and see himself as competent and capable of success. I tried to do this by being emotionally attuned/sensitive to him on a moment by moment basis, join with him and share his experiences when he permitted, and use this contained/accepting connection to model new strategies for succeeding in school and with peers.

My goals were thus to:

1. establish a cooperative relationship;
2. increase Timmy's attention span;
3. encourage and assist in the development of self-regulation skills;
4. assist in the development of appropriate social skills and supportive social networks; and
5. help Timmy develop a positive sense of self (including a healthy bicultural identity) and increase his sense of competence and self-efficacy.

In the family, I felt it important to educate them about ADHD and help them structure the daily routines and physical home environment in a way that would optimize Timmy's functioning. I believed that this would include being empathic with the mother (and in this case, sibling, who had many primary caretaker responsibilities) regarding the strain inherent in having a child with ADHD. I also wanted to teach them better skills in managing Timmy's behavior, and assist them in implementing these new parenting practices.

I also let Mrs. J. know about the many services available to Timmy at the school such as formal evaluation by a school psychologist, alternative classroom placement, tutoring, or being seen by a resource specialist. I felt that by informing her of the services available and working with her and the school to find the most appropriate classroom placement for Timmy, I would empower her to be an advocate for her son. In this way she would also be experiencing success as a parent, one avenue toward reversing the failure-depression cycle that she had been stuck in.

The goals with Timmy's family were thus to:

1. educate the family about ADHD and the interventions necessary to improve family and social relationships;
2. help the family develop a structured and consistent routine for Timmy;
3. set up a behavioral intervention program that reinforced compliance with family rules and expectations, while giving Timmy increasing ownership of the program's goals;
4. be a resource for his mother and sister and provide for them information (including support groups, parent-education groups, and individual therapy) to improve their quality of life; and
5. encourage positive interactions between family members such as playing games and having fun together.

In the school setting, my goals were to:

1. help find the appropriate classroom for Timmy; and
2. be a resource to his teacher and help her manage his disruptive behavior more effectively.

The school and family were both open to and welcomed my involvement. I obtained written permission from Mrs. J., which allowed me to interact freely with the school on all matters regarding Timmy.

Intervention Strategies

Timmy (Individual Counseling)   I tried to learn about Timmy's interests and allowed him to choose activities he enjoyed. I was very aware of the fact that as a biracial child with ADHD, Timmy had experienced a significant amount of rejection, social isolation, and control. It seemed important that he experience me as warm, accepting, and not focused solely on his problems. In the early phase, Timmy was unfocused and highly active. When left to his own devices, Timmy emptied all the toys on the floor, creating a level of chaos that was probably characteristic of other parts of his life. He played with different types of toys such as cars, trucks, animals, action figures, transformers, but only for very brief periods. During these times he talked to himself and occasionally to me as he flew around the room. In this early stage of counseling I was aware of how often I had to remind him to put things away after use. My hope was that this would help him develop some order and also that putting things away would become a new habit. As time progressed, Timmy began to internalize this process and my reminders to put toys away were needed less. I was usually positioned at Timmy's level on the floor, eye-to-eye, and readily accessible. When Timmy approached me or offered me a toy, I would take it and join him in play. We would talk about the pirates about to attack the ship and the captain of the ship coming up with a plan to save his crew. We'd "brainstorm" solutions to the trials and tribulations faced by these brave sailors. In the context of play, we would make up adventures with solutions to the various difficulties our characters faced. An important theme in these scenes was to have the hero think, plan ahead, and anticipate the consequences of their behavior. Although Timmy was not a child who would have tolerated being read to, storytelling and playacting in this setting became one way we could be together and describe interpersonal relationships and the various ways people can negotiate these. In these stories, and in our playing, we often talked about people who looked different from each other, people who had different likes and dislikes, and people who were good at doing some things but not good at doing others. I hoped that as we did this Timmy would understand that *different* did not mean *inferior* and that he would begin to appreciate himself and his uniqueness, and thereby develop a positive biracial identity.

Routinely, Timmy would come in having had a difficult day at school and would be angry and test the limits. Once, for example, he angrily emptied several containers of toys on the floor. I remained calm as I asked, "Would you like to pick those up by yourself or would you like me to help?" (I think children attend as much to the affect in our voice as to the words we say.) He yelled, "I'm not going to pick them up." I gently took his arm and one container, sat with him on the floor, and began handing him the toys that belonged in that container. He glared at me for a few moments but then began to put the toys in the container. He seemed to be fighting back tears which I acknowledged by saying, "Thanks for putting the toys away Timmy. You seem sad, are you?" Timmy's response, between the tears, was "I can't do anything right. I hate school, I hate math, I hate myself, this is the worst day of my life." In a soothing voice I let Timmy know that it sounded like he'd had a hard day. I also let him know that we could find a way to help him with his math if he wanted that. (He got a math tutor after this incident.) I asked him to tell me about his day and what happened. I believe that being calm yet fully engaged gave Timmy a new and healing experience. In most relationships, Timmy's tantrum would have begun a negative escalating cycle with a teacher, parent, or coach yelling at him or totally disengaging. Timmy seemed aware of my different response and asked me:

TIMMY: Don't you get mad?

THERAPIST: What makes you ask that?

TIMMY: You didn't yell at me when I threw those toys down?

THERAPIST: I do get mad but find it's better to talk about it. Do you think you can tell me when you're mad or sad instead of throwing the toys like you did?

TIMMY: Okay.

THERAPIST: Besides, what I really wanted was for you to put the toys away. I thought that if we worked on it together it would be much better than my yelling. It worked. You did a great job.

In my interaction with Timmy it felt important that I be responsive and involved but not intrusive. Timmy's life had been filled with demands and rejection. Thus, minimizing rules, setting reasonable limits, and accepting Timmy's choices about what to do during our time together seemed to increase his feelings of being worthy and his willingness to engage in new activities. As mentioned earlier, I usually sat on the floor to be at his level and followed his lead. I often had in my hand toys that matched his (e.g., car, pirate) but joined him only when invited. Occasionally, I would verbalize our process: ". . . that truck sure is crashing into the van"; "Michelangelo (a ninja turtle) is really shooting that weapon"; "Looks like Tyrannosaurus is attacking Brontosaurus." Sometimes Timmy would join me and say, "Rafael is going to smash his teacher." As time progressed, we would try to help Rafael find ways to let his teacher know he was mad and to appropriately communicate what responses he needed from the teacher.

Among the important goals in our work together were to (1) increase his attention span; (2) encourage him to develop problem-solving skills; and (3) increase his ability to think before acting. Attention span was slowly increased as we colored more complex pictures, made increasingly intricate Play-Doh characters, and built with more complicated Lego sets. Problem solving was modeled as I made "mistakes" in my coloring or building and then talked myself through "fixing" the problem—telling myself to slow down, take a deep breath, take a break if needed, do one part at a time, and think before acting. I would verbally describe my feelings of frustration and encourage myself to calm down. I would also celebrate out loud completion of parts of the project so that there could be more success experiences and self-affirmation. When Timmy began to imitate me and talk himself through his own projects in the same way, I felt great joy at his decreased impulsivity and increased frustration tolerance. I was also pleased to see Timmy learning that most problems are solvable.

In addition to increasing Timmy's attention span, helping him develop interests that he could share with others seemed important. Various art, craft, and building supplies worked well because completion demanded greater attention, decreased impulsivity, and provided opportunities for problem solving when errors were made and feelings of frustration were evoked. They also became potential hobbies that could be shared with others, thereby lessening his social isolation. Timmy and I completed many projects together such as making books about dragons, pirates, and sailors; making "African" masks; building with lincoln logs, and so forth. Timmy's impulsivity was especially evident in the early stages—he would get frustrated and want to quit. One common phrase was "I can't do it" or "I won't be able to do it right." Poignantly, he clearly had developed a sense of himself as incompetent and incapable. I would gently suggest we "breathe deeply and take a break" and return to the project later. "Breathe deeply and take a break" became our coping slogan. This became our equivalent of the "Stop, look, listen, think" sequence often used to slow children with ADHD down and encourage a more thoughtful and less impulsive approach to tasks. Success experiences were increased by highlighting the completion of various segments of the project we were working on. Thus, in the early stages each accomplishment was commented on as it occurred ("Wow! That's a fierce looking dragon you made with the Play-Doh. Would you like to put him on this plate to dry?"). As time progressed, we were able to increase the length of time between positive comments. In addition, Timmy began to show greater ability to slow down, think before acting, and talk himself through frustrating experiences.

Timmy's interest in pirates and dragons inspired me to bring in a Lego set, which had pirates and dragons. I suggested we work on it together over several weeks and indicated that he could take it home when completed. He was very excited but his ability to attend was quite challenged by this project. He wanted to take it home that very same day but had great difficulty staying focused in order to complete it. We acknowledged the feelings of frustration and practiced "breathe and take a break" many times in the following weeks. To his (and my!) great delight, we completed the project and took several Polaroid pictures of it. He was beaming when he took it home and to school where he shared it with his teacher and friends. Timmy's sense of efficacy was enhanced by this experience and he found a new avenue for relating to his peers—dragons, pirates, and Legos became shared topics of interest with his classmates.

One of the major changes I saw in Timmy was his increasing willingness to try new things. I believe the structure, predictable environment, and warm relationship we had gave Timmy a sense of safety and acceptance. "Errors" and "mistakes" were just learning experiences and did not warrant rejection. This issue, of doing things "the right way," was one Timmy and I worked on repeatedly in our play and discussions. As a child with ADHD, he had often been reprimanded for not doing things "right." As a biracial child, he also had to contend with how to "fit." Who was he? Which values should he adopt? What was the "right" way to be? I wanted Timmy to understand that although there were some basic rules that people were expected to follow (e.g., not hurt others), there was no *one* right way to behave at all times. We talked about and demonstrated different ways to play games, to solve problems, to make friends, and so forth. We also talked about our similarities and differences. In this process I tried to convey to Timmy how special he was—he had relatives in different parts of the country, he had relatives who had different skin colors, and so forth. Having spent my early life in Africa, Timmy and I were able to talk about that and about my relatives who were African, European, and American. In this process I was trying to help Timmy appreciate diversity and celebrate his own multiple heritages.

About six months after starting counseling, Timmy asked that his sister Patty join us. We did this once a month. Timmy and Patty had a positive relationship that was probably due to Patty's easy-going temperament and readily apparent sense of humor. Together we established a style of interacting that was cooperative, orderly, and fun! Timmy and Patty both recognized how organization facilitated play—things were easy to find and clean up was a snap. They then decided to organize Timmy's room at home. Timmy's "ownership" of the positive aspects of structure and organization made me feel hopeful that the interventions we were engaged in would endure and generalize or extend to other parts of his life.

We got boxes, which Patty and Timmy decorated, to organize his toys. We worked together to find ways to impose some order, for example, by putting vehicles in one box, animals or dinosaurs in another, action figures or cartoon characters in another, and robots in another. Although Timmy was still prone to leave things lying on the floor, the organization improved the chaos tremendously. One of the by-products of this project and of Patty's monthly sessions with us was that she and Timmy were learning to cooperate and have fun together a lot more. Patty learned that Timmy did more of what she asked when she used humor, let him see how reasonable her requests were, and offered to help him with the chore.

Family   One of the goals was to help Timmy's family understand ADHD and make it clear that all families struggle when a member has this problem. Frequently we talked about how children with ADHD have a biologically based temperament (constitution) that predisposes them to inattentiveness, impulsivity, and excessive activity levels (Anastopoulous & Barkley, 1988; Barkley, 1985). Further, we discussed that these children have difficulty following rules and controlling or regulating themselves and their behavior. This explanation seemed to help them (as it does other families) feel less to blame for their child's problem behaviors. It also made them more open to discussions of how Timmy's behavioral tendencies interacted with family characteristics and life experiences (e.g., feeling overwhelmed and emotionally stressed) and family structure (e.g., chaos, inconsistency) to make symptoms worse. Mrs. J., like other parents, was able to have more empathy for her child—that is, that he was not deliberately out to make her life a misery.

For families who have children with ADHD, a brief (10 to 12 week) multifamily educational/therapy group (consisting of three to six families) is often helpful. Being in a group helps the families feel that they are not alone or different. The groups, which incorporate some of the ideas presented by Barkley and his colleagues (see Anastopoulous & Barkley, 1989), typically involve discussing the three core characteristics of ADHD (inattention, impulsivity, and hyperactivity) and related features (such as oppositional behavior, aggressiveness, academic underachievement, social skills deficits, etc.). Most families quickly recognize their own children in these descriptions and are able to talk about how their families have been affected by the disorder. During this time, other family processes such as family conflicts, control battles, lack of consistent routines, and so forth are discussed. Then, principles of behavior management are discussed and parents are helped to see how their child's behaviors can be changed. They learn to reinforce (praise, reward) behavior they approve of and ignore or redirect behavior they disapprove of. For example, a child jumping on furniture can be directed to jump on a trampoline instead. Or, children arguing over one toy can be engaged in an alternative activity (e.g., go ride a bike). It is emphasized that consequences (rewards and penalties) *must be dispensed immediately and consistently.* Daily routines are then examined and they are encouraged to develop more consistent and predictable home routines. The calming effect of order on children with ADHD cannot be overemphasized. Parents can get help setting up daily routines by giving them charts that have each day of the week listed. Each day can then be broken down into components (mornings, afternoons, evenings, or further into hours as needed). The "must do" tasks for each section of the day are identified and there is a space to indicate completion of the task. Various levels of rewards (requiring different numbers of completed tasks) are also identified. An important note is that children are not expected to have 100% compliance in order to earn rewards. For some, 40% completion represents "success" while the levels will likely differ for others. It is important to remember that these children have already suffered many failure experiences, so the possibility of success must be maximized.

Sometimes parents need help understanding that when their child has problems with attentiveness, it is important that their commands be direct, specific, brief, and face-to-face. For example, "Timmy, stop jumping on the couch and come sit at the table." is more effective than the more global, "What are you doing? What's wrong with you—knock it off!" It is also important that parents check to see if their child did hear and understand what he/she is expected to do. In addition, letting the child know what the consequences for not following through will be very useful (e.g., "Timmy, if you are not in this chair before I count to 5, there will be no Game Boy after lunch.") Finally, parents themselves *must* follow through consistently when their child fails to comply.

Parents are encouraged to present time-out as an opportunity for both the child and the parent to recover and think about what just happened, and to think about how to do things differently next time. They are encouraged to:

1. identify the time-out location (e.g., in the study);
2. determine how long children will be there (usually 1/2 to 1 minute for each year of age); and
3. decide how compliance problems will be dealt with. (Does the time-out chair need to be placed in the corner of the room? Does the parent need to stand behind the chair to make sure the child stays there?)

Pleasurable parent-child time is a very important part of the intervention. Parents are asked to identify one time during the following week when they can give their child 15 minutes of their undivided attention. Parents are asked to use this time to engage with the child in an activity that the child would enjoy (e.g., play hide-and-seek, ride a bike, play with cars and action figures, build with Legos, but avoid activities like TV or video games that limit talking and sharing). The parents' task is to enter the child's world and join, to the extent possible, the joy of being playful. They are to try to ignore negative behavior (don't worry about cleaning up, for example, until the *end* of the special time) and verbally reinforce all the positive things they notice (e.g., "I like soldier Joe's strong voice."). Parents oftentimes need help knowing how to interact in a playful way with their children. The special weekly time is presented as an opportunity for parents to learn about their child's interests. Sometimes parents are invited to join their child and me as we play, where I try to model joining and simply playing. Timmy's mother joined us a few times and, like most parents who receive a little instruction and encouragement, quickly progressed from being awkward and uncertain to laughing and helping us create stories about the adventures of pirates and sailors as they journeyed from one place to another.

Finally, the group provides the opportunity for discussing and devising plans for handling the most repetitive or central problems that keep coming up in their family—usually having to do with discipline and with having the child listen and respond to the parent.

Although Mrs. J. was initially hesitant to join the multifamily group, my empathy for her challenge as the mother of a child with ADHD seemed to engender hope in her. It also decreased her sense of isolation and contributed to her commitment to counseling and follow-through on the plans we developed for Timmy. It was rewarding to see her increasing sense of competence in dealing with Timmy and her decreasing sense of guilt and shame around her parenting. It was a pleasure for me to acknowledge to her how effective her new parenting approach was. The increased structure in the home, especially the consistent daily routines, also contributed to Timmy's improved behavior.

As mentioned earlier, one of the very concrete things we did was outline a typical day for Timmy. Looking at this daily schedule, we were able to identify times of high conflict (e.g., early mornings), issues of high conflict (e.g., homework, picking up the room), as well as appropriate behavior (e.g., putting clothes in the hamper). We then set up a chart of tasks for each day (e.g., meal times, homework times, bath times), which was put on the refrigerator. In order to empower Timmy he was given the responsibility for putting "smiling face" stickers on the chart for successful completion of tasks. Varying numbers of stickers earned different rewards—in this way, Timmy learned to delay gratification for the more desired rewards that needed more stickers (e.g., a trip to an amusement park).

As mentioned earlier, Timmy was evaluated by the agency's psychiatrist and was prescribed Ritalin. Compliance with the medication regime was emphasized and this was added to Timmy's task chart. He took the noon dose at school, administered by the school nurse. The psychiatrist also discussed possible side effects (potential weight loss, insomnia, growth retardation, and so forth) and recommended that Timmy be off Ritalin during school holidays. The medication seemed to be effective in helping Timmy to calm down somewhat. As typically occurs, however, his ability to focus at school improved but this did not translate into improved academic performance until this aspect was specifically attended to (i.e., his teachers and tutors worked more intensely with him using the increased attention span provided by the medication).

School   An Individualized Educational Program (IEP) meeting was held and Timmy was moved to a classroom with a lower student-to-teacher ratio. Timmy's new teacher was highly competent at implementing behavioral management techniques and her classroom was very well structured. The students had special cards at their desks, which she starred throughout the day as reinforcement for good behavior. A fully starred card yielded a special treat, such as a popsicle, special pencil, funky-looking pen, markers, or small book. Interpersonal skills (fighting, taking other people's things, learning to share, being kind by saying something nice or helping someone) were addressed frequently throughout the day, often in the context of verbally reinforcing someone for sharing or being kind. She also broke Timmy's work assignments down into smaller, more manageable components. For example, instead of asking him to complete a whole page of math, she asked him to do two or three problems at a time. In this way, Timmy was able to experience frequent completions or "successes," which increased his sense of self-efficacy. In the later part of the school year the teacher also had students work in pairs on small projects which fostered cooperation and social skills.

Timmy also had access to a tutor, who worked with him in a small (two to four) group setting. Timmy's math skills were his weakest. The tutor helped with how to approach the problems and how to cope when frustrated by modeling working through frustrating problems. She would:

1.   describe what needed to be done (e.g., I have to sum the numbers first and then I have to take 20 away from that);
2.   anticipate potential feelings evoked by the task (e.g., there's too much to do, I can't do it, I feel like screaming);
3.   suggest coping strategies (e.g., OK, I need to calm down, take a deep breath, do only the first part); and
4.   then walk through solving the problem in a step-wise fashion.

As Timmy followed this model and practiced these self-regulation skills, he and I discussed in our individual sessions how this same approach would work and be effective in his regular classroom and in social settings.

TERMINATION AND SUMMARY THOUGHTS

Timmy's improvement occurred slowly but consistently over a period of a year, with joint efforts by his family, his school, medication, and individual counseling. His mother and sister improved the structure at home, and his teacher provided him with a predictable learning experience where the limits, expectations, and consequences were clearly established in advance. In counseling, Timmy learned how to cooperate better, developed further his self-regulation skills, and had successful experiences that enhanced his sense of efficacy ("I can!!"). His temper outbursts were shorter and less frequent (he had learned to "talk" to himself and remind himself to "breathe and take a break"). As his behavior improved, his social isolation began to decrease. In particular, as his self-regulation began to affect his impulsiveness, he became less intrusive with peers and more able to wait his turn. Timmy's church played a very important role in his progress. He became more involved with his church's youth group and developed a "big brother" relationship with the youth group leader, who became an important male role model for Timmy. Timmy's mother was also encouraged to involve him in sports activities. Little league and AYSO soccer provided low-cost social outlets for the whole family. Being a team member for the first time also gave Timmy, a biracial child with ADHD who had experienced much isolation and rejection, the experience of being accepted and belonging. It said a lot when his mother told me that he wanted to sleep in his team jersey every night.

I saw Timmy once a week for a year. Although he still could have temper outbursts when frustrated and was often physically restless, he was much more composed and manageable and seemed happier. I was able to meet his new fourth grade teacher and provide information that I felt would assist his transition to that class and be useful over the next academic year. Both Timmy and his family had many challenges yet to face, but we all felt that the tide had turned and that Timmy's chances of success were greatly improved.

Questions for Thought and Discussion

1. Recall a time in childhood when you failed to meet others' expectations about something and frustrated or disappointed them. How did they respond to this? How did it make you feel about yourself? Looking back now, what do you wish they would have said or done?

2. Think of yourself as a parent, teacher, social worker, or counselor. What would be the most challenging aspect for you in responding to a child with ADHD? What qualities do you possess that would help you respond effectively and what qualities do you possess that would hinder your effective response?

Suggestions for Further Reading

Barkley, R. A. (1995). *Taking charge of ADHD*. New York: Guilford. For parents who have a child with ADHD. Provides practical and concrete information on how to behaviorally manage the child's behavior.

Barkley, R. A. (1998). *Attention deficit hyperactivity disorder: A handbook for diagnosis & treatment* (2nd ed). New York: Guilford. Provides useful information on the most current findings on the nature, assessment, diagnosis, and treatment of ADHD.

Briesmeister, J. M., & Schafer, C. E. (1998). *Handbook of parent training: Parents as co-therapists for children's behavior problems* (2nd ed.). New York: Wiley. Practical and comprehensive handbook on approaches to training parents as co-therapists for a variety of child problems.

Hallowell, E., & Rater, J. (1994). *Driven to distraction*. New York: Touchstone. Written with humor by two Harvard psychiatrists who themselves have ADHD. Helps you see how individuals with this disorder can go on to live successful lives.

7 CHAPTER

HENRY: A LATINO CHILD WITH SEPARATION ANXIETY FINDING SECURITY IN A THREATENING INNER-CITY ENVIRONMENT

THE DISORDER

It is Monday morning and 8-year-old Henry sits at the breakfast table, staring at his cereal. He has tears in his eyes and seems unable to swallow. He tells his mother that he is dizzy and feels sick to his stomach. She cajoles him to eat "just a little bit" of his cereal. After swallowing one mouthful, Henry rushes to the bathroom to throw up. Flushed, he wanders back into the kitchen. His mother, anxious and unsure of how best to respond, yields to Henry's request to stay home from school. Henry goes into the bedroom to lie down. However, less than an hour later, he is on the floor playing with his toys and shows no signs of the earlier illness. This scene, with minor variations, has been repeated often in this household. Henry's physician has been unable to find any organic basis for Henry's frequent "morning sickness." The psychologist consulted has diagnosed Henry as suffering from separation anxiety disorder (SAD), a disorder in which the child experiences severe anxiety when separation from his/her primary attachment figure is imminent. Why is Henry so terrified of being away from his mother? How did this problem develop? What is the best approach to helping Henry and his family? This chapter focuses on Henry, an 8-year-old Latino child, who has been unable to master the task of being physically separate from his mother without being overly fearful.

INTRODUCTION

Almost all children go through periods, in early childhood, when they fear separation from their primary attachment figure. This "fear" has survival value in that maintaining proximity to one's caregivers increases the likelihood that one's physical and emotional needs will be met. As they get older, however, most children are able to tolerate separation. Why are some children unable to tolerate this separation? It has been suggested that early relationships with primary caretakers form the basis on which children come to see the world and people in it (Bowlby, 1973, 1988). Children who are treated harshly, whose early needs are inconsistently met, or whose primary caretakers are themselves fearful and insecure, are at increased risk for seeing the world and people in it as undependable, hostile, or threatening. In other words, the primary caregiver's sensitive reading and prompt response to the infant's needs is crucial in helping the infant feel secure. When an infant has a sense of security, he/she experiences the world as a place in which his/her needs will be met and from which it is safe to explore and master the environment. This "secure base" becomes the basic building block on which the child can develop a sense of initiative and competence. *When the mother or attachment figure models power and confidence in her negotiation of the world, the belief that the child too is capable of such mastery becomes communicated to the child.* This secure attachment and confidence about being able to succeed in the world produces children who possess a sense of confidence and joy in life's experiences.

On the flip side of this wonderful, secure attachment, is the profound *anguish* young children suffer over the threat of losing this all-important source of security. As children grow older, they begin to master their anxiety over separation in several ways. Their increasing cognitive and affective abilities allow them to hold the image of the caregiver in mind and to experience her loving feelings, even during her absence. Games such as peekaboo and hide-and-seek play a significant role in helping children understand that objects continue to exist even when out of direct view. As children learn to crawl, walk, and talk, their sense of helplessness at the caretaker's departure is counteracted by their ability to follow, as well as by their ability to leave and return to this "secure base." When normal development goes awry, however, some children are unable to manage their intense anxiety or even panic over separation, and develop separation anxiety disorder (SAD). These children have either never had a secure attachment or have experienced a loss that has undermined their sense of security. Thus, instead of approaching the world with curiosity and confidence, they remain dependent and seem unable to separate from caretakers. This excessive anxiety about separation from parents and other attachment figures is at the core of SAD. That is, the child's symptoms emerge primarily when there are demands to separate from their main attachment figure(s).

Younger children with separation anxiety disorder typically shadow, cling, cry, plead, or have temper tantrums when separations are imminent. These reactions can be so intense that they may wish they were dead, threaten suicide, vomit, or have panic attacks. However, very young children's limited ability to explain their symptoms makes a diagnosis of panic disorder difficult. Children with SAD also have nightmares, often involving separation themes. They may also exhibit exaggerated fears of animals and monsters in the dark, and often refuse to sleep alone. Common somatic complaints range from headaches, nausea, and stomachaches for younger children, to palpitations, dizziness, and faintness for older children. Older children with SAD also tend to organize their lives around avoiding separation experiences. They refuse to go to camp, sleep over with a friend, or even run simple errands like a trip to the store. Of particular importance, approximately 75% of children with SAD refuse to attend school. The distinction between school phobia and separation anxiety disorder can be confusing. Children refuse or are reluctant to go to school for a variety of reasons. Sometimes, there is something about the school environment that causes the fear. This fear of the school environment may be experienced at the level of intensity that would justify use of the term "*school phobia*." They may, for example, not want to go to school because they don't want to be subjected to new and unfamiliar rules, or alternatively, they may fear being teased or bullied at school. Occasionally, the fear is about failure or about being compared to other children. In each example listed here, the fear has been about something in the school setting. However, the school refusal can be the result of fear about leaving the parent(s). When that is the case, the school refusal is a symptom of SAD. It appears that when school phobia or refusal occurs before age 10, separation from attachment figures is typically the more prominent concern. In contrast, when school refusal occurs after age 10, the refusal itself or something in the school environment is the primary concern (see Blagg & Yule, 1994, for an excellent discussion of these issues). It has been suggested that at times the term *phobia* may be inappropriate because children presenting with *school reluctance* or refusal do not always have the same type of intense affect seen in true phobias. Under these circumstances, the term *school refusal* may be more appropriate. In addition, the refusal may have little to do with anxiety but may be due to other disturbances such as oppositional defiant disorder or major depression (see Kearney, Eisen, & Silverman, 1995, for an extended discussion of these issues).

As noted earlier, school phobia and SAD overlap. However, they are distinct from each other. The research suggests that children who fear *separation* are prepubertal, from low socioeconomic status (SES) families and, when gender differences are found, are more likely to be female. In contrast, school *phobic* children are more likely to be male, postpubertal, and come from high SES families. Further, children with SAD tend to be more severely disturbed (i.e., have more comorbid diagnoses) and are comfortable only in the presence of their attachment figure. In contrast, school phobic children are comfortable in many nonschool settings (e.g., camping, visiting friends). In addition, the mothers of children with SAD tend to be more disturbed than the mothers of school phobic children (see Albano, Chorpita, & Barlow, 1996; Last & Francis, 1988). It thus appears that one of the major distinguishing features between children who have a school phobia versus SAD is that *children with SAD are concerned that some harm such as an accident, illness, or even death will occur to their caregiver while they are away.* That is, their school refusal is primarily related to separation fears, with school-setting concerns being secondary. In contrast, issues related to the school setting are of primary concern for school phobic children.

According to DSM-IV-TR (APA, 2000), the diagnosis for SAD is made only when the anxiety over separation is beyond developmental or expected norms, lasts for four weeks or more, begins before age 18, and impairs or disturbs important areas of the child's functioning (e.g., the ability to attend school). SAD is actually a common disturbance. It is estimated that up to 4% of children and adolescents have or will have this disorder sometime during their lifetime (APA, 1994; Anderson, Lytton, & Romney, 1986; Tonge, 1994). SAD seems to occur with equal frequency for boys and girls and, when gender differences are found, more girls than boys are reported to have the disorder (Albano et al., 1996; Last et al., 1992). The average age of onset is 7 to 8 years although it can occur anytime between preschool-school and adolescence (Keller et al., 1992; Last et al., 1992).

Knowledge about ethnic differences in the prevalence and symptom presentation of anxiety disorders is sparse. However, one study suggests that SAD occurs with greater frequency in Latino compared to Caucasian children (Ginsburg & Silverman, 1996). In addition, the Latino children presenting with SAD tend to come from families with lower incomes than the Caucasian children with this diagnosis and are rated by their parents as being more fearful. Other characteristics such age at intake, gender, and proportion of school refusal appear to be similar in Latino and Caucasian children (Ginsburg & Silverman, 1996).

Some researchers have suggested that cultures that give emphasis to compliance, obedience, and inhibition may serve to increase fearfulness in children (Ollendick, Yang, King, Dong, & Akande, 1996). If that is true, then it is possible that cultural values such as these may inadvertently contribute to anxiety disorders including SAD.

SAD is routinely co-morbid with other disorders, especially other anxiety disorders and depression (Curry & Murphy, 1995; Masi et al., 1999). For example, the excessive clinging to attachment figures can result in social withdrawal, lack of interest in other activities, and lack of initiative. These behaviors result in less opportunity to have fun, learn new things, and thereby develop a sense of mastery, competence, and self-esteem. These and other symptoms often justify an additional diagnosis of dysthymia or major depression.

SAD also must be differentiated from panic disorder (Black, 1995). In SAD, the anxiety symptoms concern separation from home and attachment figures, which may escalate to panic levels. In contrast, in panic disorder, the symptoms result from concerns about being unable to function because of an unexpected panic attack. Sometimes, a childhood diagnosis of SAD precedes the development of panic disorder with agoraphobia in puberty and later years (APA, 2000). Indeed, a large percentage of adults meeting adult anxiety diagnoses report a history of childhood SAD (Manicavasager et al., 2000). SAD may also precede other psychosomatic or somatoform disorders such as hypochondriasis (Sperling, 1982). Finally, although children with SAD often are demanding and manipulative, they are not malingering or intentionally producing the symptoms—they are genuinely terrified of separation.

Etiology

The etiology or cause of SAD is not fully understood (Rabian & Silverman, 2000). As with many disorders, both genetic and environmental factors probably contribute. It is more commonly found among relatives of those who have the disorder. It is also more common in children whose mothers (and some fathers) have mood and anxiety disorders (Martin et al., 2000). In one study, for example, 83% of mothers whose children were diagnosed with SAD or overanxious disorder had a history of anxiety disorders. In addition, 57% of these mothers had an anxiety disorder while their children were being seen for similar problems (Last, Hersen, Kazdin, Francis, & Grubb, 1987b). Researchers have suggested that the likelihood of developing SAD is probably increased by having an insecure attachment, uncontrolled and unpredictable separation traumas, and by some inborn vulnerability or predisposition (Mash & Wolfe, 1999; Wenar & Kerig, 2000). Whatever the predisposing factors are, SAD usually develops following a specific life stress such as the illness or death of a parent, relative, or pet, or moving to a new neighborhood or school. As we will see in the case that follows, 8-year-old Henry's SAD became acute after his family moved across the country, a move that coincided with his mother being ill and needing surgery.

Children with anxiety disorders, including SAD, often come from families described as overprotective, overinvolved, highly intrusive, and very restrictive (Gardner, 1992; Hirshfeld, Biederman, Brody, & Faraone, 1997; Hirshfeld, Biederman, & Rosenbaum, 1997; Last & Strauss, 1990). As a result, they curtail or limit the child's opportunities to separate or individuate. These parents (often the mothers) tend to view the world as "dangerous," are vigilant about the child's whereabouts, and constantly check up on the child. The mother's own sense of insecurity becomes communicated to the child, who also comes to see the world as dangerous and becomes afraid of venturing out. Unfortunately, reality based threats of crime, neighborhood gangs, and school violence complicate assessment and treatment. Indeed, given the high levels of uncontrollable and unpredictable traumas for inner-city children, distinguishing between a mother's realistic concerns and overprotectiveness becomes difficult. Thus, counselors working with children who live in dangerous neighborhoods or schools where violence has occurred have the additional task of addressing the impact of that environment on the children and parents.

In addition to being highly controlling, these parents also seem to expect their children to cope poorly in stressful situations (Kortlander, Kendall, & Panichelli-Mindel, 1997). This leads them to shelter their children from facing interpersonal problems with peers, teachers, and others because they perceive the child as "weak," "vulnerable," or unable to cope effectively. Unfortunately, this "benevolent" act robs the child of the opportunity to learn conflict resolution, further weakens the child's initiative, and, by not taking risks or working through problems, the child doesn't learn that there are things that he/she can succeed at. The child's dependence on the mother for all his/her social and emotional needs further confirms the mother's perception of her child as vulnerable and needy of her protection. This process hinders the child's emotional and interpersonal growth and continues the unhealthy parent-child cycle of overprotection and dependence.

Both mothers and children in these families are also reported to generally be anxious and to have histories of insecure attachments (Bernstein, Borchardt, & Perwien, 1996; Manassis & Bradley, 1994; Manassis, Bradley, Goldberg, Hood, & Swinson, 1994). These families have also been described as having difficulty in problem solving, behavior control, and family roles. In the case study that follows, we will see that Henry's mother had her own history of being insecurely attached and anxious. We will also see that she was overly protective of Henry and that she communicated to Henry her sense of the world as a dangerous place. In addition, she communicated to Henry her doubts about his ability to cope. Finally, family roles and generational boundaries were not appropriately defined in this family.

Although a variety of family interaction patterns have been observed in families of children with SAD, one of the most commonly reported patterns is "hostile-dependent." That is, the child appears to be demanding, angry, and attention seeking, often dominating an indulgent mother who, by giving in, reinforces the child's behavior (Herbert, 1974). However, as we will see in the subsequent case of Henry, the close intertwining of anger and dependence is fueled or "fed" by family dynamics in which neither the child nor the parent's needs are being met. It thus becomes important that treatment include the entire family.

The importance of treating the whole family is underscored by Gardner's (1992) observation that there is often no meaningful marital coalition in many of the families where SAD is present. For example, the father may fail to provide a corrective parental influence by accepting the mother's authority passively and fail to speak up on behalf of the child. He may be as dependent on her as the child, or may simply be uninvolved in parenting altogether. In many families where there is a child with SAD, the father and child may actually be in competition with each other for the mother's interest and attention, which the mother may inadvertently fuel by encouraging each person's dependence on her. In this dysfunctional family system, a mother-child alliance or pact that excludes the father often develops. Together these factors maintain a family system that causes symptoms and limits emotional growth and maturity for all members of the family.

Sociocultural Factors

It is very important to evaluate sociocultural factors when treating separation anxiety disorder. As mentioned before, community violence, unpredictable traumas, and uncontrollable losses complicate diagnosis and treatment. Also, cultures differentially value independence. In the case study that follows, immigration and acculturation profoundly influenced the family and the problems that brought them to treatment. As will be seen, the fact that immigration includes loss of home culture, adjustment to a new culture with another language, different belief systems, and many other challenges, increases the family's fears about additional losses, fears that are often at the core of SAD. Understanding the role of immigration and the fears it evokes can help counselors working with immigrant families be more sensitive to both the parents and the children. In particular, these families are more likely than others to need help developing new support systems and a sense of community in their new environment. Further, depending on the country from which they immigrated, they may have been exposed to a great deal of violence and sudden, unexplained disappearance of family members. Thus, community violence and distrust of the authorities may increase fears about the dangers that accompany separation. Henry, the client in this case, is an 8-year-old Latino boy who lives in the inner city of a major metropolis on the West Coast of the United States. Although born in the United States, his mother was born in Guatemala and his father in Mexico. His parents' cultural background, their immigrant status, their residence in the inner city, and their low SES are all important considerations and contribute to Henry's difficulties. Before focusing on Henry, let's discuss briefly cultural factors that ought to be explored when working with Latino children with SAD.

Sociocultural factors impact both our beliefs and our experiences. For example, having limited financial resources often means being forced to live in crowded inner-city apartments where the incidence of real crime and possible harm is often greater. Many individuals living in these environments hear about gang activities including shootings, drug dealings, robberies, and other types of crimes on a daily basis and, tragically, often witness them. The fear of becoming a crime victim is a real concern and has distressing effects on those living amidst such senseless violence and exploitation. Reality based fears about the possibility of harm make it more difficult for a responsible parent to encourage age-appropriate growth and independence in a child. Similarly, counselors wanting to encourage a parent to support their child's increasing maturity and wanting the child to behave more assertively and independently have to consider how actual danger in the environment may exacerbate the psychological dimensions underlying SAD.

In the case study that follows, the family's personal history, which included immigration from Central America, further complicated the case. The impact of coming from a country with a political history of civil war in which atrocities against the poor and powerless were committed by brutal governments had to be taken into account. As will be seen, the mother, like other parents who come from a region such as this, finds it difficult to trust government organizations such as hospitals, schools, or other bureaucratic agencies. Interventions with individuals having such a history is challenging both because they are hesitant to trust and utilize government agencies (including mental health services), and because intervention with the child often means sending the child to school, another "government-related" agency. For many, informal social support is often used rather than formal social services and, as a result, their interaction with the larger community is diminished and they may become insulated or isolated (Leslie, 1992).

In addition to the political history impacting trust, psychological adjustment is affected. Posttraumatic stress disorder, depression, and anxiety are common consequences for those who have been exposed to war and multiple separations (Cervantes, Salgado de Snyder, & Padilla, 1989). These experiences heighten sensitivity to potential losses, sensitivities that may be inadvertently conveyed to their children, who then come to exhibit the fears that originated with their parents.

For immigrants from non-English speaking countries, language can be a barrier that promotes social isolation and also decreases their use of mental health services (Acosta, 1984). When everything a person understands about the new culture must be interpreted or inferred, this can evoke a sense of powerlessness and increase misunderstanding. Often, children become family interpreters or "culture brokers." In families where parents have high self-esteem and there is healthy interdependence between family members, the role of translator can provide children with the opportunity to develop positive social and language skills that increase their self-confidence (Cervantes & Arroyo, 1994). However, when parents lack self-esteem and become overly dependent on their children for their functioning, this can become a burden on the child and can result in the parent limiting the child's attempts to individuate or develop other relationships. At the same time, this dependence can further increase the parent's sense of powerlessness, undermine their already low level of self-confidence, and limit their ability to become self-sufficient. This role reversal can create a false sense of importance in the child, along with a high sense of responsibility for the parent's well-being. It is easy to see how it can become difficult for both parent and child to let go of each other under these circumstances. Thus, an important and special feature of treatment with SAD populations where a bilingual child is the family's interpreter may include addressing parental deficits in language, reading, and writing skills. Doing so will help the parent develop a sense of independence and self-esteem, which will free the child of his/her caretaking burden, as well as provide a more positive coping model for the child.

As previously mentioned, social isolation is an important consideration when working with immigrants. In many South and Central American countries, for example, families are typically large which provides children with numerous potential caregivers and parents with multiple sources of support. Thus, children and parents, by having many meaningful relationships, are less afraid of losing each other, so there is less likelihood of SAD.

Further, in diagnosing SAD, it is important to take into account family values of interdependence, neighborhood norms, and forced and multiple separations. For example, among Mexican American youth, interdependence and cooperation is encouraged and should not be mistaken as "pathological." Indeed, socialization of this sort has great value and can help individuals and groups overcome hardships and maximize their resources. This is especially relevant for Latino families who may be faced with the stress of unemployment, financial difficulties, language barriers, and adapting to a different lifestyle in the United States. Padilla, Cervantes, Maldonado, and Garcia (1988) note, for example, that social support networks for Mexican and Central American immigrants are among the most important factors in assisting their transition to the United States. As can be seen in Henry's case, the lack of extended family and community support contributed to the mother and the child's excessive dependence on each other.

Another consideration when implementing treatment plans has to do with cultural traditions. For example, in many Latino families, bearing and raising children is very important. Further, the firstborn male child has special status, which may impact parents' comfort in imposing the firm limits and consistent consequences that are often part of interventions for children with SAD. Thus, the conflict arising from what appears to be an appropriate treatment goal clashing against a cultural value would need to be assessed and addressed.

Finally, treatment of the entire family system is also made difficult by the fact that employment opportunities are rare in the inner city and, if there is hope for continuing employment, long hours, few days off, and an inflexible work schedule are to be expected. These factors make conjoint sessions with working parents, which would be helpful in establishing appropriate family roles and support systems, difficult. The impact of factors such as these will be seen in the case that follows.

CASE ILLUSTRATION

Presenting Problem

Henry came to an inner-city family health clinic with his mother. Henry had been complaining of stomach pain and headaches, refused to sleep alone at night, and was reluctant to attend school or leave home without his mother. His pediatrician had been unable to find an organic basis for his somatic complaints. At his mother's request, he was examined again by the family physician at the clinic where I worked. This physician also found no physical basis for Henry's complaints and referred the family to me, the clinic's bilingual psychologist.

According to Mrs. A., Henry's mother, Henry had a long history of difficulty with separation. During preschool and kindergarten, Henry used to cling, cry, and complain of stomachaches and headaches whenever separations were imminent. During kindergarten, Henry's family moved to the East Coast because of his father's job. Henry's sporadic school attendance resulted in him having to repeat kindergarten. With the help of the school counselor, Henry made a marginal adjustment to his school. Unfortunately, the family had to suddenly move back to the West Coast (because of a problem at his father's job). On arrival in the West, Henry's symptoms—fear of separation, stomachaches, headaches, and school refusal—escalated. It was at this point that his mother sought help.

Henry's treatment was complicated by the fact that he was behind academically in school, had no friends, was his mother's primary support system (his father worked long hours), and his mother had a pending hospitalization for her own "stomach pains" which were said to be caused by gall stones. In addition, the family had no external support and Mrs. A. had mixed feelings about forcing Henry to go to school because of her own psychological needs and separation fears, which will be discussed further in the section that follows.

Client Description

Henry was in the second grade when he first came to the clinic. He was tall, thin, and pale. He arrived neatly dressed in a T-shirt, jeans, and new tennis shoes. During the initial interview he sat close to his mother, made no eye contact, and spoke in a low monotone. He showed little emotion and answered primarily with head nods. He frequently looked toward his mother who would then respond for him. Although Henry was able to speak both English and Spanish, his mother spoke only Spanish. Mrs. A., age 42, slightly overweight, was dressed in faded shorts, T-shirt, and worn-out shoes. She was unadorned, wore no makeup, and had her graying hair pulled straight back. Although her attire suggested low SES, she carried herself with great pride.

Social Context

Henry lived with his biological parents in a one-bedroom apartment. The apartment, located in the heart of the inner city, was in a neighborhood made up primarily of Latinos who were recent immigrants from Mexico and Central America. Gangs and drugs were major problems in the area. Henry attended a crowded local public school not far from his home.

Henry's mother, Mrs. A., was born in Guatemala, the second of five children. For unknown reasons she was given to a paternal aunt who had admired her during a family visit when she was approximately 1 1/2 years old. After living with this aunt for several months, her grandparents took her to live in their home because they believed she was being poorly cared for. As a result, Mrs. A. came to view them as her parents. Her feelings of rejection and pain at being abandoned by her biological parents continued even into adulthood. She said she asked her parents for an explanation but their ambiguous responses had failed to soothe her.

Mrs. A. was in her thirties when, feeling afraid of "being alone" for the rest of her life, she began to try to conceive a child by calculating the most likely times of conception and used this to plan her sexual relations with the man she was dating. Later, although thinking she might be pregnant, she realized her lover was uninterested in making a long-term commitment to her, so she moved to the United States with members of her extended family. She was 33 years old at this time.

In the United States Mrs. A. began working in a factory to support herself. Approximately five months after arriving, she discovered that she was indeed pregnant. She was pleased and immediately began prenatal care at a county clinic. She wrote to the father of the child but received no response. She felt, however, that she could do a good job of raising the child on her own. Tragically, the female infant was delivered stillborn. Unfortunately, she was not given the opportunity to see the infant postdelivery.

She began to suspect foul play or a major error by the hospital—for example, that the infant's identification bracelet may not have been correctly matched to hers or that the infant had been switched or taken. Given her own history of abandonment and loss, this experience was profoundly unsettling and most likely was a contributor to how she later parented Henry.

Several months after this loss, she met Mr. A., Henry's father. He was 29 years old and a recent immigrant from Mexico. Mrs. A. was three months pregnant when they got married. She described him as a good, hardworking man who made her feel safe. He worked long hours in a fast-food restaurant and so was unable to attend therapy. As noted earlier, Mr. and Mrs. A. had initially lived on the West Coast but moved to the East Coast (for two years) when Mr. A. accepted a job in fast-food management. He left that position when he found out that his boss was involved with dangerous individuals, a factor that he felt could threaten his family's safety. Unfortunately, this experience only served to reinforce the family's perception of the world as a dangerous place.

Mrs. A.'s only complaint about her husband was that he was overly strict with Henry and would intimidate Henry into complying with his requests. From her description, it seemed that Henry and his father were rivals in competition for her attention, a competition that Henry typically won. For example, although Henry was supposed to sleep on the sofa in the living room, Mrs. A. felt "sad for him because he looked so lonely sleeping all by himself." As a result, she routinely had him sleep with her, displacing Mr. A. who would end up sleeping on a second mattress on the floor. It appeared as though Mrs. A.'s own childhood deprivation and insecure attachment made it difficult for her to set or follow through with firm limits for Henry. Indeed, she often undermined Mr. A.'s attempts to set limits with Henry. This only seemed to make Henry more demanding and further distanced the couple from each other. Mrs. A. seemed to inadvertently facilitate the competition for her attention by giving ambiguous messages to each. For example, she would ask Mr. A. for help with Henry, then tell him he was being too strict. At other times she would say no to a request from Henry while smiling, and then give him what he had asked for. It made sense that Mrs. A. found the competition for her attention rewarding—it was a great contrast from the rejection and abandonment she had experienced in earlier relationships.

Initial Sessions

In the first session Henry was quiet and spoke very little. I wanted to establish a connection with both Henry and his mother so I initially saw them together.

TH: Hello Henry, it's nice meeting you.

H: (Henry nods but avoids direct eye contact.)

TH: Maybe you can tell me what has been bothering you.

H: My stomach has been hurting me a lot. (long pause . . . his mother looking at me and wanting to speak but restraining herself given that I'm looking directly at Henry)

TH: Do you know what has been making you feel that way? (I wanted to see what Henry's thoughts were about this.)

H: I don't know; it just hurts me. (He sounds almost angry.)

TH: Gee . . . that must feel uncomfortable. How long has this been going on?

H: Shrugs (His mother cannot restrain herself any longer and interjects.)

M: Excuse me, doctor, but this has been occurring for a few months now.

TH: Oh . . . what happened a few months ago?

M: There are some boys in his school that have been bothering him, hitting him. One of them is bigger and despite telling his teacher nothing seems to be done.

TH: I wonder what rough things they are doing. (I speak to both of them to see if Henry will enter the conversation and report on his experience.)

M: [looking at Henry] Tell the Doctor what they do to you. (I suspect that her tendency is to "ease" all situations for him, direct him on when to speak, or step in if he pauses or has trouble finding words for his experience.)

H: (sounding frustrated and annoyed) On the playground the other day one of them came up to me and kicked me and hit me on the back. The teacher didn't do anything when I told her . . . (pause) . . . (mother interjects.)

M: These boys, Doctor, I'm worried because these are bad children who seem to be dangerous.

In the very first few minutes of my session I was faced with trying to distinguish between parental overprotection and realistic concerns given the violent nature of Henry's community. Mrs. A.'s frequent interjections, even when I asked Henry a question directly, suggested possible overinvolvement on her part. On the other hand, Henry lived in a high-crime neighborhood. In addition, there had been recent news accounts of violence at school sites, where children had been killed. In fact, in many of those cases the violence had occurred in unlikely settings. The children who committed the acts of violence had come from financially stable families who seemed well functioning on the surface. It thus seemed important that I validate their concerns and join with them, knowing that there would be many opportunities later to work through misunderstandings.

TH: Gee, sounds like the teacher not listening makes you angry.

M: Well, Doctor, I'm very worried about something happening to him. But I'm not an educated woman. But the teachers aren't putting a stop to these kinds of things and that does not seem right. I worry how safe he will be at school.

In order to understand the mother-child dynamics, I decided to meet with Henry's mother alone. Henry was directed to a waiting room next to the counseling office, which he went to with great hesitation while looking to his mother to rescue him. As Henry left, his mother breathed a huge sigh, as though she had just been released from a heavy burden.

M: Doctor, this problem of his stomachaches and not wanting to go to school is something that began since he started school. Teachers from Head Start to kindergarten were very good at understanding him and helping me with him. I was very grateful for that . . . (Mother spoke nonstop, to the point that it was difficult for me to interject questions. I sensed some desperation and experienced a neediness about her that made me want to pull away from her. At the same time, however, I was compelled by her and felt compassion for her predicament and her painful personal history.)

Before long, there was a knock at my door. Smiling, Mrs. A. said, "I'll bet that's Henry." Opening the door, it was Henry.

H: How much longer are you going to take?

TH: I know it's difficult to wait outside.

H: 'Cause you're taking a long time . . . (He sounded whiny.)

TH: You sound really upset at us for making you wait outside . . . (pause) . . . I want to talk for a little while longer with your mother. Take this clock; when the hand is here (10 minutes later), come back and knock. Then it will be our turn to talk together. (With reluctance but seeming a little reassured by the concreteness of the clock, Henry leaves.)

M: (proudly) I knew he was going to have a hard time with waiting.

TH: You did?

M: He likes being with me a lot. He wants all my attention.

TH: How does that make you feel?

M: I like it that he needs me . . . but aren't all children like that with mothers who love them?

During the time remaining, Mrs. A. provided some background history and complained that Henry did not want to do his homework. She then asked *me* to instruct Henry to complete his homework and to comply with her requests. She also asked me not to share with Henry that she was the source of this information. I immediately grasped how she developed "alliances" and could see how Henry's dad had been placed in a "no-win" enforcer role. I knew it was important that I set boundaries, clarify my role, and model being engaged yet separate in a way that did not make her feel criticized, judged, or rejected.

TH: Let's work together to find a way to encourage Henry to pay more attention to what *you* say. I also think it is best that we not keep secrets from Henry or else he won't trust us. That would make it hard for the three of us to work together. Let me meet with Henry and then we can all talk about this together afterwards.

M: OK Doctor. Whatever you think is best.

I brought Henry back into the room and told him (with his mother present) that she had told me about his stomachaches and his difficulty getting his homework and other things done. I also said that we had agreed to work together to improve the situation. I then stated that I wanted to spend time alone with Henry to hear things from his point of view and we could play with toys or talk together. (In this process I was attempting to delineate one clear boundary—i.e., that Henry and I would also have a relationship that was separate from the one I had with his mother.) I then asked Mrs. A. to agree that what Henry and I talked about would be just between us unless we felt that it was information we thought we needed to share with her. I explained that I wanted Henry to feel free to say anything he wanted including things he might be afraid to tell her. I then indicated that Henry and I would be done in 20 minutes, at which time the three of us would briefly review the session and make plans for future meetings.

Mrs. A. seemed distressed by this but agreed after I explained the importance of giving Henry the opportunity to express all he thought and felt without fear that it would be told to his mother and potentially displease her. I also noted that just as I had spent time with her alone, it was important that I spend time with Henry alone. She then reluctantly left the room. Clarifying these boundary issues was essential given the difficulty this family had understanding that having a special relationship with more than one person was appropriate and healthy.

After Mrs. A. left, I tried to interest Henry in the items in my office (toys, pictures, crayons). Henry's lack of interest or curiosity was in great contrast to other children I counsel who usually either get out of their seats to touch the toys or at the very least look at them from far away. He seemed more focused on his mother. I warmly invited him to explore the room and explained to him that the purpose of counseling was to talk openly and see if we could together find a way to help him feel safer and enjoy school and his family more. Henry hardly moved from his chair but, after many attempts to engage him, he did convey his interest in trains (his family had traveled this way from the East Coast). He also said that he might like to be a pilot when he grows up. His interest in modes of transportation was fascinating given his presenting problem: fear of separation.

At the end of this intake, we discussed counseling options and Mrs. A. chose to continue with me.

CASE CONCEPTUALIZATION

Client Conceptualization

Henry's complaints are best understood within the context of his family's history.

Parental Background   According to Mrs. A., she had been sexually active without birth control from age 17 on. Her calculated attempts to get pregnant in her thirties seemed to arise out of her fear of being alone, as well as her wish to have someone who would love her unconditionally and never leave her. Her childhood attachment to her parents had been fragile. Being given to an aunt who was a poor caretaker increased her sense of the world as an uncaring, unpredictable, uncontrollable, and dangerous place. It also increased her feelings of being somehow defective and unworthy of being loved, wanted, or cherished. Knowing this helped me have empathy for Mrs. A., whom I experienced as a desperately needy person, whose needs were so large that no one could realistically meet them. My experience of Mrs. A. also helped me have empathy for Henry, just a child, yet having to make up for his mother's suffering and meet her enormous emotional needs.

The tragic death of Mrs. A.'s first child only served to increase her suspicion of the world as dangerous, people as malicious, and relationships as tenuous and readily lost. The economic and social hardships she faced as an immigrant, and her husband's job on the East Coast with a man who was involved in dangerous activities, further increased her feeling that she was at the mercy of hostile forces over which she had limited control. Understanding life experiences that make people act the way they do helps me be more compassionate than judgmental, which is important in a case like this where a child's psychological life is being sacrificed to meet a parent's disowned need.

Mrs. A. often wondered why Mr. A. had married her, especially since she was older than he was. It seemed, however, that the age difference might have made her feel somewhat "maternal" and needed by him. Mrs. A generally felt that good things would never come her way. However, these negative expectations were disconfirmed when she became pregnant with Henry and he was born healthy. At the same time, Henry's birth reevoked her many feelings of loss. She was reminded of being an unwanted and poorly cared-for child, of being rejected by her first child's father, and of the death of her first child. Perhaps to ward off her intolerable feelings of loss, Mrs. A. continued to deny that her first child had indeed been stillborn. After Henry's birth, she spent countless hours writing to governmental agencies requesting their help in finding this child whom she believed was still alive.

In an unfortunate twist, Mrs. A. was unable to give Henry the full and total loving devotion and attention that she so desperately wanted. That is, her preoccupation with finding her daughter after Henry's birth hindered her ability to relate to *Henry's* needs. Henry was always "competing" with his dead sister for his mother's attention—he never knew when she would be emotionally available to him or when he would be shut out by her melancholy. In a similar way, Henry's father also experienced Mrs. A.'s preoccupation and emotional absence. In reality, neither Henry nor his father could compete successfully with Mrs. A.'s memories, sorrows, or preoccupation. They could, however, compete with each other for the time she was emotionally available, and this is what they did, vying for control of the small part of her that was intermittently available to them.

Mrs. A.'s history of loss and rejection made it hard for Henry to explore the environment or establish other relationships because this would represent "leaving" her and cause her great pain. So he complied by becoming anxious whenever separations were imminent. In addition, Mrs. A. communicated to Henry her view of the world as hostile, which he began to internalize. In time, Henry began to accept his mother's verbal and nonverbal messages that he could not manage his way in the world without her and that emotionally she could not manage without him.

Unfortunately for Henry, he did not have a father who was physically and emotionally present to provide a corrective buffer to counter his mother's inconsistent and insensitive parenting. Henry's father worked a great deal and, when he was home, was often fatigued. Further, Mr. A. expected Henry to be unquestioningly compliant. He also harbored some anger at Henry's intrusion on the marital dyad, particularly since Henry usually slept with his mother while he slept elsewhere. Clearly, family roles and intergenerational boundaries were not appropriately defined. Henry and his father often behaved like siblings fighting for the mother's attention. Mother had difficulty setting firm boundaries with Henry but also undermined the father when he did. Further, the marital relationship lacked strength. Mother generally took Henry's side in criticizing the father's harsh manner. While she believed that the father was too dominating, the father felt that she was too permissive. Thus, the primary alliance in this family was between the mother and Henry. The parents were not working together as a team. This indicated that it was important to work with the whole family—to increase caring and support between the couple, help develop reasonable parenting roles, and help each of them have a special, loving relationship with Henry.

Henry's Relationship to His School   Henry's perception of school was negative. He wanted to stay home in part because he was anxiously attached to his mother and in part because he wanted to avoid the school's structure and expectations. Henry and his mother colluded in this avoidance by blaming the school, the teachers, the students, and the system of rules for their problems. That Henry had difficulty with initiative, peer relationships, and completion of school tasks is not surprising. Historically, Henry's attempts at autonomy and initiative had been sabotaged/undermined by his mother who let him know that this would represent more loss and pain in her life; further, that the world was too dangerous a place for Henry to manage on his own. Any negative feelings Henry might have had regarding how his mother limited his exploration of the world and other relationships could not be directly or assertively expressed to his mother—it would only cause her further pain and he would risk losing the little connection he did have with her.

Culture   Henry, as a child of parents from two different countries, living in yet a third country, was faced with significant cultural and identity conflicts. His mother's birthplace, language, and physical features were Central American and his father's Mexican American. These differences, and the animosity that existed within his community between Mexican and Central American families, made neither community a safe haven for Henry. Further, within his inner-city home and school, Henry lacked healthy role models for relating to others and the world and this increased his sense of isolation and disconnectedness. Henry's insecure and anxious attachment in his home was further exacerbated by sociocultural factors: his family's unstable economic status; the dangerous, volatile neighborhood in which he lived; and the fact that the larger society often devalued people from his ethnic background simply on the basis of their physical characteristics. Thus Henry was faced with the tremendous challenge of integrating the cultures of his mother, his father, and the community within which he lived (Garcia-Coll & Meyer, 1993).

Orienting Constructs

Mrs. A.'s history of disrupted attachments made it difficult for her to provide Henry with a secure base from which to launch and become an autonomous, curious, active, joyful child. Without really being aware of this role reversal, she wanted Henry to give her the utter devotion she had lacked as a child—a daunting task that he could not realistically fulfill, of course. Henry also was placed in a position where he could not have any interests that excluded his mother because she would experience these as rejection. Henry had nowhere to go: he did not have permission to move out into the world and have his own life; at the same time he was emotionally deprived in this binding tie to his mother since she was unable to attend to or respond to Henry's real needs. She was often preoccupied with thoughts of her dead daughter and with questions regarding her parents' reasons for giving her away as a child to a relative who was negligent. Such double-bind or lose-lose conflicts are often in play when children have serious long-term problems.

Beyond the complex issues in these convoluted familial relationships were the real and imagined dangers in the environment. Their living situation was unstable—they lacked economic security, had little social support, lived in a dangerous neighborhood, and felt alienated in the school setting. Their predisposing bias to perceive the world as dangerous and people as likely to be malicious made sense in some reality based ways and interacted to increase Henry's fear of venturing out and exploring his world. Staying close to his family was the "safest" alternative, yet it robbed him of developmentally appropriate experiences that would facilitate growth and emotional maturity. Henry lacked the language, emotional support, and psychological awareness to express or even recognize his feelings and needs, such as anger at his mother who was inadvertently emotionally crippling him by her neediness. Henry was in a no-win situation—his only "safe base" was inconsistently available to him but he was not allowed to seek security or rewarding relationships elsewhere because this would wound his mother and threaten their fragile relationship. Given these circumstances, Henry's "solution"—separation anxiety—made great sense.

TREATMENT PLANS AND GUIDELINES

Although there has been some empirical support for the use of the tricyclic antidepressant imipramine in treating SAD (Gadow, 1991), these studies are often confounded by the fact that SAD tends to be co-morbid (co-occur) with other disorders such as depression. It is painful to see these children's intense suffering as they perspire, become sick to their stomachs, or begin to hyperventilate at the thought of leaving for school. Fortunately, SAD is readily responsive to psychological interventions.

One of the first treatment goals for children who have SAD is to help them return to school *as soon as possible.* They need to catch up academically but, more importantly, the longer they avoid school, the harder it is to get them back in the classroom. School also provides a setting where they can begin to develop peer relationships and social skills. However, returning the child to school often evokes significant family dynamics (e.g., the mother's sense of loss and increasing depression) that must be addressed or the intervention won't succeed. Parents who have a child with SAD often have their own history of insecure attachments, disrupted relationships, and separation fears. It thus becomes very important that the therapist become a safe, empathic, secure base for the parents so they can learn better ways to cope with these problems (e.g., talk about these anxieties with the therapist rather than have the child express these in his/her behavior). When the parent has an appropriate adult resource, such as an emotionally responsive therapist, he/she is less likely to "hold on" to the child. The therapist's "holding environment" for the parent does not resolve the long-standing dependency problems, of course, but it does provide temporary relief that can allow the child to return to school and for other family changes to begin. The parent can also be reassured that being firm and following through with sending the child to school, even though the child protests mightily, is in the child's best interest. The child's return to school will be successful *only* when the parent can say in a firm and unambiguous voice (i.e., without weeping or looking forlorn while they are saying it): "I will be fine while you are gone, and I want you to go to school now." This core intervention sets many other changes into motion, such as propelling the parent to build a stronger relationship with his/her spouse, to develop other adult sources of support, and to find new interests that will increase his/her sense of esteem and self-efficacy.

In addition to addressing family dynamics, school issues will need to be focused on. Realistic concerns regarding safety in the school setting must be addressed. School personnel can be very helpful in making reality based assessments of the actual degree of danger and suggesting concrete steps to increase safety (e.g., recommending that the child stay close to the playground supervisor, avoid certain areas at school, sit in the front seats of the bus). In addition, the child is likely to have already missed a lot of school and will be academically behind, which might mean finding a tutor or other resources. Teachers can also help the child develop friendships and begin to find activities that this particular child might enjoy and have success with.

The process of returning the child back to school may need to be gradual so the child is not retraumatized and successful reentry is more likely. This plan requires a timetable for returning the child to school, which will call for a certain amount of patience and collaboration from the teacher. Finally, if the child cannot attend school at all, she/he must spend the time at home away from positive reinforcements such as TV, toys, and computer games.

SHORT-TERM GOALS

1. Provide a holding environment (harmonious, empathic, understanding relationship) for Henry's mother.
2. Explore issues and role-play interventions so Mrs. A. can unambiguously encourage Henry to return to school.
3. Use understanding and avoid blame while helping Mrs. A. learn how she may inadvertently be contributing to Henry's separation fears.
4. Assess and differentiate real from imagined danger in the school and formulate a plan for Henry's return to school.

INTERMEDIATE GOALS

1. Provide Henry with a safe counseling environment where he can play and express himself, including his insecure and anxious attachment to his mother and his fear of the world as dangerous.
2. Help Henry identify his needs, interests, and abilities, while supporting all attempts at autonomy and initiative.
3. Strengthen the marital relationship and encourage Mrs. A. to seek support from her spouse rather than from Henry.

LONG-TERM GOALS

1. Help the family identify interests and support systems in the community.
2. Increase positive contact between Henry and his father.
3. Support appropriate family roles (parental, spousal, child).

Short-Term Goals

Mrs. A.'s history of frequently disrupted attachments made it clear that she needed therapy in order for her to allow Henry to individuate. Since our center lacked another Spanish-speaking therapist, I decided to divide each session into time alone with Henry, time alone with his mother, and time with both together. I planned to eventually include Henry's father so that we could have the whole family working together.

In my sessions with Mrs. A., I wanted to convey my consistent availability while still maintaining my separateness. So I was always focused, attentive, and responsive—and frequently highlighted how we could see things differently yet still be connected and caring. I hoped that the security provided by our relationship and insight into the origin of her own (and Henry's) anxious attachments would make it possible for her to unambiguously encourage autonomy and initiative in Henry.

The initial "mother only" segments of the sessions were thus spent building the relationship which included listening, being empathic, and validating the disruptive nature of her losses. Mrs. A.'s tremendous need to be heard and responded to was evident in the way she drew my attention to her dramatic stories. It was often difficult to end the counseling segments with her in order to meet the whole family. I felt both compelled by her and overwhelmed by her. As before, my own strong feelings of being overwhelmed told me much about the great pressure Henry was living under. Trying to meet some of her needs and free Henry from this weight, I often verbalized what I thought was going on: "It sounds like you have so much pain at times that you feel desperate to be heard." She seemed to feel comforted that the emotions below the words were being seen and responded to.

Mrs. A.'s difficulty setting limits was evident in her requests that I tell Henry to do his homework and in other requests that I assume the authority/parental role with Henry. I suspected, however, that if I did this I would come to be perceived as harsh and stern like his father. In addition, by having me take on the parental role, Mrs. A. could avoid the psychological conflicts that would be activated if she set limits with Henry. I suggested that the best long-term solution was helping her set limits. I worked with her on her deep fear that Henry would become angry and reject her. I also highlighted how appropriate limit setting was already contributing to Henry's social and academic progress as he was now completing tasks more and making friends at school. Mrs. A. also talked about her fear that something might happen to Henry when he was away from her. We were able to address these fears and acknowledge that the loss of her daughter and the neighborhood instability and violence added to her fears. We talked about ways to increase her sense of security regarding the realistic dangers in the neighborhood (e.g., get to know the neighbors so they could watch out for each other's children, involve Henry in supervised activities, walk him to and from school). We also *differentiated* Henry and his life situation from that involving her deceased daughter and from her own childhood, noting that Henry had two loving parents who would never give him away and who wanted him to succeed in life. I encouraged Mrs. A. to pay close attention to how she expressed (verbally, emotionally, and behaviorally) her fears about the dangers of the world, and what she communicated to Henry regarding his ability to manage in the world. I highlighted the long-term benefits of independent functioning for Henry and encouraged her to share her fears with me or with her spouse, instead of acting them out with Henry.

In the "child only" segments, Henry was encouraged to find toys and play. The goal of this process was to provide Henry with the opportunity to identify interests that were *his* own. In addition, this was presented as a safe place for him to play and master his fears. I did not want to reenact his experiences with his parents so I was careful to not be demanding, controlling, or intrusive. Whenever he expressed an interest in an activity, I was supportive and affirming of that. Henry often seemed conflicted about the extent to which he wanted to include me in his play (e.g., sometimes he would turn his back to me or exclude me in some overt way). However, he almost always came back to me and handed me the toys at the end of our sessions. I would always respond warmly so he knew that I harbored no anger at the exclusion. Henry, like most children with SAD, needed to experience full acceptance of how he chose to structure his time. When he handed me the toys I would say, "I'm glad you came in today, let's put these away together." Putting the toys away together felt important because it communicated behaviorally Henry's responsibility for completion of tasks—including this one.

Henry's sense of himself as a victim (i.e., that teachers were unfair and demanding, that his father was harsh and stern), which was often supported by his mother, was replayed with me when he accused me of picking on him and making his parents be mean to him. I acknowledged his anger and invited him to share this with me. During one individual session, after Henry's parents had implemented my suggestion that they block out time to be alone, Henry had difficulty containing his anger at me. He yelled, "I hate you, I don't want to come here anymore" and used several foul words. I let him know that I appreciated him letting me know he was angry but that the foul language was not okay. I continued to interact with him and asked if he wanted me to join him in the game he was playing. I believe my ability to set limits (regarding the foul language) *and* remain involved and interactive was a critical turning point. After this, Henry began to act out his anger in play (cars crashing, action figures fighting, etc.). Over time Henry's play became more controlled (the cars would, speeding toward each other, say "watch out" and not crash; the figures would help each other build armies and discuss strategy for beating the other side). By this time Henry was including me in his play more consistently and I had the opportunity to suggest alternative strategies for "winning."

In the initial "family segments," we focused on getting Henry back to school. We discussed Henry's fears about the school setting and his complaints that several boys were bothering him. It turned out that they were not gang members and that there had been no reports of violence on Henry's campus thus far this year. Henry acknowledged that he could avoid these boys by spending his recess elsewhere. It seemed, from his description, that they enjoyed pushing him around, throwing sand at him, and teasing him because he was easily upset. They often called him a "baby." Henry and I role-played and rehearsed him saying, "I don't like you teasing me," without crying. I also called the school while Henry was in my office and talked to the vice-principal, who agreed to talk to the boys in question. Henry seemed relieved by this and told me the following week that the vice-principal had told the boys that they would lose their recess if they hit him or threw sand at him. The vice-principal also suggested that Henry try to avoid these boys and stay close to the playground supervisor during recess.

I accompanied Henry's mother to a school conference where it was decided that Henry would be placed in a smaller class. I also asked the school about programs that were available to Henry (tutoring, free lunch, etc.). With my support, Mrs. A. was able to assertively request the services she felt were appropriate for Henry. One recommended program was the Student Study Team (sometimes called the Child Study Team). The team included the parent and school personnel (i.e., the referring classroom teacher, another classroom teacher who is an ongoing member of the team, the bilingual resource teacher, the resource specialist, the Chapter I learning/reading specialist, the school nurse, and the principal). The team meets regularly, either weekly or bimonthly, to discuss student(s) who are not succeeding. Tests, student work samples, and anecdotal information are analyzed, and suggestions for remediation are made. Progress is monitored on a regular basis.

Some examples of interventions that were proposed included having the classroom teacher develop, monitor, and reward Henry for improved school attendance, using a Student Behavior Contract signed by the student, the teacher, the parent, and the principal. The resource specialist arranged for Henry to take a battery of tests to determine grade level proficiency of basic skills and appropriateness of current grade placement. Based on this, Henry's needs for special services including tutoring, reading or math lab, or special education was determined. Henry received many of these services and the Chapter I reading specialist (a bilingual resource teacher) provided Mrs. A. with a copy of the school's multicultural activities listed in the School Improvement Plan. Henry was matched with the teacher who they felt would be the most compatible both academically and emotionally. In Henry's new class, the teacher used a variety of strategies to facilitate his success. She modified the time he was allowed to complete his assignments, did a "time-on-task" assessment so she could identify ways to help him increase task completion, and set up cooperative learning experiences to improve peer relationships while increasing task completion. She made the learning experience more pleasant by setting up small group instruction and "hands-on activities," and integrating topics that were of interest to the children in her lesson plans. By using a multifaceted approach, she was able to facilitate learning, and Henry's progress was shared at subsequent Student Study Team meetings. The teacher and the team felt strongly that Henry's small groups experiences were helping him begin to build some bridges toward developing new friendships.

Mrs. A., Henry, and I met with his new teacher and we devised a "return to school" plan. During the first week, Mrs. A. would accompany Henry to his classroom but stay in the back until recess. At this point, the teacher would walk Henry out to recess and be his transitional object. I asked the teacher if there were any children in the class who might be able to respond supportively to Henry and include him in their activities. Looking back, finding at least two responsive classmates may have been the most helpful intervention in this case. Nevertheless, working to build peer relationships, I noted Henry's interest in trains and airplanes in order to help the teacher identify another student in the class with similar interests. Thus, during this first week, the teacher engaged both Henry and this other student (Robert) in conversations about trains during recess. Although Henry continued to be distressed by his mom's absence following recess, he did stay at school all week. He continued to complain about stomachaches in the morning but he was less resistant to getting ready for school.

During the second week Mrs. A. stayed only for the first 45 to 60 minutes and, at the teacher's signal, left. The teacher would signal Mrs. A. to leave at a time when she was able to be close to Henry's desk so she could again be the transitional object. The teacher would then walk Henry out at recess (preferably with Robert also) and tell Henry where she could be found if he needed her. During the third week, Mrs. A. would take Henry to school but leave as he entered the classroom with the teacher.

An important part of this intervention was to coach Mrs. A. on how to deal with Henry each morning. She was instructed to respond to his functional needs (getting dressed, getting breakfast, etc.) and clearly state "I want you to go to school today." She was to *ignore* his complaints (even though this would be very difficult for her) and, at the end of each day when she picked him up, tell him how proud she was that he was going to school. Knowing how difficult it was for her to deny Henry anything (in this case refusing to let him stay home), I told her that I would check in with her at a certain time for five minutes during the first week. During those calls I would say something like: "I can understand that you are questioning if you are doing the right thing and are worried that Henry might become angry at you. As you and I have talked about before, Henry will be much better off in the long run if he has an education and can manage on his own. Going to school will help him later when he is ready to find a job. You are being a good mother even though it feels hard right now." Mrs. A.'s involvement in this return-to-school plan seemed to help her realize that she had the power to help Henry. I also found out later that Mrs. A. developed a good working relationship with Henry's teacher and would frequently talk to her about Henry's progress. This was also facilitated by the school's efforts—they placed Henry with a teacher who spoke Spanish, invited Mr. and Mrs. A. to observe the classroom whenever they wished, conducted testing to evaluate more formally Henry's educational needs, and monitored the boys who had been bullying Henry.

Mrs. A.'s issues with boundaries became apparent in her frequent distress calls to me, which she generally began with "I'm really sorry to bother you, Doctor." I needed to balance being available and supportive while setting limits. I compromised by acknowledging my inability to continue responding to the calls but indicated that I could see them twice a week instead. This turned out to be an excellent solution since it seemed to provide Mrs. A. with a greater sense of security and continuity from session to session. Knowing she would see me in a few days made it more possible for her to contain her anxiety with Henry and save it for me.

Mrs. A.'s improved relationship with bureaucracies (including the agency I worked for and the school) made her less suspicious and distrustful of her environment. Her decreased anxiety about the malevolence of others was conveyed to Henry by her attitude—she was able to send him to school and let him know she believed the school could provide adequately for him. This change came, of course, later in the therapy process.

Intermediate Goals

As treatment progressed, Mrs. A. became less preoccupied with her deceased daughter, her parents having given her up, and Henry's safety. With this very significant progress, we then began to focus on her marriage. I invited Mr. A. to the sessions and we were able to arrange times so that he could come occasionally. The mother only segments during these times became devoted to couple issues. They were encouraged to share more parenting responsibilities as well as find time to be alone as a couple. Mr. A. was eager to have greater intimacy and privacy with his wife. He also felt that his wife was unable to discipline Henry but undermined him when he did. She was able to point out that his interaction with Henry was largely disciplinary. Together we were able to develop guidelines for discipline, as well as for having fun together.

In my individual sessions with Henry, we began to talk more to each other. I would ask about his interests, whether he had made any friends at school, and about wishes/dreams he had (e.g., "If you could wish for any three things, what would they be?"). I was attentive to both verbal and nonverbal language. I often tried to verbalize what I thought he was communicating (e.g., I might ask, "Would you rather play alone right now?"). During one memorable session, Henry was lying on the floor and playing with two action figurines. Suddenly, one of the figurines said (Henry doing the talking for each figure, in Spanish) "I don't want to play with you anymore." The other figure then doubled over and said, "When you say that you hurt me so much. Don't you know that you are my best friend?" At this point, Henry stopped and seemed frozen. His eyes filled with tears. I moved closer to him and said, "People can do different things and have different interests and still care about each other. Sometimes even best friends want to do different things. It's OK to be different. It doesn't mean you don't love that person."

During the family segment that followed, Mrs. A. stated that Henry had been rude to her earlier in the week and had yelled that he hated the television program she was watching and wanted to do something else. She reported that she was so upset by his tone that she went to the bathroom and threw up. She then told him how his rudeness made her sick. Henry had, for the rest of the week, been subdued at home. This event illustrated so powerfully the conflict Henry was faced with: expressing his differences with his mother would make her sick—he needed to contain himself and follow her lead if he wanted her to be healthy. With clarity, firmness, but genuine caring, I explained to Mrs. A. that when Henry heard her say that, he could easily come to believe that he was responsible for her physical illness and that he had the power to control her health. Over time, Mrs. A. began to understand that Henry often felt that whenever his interests did not match hers, she would become sad. As a result, Henry was often afraid of expressing himself, developing his own interests, and becoming an independent, assertive human being. She also began to understand that success, especially in U.S. society, was based on Henry's ability to develop initiative and to be able to be respectfully assertive. We did address the need for Henry to learn to express himself in an assertive and nonaggressive manner. We spent many sessions focusing on this issue of being separate (having separate interests, needs, etc.) *and* still being connected. Henry and his mother each began to identify their likes and dislikes and were able to see that the differences here made them no less caring about each other. Henry was relieved that he could develop his own set of interests, *some* of which might be similar to mom's, some to dad's, and some to none of them.

Although encouraging assertive self-expression in Henry was a reasonable goal, I had to be careful that this goal not violate culturally sanctioned humility, especially in regard to interacting with elders. The emphasis was on being both assertive and polite (e.g., "May I choose a TV program today?" versus pouting or angrily demanding to choose the program). Henry and his mother came to notice that negotiating politely was more pleasant than not expressing their wishes and feeling angry that their needs were not being met.

I monitored Henry's school progress during the first month of his return to school by making a weekly call to his teacher. After the first month, Henry was attending regularly although he now showed some dependence on the teacher. There were both successes and failures with other children, but Henry was slowly developing age-appropriate relationships.

Long-Term Goals

A major portion of my work with Mrs. A. was to highlight the importance of letting Henry know that she saw him as capable of doing things for himself and by himself, and that she could function in the world without him. She was encouraged to share the details of her physical problems (e.g., stomachaches) and her fears about them with her husband and other adults so they did not threaten the security of Henry's world. We explored establishing supportive relationships with members of her extended family, making friends with neighbors, joining support groups, or getting more involved in the church. In giving Mrs. A. individual time in session, she was beginning to explore her own issues and her levels of depression and anxiety were decreasing. It was clear that her comfort and sense of effectiveness within her environment was setting the stage for Henry to feel more comfortable about exploring his own world and establishing new relationships.

Mrs. A. also began to develop more self-confidence and began to learn to assertively ask for what she needed. Initially, she had difficulty communicating clearly and giving direct instructions about what she wanted. She began to see, however, that speaking firmly with conviction would help give Henry a model of assertive communication and would likely be rewarded by increased compliance. I had concerns that if the mother was not effective in communicating her own needs, she might express her anger in passive-aggressive ways. Thus, an additional aim of counseling for the mother was to help her become more assertive, to express herself more clearly, and to identify her needs so she could develop her own interests and become more independent.

Mrs. A. decided to take English classes through adult education. Her successes here prompted her to seek assessment of vocational interests with the goal of obtaining some training so she could develop marketable skills and eventually contribute to the family's finances. She was enlivened by this process and even became an active member of the PTA at Henry's school.

In our individual sessions Henry and I began to address more overtly the bind he had been in—that if he developed as a separate, autonomous being he would hurt his mother and ultimately fail anyway since he was weak and the world was dangerous. We did this as we built model airplanes or played with train sets. I hoped that in counseling Henry would have the experience of being separate but still connected. That is, I hoped that he would identify interests and engage in activities that were of *his* choosing, know that I felt no anger, and know that I felt great pleasure at seeing him find things that brought him enjoyment. Together, Henry and I played a modified soccer game in the office. For several weeks we would push the furniture to the side and establish the game rules. As we played, I would cheer Henry on as he tried to get the soccer ball away from me. I would then draw connections between our play and the outside world—that when Henry very much wanted something (like he did when he was trying to take the ball away from me), he needed to be able to "challenge" and go for it assertively. Similarly, when he had something that he wanted to hold onto, saying "no" and keeping it away and to himself (just like he fended me off from taking the soccer ball) was not hurting anybody but was quite appropriate. Henry and I also talked about how asserting one's self was part of learning how to get along with others.

Henry was in the process of changing from a passive and angry child to one who was more assertive and confident. He told me that on one occasion a kid had pushed in front of him in the class line and Henry had told him not to and took his place back from this kid. Henry had also begun asking his father if he would play soccer with him and they were doing this several times a week. I enjoyed hearing how Henry wanted to repeatedly engage his father in the same "challenge the ball" exercise that we had been practicing in my office. Henry seemed to relish being able to challenge his father in this physical way and delighted in seeing his father's determination to protect the ball. What an appropriate arena in which to compete, rather than for Mrs. A.'s attention! Some of the neighborhood kids had also begun to join Henry and his dad playing soccer and Henry had been invited to one of those kids' birthday party. To further these important gains, Henry's parents were encouraged to involve Henry in a city soccer team where Henry could be involved with other boys his age.

Mr. A. continued to attend the sessions as his time permitted. Mrs. A. was discouraged from letting Henry sleep with her. Instead, she was encouraged to make an alternative sleeping space for Henry that was as pleasant as possible. For example, I encouraged her to let him have a train night-light and, if possible, to buy him a quilt with airplanes or trains on it. Mr. A. was very much in favor of this and even worked an extra shift to purchase these items!

Mrs. A.'s fear of Henry's anger and possible rejection if she was firm with him was directly addressed. This process was reframed to make her see how, at times, painful or difficult processes were necessary for good outcomes. I used the example that for her to get her gall stone problem healed she would need to go through treatment—which would likely be painful or difficult, but that the treatment was necessary for her to get fully healed.

Thus, appropriate family roles became focused on more as time progressed. Mr. and Mrs. A. were coached on parenting issues (implementing a time-out program, withdrawing certain reinforcements when Henry was rude or noncompliant with their requests, rewarding him for appropriate behavior, giving him clear and unambiguous directions about what was expected of him, etc.). Mr. and Mrs. A. were also encouraged to discuss their differences about parenting in privacy and not allow Henry to manipulate them based on these differences, as had occurred in the past.

TERMINATION AND SUMMARY THOUGHTS

Termination was addressed when Mr. A. found a job with medical benefits in an adjoining city. The family realized that while they could benefit from further counseling, their overall functioning was significantly improved. We thus agreed to schedule sessions once a month until they were settled in the new city and Henry was settled in his new school. I was able to support them psychologically as they made the move and Henry's teacher and school psychologist were very helpful in facilitating his transition to the new school. Although Henry complained of stomachaches the first week at his new school, these complaints had all but disappeared by the time I saw them a month later. Probably the most important factor in adjustment was his mother's improved mental health and her unambiguous encouragement that Henry go to school.

I saw Henry and his family for a year, sometimes seeing them twice a week. We terminated after his family moved to a new city although I did have one final session with them after they had moved. Mrs. A. was encouraged to join a support group for parents who had had a child die (e.g., Compassionate Friends). Henry's school psychologist had suggested he become involved in a school based counseling program that included group therapy. The opportunity for increased contact with peers seemed like an excellent one. Henry was also on a soccer team and his success as a "strong player" increased his self-confidence greatly. It also provided him with the opportunity to develop friendships with children his age and there was no mention or concern about bullies for the first time.

Henry and his parents liked the teacher at his new school and Henry was especially fond of the cafeteria food! Although Henry's report card confirmed his improvement, he continued to have some academic deficits and would continue to receive special academic assistance.

While Mr. and Mrs. A. would occasionally struggle to respond as a parental team, they had made great progress. Their marriage was much improved and they were spending more time together. Mrs. A. still felt guilty when setting firm limits with Henry but was able to tolerate this better. And although Henry was still occasionally passive-aggressive and resistant to limits, this had lessened. I was sad to see them leave at this point just as the major changes in their lives were occurring. I felt honored by the trust they had shown in sharing details of their lives with me.

Questions for Thought and Discussion

1. Recall a significant loss in your childhood. Which responses from important adults in your life were helpful and which were ineffective? What specifically did they say and do to make things better or worse for you?

2. What was your most significant or enduring childhood fear? What did caregivers say and do that increased or diminished your fear? Does this childhood fear relate to any situations that create anxiety for you today?

Suggestions for Further Reading

Blagg, N., & Yule, W. (1994). School phobia. In T. H. Ollendick, N. J. King, & W. Yule (Eds.), *International handbook of phobia and anxiety disorders in children and adolescents* (pp. 169–186). New York: Plenum. Provides a discussion of the issues and the intervention approaches used with school phobic children and adolescents.

Falicov, C. J. (1998). *Latino families in therapy: A guide to multicultural practice.* New York: Guilford. Provides a well-written, thoughtful framework for culturally sensitive interventions with Latino families.

ELIZABETH: AN ASIAN AMERICAN ADOLESCENT RESOLVING RAPE TRAUMA

CHAPTER 8

INTRODUCTION

The Prevalence of Date Rape

Every three minutes a rape occurs somewhere in the United States (National Crime Victimization Survey, 1995). Yearly, approximately 500,000 women are sexually assaulted. The evidence suggests that 14 to 25% of all women in the United States will be raped at some point in their lives (Calhoun & Atkeson, 1991; Koss, 1993). Rape is a grimly prevalent but widely underreported crime. For example, Martin (1992) found that among individuals raped each year, 84% did not report the rape to the police! Why? Many victims of sexual assaults fear that others will blame them for the assault, others are concerned that they will be humiliated by the criminal justice system, and others fear reprisals from the rapist and disdain from those who hear about the rape.

The underreporting by victims is further highlighted by the difference between the number of rapes reported to the police and those reported to community crisis hotlines. For example, in a northwest city, reported rapes totaled 55 for 1992 and 53 for 1993 (Department of Public Safety, 1994) while that city's sexual assault service actually responded to calls from 3,600 victims during the same time period (Sexual Assault Support Services, 1993). The incidence of rape is also underestimated because a significant number are not considered rape and are therefore not counted (Bart & O'Brien, 1985; Martin, 1992). Rape is especially likely to be discounted or "legitimized" if the victim has had personal involvement with the perpetrator. In dating situations, the victim is likely to be blamed for the rape if she fails to protest early rather than late during "foreplay" (Shotland & Goodstein, 1983).

Although perpetrators of sexual assaults may be strangers, the risk of a woman being raped *by someone she knows* is four times greater than the risk of being raped by a stranger (Warshaw, 1988). According to the National Crime Victimization Survey, 80% of rapes were committed by someone known to the victim (Schafran, 1995). Similarly, in Warshaw's (1988) study, 84% of those raped knew the rapist, in many cases as classmates or on a first date. According to this report, 57% of the rapes occurred on dates. Focusing more specifically on teenagers, Ageton (1983) found that almost all of the female teen victims she interviewed knew the perpetrator: 56% had been raped by a date, 30% had been raped by a friend, and 11% had been raped by a boyfriend. Sadly, 78% of the teenaged victims in this study reported that *they did not tell their parents about the rape* and only 6% reported the assault to the police (Ageton, 1983).

Clearly, the sexual assault of teenage girls by classmates, boyfriends, casual friends, and co-workers is commonplace and hidden. In Warshaw's (1988) survey, 38% of the rape victims reported that they were 14 to 17 years old at the time of the assault. Since the prime dating age for females is between 16 and 24, and the risk of rape is four times higher for this group than for any other population group, developing effective clinical interventions for teens and young adults is essential.

While the majority of rape victims are believed to be female, some estimates suggest that one in ten rape survivors is male (Gibbs, 1991). Very little is known about male rape that occurs outside of prisons because most of these do not get reported. Most male rapes that we know something about occur in prisons where men who rape other men are usually heterosexual and are motivated by domination, control, revenge, sadism, and degradation (Groth & Birnham, 1979). Multiple assailants and greater physical injury is more common in male compared to female rape (Gerrol & Resick, 1998; Kaufman et al., 1980; Myers, 1989).

Cultural context plays an important role in determining whether rape, especially date rape, will be reported. Cultural values and beliefs affect women's willingness to share details of rape experiences (Holaday, Leach, & Davidson, 1994). For some groups like Asian Americans, reporting the rape or seeking services are often avoided because of the shame they feel and their fear that they will also be bringing shame to their family and community. As we will see in the case study that follows, even when psychological services are sought, the cultural sensitivity and skill of the mental health professional will greatly influence whether the client will stay and get the help she needs or whether she will stop treatment prematurely after one or two sessions.

Rape Trauma Syndrome

In addition to cultural sensitivity, counselors will need to be aware that even when rape victims do seek help, many do not identify the sexual assault as the presenting problem. Commonly, rape victims will present with symptoms of anxiety and/or depression without describing or identifying the precipitating sexual assault. Counselors therefore need to become sensitized to a pattern of symptoms fitting what is commonly referred to as *rape trauma syndrome* (Burgess & Holmstrom, 1974).

Rape trauma syndrome is not a diagnostic category found in the Diagnostic and Statistical Manual of Mental Disorders (DSM-IV-TR APA, 2000). The diagnostic categories described in the DSM-IV-TR are based on symptoms rather than on precipitating events. However, one DSM-IV-TR category, posttraumatic stress disorder

(PTSD), is often observed in sexual assault survivors. These PTSD symptoms include sleep disturbances, flashbacks, emotional numbing, and hypervigilance. Another DSM-IV-TR category that may be observed in survivors is adjustment disorder. These symptoms include diminished occupational, academic, and/or social functioning, accompanied by emotional reactions such as anxiety and depression. Unlike these broader categories, rape trauma syndrome focuses on the behavioral, somatic, and psychological reactions specific to victims of forcible and forcibly attempted rape. These reactions are noted to occur in three distinct stages: the *acute stage,* the *outward adjustment stage,* and the *renormalization stage.* The period of time spent in each stage will vary across individuals based on their prior psychological history and current support systems.

In the period immediately following the assault, referred to as the *acute stage,* survivors typically go through a phase of disorganization where they present with symptoms of acute distress that resemble a state of emotional shock (Tyra, 1993). Cognitive impairment may be seen in diminished alertness, dulled memory, disorganized thinking, and even bewilderment. Emotionally, the victim may be numb, paralyzed with anxiety, and overwhelmed, or seemingly calm and collected. A wide range of contradictory feelings may be expressed at the same time, including fear, humiliation, anger, and guilt.

In the second stage, referred to as the *outward adjustment stage,* the survivor attempts to convince herself and others (often prematurely) that she has resolved the crisis and has returned to a normal lifestyle. Emotionally and interpersonally, however, the rape may still be having an enormous impact. The survivor's activities may range from minimal involvement in work or school activities to overcompensation with extreme involvement. Socially, survivors tend to withdraw from other people, even breaking off contact with relatives and friends who are accepting and loving. Survivors distance themselves for a host of reasons, including a damaged sense of personal safety, distrust of existing relationships, reluctance to enter new relationships, disturbances in previously rewarding sexual relationships, and fears and phobias related to the circumstances of the rape (e.g., the smell of alcohol).

In the third stage, referred to as the *renormalization stage,* a sense of recovery begins to solidify. The intense shame, fear, and self-blame subsides as the survivor begins to appropriately direct anger toward the perpetrator. As a fundamental sense of trust is restored and fears are resolved, the survivor is no longer plagued by obsessive memories of the attack or by the concomitant nightmares. The concept of renormalization does not imply that the survivor's life goes on as if the rape had never occurred. For most, significant scars remain and many report that, years later, "life is never the same again." Kilpatrick (1985) reports that at some point following the rape, 19% of rape victims had actually attempted suicide and 44% had reported suicidal ideation (thinking about the possibility of committing suicide and ways of doing it).

Cultural Influences in Date Rape

Only one of nine Asian American rape survivors I have worked with attempted to report the assault to the police, even though all displayed symptoms of rape trauma syndrome. For these survivors, as is often true for many date rape survivors, previous involvement with the perpetrator tended to "legitimize" the relationship. Sadly, this then comes to be seen as "proof" of the "badness" of the individual, both to herself and to others.

While cultural factors are likely to shape how each client moves through the rape trauma syndrome stages, there is little research concerning cultural differences in the symptom presentation of rape trauma syndrome. Becoming familiar with cultural values, such as preserving the family's honor at all cost, not bringing shame to the family, not discussing personal or family issues outside the home, and not talking about sex, is important because it will greatly influence the treatment process.

The case that follows is about Elizabeth, an Asian American rape survivor, who was left feeling profoundly disempowered and isolated. As a minority, having to come to terms with her bicultural identity, prejudice, and stereotypes, Elizabeth was also faced with further disempowering experiences at the community level. As we will see, this exacerbated her problems and further isolated her from the support she needed.

While the research suggests that the majority of perpetrators are known to the victim and are the same race, sometimes they differ, which adds complexity. For example, the cultural stereotypes of men as having power and sexual prowess and women, especially Asian women, as submissive and compliant, heightens the likelihood of rape. Even when the woman says "no," the perpetrator may see this as "playing coy." The woman, feeling afraid and powerless, may then blame herself for somehow being in this situation. She may question if there was something about her—something in the way she looked, dressed, or spoke—that made her a target. While struggling with this self-blame, she will be alone with her feelings, believing that it is best to be stoic and not further shame herself or her family by making the rape public.

Counselors who are sensitive to the impact of culture on client's presentation and management of symptoms will be able to form a stronger therapeutic alliance and develop treatment goals that are culturally acceptable. In the early phase of treatment, for example, it is important for counselors to know that many Asian Americans differ in their communication styles. That is, they tend to be less direct, use fewer verbalizations, show less emotion, and are comfortable with silence. This awareness will reduce the likelihood that the client will be misperceived, misdiagnosed, or misjudged. In particular, silence is awkward for many counselors and they may attempt to manage their own anxiety by ineffectively working hard to fill the silences with words.

Counselor-client differences or similarities could also affect their ability to work together. Addressing this directly can be helpful with many clients, and can be done by asking the client about potential differences in culture that may exist between them, by acknowledging that these differences can have an impact on their relationship, and by encouraging the client to talk about any misunderstandings that may arise. By inviting the client to educate the counselor about cultural differences that may emerge in their work together, the door is open for future exploration and gives the client "permission" to raise these issues in the future. This is especially important if misunderstandings emerge based on cultural/ethnic/religious differences.

Generic Considerations in Treating Asian American Clients

Asian Americans represent one of the fastest growing and most diverse American populations of color. They are from backgrounds representing more than 20 different countries and are comprised of at least 29 different subgroups (Yoshioka, Tashima, Ichew, & Maurase, 1981). As a result, their immigration patterns, native languages, command of English, degree of assimilation and/or acculturation, family intactness, cultural values, and political and religious beliefs and practices vary (Wong, 1985). In addition, a majority of the Asian population in the United States, with the exception of Japanese Americans, are foreign born (McLoed, 1986). Despite this diversity, which means that differences in social, emotional, and economic status exist between Asian Americans, they are often viewed as a "model" minority with tremendous educational and economic attainment (see Sue & Sue, 1999). They have also been reported to function well in society with low criminal, psychiatric, or divorce rates. These factors, in addition to their high rates of intermarriage with Whites, has led society to erroneously believe that Asian Americans are less prone to the negative impact of prejudice and racism (Sue & Sue, 1999). Historically and currently, however, Asians have experienced tremendous prejudice and racism (see United States Commission on Civil Rights, 1992). Examples include denial of citizenship rights (e.g., The Chinese Exclusion Act of 1882, which was repealed only in 1943), internment camp placement during World War II, and harassment and physical assaults (examples include labels such as "gook" and "the Yellow Peril"). Further, close inspection of Asian enclaves such as the Chinatowns and Japantowns in San Francisco and New York illuminates the fact that many Asians experience poverty, juvenile delinquency, and myriad physical and mental health problems. Sue & Sue (1999) suggest that the discrepancy between "official" and "real" rates of social, economic, and psychological difficulties in the Asian population are probably due in part to cultural factors. These factors include the way in which symptoms are expressed (i.e., somatic symptoms such as stomachaches or internalizing symptoms like worrying rather than externalizing ways such as getting angry), family preferences for handling problems themselves rather than seeking outside assistance, and the shame or disgrace associated with having others know about one's social and economic problems.

Clearly, Asians in America are a diverse group with varied social and economic backgrounds, family experiences, and cultural values. Therefore, counselors must be careful in how information about Asians or any other group characteristic is applied to individual clients, since *each person's experience will likely be unique.* Having said this, however, it is helpful for counselors to be aware that some commonalities exist. For example, Asians may have a tendency toward emotional restraint; deference to authority; specified family roles, including a hierarchical family structure; and an emphasis on the family and extended family as important units (Tsui & Schultz, 1985). In addition, Asians are more likely to express psychological distress in somatic or bodily symptoms and, typically, the culture does not value seeking counseling for emotional or personal problems (Sue & Sue, 1999).

Counselors working with Asian clients would benefit from learning as much as possible about each client's historical and sociopolitical experience and keep each cultural context in mind as they try to establish their credibility as effective helpers. Sue and Zane (1987), in particular, write compellingly about the importance of having therapy goals and the treatment process consonant with the client's cultural values.

Other important cultural value differences exist between Asian Americans and the mainstream culture. One example would be differences regarding successful attainment of developmental tasks. That is, most Asian Americans do not encourage the development of autonomy as much as European Americans. For Asian Americans, there is a strong focus on family, which emphasizes enduring attachments to the extended family and close ties to the mother. From birth, the fostering of dependency and interdependency is valued in child-rearing. Consequently, there is a strong sense of duty or obligation to one's parents. The direct expression of conflict between Asian American parents and their children should not be expected since questioning authority is typically not permitted. In particular, it is generally not acceptable to express anger, resentment, or frustration toward a parent or toward authority figures. Clients thus have to find respectful ways of developing their sense of self within the context of honoring the family. For example, counselors may need to help clients frame disagreements in congenial ways (e.g., to parent, "I hope that my becoming a teacher rather than a physician, as you wish, can still bring honor to our family.").

In addition, the Asian American culture discourages the development of intimate relationships with the opposite sex. Typically, Asian American parents discourage their children from dating, and encourage the suppression of sexuality with the goal of maintaining their children's focus on educational achievement. Clients from Asian American cultures can also place a premium on placing others' feelings over one's own, on not verbalizing one's feelings and thoughts, and on being humble and modest. Counselors will be more helpful to their Asian American clients when their interventions are congruent with these cultural values (e.g., "It may not be helpful to tell your father how angry you feel when he treats you like a child. Instead, maybe you can write your thoughts and feelings down. Then we can talk about them in here and you may be able to let them go or, working together, maybe we can find more effective ways of talking to him about them. We can also help you develop some coping strategies to manage during the conflict—for example, being able to take deep breaths and consider how his own developmental/cultural experiences have shaped him.").

In sum, the emphasis on role, status, and hierarchy in the Asian American culture has great implications for counselors working with this population. As we will see in the following case study, these cultural factors often play a significant role in treating Asian American victims of date rape.

CASE ILLUSTRATION

Presenting Problem

In the fall quarter of her sophomore year, Elizabeth, an 18-year-old Chinese American college student, was sexually assaulted by a male classmate. She had read in a college bulletin and heard from professors that one can make friends by studying with others. In one of her first attempts to establish a friendship with a male peer, Elizabeth met with the following traumatic event.

With a midterm exam approaching, Elizabeth asked her classmate, Rod, if he would be interested in studying together at the library. Just prior to the library's closing Rod informed Elizabeth that he had copies of audiotapes with information that was needed for the exam. He suggested that they go to his apartment to listen to the tapes and continue their work.

When they arrived at Rod's apartment, Elizabeth suggested that they use the tape deck in the living room. Rod responded that doing so would disturb his roommate and insisted that they use his bedroom. As soon as he closed the door of the bedroom, Rod jumped on Elizabeth and covered her mouth with his hand. In spite of her attempts to fight him off (she bit him), Rod stuffed her mouth with a cloth and proceeded to rape her. Rod is six feet tall; Elizabeth is less than five feet.

During the weeks that followed, Elizabeth avoided Rod. After several weeks, Rod confronted her in the lecture hall, asking why she had been avoiding him. Elizabeth responded that the avoidance was caused by what Rod had done to her. Rod denied that he had done anything, invoking the cultural stereotype that even though Asian women protest, in actuality they are ready sexual partners. He asserted that Asian American females are willing to do whatever they can to please a man. In addition, Rod told Elizabeth that she knew what she was getting into when she went to his apartment.

A few weeks later, Elizabeth called the city police department and attempted to report the rape. They informed her that it was now too late to prosecute and failed to provide her with any referrals such as sexual assault support services or counseling.

During the winter term, Elizabeth found that she was pregnant. She beat her stomach until she was black and blue. She had an abortion without informing her family of the rape or pregnancy. She confided in a friend about the pregnancy, and because she had no money, her friend referred her to an individual in another city who did abortions. For the next several months, Elizabeth was unable to concentrate. She felt no motivation to do her schoolwork and, accordingly, her grades fell dramatically.

At the end of the spring term, Elizabeth sought the services of the university's counseling center, distressed because she had been charged with larceny by the department store that she worked for. According to Elizabeth, she did not have any credit cards when she was hired. In order to charge items at this department store, she paid into a credit account. After contributing several hundred dollars to this account, she believed that she could withdraw her money from it whenever she chose. She attempted to withdraw some money from the business office. They, however, referred her to the personnel office, where she was told she could not do it and sent her back to the business office.

Elizabeth was angry because she felt she had been lied to and denied what was due her. Subsequently, Elizabeth began acquiring articles and charging them to her account—using the credit she had built up. After making purchases equivalent to the credit due her, Elizabeth continued to charge on others' accounts. Prior to this, Elizabeth had never stolen anything. In addition, she did not open the packages after she brought them home but threw them in her closet.

After several weeks of this behavior, security officers confronted Elizabeth. She was disturbed because the security officer wrote in his report that she stole the merchandise simply because she "desired to have nice things," which she felt was not true. Following the formal charge with a crime, Elizabeth was extremely concerned that her name would appear in the newspaper. She felt sure that family and friends would soon find out. She considered killing herself, since the shame of others knowing felt overwhelming to her.

When Elizabeth came to the counseling center at the end of the spring quarter, she had not discussed the details of the assault or the subsequent problems with anyone. An intake worker at the counseling center referred her to me because I am a Japanese American female with a longstanding interest in working with Asian (American and foreign-born) students. During her intake session, Elizabeth had stated that a variety of events had occurred but she was unable (or unwilling) to give details—especially regarding the rape. The intake worker and I agreed that Elizabeth met the criteria for major depression. She reported feeling depressed and had much self-blame and feelings of guilt. In addition, she reported eating and sleep disturbances and had suicidal ideation. Elizabeth was also very anxious and had symptoms suggestive of post-traumatic stress disorder, including numbness, nightmares about the rape, social isolation, and hypervigilance.

Client Description

Elizabeth, a short Chinese American student whose hair appeared uncombed, was highly distressed during our initial session. She was very soft spoken and had a lost, distant gaze. At times, she spoke so slowly that I could count to 20 between her responses.

Social Context

Shortly before the assault, Elizabeth had turned 18 years old. She was the older of two girls born to a couple who had emigrated from Hong Kong to the United States. Her father committed suicide when she was about 3 years old. After the suicide, Elizabeth, her mother, and sister moved into the home of her maternal grandparents and their three offspring. Early on, Elizabeth had been told that her father died of a heart attack. Later, when she was 16 years old, Elizabeth was told that her father had killed himself. She was told only that the suicide had been due to the difficulties of adjusting to life in the United States. Elizabeth's mother dated frequently, and Elizabeth and her sister were told to never address her as "mother" but to use her first name: Mary. When Elizabeth was 9 years old, Mary wed a European American but did not tell her new husband that she had two daughters! Elizabeth and her sister continued to live with her grandparents, while her mother moved to a separate residence with her new husband.

Mary had a child by her second husband. Sometimes Elizabeth and her younger sister visited Mary and her new family. They were still prohibited from calling her "mother." Elizabeth experienced great difficulty when she saw her half-sister being treated with acceptance and indulged by Mary. In contrast to Elizabeth and Alice (her full sister), Laura (her half-sister) had a fully decorated room and a closet full of clothes.

Elizabeth described her relationship with Mary as being "cool"; Mary had never been emotionally supportive of Elizabeth. Rather, she issued directives about what Elizabeth should or shouldn't do. Elizabeth also described Mary as only wanting to interact superficially. For example, she would discuss soap operas and movie stars but never ask how Elizabeth and Alice were coping at their grandparents' home or at school.

Elizabeth lived with grandfather and grandmother who "hated each other." They fought constantly—often yelling "I hate you"—and threw appliances such as the toaster, often breaking them. These warring grandparents blamed Elizabeth for most of their problems, even if she wasn't at home when the problem that she was blamed for occurred.

Grandfather, who spoke English, was described as "mean and domineering." He rarely spoke to Elizabeth. Elizabeth felt that her grandfather often told lies about her to her grandmother. Grandmother, who spoke only Chinese, would frequently make nasty statements about Elizabeth. Grandmother's name-calling and verbal abuse escalated when Elizabeth was in high school. Elizabeth would ask her aunt what her grandmother was saying and her aunt would translate, "You are bad . . . you killed your father."

Elizabeth's uncles and aunt were more benevolent influences in her life, fortunately, and they often provided emotional support for Elizabeth and her sister when family crises escalated.

Elizabeth's grandparents constantly threatened that when her Social Security check stopped coming at age 18, she would no longer have a place to stay. Both Elizabeth and her sister received checks from Social Security because of their father's death, which were turned over to their grandparents.

Elizabeth and her sister shared a twin bed. Until the end of her junior year in high school, Elizabeth engaged in few extracurricular activities. She had never slept over at a friend's home, was not allowed to have friends over to visit, and had never ridden a bicycle or gone bowling.

Elizabeth attended a public elementary school and did well in school. She lived in a neighborhood with predominantly European American neighbors and attended schools with few Asians. She was often teased at school for being Asian and for dressing differently. Elizabeth remembers that, as a child and preteen, she had only two pairs of trousers, which she wore continuously. Later, in high school, she tried to fix up old clothes that friends gave to her. At age 14, she began babysitting and working in restaurants to obtain money for clothing and other necessities.

At the end of her junior year of high school, a critical change occurred as Elizabeth began developing friendships. Prior to this, Elizabeth described herself as not knowing how to make friends. One especially supportive friendship that contributed greatly to her development was with a Korean American female whom Elizabeth described as being "Americanized." Elizabeth began to stay over and go on outings with her friend's family. This friend noted to Elizabeth that Elizabeth had broken out of her shell during that year.

During her senior year of high school, Elizabeth began yelling back at her grandmother when her grandmother was verbally abusive and when she tried to forbid Elizabeth from going out of the house. During most of that year, Elizabeth stayed with friends for three to four day stretches. Although her grandmother accused her of sexual impropriety, Elizabeth had never been involved in any sexual relationships.

For her first term in college, Elizabeth received all B's. During the following two quarters, her grades began to go down. This correlated with her grandparents' escalating attempts to kick her out of the house because she was turning 18 and her Social Security checks were about to cease. After her grandparents insisted that she leave, Elizabeth's aunt invited her to their home. Elizabeth greatly appreciated the offer but stayed with friends during the spring of her freshman year, after which she moved to an apartment with another female friend.

Preimmigration and immigration history reveals that, as a young child, Elizabeth's grandmother saw her own mother killed by Japanese soldiers. The grandparents immigrated to the United States when Mary was 9 but left Mary with an aunt. Mary joined her parents in the United States when she was about 15 years old. By that time, Elizabeth's uncles and aunt had been born.

Mary was invited to Hong Kong to meet an eligible male friend of the family. After reluctantly going to meet him, she was forced to marry him because his family said that they had spent a "fortune" to bring her to Hong Kong. Mary's family also pressured her to marry him to avoid the shame and disgrace that would result if Mary refused and the intended husband's family felt rebuffed.

Initial Session

Elizabeth appeared very distressed at the beginning of our initial session, but her crying was quiet and restrained. I could feel the weight of her sadness and anger for the losses that she had experienced throughout childhood and for the trauma she had recently endured. I was deeply affected as I learned more about all that had happened to her, but also felt great respect for the resiliency within her that had allowed her to cope as well as she had with so little support.

I believe that, at the start of counseling, it is important to describe to clients what counseling is all about. Asian American clients, in particular, tend to have had minimal experiences with counseling and think counseling is only for "crazy" people. Thus, it is important that counselors explain how counseling works, what they will do together, and what the client can expect. It is important to address the client's questions, concerns, and expectations about the treatment process in a friendly but direct manner. Using humor and culturally familiar terms, I often explain to clients the differences between being "crazy crazy" (psychotic) and "crazy" (neurotic). Usually, I ask them if they are hearing voices coming out of the air or are seeing things. Clients who are not psychotic usually giggle or look at me in amazement. I also explain that many people have phases in their lives when they need the support and counsel of someone—and that counselors can provide this in much the same way that teachers, coaches, ministers, and others give their input and guidance when needed.

In view of Elizabeth's presenting problem and history, I shared with Elizabeth my backpack metaphor, which is a simple but concrete way of describing what treatment involves. I explained that the process of counseling included exploring:

1. what historical rocks/boulders/mountains of feelings were in her backpack and causing her to feel depressed—looking for rock piles of different issues and taking them out one by one and allowing the thoughts, memories, and especially the feelings to be expressed;
2. dealing more directly with present rocks/issues in her life;
3. learning how not to put more rocks in her backpack and to deal/cope in different, more healthy ways (i.e., assertion, communication, negotiation skills); and
4. examining sources that had helped hold her up (e.g., friends, aunt), pushed her down (e.g., mother, grandparents), or needed to be developed (e.g., laughing, having fun, relaxing, and getting emotional support from others), or needed to be discarded (e.g., negative self-talk).

Where to begin counseling was a major question. Obviously, there had been many recent stressors and traumatic events, and each of these was exacerbated by her difficult family history. At the end of the first session, I stated that she had certainly been through a lot and recounted what the major issues were that she presented: the rape, abortion, failing academic status, theft charges, and the upcoming trial. Added to these mounting situational stressors were her painful family history and the most recent familial crisis of being kicked out of her grandparents' home. I was also aware that cultural factors might be having an impact on these events and how they were being coped with. I told Elizabeth that at some point we could get to each one of these issues if she wished.

I viewed Elizabeth as being in crisis because of the rape and felt that she needed the active, focused approach to treatment that crisis counseling provides. The upcoming trial and the presenting problem of theft that finally brought her in had to be a priority, given the extent of her shame and fear of exposure. Although I felt pulled by her poignant developmental and familial history, I knew that it was essential for her to take the lead in setting our agenda:

> THERAPIST: I feel so touched as you talk about your past, the rape, the abortion and all of these painful things that have happened. We can talk about any of these things if you wish, and work together to find some better ways for dealing with them. But right now, I'm feeling it would be best if you could choose where we begin. What would you like to focus on first?

Elizabeth paused a moment, but seemed to enjoy having permission to do what she wanted to do for a change. She opted to talk about the upcoming trial. Elizabeth stated that charging merchandise to other accounts was wrong, recognizing that this was something that had never crossed her mind prior to the rape. She could not believe that she had done it. We began talking about what was going on with her psychologically prior to, and during, the theft:

> THERAPIST: It seems as though you've had so much pain during the past nine months, and so little support to help you get through it all, that when you were not given your money by the department store it was the straw that broke the camel's back. These events were like large boulders being thrown in your backpack. Now, you already had in your backpack the mountains of feelings you suffered from losing your mother and your father in childhood, and the hurt and anger from living with your grandparents. In combination with the rape, abortion, and theft charge, I can see how it has all become just too much for you to bear. And you have had to deal with all of this with so little support.

Her pained expression told me that she believed that I understood her. For the first time, the tension in her face softened; I felt that this empathic link allowed our relationship to begin.

Regarding the rape, I conveyed to Elizabeth that she would have control over what details she wanted to share and when she wanted to share them. She then proceeded to tell me the details of the events leading up to the assault. Sadly, Elizabeth blamed herself for the rape and thought that she had not fought hard enough. In light of the self-blame, it was imperative that I validate that she had been raped against her will and that it was not her fault. I acknowledged her courage and emphasized the fact that she did the best that she could under the circumstances. I also affirmed that it was ludicrous for the rapist, Rod, to claim that she wanted sex—highlighting that a willing sexual partner does not struggle with and bite her lover's hand! Elizabeth said that this validation was "good to hear" as she felt a sense of relief from the guilt. I told her that many victims of sexual assault feel guilty and blame themselves. I again assured her that she had done the best she could, and I told her directly that Rod was the one with the problem. Victims of assault need to hear unambiguously where the responsibility for the problems really resides. Although it may seem so obvious to the counselor that it doesn't bear emphasis, the client is traumatized and is not thinking clearly. Her shame and guilt necessitate clear, direct, and repeated clarifications. Before we ended, I explained to Elizabeth the following:

> THERAPIST: There may be times during our work together when you feel that I don't understand you or even hurt your feelings. If that happens please let me know. I know this could be hard for you to do, given your culture and family. I know that you have not had much practice at this but I hope you will try. If you don't tell me about the problems that

might come up between us, I'm afraid that it will make it harder for you to trust me or keep working with me. I hope you will practice with me—talking about things so I can help you carry the load you usually manage on your own.

A statement of this sort is important in that it explicitly gives permission for a different type of communication and relationship than clients like Elizabeth have had with others. It also reframes questioning authority figures and expressing disagreements as an opportunity to develop a healthier relationship, which is especially important for Asian American clients because many will find it difficult to disagree with or question an authority figure such as a therapist.

Case Conceptualization

Elizabeth is a late adolescent who experienced significant losses and deprivation throughout her childhood. She had little support from her narcissistic mother and lived in fear of her combative and rejecting grandparents. Elizabeth was also teased and rejected by other children because she was Asian and poor. She was lonely and isolated until her mid-high-school years, and Elizabeth had minimal opportunities to explore and experience all that there is for children and adolescents to do.

I believed that the recent expulsion from her grandmother's home, the rape, and the abortion represented further loss, rejection, and abuse. These factors, it seemed, triggered her credit card rebellion. The department store's response to Elizabeth wanting to use the money she believed was rightfully hers seemed to evoke a rebellion and defiance. Her felt injustice seemed to repeat aspects of her family experiences, where her Social Security check was used and all she received in return was rejection and abuse. In some ways, it made sense to me that Elizabeth wanted to act out her feelings of anger and, lacking appropriate language for redressing the unfairness, she responded by taking/stealing from the store.

Compared to other Asian immigrant families, Elizabeth's family was atypical in several ways. They were not supportive of her educational achievements and goals; family cohesion and support were lacking as seen in Elizabeth's mother's abandonment of her two daughters; and her grandparents had forced Elizabeth out when her Social Security check stopped coming. The verbal confrontations between family members was also unusual—likely more disruptive given the cultural context in which they were occurring.

Like many immigrant families, Elizabeth's family faced many difficulties in their quest to create a new life in America. Elizabeth's father spoke little English and felt estranged from his new country. Shortly after the birth of his second child, he killed himself by jumping off a bridge. His dream for a new and better life had gone tragically wrong. As so often occurs, sadly, he inadvertently left his children a legacy that mimicked his—loss, shame, and unmet needs.

Mary too had experienced loss and abandonment. She had spent much of her childhood separated from her parents and in adulthood was pressured into a marriage she did not choose. Her lack of identity and sense of belonging probably contributed to her later marriage to a European American man, thinking this would provide a sense of security and stability in her new country. Mary also repeated the legacy of giving up/abandoning her first born children. Sadly, these themes of abandonment and loss are frequently replayed in many immigrant families as they struggle to adjust to a new country and culture. Tracking the generational patterns, Elizabeth's grandmother lost her mother early in her life; Mary was separated at about 9 years of age from her mother; and Elizabeth, in turn, lost her mother when she was 9 years old. Attachment bonds were fragile and important relationships were broken in all three generations.

Elizabeth was in the conforming stage of racial/cultural identity development, a stage characterized by self-depreciation and rejection of one's own cultural identity (Sue & Sue, 1999). She said that she hated being Chinese and did not want to learn Chinese because she heard her grandmother say hateful things about her in Chinese. The racial taunts she heard as a child also had a negative impact on her identity, and the trauma of the rape was also overlaid with cultural stereotypes—all of which blocked Elizabeth from achieving a positive cultural or racial identity.

Orienting Constructs

In general, I view life from an Eastern orientation. I believe negatively and positively charged forces—yin and yang—operate. At times certain characteristics predominate while others are in the background waiting to be developed. The goal is to attain balance and develop the ability to move back and forth flexibly. Counseling thus focuses on the client's imbalance with the goal of affirming and helping support the side that needs to develop.

I find visual metaphors helpful to many clients. For example, I sometimes use the metaphor of plants to help understand clients' problems. I ask the clients what kind of gardeners they had to help them grow. Did they have the water and shelter they needed? Did they have enough sunshine and fertilizer? Were they pruned too much or left untended? What does the client's tree look like now? If different parts of the tree represent developmental areas, such as personal, interpersonal, and academic/career, what branches are blossoming with flowers and leaves? Which sides have buds yet to bloom? In what areas has growth been stunted? Are there knotholes in the tree that serve as scars to cover old wounds?

I also ask myself, if this client started off in life with an empty backpack on her back—standing straight up to the world, emotionally responsive and open to new experiences—what happened along the way to make her feel the way she does now? What kind of rocks (feelings) did Elizabeth throw in her backpack because she faced rejection from her mother and denigration from her grandparents? What are these feelings? Are they rocks of sadness, anger, insecurity? What piles of rocks have accumulated into mountains? How heavy are the rocks? How has she protected herself from further pain (defenses)? Has she built walls to protect herself? How high and thick are the walls? What support has she had to hold up the backpack? Is she able to acknowledge her feelings and assert her thoughts and feelings to others? How much practice does she have doing this? What impact does this backpack of rocks have on her present relationships? Such visual metaphors often sound unsophisticated, but with certain clients they can facilitate a working alliance.

In Elizabeth's case, her primary gardeners had abandoned her, physically and emotionally. The substitute grandparent gardeners gave minimal water and almost no fertilizer or sunshine. At times, it seemed as if they had pruned her with an ax. Her aunt and several friends had been better gardeners who had tried to help her grow. Elizabeth resonated with these metaphors and came to life emotionally as I used this visual language with her.

Elizabeth had a heavy backpack that had chronically depressed her. She had thrown in rocks and boulders filled with all her sadness, anger, and shame and they had piled up into mountains. There were mountains of losses and mountains of having been rejected and blamed. The walls built by these mountains kept Elizabeth from getting close to others emotionally. She had stored these feelings for so long now that she was no longer able to acknowledge that she even had feelings! Elizabeth had little support to help her with her load and she had difficulty standing up straight, literally—the recent events made it almost impossible for her to even hold her head up.

Perhaps the core of the problem was that Elizabeth had a shame based sense of self. Believing that she was unimportant, unlovable, or worthy of rejection, there was no validity to her own needs and no expectations that others would understand or care. Despite this low self-esteem and feelings of worthlessness, however, Elizabeth was a survivor. I observed that the validation I offered to Elizabeth, my willingness to take her seriously, and my efforts to actively try and help her solve her problems all were received with disbelief. There was an initial questioning that I would actually want to do something for her. This was followed by expressions of appreciation that were accompanied by deep sobs that revealed the depth of her shame and deprivation. Although it had been difficult for Elizabeth to express any feelings before this, she soon expressed her happiness about having our relationship as well. Elizabeth now felt safe enough to take the risk of allowing me to care about her and help her.

Treatment Goals and Intervention Plans

Counselors need to have a *treatment focus*. That is, they need to know where they are going in treatment and how they plan to get there. Thus, my first goal was to address the theft charges and upcoming trial and sentencing. It was the theft charges that had originally thrust Elizabeth into crisis and propelled her to seek help. The possibility that her family or friends would find out about the charges terrified her to the point that she regarded suicide as a viable solution. The risk for suicide was especially significant because her father had modeled this heartbreaking way of escaping problems. I suggested a referral to the Student Health Center for a medication evaluation, but Elizabeth would not take medication because she was "afraid of becoming addicted." It was critical to help her find alternative cognitive and behavioral strategies for dealing with the overwhelming feelings she was experiencing.

Second, I wanted to stabilize her rape trauma and abortion-related symptoms. I wanted to do this by helping her with the shame and hopelessness evoked by her violation. As emphasized earlier, Elizabeth needed to develop new ways of coping with such overwhelming feelings or the immobilizing depression would continue, and accompanying school failure and dropout would follow. To work effectively toward this goal, I needed to give Elizabeth permission to feel her sad, hurt, and angry feelings, reframing the ability to experience and share them as a pathway to being able to "stand up straight" and approach the future with pride. I did this because I know that many Asian Americans think it unacceptable to cry or express their needs so they suppress these. Yet, in time, their impact often emerges in self-defeating ways, as in Elizabeth's stealing, and in her depression and withdrawal. I felt that talking-out, rather than acting-out, these feelings of betrayal, deprivation, and outrage would be more adaptive in the long run.

My third goal was to stabilize Elizabeth's current life structure by helping her succeed academically. To do this, I planned to connect Elizabeth with additional support systems on campus that could continue after counseling stopped. For example, I helped her to find tutoring through the International Students Association to help with her academic standing, and helped her to join an ongoing support group at the Women's Resource Center on campus. Academic achievement was very important to her, and her inability to concentrate, her decreased motivation, and her declining grade point average were constant reminders of the sexual assault and contributed to her low self-esteem and depression. The personal and academic support she received from these two resources proved invaluable.

Fourth, I wanted to help Elizabeth problem solve with regard to the issues arising from the rape and abortion. The goal here was *empowerment*. One option included taking action against the perpetrator (e.g., report the rape and the perpetrator's use of cultural stereotypes in justifying his behavior to the Affirmative Action Office and the Dean of Students). For rape survivors, reporting sexual assaults can be significant in helping them appropriately place the responsibility and blame on the rapist, where it belongs, and no longer on themselves. I broached this issue carefully, however, because there are often cultural prohibitions against sharing information of this sort. I wanted Elizabeth to feel empowered to act when and how she chose, and to be certain that she did not do what I might think was best.

Fifth, I also planned to focus on the cultural stereotypes that were a part of the rape, because Elizabeth was very disturbed by the rapist relating this to her. Elizabeth's rape was in part an act of bigotry that was powerfully violating and defiling. It further wounded her fragile racial identity, aggravating her previous experiences with bias and disaffection, and fueling a sense of cultural shame.

Given her history of emotional abuse, Elizabeth had an inordinate amount of negative self-talk and self-blame. Thus I wanted to teach her how to assert herself more effectively, and I wanted to teach her techniques for dealing with the negative self-talk (e.g., thought stopping). I believed that Elizabeth's negative self-talk and self-blame had its roots in her history of abuse and in the Asian worldview. Among Asians, in particular, the inability to solve problems on your own is often seen as a lack of determination and evidence of personal failure (Ichikawa, 1989). I needed to find culturally consonant ways to help her advocate on her own behalf more effectively and respond to herself in more affirming ways.

Finally, underlying each of these goals was the need to develop a collaborative treatment relationship in which safety was established. Developmentally, Elizabeth had been given little in life, materially or emotionally, and she needed a safe harbor for awhile. With all clients, but perhaps even more so with Asian American clients, what you *do* demonstrates your care or concern in far more important ways than what you say.

Treatment Process

Reaching Out   In order to provide culturally sensitive treatment, counselors working with people of color cannot always limit themselves to the conventional role of working only in the "50-minute" hour. According to Atkinson, Thompson, and Grant (1993) there may be times when it is beneficial for the counselor to assume alternative roles, including adviser, advocate, and facilitator to indigenous support systems. For example, a counselor in the role of cultural mediator would help to point out and interpret perspectives of Asian American culture to individuals outside the Asian American culture and also help to point out and interpret perspectives of European American culture to the Asian American client. The counselor's role would depend on the client's level of acculturation and the nature of the problem.

Recognizing the power imbalance that Elizabeth experienced with the majority culture and the emotional deprivation and personal denigration she experienced in her family, I felt that it was critical for her to have the experience of someone reaching out to her. As things unfolded with the court case, it became clear that she needed me to actively extend problem-solving help and consultation in dealing with the judicial system. Her family's immigrant status and her level of acculturation seemed to require that she have an *advocate* in this important arena, where she had little knowledge and felt disempowered. At Elizabeth's request, I agreed to contact her public defender and explain the events that led up to her being charged with theft. He asked that I write a letter that described her history, the rape, the abortion, and her psychological state at the time of the thefts. This letter was to be presented in court on her behalf.

Elizabeth and the public defender asked me if I would go to court with her on the day of the trial, and I agreed. She looked visibly relieved that I would attend the trial with her, along with the leader of her support group at the Women's Resource Center. Our presence proved to be a watershed event in Elizabeth's recovery. Elizabeth's focus changed from how she would commit suicide to how she would deal with each issue that arose, including the sentencing, which might include jail time and a work detail. Much to her relief, by some good fortune, her name never appeared in the newspaper section of court proceedings—sparing her excruciating humiliation.

I have come to believe that when one works with individuals who have been sexually assaulted, one must be knowledgeable about the relevant institutional grievance procedures and the effectiveness and fairness of these systems. Without this understanding, one might encourage clients to go alone to report the rape. Telling their stories to persons who may be insensitive or unresponsive further traumatizes the victims. It is usually important for counselors, support group leaders or members, friends, ministers, or others to go with victims whenever possible to provide emotional support, to help clarify questions asked of the survivor, or to help explain to the investigator details that are necessary for thorough reporting. At times, counselors may be the only persons whom the survivors have trusted enough to tell the details.

As a result of the rape, abortion, and subsequent distress and depression, Elizabeth's motivation and concentration had decreased considerably. Reflecting the severity of her depression, she was unable to get out of bed at times. Her GPA for the quarter following the attack was 0.7. She despaired that no one would want to help her, as the police had not helped her when she telephoned them. Given that Elizabeth had not received support or help with her problems throughout her development, I felt it necessary to reach out more actively than I would with some other clients. I offered to help her prepare by role-playing, and then to have her contact her professors with me to see if she could retroactively withdraw from the previous quarter's classes. She found the role-playing useful, called the professors from my office while sitting next to me and, fortunately, was able to work out a solution with each of them. Elizabeth wanted to attempt to finish the current quarter, and we were able to find a way for her to do that.

Responding to Feelings   The first step in this process is to explore the kinds of response the client has had to expressing her feelings. With Asian clients, I acknowledge family and cultural norms of giving and receiving support:

> THERAPIST: I know that in many Asian families (that includes Japanese, Chinese, Korean, Vietnamese, etc.) people don't share feelings, or receive support for these feelings. I had one Asian student say, "All my parents care about is my head and stomach." Many of us have been taught to hold our feelings in, have a blank face, accept the situation, and move on. How was it for you?

In Elizabeth's case, she had had no experiences of getting emotional support for expressing sad and painful feelings. Initially, she wanted to know what could be accomplished by crying with another. I answered her question directly, using the backpack metaphor. I took time to explain to Elizabeth that she had lived many years, during which she had accumulated rocks, and that these rocks were filled with feelings that had never been expressed. I suggested that, if she began to unload (share) the rocks, boulders, and mountains of feelings, she would begin to feel lighter. I warned Elizabeth that she may, in fact, feel worse in the beginning. However, I likened it to carrying heavy shopping bags around. When one finally sits down, one does not immediately feel great; rather, we may moan and groan, feeling the aches and pain, and then we feel better.

I then wanted to address with her why I thought she was having difficulties expressing her feelings to me, given her history. My being Asian made it easier for her to relate to me, and she expected me to understand because I was a counselor. I thought that my being Asian, however, also made her hesitate to express feelings because she expected me to respond like her mother or grandparents. I could really feel the conflict she was experiencing, as I recalled how difficult it had been for me to directly express my negative feelings in front of someone else, even to my counselor, given my Asian background. I told her that she might have to work at learning how to express her feelings and suggested that she could practice with me.

Elizabeth had been particularly restrained in expressing her feelings regarding the rape and abortion. As she began to feel safe with me, Elizabeth indicated that when she found out she was pregnant, it was clear to her that she would have an abortion (she viewed the pregnancy as an extension of the rape). As we talked about Elizabeth's experiences with abuse and violation, her feelings fully emerged. During these times, we would sit together in silence as Elizabeth struggled to find ways to put her feelings and experiences into words and begin to metaphorically empty her backpack. With just a little patience and affirmation, however, Elizabeth soon made much progress in identifying, sharing, and ultimately coming to terms with the mixture of difficult feelings that emerged.

It is especially important when working with Asian American clients to pay attention to nonverbal cues, since many of these clients tend to place less value on direct emotional expression. I usually watch the eyes: one can often see a flash of feeling signaling that something is going on. As I watched Elizabeth's nonverbal cues, I was able to tell when it was acceptable to go deeper into feelings or that some impact had been made. Conversely, it is critical that counselors be mindful of their own nonverbal expressions, since Elizabeth and other Asian American clients often attend more to our actions than our words.

In response to my affirmation of her experience, Elizabeth increasingly allowed herself to feel angry at the male who raped her. As she risked experiencing this previously taboo feeling, she began to decrease the self-blame and negative self-talk that had permeated her responses in the initial phase of treatment. She was, however, still fearful of seeing him. He apparently had transferred to a school in the South after Elizabeth told him she was going to report him. At the end of winter term, right before finals, Elizabeth ran into Rod's roommate on campus. The roommate assumed that she had had a positive relationship with Rod and informed her that Rod would be coming into town. Elizabeth was in a panic for the next week and, on her way to a final exam, she was sure she saw him walking with his roommate. Elizabeth "fell apart." She was unable to take the exam, as she was flooded with fear and memories of the rape.

As we processed this crisis, I suggested how things could be different for her now than they had been in the past. We began to explore and define what she might need and what she might not want from me and from others when difficult feelings emerge. The concept that her thoughts and feelings were valid and acceptable and that she deserved to have things given to her emotionally was foreign to her. This new way of thinking and caring I conveyed to her was necessary for Elizabeth to begin thinking about other possibilities for relationships:

> THERAPIST: Your family expressed feelings to each other and to you in a certain way—some because of culture, some because of the family you grew up in. Even though you grew up with this, you can learn a different way now. You can choose a way that is going to be the best for you. What do you think someone could do for another if they were crying? What would be a good way to respond to someone who is hurt? What would you like others to do for you?

I had Elizabeth begin to write up a list of what she needed in relationships. I told her it was important that she write down concrete details. For example, "I need support" was not enough. She needed to write down, "I need someone to really listen to me, ask me questions about how I feel, or validate my feelings. I do not want others to tell me that "it will be okay, don't worry about it," or to tell me what to do.

I also taught Elizabeth a method of asserting her feelings, thoughts, and needs using the DESC method (Bower & Bower, 1976). DESC is an acronym for: **D**escribe the situation or behavior, **E**xpress her feelings and thoughts, **S**pecify her needs and changes in the behavior she desires, and consider **C**onsequences—positive and negative to her and the other individual. Elizabeth was able to begin using this method with me and then with others in her life. Since many Asian clients often feel that any direct expression is aggressive, differences between assertiveness and aggressiveness had to be clarified. In particular, I worked hard to help Elizabeth find ways that she could be more direct or assertive in expressing her needs and feelings while still ensuring that she was being respectful at the same time.

One of the most important reasons that Elizabeth needed to learn how to assert herself was that her Asian American communication values ran counter to what is valued in the majority European American culture. Elizabeth would need to be able to assert herself to be successful, to advocate for herself (e.g., with professors or employers), and to deal with the probability of sexual or racial harassment or discrimination in the future. Elizabeth, like many Asian American clients, needed to understand the importance of dealing *flexibly* with others and how cultural factors influenced these skills (i.e., finding ways to remain *respectful* to others was often the key). I encouraged Elizabeth to learn to selectively use different behaviors depending on the situation. I noted that learning assertiveness and communication skills, which are valued by the majority culture, in no way devalued her Asian values. I wanted her to appreciate the fact that rather than being disadvantaged, students of color are enriched when they have bicultural communication competence and can function effectively in multiple cultural contexts.

I also explained to Elizabeth that she needed a lot of practice—and that I was the right person with whom to begin practicing all of these new ways of communicating. Because so many clients think that something is wrong with them because they do not communicate or address interpersonal problems well, I try to help clients like Elizabeth appreciate the fact that they did not have very effective models for learning positive communication skills.

Finally, Elizabeth needed to weed out those individuals in her life who were not supportive of her. At the same time, she needed to become more active in seeking out new relationships with people who were willing to listen to her and wanted to have a mutually responsive relationship. As treatment progressed, I was happy to see Elizabeth increasingly act in ways that reflected her new belief that she deserved to have her needs considered and feelings respected by others:

> THERAPIST: You can't make someone change, but if the other person can't or won't respond to you, then perhaps you need to find others who can. If the other person doesn't want to change, then you have to consider what the consequences are for you. Nobody is perfect, of course, but the other person's willingness to meet you in the middle and try to work out the problems that come up between you is important.

Relational Patterns   From the beginning, issues regarding family experiences and how these were affecting current relationships were identified and worked with. With regard to her family history, for example, I shared with Elizabeth the metaphor about her being a plant. She chose to be a rose. We explored how her rose bush was first neglected and, at times, even trampled on by her gardeners. Not wanting to blame her caregivers but, at the same time, to help her make a more realistic assessment of what had actually occurred in her life, I presented Elizabeth with this:

> THERAPIST: I'm not saying that your parents and grandparents were bad people who wanted to hurt or deprive you. But in my assessment, they could not be better caregivers because of problems in their own lives. Better parents not only provide a roof over your head and clothe and feed you, but they also take pleasure in your accomplishments, support your interests, and give you the help you need when you have problems. From what I know about you, it seems that you didn't feel cared for by them or got the help you needed often enough. I'm hoping that you will start to develop different relationships in your life now—choose better ones that will give you the good things you deserve. In fact, I hope you and I are forming this more rewarding kind of relationship right here in our work together. What do you think?

Understandably, Elizabeth was deeply convinced that something was wrong with her because her father killed himself, her mother would not claim her as her daughter, and her grandparents would kick her out of the house once her financial contribution ended. Elizabeth needed to hear from me, in explicit and unambiguous terms, that she was not responsible or to blame for any of this. She needed to have her false belief that she was not lovable repeatedly disconfirmed by finding that I, and that others, could care about her. An opportunity soon emerged that helped Elizabeth and me grow closer.

Elizabeth dropped out of an ethnic studies class after the sexual assault. However, she retook this class in the spring quarter of the following school year. I happened to be a guest lecturer in her class one day on "Asians in America—Prejudice and Racism." Following this, Elizabeth had much to talk about in the next session. I asked her how it was for her to see me in her class and she said that it had been "great." Elizabeth said that she was very moved by some of the things I spoke about during the presentation.

We began talking about her experiences growing up in a West Coast community. We talked about her family's immigration to and adjustment in America, the racial issues that might be involved in her mother marrying a European American and abandoning her children, what her experiences had been as an Asian American, and the emergence of racial stereotypes in her sexual assault. Soon afterward, Elizabeth decided that she wanted to pursue a teaching credential, hoping to bring ethnic studies into the traditional social sciences/history curriculum in public schools. Clearly, Elizabeth was now developing a positive cultural identity. I was pleased because I felt that this would leave her feeling better about herself and capable of establishing more rewarding relationships in her future.

Stress Management   I often give my abuse clients relaxation skills training and, as our working alliance solidified, I became increasingly interested in teaching Elizabeth how to manage stress more effectively through relaxation. She continued to have difficulty falling asleep and spent many hours worrying about her problems. Early on, she had rejected a referral for medication that might have helped to alleviate these symptoms. So I taught her exercises that I felt would help her achieve the relaxation state as a way of coping with this difficult period. I also felt it would increase her resilience in dealing with future stressors.

Using an educational approach, I first discussed with her the impact of stress on one's body. I noted how relaxation brings one's body back to a balanced state. I then instructed her on how to attain the relaxation state, and how to incorporate relaxation exercises into her daily life. I explained to her that this was an inexpensive, nonharmful way to narrowly focus her brain for a while and that she had total control over this process. During our sessions I guided Elizabeth through different relaxation exercises, such as the use of imagery, meditation, and self-hypnosis. I also taped the relaxation exercises so that my voice would be a continuing source of comfort to her at home. Elizabeth responded to these exercises with an increased sense of calm. Since many Asian Americans tend to somaticize their problems, using imagery that focuses on relaxing internal organs, muscles, and nerves is especially helpful. On the self-hypnosis tape I also presented affirmations and goals for positive changes in her life, such as increased relaxation, self-confidence, and the ability to concentrate.

Elizabeth used the tape religiously and stated that it helped her fall asleep at night. She also reported that she once felt panicked when she thought that her roommate had recorded over the relaxation tape. The tape represented a concrete way for me to provide a secure connection for Elizabeth, which was a primary treatment goal given her history of such profoundly insecure attachments.

Balancing Goals   Counselors are often struggling to balance seemingly appropriate treatment goals with the client's concerns, capacities, and cultural context. For example, one issue I had to try and balance was Elizabeth's need to become more assertive in order to better protect herself, and how her cultural values might impact this. As mentioned earlier, I tried to work with this by helping her understand that she could assert herself and have her needs met without becoming self-centered or culturally inappropriate. Although I was able to successfully balance this goal by emphasizing *respect,* other goals were not balanced so readily.

I also had to walk a fine line between my belief that reporting Rod to campus officials would empower Elizabeth and her reticence to file this report. I chose to deal with this by suggesting that she could report if she chose, giving her information about reporting avenues, and exploring together what either choice would mean for her and how it would feel over time. My internal struggle was to ensure that I did not subtly pressure her—I wanted to honor whatever choice she made. Elizabeth had experienced victimization in the past but, this time, she could take some action. I believed that doing so would diminish the helplessness (and resulting depression) that such victimization experiences usually engender. However, Elizabeth did not feel that she could do this because the rapist had left campus and she believed that it was too late to do anything. In addition, I knew that she was still blaming herself and that publicly talking to others about the rape would add to her feelings of shame. Pressing her to report would only thematically replay the demand/compliance dynamic that she had suffered in the rape and, in lesser ways, in many other relationships throughout her life. *I did not want to evoke these same problematic themes about control in our relationship.* Clearly, this decision needed to be her own. Recognizing that my goals might be differing from hers at times, I wanted to check how our process felt to her:

> THERAPIST: How did you feel about me suggesting that you could report the rape to the dean of students? Does this feel similar in any way to when your mother or grandmother tells you to do something? I guess what I'm really wondering about is if you ever feel you have to do things my way, or worry about what will happen when we disagree about something?

She said she didn't feel the need to do things my way because she felt that I cared about what happened to her. I was glad to hear this, of course, but thinking about how much she had had to comply with others in her life, I again invited her to tell me if ever she felt pressured by me to act in a way she was not comfortable with.

I relinquished my "goal" of pursuing consequences for her rapist after suggesting once that she could write a letter to the dean of students at Rod's present university if she wished. However, I did suggest to Elizabeth that she could think of ways that he could "pay," even if this was limited to fantasizing. Elizabeth said that she had been thinking of this and thought of writing his name on all the women's bathroom walls saying that he was a rapist. Together we elaborated on this fantasy, giving her an opportunity for ventilation through fantasy as a means of further shifting the blame and shame on to the perpetrator rather than keeping it on herself.

Resistance to Treatment   At the beginning of treatment, Elizabeth often arrived 10 to 15 minutes late for her 9:00 A.M. sessions and always apologized for being late. I understood the severity of her depression and could see that she was having difficulty even getting out of bed and taking care of herself. I also understood the ambivalence she had about coming in. She had sought services at the counseling center when she felt desperate, as she had been "crying all the time," although these tears were never shared with another. I don't think she believed that someone would really want to support and help her. To have someone listen to her would be significant, given her history. Further, up until this point, she had never shared with anyone in or outside her family the details of the sexual assault and resulting abortion, the theft or criminal proceedings, and so forth. Her reluctance to share was partially based on Asian cultural values, which discourage the disclosing of problems outside the family. Not bringing shame and dishonor to the family is more important than responding to one's individual needs.

I chose to address the issue of Elizabeth's lateness by acknowledging how difficult it must be for her to get out of bed, given her depression. I wanted to normalize her experience and use empathy to provide an understanding response. At the same time, we focused on how hard it must have been for her to keep inside all that had happened to her. I also acknowledged that she had so little practice expressing her feelings and thoughts. I told her that, given all of that, trusting and believing that I wanted to help would take time. The only thing about her being late was that it gave us less time to talk and work together. Addressing resistance with empathy or understanding, and ensuring that she did not feel blamed or criticized, allowed Elizabeth, like it does for many other clients, to become more punctual.

How might a non-Asian therapist similarly establish rapport with an Asian American client like Elizabeth and successfully engage him or her in treatment? My primary suggestion is that obvious cultural differences, such as race, can be acknowledged. The counselor can ask clients how they feel about working with a counselor who is different, and by asking clients to tell the counselor anytime they feel that the counselor is not understanding their personal experience or cultural perspective. This invitation will signal to clients the counselor's respect for cultural influences, and invite a more honest discussion about any misunderstandings that may occur.

TERMINATION AND SUMMARY THOUGHTS

Elizabeth and I had worked together on a weekly basis for about 25 sessions. The anxiety and depressive symptoms that she had initially improved markedly. She had moved from the outward adjustment stage to the renormalization stage of rape trauma syndrome. For example, she was reaching out and establishing closer relationships with females, and was reestablishing a high school friendship with a male friend. She was beginning to have "first" experiences such as learning to ride a bicycle, going bowling, going out of town to the coast, and going to a Shakespearean Festival.

Developmental and relationship crises push students to seek help during these times. Issues emerge at various points during a student's tenure at the university. Termination with an individual counselor may mean that they will reconnect with the same or a different counselor at a later date. It is important to convey to clients that there will be occasions in the future when they may benefit from seeing a counselor again and frame this as a strength they have in recognizing when they need the support. Often, counselors come to be seen as an extension of the client's family, especially for clients of color, and they may in the ensuing years stop by occasionally to maintain ongoing contact.

Although session limits at the counseling center prevented me from being able to continue treatment with Elizabeth, I told her that she could drop in and visit with me occasionally if she wished. I also let her know that she could have a similar positive experience with another counselor in the future, and that it would make me happy to know that she was getting the help she needed. I also expressed that there still were issues about family history that she might want to deal with in time. Elizabeth still had a long way to go in terms of getting rid of the rocks in her backpack; there was still much pain and difficult issues to be dealt with.

When I said this to Elizabeth, my affection for her was evident. She thanked me and then said something that surprised and touched me greatly:

ELIZABETH: Sometimes, I wish you were my mom. She began to cry and I reached out and held her hand. She continued to stay with her feelings as we sat together in silence. I searched to find a way to tell her that she could keep me, and all of the good things we had shared, inside of her even though we would no longer see each other:

THERAPIST: Someday soon, you will leave for Hong Kong or go to graduate school or a teaching job somewhere, and you will not see me. Even though we will have said goodbye, I would like to think that our relationship will live on inside of you, just as I will keep the good memories I have of you and our time together. You are a brave and resilient person, and our relationship has been important to me.

I saw Elizabeth one more time before the school year ended. Although Elizabeth would still be facing many challenges in the years ahead, I felt strongly that she had a much brighter future. Elizabeth had enriched my life, and I was honored to have shared so much with her.

Questions for Thought and Discussion

1. Rape is a crime that is vastly underreported. Suppose you (or your partner) were a victim of this crime, would you report it? Explain. Note in particular the circumstances under which you would report and those under which you would not report. What cultural and familial beliefs might affect your decision?

2. Imagine you are a teacher, social worker, or minister. How might you respond if a young adolescent told you she had been raped on a date? What would you say and do to try to help?

Suggestions for Further Reading

Atkinson, D. R., Thompson, C. E., & Grant, S. K. (1993). A three dimensional model for counseling racial/ethnic minorities. *The Counseling Psychologist, 21,* 257–277. This article helps therapists use nontraditional methods to work more effectively with peoples of color.

Ottens, A., & Hotelling, K. (Eds.). (2000). *Sexual violence on campus: Policies, programs, and perspectives for the 21st century.* New York: Springer. This comprehensive volume will help counselors and administrators prevent sexual assault on college campuses.

Takaki, R. (1989). *Strangers from a different shore: A history of Asian Americans.* New York: Penguin Books. This excellent book helps counselors treating Asian Americans know their history in America from a perspective that is not Eurocentric.

9

SAM: DEVELOPING RESILIENCE IN GROUP THERAPY AS HE COPES WITH ABANDONMENT BY DRUG ABUSING PARENTS

INTRODUCTION

When I met Sam, a handsome, 9-year-old African American male, dressed in fashionably baggy clothes, sporting a hairstyle that included a flattop with a ponytail, it was hard to believe that the history I had just read was his. According to Sam's records, he was oppositional, aggressive, had used drugs, and might even be in the early stages of a psychosis. Sam had just been placed in the private education/ treatment facility for children and adolescents where I worked, following a physical assault on a teacher's aide. Over the years he had been given multiple diagnoses including attention deficit/hyperactivity disorder, oppositional defiant disorder, and it was believed that he had a learning disability. These problems, and his poor school performance and adjustment, had resulted in his designation as severely emotionally disturbed (SED) (Morgan, 1989), a term used in public school settings for many different kinds of difficult to manage children. Placement in special education classes on the public school site near his home had not been successful, which warranted Sam's transfer to our facility, where we specialized in educating children and adolescents in a counseling environment.

Seeing Sam made me wonder once again: What makes a 9-year-old child aggressive? What makes him use drugs at this early age? What had he experienced to make him become so angry, defiant, and unmanageable? To what extent had his mother's drug use impacted him neurologically? I wondered also about what Sam would need from me to make the "turnaround" to become a successful, productive, and happy child, adolescent, and adult. I knew that I would have to explore and understand the specific challenges that Sam had faced in his family, his community, and his school, so we could work together to help him develop resilience and successfully adjust.

This chapter describes Sam's treatment in group therapy for preadolescent, acting-out boys. The group consisted of boys from various ethnic and cultural backgrounds. As a Caucasian female counselor, I knew that a major task was to establish my credibility given the racial, gender, socioeconomic, and other differences that existed between the group members and me. I wanted to establish with them mutually respectful relationships, where expectations were clear and responses consistent. I hoped that these boys would have the experience in counseling that would give them hope for a more stable future, help them make healthy life choices, and help them find ways to set and accomplish meaningful goals for their lives. The clinical literature clearly suggests that children who have at least one consistent, caring, emotionally supportive adult in their lives are more able to develop resilience. This means that they are more able to cope successfully even when faced with significant life stress such as poverty, crime-filled neighborhoods, abuse, and so forth (Cicchetti & Rogosch, 1997; Kendall-Tackett et al., 1993; Masten & Coatsworth, 1998).

I will first discuss the concept of resilience, followed by a discussion of the clinical features of group therapy with children. Because an integral part of my counseling with Sam occurred in a multicultural context, I will also present a brief overview of some of the relevant sociocultural factors to consider when working with African American children. Finally, I will discuss Sam's developmental history, the problems he faced, and the work we did together.

Resilience

Over the years, researchers have noted that children who are exposed to many stressors at the same time (e.g., family conflict, poverty, child abuse, poorly staffed schools, high crime in their neighborhoods) are at risk for developing psychological problems (Garmezy, 1991; Garmezy & Rutter, 1988; Kazdin, Kreamer, Kessler, Kupfer, & Offord, 1997; Masten & Coatsworth, 1998; Rutter, 1985, 1990; Shaw, Vondra, Hommerding, Keenana, & Dunn, 1994). However, not all children exposed to these types of difficult life circumstances suffer negative psychological effects. The ability to cope or recover quickly from hardships of this type is called *resilience.* In recent years, researchers have dedicated a great deal of effort to identifying factors that help children become resilient (Cicchetti & Garmezy, 1993; Masten & Coatsworth, 1998).

According to the research, there are important aspects of the child, his family, and his community that affect risk and resilience. Risk factors for negative outcomes under stressful situations include gender (boys exhibit more behavior problems than girls), difficult temperament, not having a good relationship with parents, poor planning ability, and poor social skills (Rutter, 1990). Characteristics such as being intelligent, having an easy temperament, and having skills valued by society, such as being athletic or artistic are considered "protective" (Fonagy, Steele, Higgitt, & Target, 1994; Masten & Coatsworth, 1998). In addition, having families who are warm and provide structure, having a supportive extended family, and having financial security are also considered protective and help children make good adjustments when exposed to traumatizing or challenging situations (Masten & Coatsworth, 1998). This ability to adjust well under difficult circumstances is called resilience. Since the family serves as the child's major support system, the parent's ability to provide effective parenting is very important. Unfortunately, when parents have psychological problems (e.g., depression), engage in antisocial behavior (e.g., use drugs), and have stressful life circumstances (e.g., are unemployed, have many children), they become less able to provide adequate supervision, consistent discipline, and emotional responsiveness (see Fonagy et al., 1994). Thus, when children do not have this consistent and responsive parenting, and when they lack attachment to a significant caregiver, their development goes awry and they are more likely to develop psychological difficulties. Secure attachment to a warm and structured caregiver affects children's beliefs about themselves and others (e.g., they feel worthy of being cared about and see people as trustworthy and dependable). When children feel connected to someone, they are more willing to internalize that person's values and show an increased ability to self-regulate. Self-control, including behavioral and emotional regulation, is essential to normative functioning and the lack of this ability increases risk for behavioral problems including conduct disorder (Cole, Zahn-Waxler, Fox, Usher, & Welsh, 1996).

As will be seen in the following case of Sam, kids who lack a secure attachment to a loving, law-abiding, nonabusive, emotionally responsive caregiver, are more likely to engage in antisocial (even violent) behavior, don't feel good about themselves, and are hypervigilant for cues related to hostility. They will have difficulty taking other people's perspectives, problem solving, controlling their emotions and behavior, and be more likely to interpret behavior from others as hostile. This will often result in rejection by their peers and in a drift toward other, similarly disenfranchised or deviant peers (Patterson et al., 1992), which will further increase their risk for delinquent behavior (Fergusson & Horwood, 1996, 1998; Keenan et al., 1995).

In summary, positive attachment to a caring adult will enhance resilience in several ways. These children will:

1. feel good about themselves;
2. trust others;
3. be more likely to see benevolent (positive) rather than malevolent (negative, hostile) intentions in others' behavior;
4. be more likely to value affiliation or connection rather than dominance or revenge;
5. have empathy for others; and
6. be realistic about their own level of aggressiveness and its negative consequences (see Crick & Dodge, 1994).

In other words, self-regulation, self-control, positive self-concept, empathy for others, and choosing to behave appropriately all come from having a secure attachment to a caregiver who provides warmth and consistent discipline. When a child has a relationship such as this, he/she is likely to internalize the attachment figure's values and engage in prosocial behavior.

Group Counseling

For the past five decades, group therapy has gained acceptance as one of the most corrective counseling approaches for children (Callan-Stoiber & Kratochwill, 1998; Schiffer, 1984). The group approach is seen as particularly effective for children during middle childhood (ages 6 to 12) because they are developmentally in a phase when socialization and peer relationships become a prominent feature of their lives. In fact, Parker et al. (1995) suggest that "children who are successful with peers are on track for adaptive and psychologically healthy outcomes, whereas those who fail to adapt to the peer milieu are at risk for maladaptive outcomes" (p. 96). During these years, children spend increasingly more time with peers, who exert an enormous influence on their prosocial or problematic behavior. As such, peer relationships act as a "major psychosocial pathway" toward the development of the child's identity and self-concept (Schaefer, Johnson, & Wherry, 1982). Because children's personalities are so strongly developed within social contexts, group therapy is an excellent arena for the examination and modification of both social and personal problems.

Thus, group therapy may well be the preferred mode of treatment for many children. This may be especially true for children who come from multicultural settings. First, many minority cultures have traditionally depended upon a variety of group activities to bring families, clans, and tribal groups together for cultural, religious, and social activities. As a result, the development of ethnic minority children is often embedded in an interdependent or cooperative orientation (Ho, 1992). Group therapy, therefore, may represent an extension of this relational orientation frequently observed in ethnic minorities. Second, groups consisting of individuals from diverse ethnic backgrounds may permit members to value their similarities *and* their differences with others, learn that people communicate in different ways, and have the opportunity to practice a variety of problem-solving and coping strategies (McKinley, 1991). In particular, children who live or go to school in ethnically diverse environments need the opportunity to learn how to interact cooperatively and to appreciate similarities and differences so they can "find their own place in the world" with others. However, despite the benefits of group therapy, a child's appropriateness for this interpersonal encounter has to be assessed and depends, in part, on his or her attachment history.

Appropriateness for Group   In order to benefit from group therapy, a child must have formed in his or her early history a significant attachment with at least one primary caretaker. Since attachment affects children's ability to establish relationships, have empathy or feel for others, and be able to both give and receive feedback, it plays an essential role in group therapy. In addition, it is helpful if the child has demonstrated the ability to successfully join and sustain participation in some other type of group activity (e.g., sports team, Scouts, or other organized club). For children with histories such as this, group counseling is often effective. Here children can develop insights, build social skills, bond with others, get help solving problems, see that other children share similar problems, and receive feedback on how they affect others. In this caring, interpersonal context, the counselor can create the safety children need in order to try out or, more importantly, practice new and more effective ways of relating to others (Vinogradov & Yalom, 1994; Yalom, 1995). However, children will not be appropriate for group therapy if they are unable to trust others or are unable to establish relationships with others. In addition, children who act out, bully, or scapegoat others can be inappropriate group members because this behavior may continue in the group as well. When this occurs, the pivotal task of the counselor is to stop the scapegoating process and keep the group from teaming up against the weakest member. Some victimized children have such a compulsion to victimize others that the counselor can't always stop this in a group format and must assess carefully whether to include these kids in the group.

Due to the extended nature of many ethnic minority families, children of color often have a history of bonding with other family members if their biological parents are not readily available. The extended kinship patterns and flexibility in caretaking roles within minority families makes it possible for a variety of figures in the child's life (e.g., grandparents) to perform nurturing and caretaking functions in the absence of the child's natural parents. This rich and adaptive heritage of collective development makes it likely that ethnic minority children have had a prior sense of belonging or bonding to some group or person.

Sociocultural Factors

Counselors who work with ethnically diverse clients will benefit from having some familiarity with the cultural values and expectations of those groups. Although individual differences exist within groups, sensitivity to potential cultural factors (e.g., possible differences in communication style) is critical for effective treatment. Although counselors will want to consider the ethnic background and cultural context of each of the children in a group being formed, I will focus only on Sam's African American sociocultural concerns.

The family structure for many ethnic minority individuals is established within a deep relational and cultural context (Fuller, 1997; Sue & Sue, 1999). For most African American families, this structure is based upon strong kinship ties, which may extend beyond the immediate family to include extended family and members of the community. For example, involvement in church and a strong commitment to religious and spiritual values are frequent characteristics. Further, role flexibility, where family members share various tasks frequently occurs. For example, males and females may be equally involved in child-rearing activities and in contributing economically to the family. In addition, it is not uncommon for African American girls to be socialized to be assertive and aggressive and for boys to be socialized to be emotional and nurturing. African American families are also less likely to openly express conflict, more likely to believe that family business should be kept in the family, more likely to use physical punishment, and more likely to value achievement (see Gibbs & Huang, 1997).

In working with African American children, it is important to be sensitive to economic issues and to the impact of racial discrimination on their lives. Poverty, financial worries, and high unemployment rates place excessive demands on parents who may have to devote much energy toward their economic survival, diminishing their ability (in time or energy) to be with their children. For single- or teen-parent families, these demands become extreme. As will be seen in the case that follows, Sam's life circumstances, including his family's low socioeconomic status, parental drug use and absence, lack of resources for positive extracurricular activities such as sports, and insufficient adult supervision all contributed to his presenting problems.

African American families are also faced with the dual responsibility of teaching their children how to function successfully both within their own culture, and in the broader culture, where they have often experienced prejudice and racial discrimination. While the task of establishing a positive identity is challenging for all children, it is more so for those African American children who are poor, and those whose values, communication styles, expectations of others, personal sense of efficacy, and so forth differ from those of the mainstream culture, if that culture devalues these characteristics.

That is, if the mainstream community sees differences as deficiencies, children exhibiting differences have to confront this negative characterization as they try to forge self-affirming identities. The task of developing a positive and self-affirming identity is even more difficult if the children lack appropriate role models or effective and nurturing parenting.

Given African Americans' history of slavery and discrimination, many are appropriately distrustful of police and other governmental agencies. They are as a result cautious about seeking mental health services also. Sam, in the case study that follows, is clearly distrustful of authority figures and of the school system. Many African Americans seek counseling only if in crisis and often prefer to see African American counselors, in part because they feel that they might be able to identify with these counselors, at least racially. Trust issues are salient and premature termination is common, especially if clients experience the counselor as insensitive to their family and cultural background (Sue & Sue, 1999).

All counselors need to be sensitive to clients' sociocultural backgrounds. It is important that counselors have the personal flexibility to be open to the differing worldviews presented by their clients. That is, counselors need to provide a secure, nurturing environment that is accepting and affirming of the differing needs and behaviors clients present, understanding that these will differ because clients all have different personal, family, and cultural experiences. Counselors will be more effective at this if they have explored their own worldviews and the factors that have contributed to the filters and lenses that shape what they see and hear. Only then can they de-center from their own point of view and enter the child's subjective worldview more empathetically. Becoming more aware of one's own worldview will also help counselors develop a nondefensive counseling stance. That is, when counselors are open and accepting, it invites children to express their similarities and differences, as well as agreements and disagreements, more openly. In this way, counselors will be able to encourage children to be more open to accept others who are different from them, accept their own differences from others, and be more willing to try a variety of coping approaches. Counselors who are sensitive to differences in values, communication styles, family constitution and structure, identity development, and normal developmental milestones will be more effective. Finally, attention to the potential impact of racism, poverty, and cultural conflicts on the family and child is very important.

CASE ILLUSTRATION

Presenting Problem

Sam began to receive counseling services shortly after he was designated by his school's psychologist as severely emotionally disturbed (SED) (Hagborg & Konigsberg, 1991; Morgan, 1989; Trupin, Forsyth-Stephens, & Low, 1991). SED is a label used by school administrators to refer to children whose psychological problems are greatly impacting their educational adjustment. These psychological problems may include conduct disorder, attention deficit/hyperactivity disorder, oppositional defiant disorder, mood disorders, and a variety of other disorders. A majority of children labeled SED have a history of aggression or acting-out at school. Sam, who had received multiple psychiatric diagnoses over the years, and had been given the SED label, had experienced both physical and emotional abuse in his home. Sam also lived in a neighborhood where gang activity and drug abuse were rampant.

Sam, like other children diagnosed as SED, had first been placed in a special classroom in his public school district for children with similar problems. When he failed to show improvement in this classroom, the school district referred him to our specialized, highly structured treatment facility for education and counseling services. In our facility, children are placed in small classrooms (six to eight children per classroom) which operate according to a behavior modification model. In addition, children receive individual or group therapy, which may use a variety of treatment approaches.

With Sam and the other children, an interpersonal approach to treatment that focused on the interaction that occurred between us was used (Kiesler & Van Denberg, 1993; Strupp & Binder, 1988; Teyber, 2000). This relational approach incorporated sensitivity to ethnic and cultural socialization norms. In other words, I believed that Sam's problems were the result of his attempts to cope with the pain he had experienced in his relationships with important caregivers. My goals in treatment, therefore, were to help Sam recognize that his coping strategies were no longer being effective but rather were resulting in negative consequences for him. It seemed that Sam needed to see that there were other ways to cope that would bring about more positive outcomes. My belief was that if I provided Sam with the experience of being cared about and consistently responded to, he and I would develop a strong bond. Further, I believed that out of experiencing this secure relationship with me, Sam would begin to experience a sense of being worthwhile, increase his self-esteem, develop empathy for others, and be willing to try out new ways of interacting with others. For Sam, as with most clients, change does not simply come about by being told they are worthwhile. Instead, they change by experiencing respect and high regard in their relationship with the counselor.

Developmental History

Although Sam was placed in a fourth grade classroom, his grades and achievement scores indicated he was far below the fourth grade level in most academic areas. This was not due to a lack of intelligence but rather due to the fact that Sam had actually spent very little time in the classroom over the past four years. For example, in kindergarten, he was sent home frequently because of his aggressive behavior (i.e., fighting with other children, breaking classroom toys) and lack of attention (which often resulted in Sam disturbing or picking on other children). Although Sam was promoted to the first grade, he was often tardy, missed many school days, and sometimes was sent home from school for acting-out (e.g., fighting, breaking toys, taking things that did not belong to him, refusing to follow instructions). Teachers continued to promote Sam rather than hold him back despite his academic problems because no teacher wanted him to repeat the year in her classroom. By the third grade, Sam's oppositional and aggressive behavior and his poor academic performance warranted his placement in a SED classroom at his public school. Here, Sam's problems continued. In particular, his aggressive behavior escalated. Finally, when Sam became physically threatening to a teacher's aide, he was referred to our program. Sam arrived at his new placement angry and withdrawn. On his very first day at this new school Sam tried to assault another student.

Client Description

When I first met 9-year-old Sam, I was struck by the image he had created for himself. He was wearing baggy denim jeans and expensive sneakers. His hair was cut with a flattop and he had a small braided, beaded ponytail in back. He wore a gold hoop earring in his left ear and a large gold chain with a BMW medallion around his neck. Sam swaggered into my office, sat down, and initially refused to talk to me. Rather than "forcing" him to talk, I told him I was willing to "hang out" with him. I also said that if he chose to, he could help me decorate the bulletin board in my office. After about five minutes of stony silence, Sam got up and began to hand me pieces of construction paper while I stapled. Before leaving my office, Sam made reference to the fact that I was not much taller than he was (I am a little over five feet tall). He said this with a smile that lit up his entire face. I surmised that my physical size and casual style reduced any sense of judgment or threat he may have anticipated from me or, perhaps, that he could readily control our relationship. I guessed that Sam's previous experiences with authority figures had probably taught him to be wary and that if I had insisted on somehow forcing him to engage with me, he probably would have shown more anger and hostility. It seemed that in my relationship with Sam, I would need to emphasize respect and cooperation rather than hierarchy and authority. At the same time, I felt that Sam also needed to know that there were rules and expectations that he needed to abide by. Sam's previous experiences had been either punitive or permissive, lacking a middle ground where rules were enforced with respect and warmth. With Sam, as with most kids, empowerment to make positive choices for his life would result primarily from experiencing a relationship that was caring and emotionally responsive, where rules and expectations were clear, and where consequences were logical and consistent.

Sam believed he was placed in our facility because he was a "bad" child. He wanted to attend school on a half-day schedule so he could go home and play without adult involvement or constraints. His plan, which he told me about early on, was to "get into lots of trouble" so the school "would have to place me back on half-day." Although the principal told Sam from the outset that half-days were not an option at our school, Sam was out to prove him wrong.

Social Context

Sam's parents, Morris and Chantae, were 16 years old when Sam was born. They both dropped out of high school and did not return to earn a diploma or GED. His parents never married and remained together only sporadically in subsequent years. Chantae's own mother was also 16 years old when she gave birth to Chantae. Chantae had little contact with her biological father. When Chantae was 6 years old, her mother got married and moved to Tennessee. Chantae remained behind and was raised by her maternal grandparents, Raymond and Annie. Raymond and Annie had three other children living at home (two daughters and one son) who were 10 to 15 years older than Chantae. Raymond died when Chantae was 10 years old. Chantae continued to live with her grandmother until Sam was 5 years old. At that time, she and Sam moved in with Luke, Chantae's boyfriend. Chantae had an unstable relationship with Luke—she was sometimes with Luke and at other times returned to Morris (Sam's biological father). For the next two years, Chantae and Sam moved back and forth between Luke's house, her grandmother's house, and Morris' parents, depending upon the status of Chantae's relationships. During that time, Chantae often left Sam for days, even weeks, with her grandmother or with Morris and his parents.

Chantae never worked—her primary support came from Welfare and Aid to Dependent Children. During her late teenage years, she got involved in illicit drug use. By the time Sam had started school at our facility, Chantae was rumored to be on crack cocaine. Morris sporadically worked on construction jobs. He had a police record beginning in adolescence for petty theft, carrying a weapon, and noncompliance in school. Two years prior to Sam's enrollment at our facility, Morris was arrested for holding up a convenience store. Sam was found asleep in the back seat of Morris' car during this robbery. Following his arrest, Morris was jailed in a state penitentiary and was due to be paroled sometime in the next year.

During the year prior to Sam's placement in our facility, Chantae began leaving Sam with Annie for longer periods of time, sometimes for months at a time. She had another child, fathered by Luke, named Yazmine, who was 11 months old when Sam started at our school. According to Child Protective Services (CPS) reports, Chantae had been accused of physically abusing Sam on numerous occasions. He had, for example, come to school on a number of occasions with untreated welts and cuts. There was no school record of sexual abuse. As a result of the abuse and Chantae's inconsistent living situation, Annie was given primary parental custody of Sam (although Chantae was still able to live or visit unsupervised in the home). Sam had a social worker assigned to him who visited the home once a month.

Although Sam reported a close relationship with his great-grandmother, he was also very protective of his mother and baby sister. He expressed concerns about his mother's health and welfare and believed that once his father was released from prison, the two would get married so "we could all be a family."

Annie loved her great-grandson but she was in her mid-sixties and was having increasing difficulty managing Sam's behavior. She tended to be permissive and used very little discipline. Although Sam never assaulted any of his family members, he often ran away for hours at a time when angry. He denied involvement with gangs and said he had "tried" alcohol and marijuana a few times. His family was, however, concerned about future drug use and/or gang involvement. Sam's uncle Markus had been a stable male figure in Sam's life up until Sam was 6 years old, at which time he joined the army and now had only occasional contact with Sam.

Sam's school performance was poor, due largely to his unstable family life and disrespect for teachers and rules. Within the first week at our facility, Sam began to demonstrate a certain amount of "street smarts." For example, his new teacher reported that while accompanying Sam to recess on the first day, another teacher was in the hallway counting the children's lunch money. Without stopping or changing his walking stride, Sam was able to glance once at the teacher's hands and report how much money she was holding in one and five dollar bills. The next day Sam was caught breaking into the classroom's computer security lock in order to play Nintendo instead of practicing his math on the computer.

Sam was also well coordinated and enjoyed sports—especially basketball. Despite Sam's bravado and hostile presentation, he was also bright and could be sociable with others. As a result, the staff felt positive about his appropriateness for our program and his potential for future success.

Individual Counseling

Before placing Sam in group counseling, I saw him for four individual counseling sessions. Whenever I work with children or adolescents, I try to do both individual and group therapy. I find that there are issues that children can best address in individual counseling first (e.g., sexual abuse or other issues that evoke deep shame). Later, group therapy becomes most appropriate—it provides children with the opportunity to feel understood by others, develop empathy for themselves and others, build social skills, and receive constructive feedback about how others experience them. As part of this process, they begin to develop self-esteem and feel empowered to make healthier choices for their lives. Sam, as a preadolescent, was a good candidate for group therapy as the primary treatment, with individual sessions providing the opportunity to further process relevant issues from the group.

I knew that establishing a working alliance with Sam would be critical. Minority children, like Sam, have often had negative encounters with authority figures so that Sam's skepticism regarding any "White" or "authority" person's ability or desire to be helpful made sense. Strict authoritarianism, which would put Sam in a victim, powerless role, which he had likely experienced during his many years in the system, would not be effective. Yet, Sam needed structure, consistent rules, and a clear sense of expectations within a warm and caring relationship. Thus, in our work together, the treatment goals and techniques were secondary—I knew these could not be implemented until Sam came to trust me and feel safe with me. It felt important that Sam experience, by my words, tone of voice, and other body language, both my respect for and interest in him. At the same time, he needed to know that I would not be manipulated by him and would remain effectively in charge. In our work together, I communicated this by clearly conveying my expectations (e.g., that stealing, being assaultive, and being disrespectful were unacceptable) and that the consequences for inappropriate behavior would be consistent (e.g., time-out, loss of special privileges; in contrast, he would be rewarded with special activities when long periods of appropriate behavior were sustained).

Most children are unaware of the role of the counselor. Due to his experiences with the school and social work system, however, Sam had some idea of what a counselor "does." To him, a counselor was a person who "meddles in your family stuff" but at the same time "could be fun." During our individual sessions together, it appeared that my initial credibility as a helper was going to be based upon whether or not the "fun" was worth the "meddling."

In my office I have only a few rules: no taking or breaking my toys and the sand needs to stay in the sandbox. Although the facility I worked for followed a strict behavior modification program, coming to counseling was available for all regardless of their behavior. As a result, most children enjoyed the refuge of the counseling hour. Furthermore, my simple rules made sense to the children and I had relatively few behavioral problems.

Occasionally, however, the children engaged in testing, which usually had a physically threatening quality to it. With Sam this occurred at the end of our second session together. Sam and I had spent the session playing basketball with my small indoor hoop and sponge-like basketball. I typically remove my shoes and jewelry when I play. When I went to find my watch at the end of our time, it was not where I had placed it. Sam glared at me, fists clenched. "You think I took it," he yelled. "You're just like the rest of them." I responded with, "Actually Sam, I was hoping you would help me look for it, it may have fallen." Sam glared at me for what seemed like an eternity. The tension in the room had suddenly escalated and it seemed as though Sam was ready to pounce. His breathing had become more rapid and his jaw quivered slightly. I began to look under a chair when Sam put his hand in his trouser pocket and threw the watch at me, "Take your stinking thing," he said. I had not accused Sam of taking it and was surprised that, having taken it, he was willing to relinquish it so quickly. Although his fury was on the surface, he also seemed close to tears. I believed Sam was testing me to see if I would become angry (and punitive) or permissive (and minimize the inappropriateness of this behavior). It was important that I let him know his behavior was not appropriate and convey that in a firm but non-shaming way.

TH: Thanks for giving it back to me Sam.

CL: And? (glaring and clenching his fists)

TH: I don't like having my things taken without permission but I hope you and I can work it out.

CL: That's it?

TH: What do you mean Sam?

CL: You're not going to take me to the principal or something?

TH: No Sam. I think this one we can work out together. There is one more thing. I did not like it when you threw it at me. But I do appreciate having it back. If there is something in this office that you would like to have, let's talk about it first, OK?

CL: (Sam unclenching his fist, seeming much calmer) Well don't you be so stupid and leave things like that around. Others might not give them back so easily.

In this episode, I was aware of how easily our interaction could have escalated into a power struggle. I wanted to convey to Sam that there were limits (stealing was not OK; throwing things at me was unacceptable) but do this in a way that was not rejecting or punitive. I also hoped that I could begin giving Sam a different language for communicating his wants (i.e., he could ask). I also wanted to model for him how to convey feelings without acting them out (in this instance, by telling him calmly and without anger that I didn't like the watch being thrown at me). Over the months, Sam and I had replays of this issue, where Sam would foul me too hard during a basketball game or throw the ball in anger toward my shoulder. During each episode, I would stop the game, ask Sam what it was he wanted to convey during these aggressive episodes, and let him know that being physically aggressive toward me was unacceptable. The game would end and we would resume it only after Sam was able to express *in words* the feelings he was experiencing and the needs he wished to convey. We spent many basketball games sitting quietly while Sam glared in anger. Over time he learned that I was not easily manipulated. At the same time, I was fair, respectful, and cared about him.

Sam and I began to establish a collaborative relationship. Together we made up elaborate basketball rules as we played in the office—rules necessary for getting around the desk, taking equal turns, and the number of points allotted for certain types of baskets. Occasionally we talked about how this was like life. To play, survive, thrive, and so forth, some rules had to be followed, and others had to be negotiated. Playing with Sam also gave me the opportunity to let him know that I valued his input on how we spent our time together and that I was willing to invest my energy to learn what he enjoyed. This process went a very long way in helping us establish a caring, reciprocal working relationship. During this time, Sam was beginning to settle into school and had taken a leadership role in the classroom (which at times had a negative quality that included provoking fights between groups of children). Sam had also discovered that the facility was one place he could not "get kicked out of." Sam appeared to look forward to our time together, and I knew our relationship was off to a good start when, as I was returning Sam to his classroom he stopped, turned to me and said, "You play pretty good basketball for a short White woman!" Gratefully, I was aware that had Sam not been reached at this young age, it might have been much harder to connect with him.

Sam and I had many other encounters that involved threat during the early phase of counseling. For example, on a morning before one of our individual sessions, Sam had a verbal altercation with another child and, as a result, was sent to time-out. By the time he came to my office he was sullen and withdrawn. He was uncommunicative and angry during most of the session so I allowed him to play mostly by himself in my office as a way to provide him with the space he needed to calm down. On the way out of our session he ran into Ron, the child he had argued with that morning. In front of my office door (with me unintentionally caught standing between the two) the two boys began to glare at one another, clenching their fists. The tension was intense and the probability of a physical altercation was high. I knew I needed some way to defuse the tension and give them each a face-saving "out." Speaking in a gentle, but firm voice:

TH: The two of you had a difficult morning together . . .

SAM: Yeah. (moving closer to Ron, seeming ready to attack) And I spent a half an hour in time-out because of this asshole. He's not going to get away with it. (Sam was now pushing against me since I was standing between him and Ron.)

RON: Man, you are *nothing.* (He too seemed ready to attack.) I have no problem making something out of this with you!

TH: Yes, you could fight and someone will get hurt. Sam, I'd like it if you would take off on that side of the hall (nodding to my left) and Ron, I'd like it if you would take off on that side of the hall (nodding to the right).

SAM: I'm not running from him!

TH: No, that's not what I'm saying. I'm asking both of you to leave at the same time to find a place—any place away from each other—and cool down. I don't care where it is—just somewhere quiet on the school grounds. You two can fight and both get into trouble and both be losers, or, you can go your separate ways and both be winners.

I slowly backed away from the boys. Sam and Ron continued to glare at one another, but they slowly backed away also. They walked away in opposite directions although they continued to peer back at each other. Sam found a place under the stairway where he sat for half an hour before he returned to class on his own. I made it a point to praise each child individually before they went home that day for making the appropriate choice to not fight under such tempting circumstances. I was also silently relieved that I did not get into a power struggle that I surely would have lost.

These two examples are intended to portray some of the realities of working with children like Sam. They are often angry and hostile but there is generally an element of self-preservation in that stance. Sam's life experiences had taught him to be vigilant. He didn't know whom he could trust. In his home and neighborhood, a "tough guy" exterior was a realistic survival stance. In addition, his experiences with authority figures (school, social services, etc.) had also been disempowering—for Sam, it felt as though they were always in control and in charge. Although Sam seemed hostile and sullen, I also saw him as a young child trying to cope with deep emotional wounds, lacking the language needed to communicate and manage his pain. Sam needed help developing a way to communicate his needs that was not destructive. He also needed to develop a greater sense of *efficacy* so he would be less vulnerable to shaming by others.

Group Counseling

The group was composed of five boys (ages 8 to 9). I had seen each boy approximately four times in prior individual sessions. All of the boys had common presenting problems involving acting-out behavior and noncompliance in school which had profoundly affected their academic performance and school adjustment. They were each designated as SED and had not been able to adjust in special education classes at their local school sites. They were also at high risk to become juvenile delinquents and, subsequently, continue an antisocial adulthood of criminal behavior if their acting-out behavior did not change.

It is probably best to have no more than five or six in a group of aggressive boys. Imposing structure and setting limits is harder with a larger group. The group first met after each child had gone through a full week without being aggressive toward others at school. This meant they had the potential to control, at least for short periods, their aggressive behavior. This ability was important because group therapy can be confrontive, requires some social skill, and is most effective when members can have empathy for others.

The group was composed of children from different ethnic backgrounds that reflected the ethnic minority makeup of the facility and of their home neighborhoods. There were two African American boys (Sam and Donnie), two Latino boys (Jose and Manuel—both of Mexican descent), and one Caucasian boy (Paul). The challenge at the onset of group therapy was to make overt any racial tension between the children while developing rules about how this tension was going to be handled by all of the group participants, including me.

First Group Meeting   Although these children often played cooperatively together during recess and in the classroom, when anger erupted they frequently used racial slurs against one another. I wanted to establish a safe and cohesive environment, where differences (racial, athletic ability, etc.) would be valued and not denigrated. During our initial group session, Sam was angry because he believed that I was no longer going to see him in individual sessions. Although we had discussed our schedule beforehand (i.e., that he, like the other children, would be seen in some individual as well as group sessions), Sam felt that my time was going to be taken away from him. As the children assembled in my office, Jose picked up the basketball that Sam and I had frequently used.

SAM: Hey! You can't play with that!

JOSE: Who says?! (passing the ball to Paul)

SAM: I say and I'm bigger than you!

JOSE: It doesn't belong to *you*, it belongs to Ms. Cassie—being bigger doesn't matter.

SAM: Listen you dumb wetback, when *I'm* here the basketball is mine 'cause I'm a better player so put it back!

At hearing the phrase "dumb wetback" Jose and Manuel looked at one another and began slowly circling Sam. In order to diffuse the tension and potential fight that was ensuing among the boys, I began to set immediate limits.

TH: (making eye contact with each of them and speaking in a firm but calm voice) Sam, Jose, Manuel, Donnie, and Paul—I need you to sit down right where you are.

TH: Sam, take a deep breath—what just happened?

SAM: (arms folded, and looking away) Jose was using *our* basketball, the one we use for our games. I think you should keep it for me and not allow anyone else to play with it.

TH: I understand that you like to play basketball, and I enjoy the special time that we spend together. I wonder if you are worried that perhaps if Jose or someone else is in my office with us for this group, maybe you and I will not be able to spend any more time together?

SAM: (still silent but turns his face briefly toward me)

TH: There are some things that we need to talk about. First, let's plan out our schedules for when I will be seeing each of you alone—just like we all talked about before. I'll get out our appointment cards, and with each of you, we will come up with a time that we will meet—just you and I together.

The boys' heated discussion was significant for all of them, but especially for Sam. He wanted reassurance that our time together was special and that we were going to continue our relationship on a one-to-one basis. Realizing that Sam wanted to "save face" with the other boys but also wanted to feel "special," I chose not to delve deeper into this issue with him right then. I then went to each child with an appointment card, kneeled down, and faced them individually to make our appointment. In this way, each boy had the opportunity to feel special while at the same time Sam could see that they were all treated equally. Sam and Jose both appeared appeased.

Next, I wanted to address the racial name-calling and the need for group therapy rules.

TH: (getting out a large sheet of butcher paper and tacking it to the wall) Now that appointments have been settled, let's talk about some rules. I need you all to help in coming up with some important rules for our group so no one feels left out or feels like others have done something to make them angry. Sometimes when we are mad at other people we call them names. What are some names that we might call people when we are angry? If you think a name is too bad to say out loud, you can spell it out for us. I'll write it on this paper.

PAUL: Um, jerk, waste-case, dweeb . . .

SAM: Bagger, retard, fool, mother fucker . . .

JOSE: Stupid, goob, asshole . . .

The boys continued coming up with all of the derogatory names they could, first with slang terms, then profanity, and later with Spanish curse words (which all the children knew). By the end, the boys were having fun coming up together with their own funny combinations such as "snot-breath" and "nose-hair-head." Now, racial slurs needed to be addressed.

> TH: What great imaginations you all have! Sometimes though, when a person *really* wants to get someone mad or in order to *really* hurt their feelings, he might call them a bad word that has to do with their race or color or religion. We're going to make the same word list, but this time we're going to do it a little bit differently. Jose and Manuel, I want the two of you to come up with a list of hurtful words that someone might call you because you are Mexican. Donnie and Sam, make a list of hurtful words someone might call you because you are African American. Paul, make a list of bad words someone might direct at you because you are White.

At first the children were hesitant about this exercise, but once we got started we were able to fill up the other side of the paper with all sorts of racial slurs and their combinations. Since all the boys had attended racially mixed schools, none of these words were new or surprising to them. What made it a different experience for them was that this time these words were discussed out in the open—in a nonangry, noncontemptuous, and nonthreatening way. In order to address this sensitive but important matter, I wanted to diffuse the heated quality of the subject.

> TH: Sam, if someone called a White boy one of these words (pointing to my list of White slurs) how do you think he might feel?
>
> SAM: Well, he might feel angry or dissed (disrespected).
>
> TH: Yes, you're right. That is how he might feel. Manuel, how do you think a Hispanic might feel if someone called him some of these words? (pointing)
>
> MANUEL: He could feel hurt inside, maybe like he is different from other people or maybe that he has to do something so no one will think he is a "woose" (sissy).

Around the room I went, asking each boy to address the racial slurs of a child from a different ethnic group. No child had to address his own feelings about his own ethnic group or risk placing himself on the line. The issue was addressed and together, in a collaborative fashion, we decided that our first rule was "no capping" (name-calling). We took the paper off the wall, rolled it up, tied a ribbon around it, and placed it in my closet in case we ever needed to turn to it for future reference.

Working Alliance   The relationship between counselor and client is a central feature of treatment. The effectiveness of the counselor's interventions pivots on the quality of this relationship and the interaction or process enacted between counselor and client. As a result, the counselor needs to convey to clients that they are valued and that the counselor has good intentions toward them. On the client's part, he must be motivated to change and trust that the counselor is willing and equally motivated to help in this change process. For ethnic minority children working with a counselor who is from a different background, racial issues and how these are managed become important to the developing relationship. For a collaborative relationship to develop, the child's understanding of the counselor's achieved credibility (i.e., effectiveness and trustworthiness) and ability to provide help in spite of any racial differences, is significant (Sue & Zane, 1987). Although I genuinely liked Sam and saw psychological strengths in him, I initially struggled with my own feelings of inadequacy—could I, a White female counselor, establish credibility with him and convey my ability to help?

During the first few individual and group sessions with Sam, I tried to convey a nonjudgmental and nonpunitive stance but at the same time also set clear rules and was firm in my expectations (e.g., letting him know that taking things like my watch without permission was not okay). While I felt that Sam was beginning to recognize that our relationship was different from other relationships he had experienced (ours was caring and nonjudgmental but still firm), I did struggle at times with my ability to handle our racial, cultural, and economic differences. Sometimes I felt overwhelmed by the cycle of poverty and discrimination that Sam faced. While my lower-middle-class upbringing was not easy, my status as a Caucasian or "majority" member of society gave me the belief or hope that as bad as life can be, circumstances can always get better if you worked hard enough. I knew that I needed to explore if Sam, given his life circumstances including a drug-addicted mother, multiple drug using males entering and exiting his life, lack of effective home discipline, and poor social and school adjustment, had *hope* that good things could be part of his future. Did Sam believe that his life could change and be better?

Because Sam was a young African American male, living in a high-crime neighborhood, having drug using parents, lacking effective parenting or healthy role models, the challenges he had to face were overwhelming. I found myself wanting to protect Sam from his environment and from a potentially menacing future. Interestingly, *Sam shared the same protective concern for me.* That is, he had his own desire to protect me from what he believed was my own inability to take care of myself. Based on my knowledge of Sam's history, I knew he felt he needed to protect the other women in his life (i.e., mother, great-grandmother, baby sister, and others, perhaps because he had seen them being hit). I began to wonder if this role of protector was one of the arenas in which Sam felt some sense of importance and could exert some control. It thus became important to understand how this had developed and the meaning it held for Sam. I didn't want Sam to feel he had to parent me—he needed to be a child and have *his* needs responded to. At the same time, however, I realized that an important part of Sam's identity revolved around being a protector of others because this protected him from further physical abuse from his mother and it was a role in which he received affirmation from others.

The following dialogue demonstrates how Sam's desire to protect me was played out. During one of the first few group sessions together, a few of the boys began to test the limits of the group. Although they spoke in low voices, they were intentionally loud enough for me to hear.

> DONNIE: I don't want to be here or even in school today. Will someone run with me? Let's go to the arcade or something?

> MANUEL: I'd run, but I've got a home visit this weekend, and I don't want a demotion in points. Maybe next week.

> JUAN: I'll run. If we do it soon from this office the hall monitors won't be able to get us right away, and we could be there for awhile and move on. This gringa can't stop us.

PAUL: I'll get food from her desk. Sam, you coming?

SAM: That's stupid! What if she *does* try to stop you? I'm not going to hurt the lady and you're not neither. She's been real nice. In fact, if you touch her, I'll be *on* you.

DONNIE: You're just saying that because you *like* her. You're the one who's stupid—there's three of us and you. What you gonna do about that?

SAM: I told you—I will be *on you* faster than you think!

TH: I'm not hard of hearing. I can hear all of you just fine. Manuel and Sam, you are both making a good choice not to run. Donnie, Juan, and Paul if you want to run—okay. I'm not going to stop you— there's the door. But first, I'd like you each to think about your choices. Donnie, you go up a level tomorrow and running will jeopardize that. Juan and Paul, you both have basketball tryouts after school. If you choose to run you will be off the team.

JUAN: I'm not—I'll run another day. I want to play ball after school. They're giving out uniforms. Paul?

PAUL: Maybe I'll stay then—Donnie, we'll go another day.

DONNIE: (loudly, speaking directly at me) I'm running anyway. Those are all stupid reasons to not run and you're stupid for thinking that moving up a level will keep me here!

SAM: (approaching Donnie) You're dissing her—you *can't* do that and I won't let you.

TH: Sam, I appreciate your concern but I can take care of myself. Move away from Donnie. You have been doing fine up until now—you don't want to get into a fight and have to go into time out. What I do need you to do right now is to move away from Donnie, let him leave if that is his choice, and go about your own business. The same goes for everyone else. You know your choices—make them now and let's get on with our group.

A potentially assaultive situation in group counseling is always a spur-of-the-moment circumstance. All the boys except for Donnie wound up staying in the group. Donnie left to save face. After sitting in the hallway for five minutes he returned to the group. Sam spent about the same amount of time saving his own face by sitting in the corner of the room and tapping the wall with his foot. Both boys needed to cool down and, as they did, I continued with our group activity for the day. Sam and Donnie eventually calmed down and returned to the group. I waited until our next group meeting before I began addressing this incident.

I added a new group rule about having the boys leave for a cool down period rather than act out. I then wanted to explore the issue of Sam's apparent need to take care of me. I wondered if this was an expression of Sam's transference (i.e., had Sam transferred to me the same protectiveness he felt toward his mother and other female relatives?). Was this a coping strategy Sam used at home to stave off abuse or punishment? Did he witness caregivers like his mother or grandmother being mistreated? In addition, I was concerned that perhaps Sam's protectiveness toward me was actually in response to some expression on my part of needing protection. It seemed important that I explore this as I examined my own concerns regarding protectiveness.

To reinforce group cohesiveness, during this session I suggested a group drawing activity. I had all the boys share a large sheet of butcherpaper and asked them to come up with a scene from school. I then instructed them to draw the scene together with each of them cooperating in some activity. They chose to draw an afternoon kick-ball game.

TH: I really enjoy having you all cooperate together today with your drawing. I especially like the scene you're drawing with all of you having fun together at the party. Can you each tell me what you are doing in the picture?

JUAN: I'm getting ready to play kick-ball. I get to be team captain and Paul's on my team.

PAUL: (laughing) Yeah—and when we win, we get a trophy, and sponsored by Nike!

MANUEL: We could all be on the same team—just us from the group and we'll play against some other kids.

DONNIE: Sam and me will play—I'll draw me practicing with you (pointing at Sam). What do you think?

SAM: Okay—but I'll draw Ms. Cassie in the picture. The staff is boring and she will probably have more fun with us.

TH: Sam, you seem to think that it is pretty important that I am taken care of at this game. Can you tell me more?

SAM: Well, I don't know—we're having more fun than the staff and maybe you don't want to be alone.

JUAN: She's a grown-up. Grown-ups like to be with other grown-ups, not shorties.

TH: Sometimes grown-ups like to be with kids and sometimes they like to be with other grown-ups and still other times they like to be alone. What do some of you others think?

PAUL: My mom is alone a lot since my dad left. She says she's busy all day and being alone is *good* for her.

TH: Do you ever worry about her?

PAUL: Sometimes. I used to feel that maybe she was lonely and that I should stay with her more when she was home and stuff, but she says she's okay and that she needs to worry about *me* and not the other way around. I think she's okay.

SAM: My mom is by herself without nobody a lot. Sometimes she gets sick or gets in trouble with the police or with bad people. She can't help it—Grandma says it's because she and my aunts never learned to take care of themselves. With my dad gone, she just gets in trouble more. My dad and grandma say I'm now the man of the house so I have to look out for her.

With this session, Sam's protectiveness toward me began to make sense. Sam saw his mother and aunts as helpless. This belief was reinforced by his grandmother and by his father who reminded Sam, during prison visitation days, "You're the man of the house—look after your mother and your grandma—they need to be taken care of." In Sam's neighborhood, "being taken care of" often meant protection from physical harm. Sam's family often praised him for protecting his "helpless" mother. In short, Sam's own worth was attached to his ability to safeguard the women in his family. Although I certainly had my own reasons for wanting to protect Sam, his protective behavior toward me had to do with his own beliefs about how he viewed his own self-worth and how he saw his mother and other "alone" women such as myself. These two sessions helped me to understand a number of relational themes for Sam: how he saw his "worth" in the world, how he saw himself in relation to his mother, and how he behaved toward people (at least women) he cared about. I realized that a principal goal of our work together was to involve Sam in learning that he could relate to me differently than to the other women he had been close to. Sam needed to know that *he* could be responded to rather than be the caretaker. I also wanted him to know that he did not have to protect me in order to protect himself from being punished, abandoned, or abused—that I would remain consistently engaged regardless of his behavior. I felt that Sam would benefit from finding other ways of receiving positive attention (e.g., academics, sports, drama). I felt that if Sam developed this *flexibility* in relating to others it would enhance his resilience.

Sam's developing resilience was evident in the success he was experiencing at our facility. Despite his challenging history, he was improving his grades, making friends, and identifying enjoyable activities (e.g., sports) that involved cooperation rather than conflict. I realized that this had developed in part out of his growing attachment to me. Out of this attachment, Sam was more willing to try new behaviors, feel empathy toward others, and acknowledge some of his fears, struggles, and wishes. I was pleased by his progress and wanted to help him access more fully whatever resources were available to him in his family and in his community.

CASE CONCEPTUALIZATION

Client Conceptualization

Sam was raised in an impoverished household and in a neighborhood marked by gang and drug activity. At home few rules or behavioral constraints were placed on Sam. By the time Sam started school, he was an unruly, angry, and an acting-out child. In addition, his mother frequently physically abused Sam. Like many abused children, Sam had learned to "read" his environment well. He was vigilant for what others might be thinking, feeling, or what they may be likely to do next. On the one hand he was sensitive to the needs of others but was also frequently "sneaky" and deceitful. Thus, while Sam was likable and enjoyable to be around, he could also be hurtful toward others. At those times he would lash out, using what he knew about their vulnerabilities against them. This social/antisocial presentation seen in Sam probably developed out of his deeply ambivalent feelings toward his mother. On the one hand, he loved her deeply. On the other hand, he felt shamed and outraged by her physical abuse of him. As a counselor, it felt important to affirm Sam's love for his mother as well as his outrage toward her behavior. It seemed that only then would Sam feel free to relate to others in a more even or composed way.

Sam's mother was 16 when he was born and was unable to take care of her own emotional needs, let alone the physical and psychological needs of her young son. Sam was inappropriately placed in the position of parent when, at a very early age, he began to meet his mother's need for protection from others. While parentified children such as Sam may feel special and grown-up for being their family's little man, they miss out on the opportunity to be children themselves. Given this parentification, compounded by the vigilance learned and shame engendered by an abusive environment, children (such as Sam) can only be adult for so long before their own helplessness and rage erupts into anger and acting-out behavior. Indeed, given his age and limited sociofamilial resources, much of Sam's early acting-out behavior could be seen as a cry for help being expressed in ways consonant with his developmental level. Given Sam's range of behaviors—withdrawal, cooperation, and rage—that seemed to shift without warning, it was no wonder that he had a host of different diagnoses from various professionals throughout his young life.

In addition to his family problems, Sam lived in an impoverished and violent inner-city neighborhood. He had repeatedly witnessed crimes—both petty and violent. Both his home and his neighborhood were turbulent, inconsistent, and violent. Sam's tough guy exterior may have been an externalization of anxiety (possibly PTSD) and/or depression, borne out of his inconsistent and frequently violent sociofamilial circumstances. Given Sam's developmental level and inadequate parenting, his ability to convey his feelings and needs was greatly limited. Thus, his symptoms of hypervigilance, withdrawal, sullenness, anger, and assaultiveness, coupled with moments of cooperation and warmth, were reflections of his courageous and creative attempts to cope.

One of the most destructive legacies of physical abuse is a *shame-rage cycle* that develops. Shame develops out of the sense of powerlessness to stop the abuse—the humiliation that someone can do this to me and I cannot make them stop. In a flash this then leads to rage—partly as an attempt to disprove the defeat and restore a sense of self as powerful—a rage that is very hard to modulate or regulate. Although Sam continued to have difficulty controlling his anger, he demonstrated that he could learn from past experience and that he could take on another person's perspective. These were far-reaching accomplishments that held out the promise that Sam may be able to escape a life of violence and crime. For example, Sam was no longer automatically assaultive when he was angry but was often able to walk away or verbally joust. I believe he saw that I set limits with him and stopped him from fighting with others in the group because I cared about him, not because I thought he was a bad kid who needed to be put down. This increasing ability to control his anger and his growing ability for accurate empathy made me hopeful that Sam would not become a sociopath. In fact, the capacity he had to trust and engage with me, coupled with the absence of stronger pathology, indicated to me that there was some strength in his home life that mitigated against the problems. These healthy features, perhaps from his great-grandmother, were important to pursue and affirm.

Orienting Constructs

Sam's sense of self was borne out of his individual, familial, and cultural experiences. He was born to a teenage mother who had difficulty providing him with a sense of security and safety. His mother was frequently absent. When present, she was physically abusive. In addition, the family had limited financial resources and lived in a neighborhood where threat of physical harm was a daily reality. Furthermore, Sam was referred to as the "man" of the family. For Sam, this meant protecting the women in his life, including his mother, the woman who had hurt him most! A paradox that is frequently observed in children who have been abused is the intense love and loyalty they express toward their abusers. This occurs, in part, because their abusers do show momentary affection; further, the child tries to defend against facing the shame that comes from being hurt and denigrated. It is also difficult for children to maintain a view of the world as just when they are being hurt—so they have to deny the reality of the abuse and its emotional impact on them, and often develop idealized images of their abusers.

Sam's task, to protect the women in his life, was impossible given his developmental level—no child can actually succeed in shoreing (as in "holding up" or supporting) up their failing parent. This experience must have engendered a further sense of helplessness and inadequacy in him, which likely contributed to his shame-based sense of self and the rage he sometimes exhibited.

For Sam, being a child meant being vulnerable and at risk for abuse. This often became translated into attacking others—turning the tables and having *them* experience the vulnerability and abuse he endured at home. Sam was often hypervigilant—which gave him a sense of being in control. He took this stance one step further and was frequently on the offensive, a stance that made him feel safer and less vulnerable to attack. This then became his template for coping with the world—that is, Sam was going to provoke and attack before others could do that to him. In addition, Sam's experiences of failure and reprimand in a variety of educational settings validated further his need for this hypervigilant attacking stance. As I increasingly understood why this coping strategy was necessary and worked for Sam in the past, it made it easier for me to remain firm but calm as I repeatedly set limits on his attacking behavior with me.

Sam's only source of affirmation in his family was when he took the role of protector. It was an impossible task, of course, *to try to take care of and protect the person who is hurting you and from whom you cannot protect yourself.* His pathway to efficacy and self-esteem was a hopeless one. Sam was desperately in need of finding new pathways to developing a sense of efficacy and receiving affirmation.

Given Sam's history, it made sense that he would be vigilant and test my trustworthiness by provoking and challenging me, on the one hand, and be anxious to please and be my protector on the other hand. It was crucial that I maintain my ability to:

1. set limits and follow through consistently without being abusive or authoritarian;
2. respond to his acting-out without leaving or abandoning him;
3. welcome his expression of needs and feelings (especially those beneath the attacking stance) without asking him to respond to mine; and
4. help him identify the multiple possible pathways to a greater sense of efficacy (e.g., making and keeping friends, sports, academics).

Sue and Sue (1999) aptly discuss how African American values have been heavily shaped by social class variables such as racism and discrimination, which may affect an African American's ability to trust a Caucasian counselor. It appeared that in Sam's case, distrust of me was further due to the abuse and neglect he had received from his mother. Children who have been abused or neglected will often demonstrate a pattern of hypervigilance and "pseudoadult" behavior in which they read the environment well and present in ways that seem mature, at least for short periods. Underneath this highly responsible veneer, however, normal development is impaired (the children do not learn to communicate effectively, have difficulty trusting or bonding with others, and have little curiosity and initiative). Although, in counseling, they initially come close to the counselor, they later damage or sabotage this relationship (by being angry, sneaky, etc.). Often, they believe that, "If I allow myself to feel close to the counselor, she may eventually leave or hurt me." This internal state reflects a core issue of worthiness: "If I were somehow different (i.e., a smarter, better looking, or a perfect child) I would never have been physically hurt or abandoned in the first place." For many seriously mistreated children, the child's message to him or herself as a result of this abusive treatment may be simply, "I am a mistake. I should never have been born." This shame based sense of self may be the most tragic legacy of an abusive childhood.

This approach-avoidance behavior and toxic self-image was demonstrated in everything Sam did. A typical example of this occurred about four months into group therapy. Even though the children in the group had all been labeled delinquent, it was rare for them to steal toys or materials from my office. My office had become a refuge for them. As such, it had developed into a space that they had come to value and appreciate. Given this context, when Sam stole a small mechanical action figure, it became a therapeutic issue. Not only had he stolen the item, he had also bragged about it to the other groups members during recess after one of our sessions. The children were agitated, not impressed, by this behavior. They had come to like Sam and felt violated when he took the toy they saw as belonging to all of them. The following group discussion illustrates how, once again, this same repetitive theme or conflict was addressed in the group. Following this, Sam and I also returned to this recurring pattern in our next individual session.

DONNIE: Um, what do you think should happen if someone steals something from the group? Like a toy or something.

TH: Well, do you have something in mind?

DONNIE: I think that if someone takes something that he should be punished. He should lose points and should have to leave the group.

TH: That sounds pretty harsh, Donnie. You sound kind of mad.

DONNIE: Well, yeah. I mean we all share in here, and if people take things, then we'll have nothing left.

TH: What do others think or feel—about what should happen if someone steals something from the group?

JUAN: I think it depends. If it's something big like a radio, you should call the police. If it's a toy, then the person should just be kicked out.

MANUEL: Yeah, he should be kicked out because nobody can trust him again.

PAUL: Maybe he should be just temporarily kicked out—maybe for just a couple of times. I mean *something* has to happen to him.

TH: Can any of you think of a reason that someone may take something from the group that doesn't belong to them?

PAUL: Because maybe they don't have nothing at home. Or maybe because they wanted to just do a dare.

MANUEL: (looking over at Sam) That's a stupid dare! Nobody will like someone who steals something that we can't use anymore!

TH: (quietly) Sam, I've noticed that you haven't said anything. What's up?

SAM: (pulling the item out of his pocket and throwing it across the room) Nothing's up! You are all a bunch of "narcs"! It was just a stupid toy, and I was going to put it back!

TH: Sam, thank you for returning the toy. I understand that you are upset right now. You can leave for some quiet time if you'd like or you can stay—it's up to you.

Sam chose to remain in the group but moved to a corner of the room to get some space. I wanted to address the other boys' feelings, including anger and mistrust toward Sam. At the same time I wanted to address how Sam was managing the process of getting caught and what feelings he might be experiencing. Perhaps Sam was testing me publicly to see if I could impose limits and still remain caring and emotionally connected to him. I felt that if I passed this test, Sam would feel safe enough to delve beyond the surface feelings of anger. I hoped he would be able to move beyond the reactive feelings of anger and deal with the hurt and shame that were underneath. The effectiveness of my response (i.e., limit setting with respect and care) let him know behaviorally that this was a safe place to begin dealing with the more vulnerable feelings.

An *affective constellation* or sequence of feelings such as reactive anger, which defends against unacceptable feelings such as sadness or hurt, often emerges in counseling (Teyber, 2000). Sam was readily in touch with the anger he felt as a result of his abuse and neglect. What was becoming increasingly clear to me was that his anger masked the deeper feelings of hurt and vulnerability. Sam's mother had been unable or unwilling to take care of Sam's natural childlike needs. I suspected that underneath Sam's sadness and longing to be cared for were even deeper feelings of shame over unmet attachment needs. These needs included being loved, cherished, and protected by his mother and family. For a child like Sam, to be vulnerable but not responded to, is simply too painful to tolerate. As a result, anger becomes a much easier emotion to express and serves as a way to protect one's self. The following dialogue illustrates how Sam was permitted to express some sadness over the rejection by his friends when he was caught stealing.

TH: So, have any of you done something that you later regretted? Maybe something that when you did it was not-so-smart that you didn't really think through—that when you think about it now you kinda say to yourself, "Ugh, why did I do that?"

JUAN: One time after I got my room painted I put stickers on the wall that wouldn't come off. Now, I have these stupid stickers in some places and peeled paint in other places.

TH: What did your family do when they found out?

JUAN: My dad was mad! He hollered like crazy until he caught me and spanked me.

PAUL: Once when I was supposed to be minding my sister I went across the street to play with my friend and she followed me. A car almost hit her!

TH: What happened then?

PAUL: My mom yelled at me and didn't talk to me for almost a week!

TH: How did you feel?

PAUL: Bad man. I mean my sister is a pain and all but I don't want her dead or nothing.

TH: What do any of you think Paul's mom should have done when she found out that his sister almost got hit by a car and it was *his* fault for not watching her?

MANUEL: I think being put on restriction is good.

TH: Then what?

MANUEL: That's it. I mean it's not like he didn't already feel bad.

TH: So you're saying that sometimes we do things that we regret and make us feel bad inside?

MANUEL: Yup.

TH: Do you think that maybe that's how Sam feels—that maybe he didn't think first about stealing the toy and now he feels bad?

JUAN: Maybe.

TH: Do you think that maybe it's okay to do something you regret and that sometimes we just make mistakes? Maybe friends would understand that?

PAUL: Yeah, I guess. We all do stupid things. Like you said—that's okay.

At this point Sam shyly and unobtrusively became more engaged in the group. Later, during our individual session together, he confided that making mistakes was not okay in his family and that often his mother would stay angry at him for days when he did something stupid. She would also yell and sometimes hit him. He also suggested that he believed she left him so much because he did "dumb" things. After finding that he could do "stupid" things with me like stealing, and still receive firm limits and care, Sam felt safe enough to risk experiencing and revealing his sadness. I offered him the corrective experience that he had not received often enough: I did not threaten to leave, I did not diminish his feelings, and I let him know that regardless of his "bad" behaviors I was still with him and for him.

SAM: (upset) Maybe if I were good, you know—like kids on TV my mom wouldn't get so angry—or leave . . .

TH: . . . because somehow it's your fault that your mom gets mad at you?

SAM: (nodding his head)

TH: . . . and only if you were perfect like actors on TV your mom might be like those moms on TV and everything would be okay.

SAM: (crying and nodding his head)

TH: Even though Sam—and this is important so I'd like you to listen carefully—there is no such thing as a perfect child or grown-up. Actors pretend—they're not real. Just like your friends here said, they make all kinds of mistakes—*that* is real.

SAM: But if I could be good—I mean, sometimes I am for a long time. But then I mess up . . .

TH: Yes, like today you messed up. And that's it—you messed up, just like Juan has done, and Paul, and Manuel, and everyone else. And I still like you and I'm not going anywhere . . . and I look forward to having you come back.

TREATMENT PLANS

Initial Treatment Plans

My initial treatment plan included the establishment of a working alliance and the development of group cohesiveness. My hope was that by establishing a positive relationship between Sam, the group, and me that was supportive and trustworthy, the foundation would be set for further, more in-depth work. These initial goals included addressing issues related to race and establishing rules for appropriate behavior in the group, such as no physical or verbal assault or ridicule allowed.

Once these initial goals were met, I hoped to use the group as a place where Sam could begin to learn more socially appropriate behaviors and the rewards that come from healthy, affirming relationships. For instance, Sam demonstrated that he could be charming and humorous. Perhaps Sam could learn to use this side of himself to take on a more positive leadership role rather than use it as a vehicle for instigating others and receiving negative attention from his teacher. In addition, it was important that Sam learn better impulse control and problem-solving skills. These included recognizing potentially volatile situations and triggers for his anger and making more appropriate responses that may include walking away. The group was an especially appropriate vehicle for dealing with these issues since the boys could together generate solutions to problems and practice with each other more appropriate responses. I hoped that the group and I might provide for Sam this consistent, safe, holding environment where he could begin to acknowledge, express, and have some of his needs met in an age-appropriate way.

Let me try to highlight further what I mean by using the group and our relationship to provide a "holding" or "containing" environment. Because Sam's family did not provide much empathy for his feelings or support for the predictable problems which resulted from his everyday experiences, Sam was unable to manage normal emotions such as sadness, anger, anxiety, or even happiness. This was greatly compounded by the physical abuse he had experienced from his mother and was further fueled by the series of humiliations he had experienced from her boyfriends and in educational and other settings. His low socioeconomic status and race were also not valued by the majority culture, further contributing to his feeling that the world was threatening and demeaning. In order for Sam to begin to heal, it was going to be necessary for him to identify and experience his range of feelings and learn to express them in more flexible ways. This time, however, it could occur in a relational context characterized by care and concern, where his feelings could be managed and "held." This meant that when Sam's feelings of need or self-devaluation emerged in treatment, I could welcome and respond compassionately to them, rather than be overwhelmed or threatened by them, as had occurred with others in his past.

Finally, the last phase of therapy included Sam's ability to internalize or take me in and keep the things I had taught or given to him. Keeping the memory of our relationship alive inside him was the best way to begin developing a sense of himself as love-worthy. More specifically, I hoped that Sam would be able to use our relationship and connection as a source of strength to draw on during times of stress. I hoped that he would be able to hear my words and voice inside him at difficult moments and use them to make good choices. Over time, hopefully, my affirming and soothing voice would become a part of his own inner voice so he could become more self-affirming and self-soothing.

Sam was increasingly able to use our relationship as a tool for security and strength. This was most evident when he began to struggle with making appropriate behavioral choices, which involved acting-out or running away. During the middle to later phases of our work together, he seemed to regress to old aggressive and withdrawn behaviors that he had previously given up. Looking back at some of these experiences, I believe he was testing the environment, and me, before he made some crucial progress in counseling. It was as if he was mulling over whether or not to risk *feeling*, and if that risk was worth some of the pain that would accompany change.

Sam was making steady progress in treatment but the depth of his pain was made evident about eight months into therapy. In this particular instance, Sam had gotten extremely angry with one of the other group members for what he believed was cheating during a game. A similar circumstance eight months before would probably have led Sam to either hit the other child or to run away from school. In this instance, Sam did not assault the child, but stood up, clenched his fists, teetered on his feet for what felt like an interminable stretch, and then ran out of my office. He headed for the back fence, which separated the school from the adjoining neighborhood. According to our facility policy, leaving the school property without permission was grounds for police and parental involvement. They also lost all behavioral points and special privileges. Sam climbed the fence and rather than jumping down on the other side and running, he stopped and perched himself. In essence, Sam was "on the fence" both literally and figuratively. If he ran further, he may have spent some time in detention. The situation, which tipped off his anger, however, was too overwhelming for him to handle in a more appropriate manner. Sam sat on the fence to cool down and think things through.

The fact that Sam could respond so intensely to what seemed like a relatively minor incident alerted me that he was in a hopelessly familiar and painful scenario. Sam was in a no-win situation in this incident: He was in a no-win situation with his mother and in a no-win situation as a Black male trying to succeed in his inner-city environment and in this sociopolitical context. Thus, this incident evoked the same feelings he had experienced in his early life (i.e., rage and helplessness). Sam was, however, beginning to respond differently to these profound affects which in the past had resulted in assaultive behavior.

I could see Sam outside my window and had asked the facility staff to keep an eye on him but to leave him alone. After about an hour it began to rain. By this time, Sam had missed lunch. I walked outside to a table where Sam could see me and I left his jacket, umbrella, and lunch, and I went back to my office. As soon as I left, Sam climbed down, took his things, and returned to the fence. A couple hours later I walked into my office from a meeting and Sam was sitting under a table drawing a picture.

TH: I'm glad you're back. Do you want to talk?

SAM: (shaking his head no)

TH: That's fine. The school bus will be here in about an hour and a half to take you home. I've got paperwork and a few errands to run until then. You can stay there until you have to go home and I'll just leave you alone. I'll leave it up to you to let me know if you need anything. One last thing: You made two good choices today—you did not hit Donnie and you did not run. I'm proud of you.

True to my word, I went about my business and left Sam alone. I went to a meeting and when I returned Sam had gone home. On my desk he left a painstakingly drawn picture of our group together. I was in the middle with the boys standing around me. I could see that Sam saw the group as a family, and that he was internalizing me as a more benevolent or inner voice.

Revised Treatment Goals

The basic treatment goals were not revised much. However, in addition to group and individual sessions, I pursued family therapy with Sam's great-grandmother and aunts. There appeared to be potential for change within the family and his great-grandmother and one of his aunts were open to receiving help in learning how to handle Sam more effectively. With the help of Sam's social worker, I also found a community anger-control program for him. The anger-control program, held at a local church, was designed to keep children such as Sam out of gangs. Through this program Sam was able to develop relationships with other children under positive circumstances and he was able to develop alternative ways of managing his anger.

There were two issues that I was aware of when I initiated counseling with Sam's family. First, Sam's great-grandmother and aunt appeared somewhat isolated from any help or support within their community. Second, I did not know how amenable they would be to having a female Caucasian therapist. As a result, I decided to run a larger family counseling group with Sam's family and two other families who had children from the same neighborhood. I also had a male, African American co-therapist to balance gender and ethnicity. The family treatment plan included parent training (e.g., effective discipline; enforcement of clear rules and firm limits; developing logical, nonabusive consequences such as cool down time, home restriction, working to pay back stolen or damaged property, while reinforcing appropriate behavior). We also explored ways to increase use of the support available in the community. In addition to having these families begin supporting one another, they also became involved in other community activities (sports at the YMCA, church based youth groups, etc.).

Balancing Goals

A major challenge was to maintain a firm but supportive relationship with Sam while helping him come to see that he did not have to "do" anything, take care of me, or "be" anyone other than himself, to receive care and nurturance from me. It seemed significant that Sam experience a relationship that was affirming and supportive, *and* had clear rules, clear expectations, and consistent consequences. I wanted to convey that while I may not always approve of his behaviors, I would remain consistent and affirming. For example, I needed to let him know that I didn't like it when he took things from my office without permission but that I still liked him and wanted to continue working with him.

My other challenge was to see beyond Sam's external angry presentation and not overreact with the same intimidation and/or counterattack this had usually elicited from others. I did this by recognizing that the extent to which Sam seemed threatening to me reflected how much he had been hurt. By responding in a consistent, nonreactive way, I was able to provide Sam with a safe environment from which he could access the other, more threatening feelings that his anger protected. Sam soon learned that the emotions of hurt, shame, and hopelessness were understandable and that I would respond to them without making him feel like an infant or shaming him further. This safety made it possible for Sam to begin developing new ways of expressing his needs and setting limits with others. For example, we began role-playing what to say and do when angry, identified cool down activities he could engage in when he felt angry (such as drawing or sports), and discussed the process of thinking through the consequences of his anger in each situation.

THERAPEUTIC PROCESS

Relational Aspects

One especially powerful replay of an issue Sam had struggled with in his family occurred in the example discussed earlier when Sam stole a toy from my office. For good reasons, Sam watched my response to this test very carefully. His mother would have used this type of behavior to confirm that he was bad and justify why she left him. The social system would have used the theft to place him in juvenile hall. In contrast, my response was to set firm limits but remain emotionally available and caring. Clearly, setting limits helped Sam know that there would be predictable consequences to his behavior. He had not felt the safety of secure boundaries in the past and he needed it now. In addition, both the group and I were able to show compassion for Sam while still disapproving of his behavior. Sam had not received this essential developmental experience from his family or the system, and it was a new and corrective experience that proved to be a watershed in treatment.

In this experience, Sam also was able to deal with me directly on issues of color for the first time (i.e., Sam: You only get mad at me because I'm Black! You wouldn't do anything if I were White like Paul!). It also revealed his ambivalence toward me in that I represented what he wanted in a parent but what he hated in the system (i.e., Sam: Man, I can't make you out. I like you sometimes, but you'll change just like the other White teachers do.). Sam also expressed this ambivalence toward his mother, whom he loved dearly but who consistently failed him by her abuse and abandonment. I understood that a huge component of what Sam hated was the arbitrariness or unfairness that he perceived in both his mother and in the sociopolitical system. For Sam, such unfairness evoked both the helplessness and rage, which led him to so many of his troubles. This issue was illustrated, for example, in the episode when Sam ran and sat on the fence when he thought that another child had cheated at a game.

Obstacles to Treatment

Initially, I wondered if my gender and race might make it difficult for Sam to develop an attachment or bond with me. We were able to do this. Interestingly, the biggest obstacle had to do with *my* feelings of protectiveness toward Sam. Although Sam was protective toward me for reasons that involved his family history, my feelings toward him included my own process of questioning our racial, cultural, and economic differences.

As I explored this issue, Greene's (1985) suggestion that there are four areas that can emerge when a Caucasian counselor is treating an African American client was helpful. These areas include racism or prejudice, color blindness, paternalism, and the unquestioning acceptance of African American power. The first area is clear: this involves the counselor's feelings of unconscious or conscious superiority over the client as a result of race. Color blindness involves ignoring any issues pertaining to the individual's race with the belief that no meaningful social or cultural differences actually occur between Caucasians and African Americans. From a paternalistic standpoint, the counselor interprets all of the client's problems as a result of race or prejudice, thus ignoring any other alternatives or contributors such as ineffective parenting or hurtful family interactions. Finally, the idea of unquestioning acceptance of Black power involves the counselor's attitude that because racism exists, any thoughts, feelings, or behaviors on the part of the client—regardless of the pathology—is justified. I considered each of these areas carefully, but none seemed to adequately address my process. I felt *both* protective toward and overwhelmed by Sam's life experiences. None of Greene's areas fit for me. As I explored this further, the issue of survivor guilt seemed relevant.

According to Niederland (1981), *survivor guilt* is a fundamental human conflict which involves a biologically based concern for and sensitivity to the pain of significant others which makes it difficult for an individual to be comfortable or successful if these others are not. Although survivor guilt is more clearly understood in the context of war (e.g., surviving the Holocaust), Modell (1971) believes that this issue occurs in a wide variety of situations. I began to wonder if I was experiencing guilt over the probability that I would never experience what Sam had experienced. By thinking about my struggle in this manner, I was able to keep this special form of guilt from operating in my relationship with Sam. In particular, I did not want to be less firm with Sam than he needed me to be. Had I allowed this protectiveness to lead to indulging Sam's provocativeness and testing without setting the firm limits that he needed, I would have been responding in a way that sounds similar to Greene's notion of paternalism and reenacted the permissiveness that Sam had experienced from his caretakers. A paternalistic stance encourages dependence, which the counselor may contribute to by focusing solely on the client's vulnerability instead of supporting the client's active strivings toward efficacy as well. I did not wish Sam to be dependent upon me. I wished for him to develop a sense of personal power that would make him less dependent on others, including me. Initially, his situation seemed simply overwhelming to me and I felt guilty over not knowing immediately what to do for him. As I grew to understand this, I was able to be warm and caring but also firm and consistent.

TERMINATION AND SUMMARY THOUGHTS

Counseling ended almost two years later when Sam successfully returned to public school. This was planned ahead of time and we spent several months making this transition. During that period, Sam began to take a few classes at a time in the public school. Since part of his day was still at our facility, we were able to address the anxiety-related issues that emerged with this process. I had contact with Sam's teacher at his new school and we were able to work together in this transition process. Two of the boys from our group were also transferring to Sam's school so they had the advantage of sharing this challenging new step together.

Sam's angry outbursts had decreased significantly at this point. He had learned to draw on a greater range of problem-solving skills when he felt angry or sad. For instance, Sam liked to sketch and color. In the group, I often had the children make pictures about their feelings or thoughts. Sam began to keep a journal of his drawings. As time progressed, his pictures were accompanied by creative stories. His drawings and writing became useful mediums for expressing his emotions. Sam was also athletic and learned to use physical activity as a way of letting off steam. Finally, Sam's social skills had improved. He had developed positive relationships with a number of the facility staff, had closer relationships with some of his peers, and had learned to express his feelings using words (although he sometimes had to be reminded that certain words, i.e., use of profanity, was not appropriate!).

The shame Sam once experienced over having unmet needs (i.e., to be loved and cared about) had diminished. He was now involved in a group at his church where his African American heritage was celebrated. Sam's family had continued in family counselor. Though they struggled with this, they were now better able to set limits and enforce these in consistent ways (e.g., restrict him when he had broken a curfew). Sam grew especially close to one of his aunts who lived with him and his great-grandmother. Unfortunately, Sam's mother continued to float in and out of his life, which was highly disruptive for him. The family tried to include her in the parenting classes and insist that she too follow the disciplinary practices they were now using, but she often failed to follow through. Fortunately, Sam now had family and community support to counteract some of the hurtful consequences of his mother's inconsistency. Despite this, Sam smiled more, performed better in school, and demonstrated more positive leadership skills, such as being voted in as class vice-president.

Sam had grown in our two years together and had the potential for continued success. He was now more aware of his "triggers," had developed a greater range of coping strategies, and was more flexible in his reaction to others. I was also pleased to see that Sam had learned to acknowledge his own achievements and felt more positive about himself. I was aware, however, that as an African American male, Sam would likely have to cope with a great deal of arbitrary unfairness of the sort that had ignited his acting-out behavior. He also continued to live in a neighborhood that was menacing and that did not support expression of his tender side. Further, his mother continued to be inconsistently available. Sam also faced the risk of becoming a drug user, given his family history of drug abuse and his own early experimentation with alcohol. This issue was addressed with Sam and with his family, and resources were provided for alcohol and drug prevention programs. I also emphasized that if Sam continued to be involved in healthy activities such as sports, associated with non-drug using peers, and was frequently reminded of how destructive drugs were, he would be less likely to become a drug user. I was pleased that Sam did have a caring great-grandmother and a supportive aunt, both of whom planned to continue counseling for Sam and themselves after he left our facility. Sam's family was also now more involved in their church and in a youth group at the YMCA where support and socialization needs could be met. I hoped that Sam's increased sense of efficacy and wider behavioral responses would serve him well in the many challenges he would likely face.

Questions for Thought and Discussion

1. What is your typical style of coping with interpersonal conflict? If you were interacting with a hostile, provocative teenager, what would your initial or automatic response tend to be and how might that affect the relationship?

2. Thinking back on your own life, what factors or relationships contributed to your resilience and the emotional strengths you see in yourself? What diminished your ability to cope?

Suggestions for Further Reading

Callan-Stoiber, K., & Kratochwill, T. R. (1998). *Handbook of group intervention for children & families.* Boston: Allyn & Bacon.

   Systematically presents information on how to plan and implement prevention and intervention groups for children, adolescents, and families.

Masten, A., & Coatsworth, J. (1995). Competence, resilience, and psychopathology. In D. Cicchetti & D. Cohen (Eds.), *Developmental psychopathology: Vol. 2. Risk, disorder, and adaptation* (pp. 715–752). New York: Wiley.

Masten, A., & Coatsworth, J. (1998). The development of competence in favorable and unfavorable environments. *American Psychologist, 53,* 205–220.

Rutter, M. (1990). Psychosocial resilience and protective mechanisms. In J. Rolf, A. S. Masten, D. Cicchetti, K. H. Neuchterlein, & S. Weintraub (Eds.), *Risk and protective factors in the development of psychopathology* (pp. 181–214). Cambridge: Cambridge University Press. Useful resources for understanding the issues of risk and resilience.

10 CHAPTER BRIAN: RECOVERING FROM THE FOSTER PARENT SYSTEM WITH CONDUCT DISORDER

THE DISORDER

Conduct disorder is a psychological term or diagnosis that is given to children and adolescents who steal, set fires, lie, kill animals, use drugs, and in some cases, kill classmates or other people they are angry with. What causes children and adolescents to become this uncaring, this callous, this vicious? Are there early signs of this very serious disorder? What can teachers, social workers, counselors and others do to reduce the likelihood that these children and adolescents will become what the legal system calls juvenile delinquents? We know that over one-half of these kids continue in adulthood to engage in destructive behavior that violates many social and legal rules and destroys the lives of many of the people they come into contact with. As they reach adulthood, this diagnosis changes from conduct disorder to antisocial personality disorder. With this change in diagnosis comes the sense that this destructive behavior now seems ingrained and represents this person's primary way of interacting with the world. At this point, the hope that this person can and will change is greatly diminished and a future that involves serious, ongoing criminal behavior is likely.

Clearly, conduct disorder is a very serious disorder and, sadly, a terribly common problem as well. Experts suggest that one-third to one-half of all child and adolescent referrals involve conduct problems, aggressiveness, and antisocial behavior (Wenar & Kerig, 2000). It occurs in about 6 to 16% of the population for males under the age of 18 years, and 2 to 9% for females in that same age range (DSM-IV-TR, 2000). What are the specific criteria for a diagnosis of conduct disorder? Conduct disorder is defined as "a repetitive and persistent pattern of behavior in which either the basic rights of others or major age appropriate societal norms or rules are violated" (DSM-IV-TR, p. 85). For a person to receive a diagnosis of conduct disorder, three behaviors—from any of the following four main groupings—must have been present in the last 12 months, with at least one of these behaviors present within the last 6 months (DSM-IV-TR, 2000):

AGGRESSION TO PEOPLE AND ANIMALS

1. Often bullies, threatens or intimidates others
2. Often initiates physical fights
3. Has used a weapon that can cause serious physical harm to others (e.g., a bat, brick, broken bottle, knife, gun)
4. Has been physically cruel to people
5. Has been physically cruel to animals
6. Has stolen while confronting a victim (e.g., mugging, purse snatching, extortion, armed robbery)
7. Has forced someone into sexual activity

DESTRUCTION OF PROPERTY

8. Has deliberately engaged in fire setting with the intention of causing serious damage
9. Has deliberately destroyed others' property (other than by fire setting)

DECEITFULNESS OR THEFT

10. Has broken into someone else's house, building, or car
11. Often lies to obtain goods or favors or to avoid obligations (i.e., "cons" others)
12. Has stolen items of nontrivial value without confrontation of a victim (e.g., shoplifting, but without breaking and entering; forgery)

SERIOUS VIOLATION OF RULES

13. Often stays out at night despite parental prohibitions, beginning before age 13 years
14. Has run away from home overnight at least twice while living in parental or parental surrogate home (or once without returning for a lengthy period)
15. Is often truant from school, beginning before age 13

Source: Reprinted with permission from the *Diagnostic and Statistical Manual of Mental Disorders,* Fourth Edition, Text Revision Copyright 2000 American Psychiatric Association.

The DSM-IV-TR makes a distinction between childhood-onset type, in which at least one criterion characteristic of conduct disorder is met before age 10, and adolescent-onset type, in which none of the criteria is met before age 10. For those whose onset is early (before age 10), as in the case of Brian, and who receive no help, severe negative consequences such as ongoing criminal behavior are more likely.

Searching for ways to better understand and treat conduct disorders, some researchers have suggested there are two different subgroups or types of conduct disorder (Baum, 1989). The first is the *undersocialized* or *solitary aggressive* type, which is defined by fighting, disobedience, temper tantrums, uncooperativeness, impertinence, and restlessness. These individuals are typically aggressive, impulsive, fail to learn from experience, and most troubling, lack feelings of guilt or anxiety. Paralleling the early-onset child, this subgroup is the most severe type, and has a poorer prognosis for adulthood that includes a greater likelihood of antisocial personality disorder (also sometimes referred to as psychopathic or sociopathic) and substance abuse disorder. As we will see, Brian was a child who fell into this early-onset category. Therefore, early intervention was very important in order to avoid the extremely unwanted possibility of an antisocial personality disorder later in his life.

Children and especially teens who exhibit the other cluster of behaviors have been termed *socialized* or group aggressive type. Typical behaviors for this group include having conduct disordered companions, being truant from school and home, being loyal to delinquent friends, stealing with others, lying, and setting fires. This group has been socialized with a deviant set of values and typically comes from environments where there is less parental monitoring and families with fewer financial resources. Sometimes children who fit this category live in neighborhoods where gang activity is rampant and individuals may be threatened with physical harm if they refuse to engage in activities of this sort. Although DSM-IV-TR does not use the undersocialized/aggressive and socialized/group aggressive categories, they can help clinicians understand how these problems originally developed (etiology), how they can be treated, and the long-term outcomes that may occur.

In normal development, children learn self-control and to care about and interact with others as a result of having a secure attachment to their primary caretakers and a sense of basic trust that their needs will be responded to. These caregiving relationships, based on affection and consistent adult responsiveness, become the most important part of the child's developing world. Keeping these secure ties intact is the most important ingredient for healthy development (Karen, 1994). When the parent-child relationship develops normally, the child internalizes or adopts the parent's rules as his or her own. More interesting, when attachment bonds are secure, the child takes on the caregiver's loving feelings for himself or herself and the child feels love-worthy. Self-esteem develops as the child comes to hold the same loving feelings for him or herself that the parent feels for him or her. The child also develops the capacity for empathy (or caring about others) that is frequently lacking in conduct disordered children. For many who love to watch children grow, being affectionate, setting consistent limits, and responding to your child's needs is the magic of childhood. However, this developmental process is as vulnerable as it is precious. There is, clearly, an all-important link between secure attachments and children's socialization, that is, their gradually increasing ability to control themselves or regulate their own behavior, accept their caregivers' directives, and care about others.

As previously stated, this reassuring relationship allows the child to form a link between parental directives (e.g., Parent: I want you to . . . You cannot . . .) and the feelings of affection that bond the relationship between the child and the primary caregivers. As this occurs, children progressively move away from their own egocentric or self-centered perspective. They become more able to take on the perspective of others and more willing to consider the wishes of parents and, later, siblings, teachers, and friends. Only in the context of this dependable and trustworthy relationship can children learn (1) what is expected of them; (2) how to develop greater frustration tolerance (the ability to delay their immediate wishes or emotional reactions); and (3) socially accepted strategies for attaining goals (i.e., "using your words" and asking rather than just taking). The parent's emotional responsiveness, along with the children's growing ability to think and remember, make it possible for them to become increasingly responsible and caring toward others.

In the child with conduct disorder, this basic socialization process has gone awry. For this child, the primary attachment bond is insecure or in some way disrupted. *Without an affectional tie to the caregiver, the toddler is uninterested in maintaining the parent's approval and unwilling to comply with the adult's requests or socialization demands* (e.g., "Don't hit your sister."). As we learn more about this disorder from the case illustration of Brian, we will see that the child's unwillingness to conform or noncompliance with adult rules, which arises out of lack of nurturance *and* lack of setting consistent rules with consequences, is the cardinal feature of this disorder.

Longitudinal data following children from early to middle childhood supports this attachment framework for understanding how conduct disorder develops (Erickson, Sroufe, & Egeland, 1985; Renken, Egeland, Marvinney, Mangelsdorf, & Sroufe, 1989). In order to maintain a secure attachment as children become toddlers, preschoolers, and older, *caregivers also must be able to effectively set limits and regulate children's behavior, but do so without disrupting ties* (e.g., Mother, calmly to child: Look in my eyes and say, "If I take the ball away from my sister again, I will go to time-out for 5 minutes." versus Mother, exasperated and shouting: "Damn it, what's wrong with you, get away from her!"). When attachment figures cannot discipline effectively and successfully manage problematic child behavior (e.g., hitting, biting), the child does not feel safe or "contained" in the parent-child relationship and becomes insecure in his or her attachment (Waters, Posada, Crowell, & Keng-ling, 1993).

Extending this, some caregivers simply do not posses the emotional stability or parenting skills to enforce limits without threatening relational ties. In contrast, other caregivers may be ineffective as a result of the *interaction* between a temperamentally difficult or otherwise challenging child and an overwhelmed or unskilled parent. For example, researchers find that active, willful, intense boys with a short attention span are more difficult to raise. In addition, they are more vulnerable or reactive to stress, such as parental conflict or a disorganized family household, than children with an easier temperament (Hetherington, 1989). In this regard, Campbell (1991) found that certain temperamentally "difficult to raise" kindergarten children who were aggressive, noncompliant, hyperactive, and inattentive, were at risk for continued problems. Thus, a negative escalating cycle often develops. The child's behavioral problems persist, which then increases stress on the family as a whole, and on the marital relationship in particular. This, in turn, increases conflict in the mother-child relationship. Campbell hypothesizes that stressed mothers become more restrictive and negative in reaction to impulsive and difficult children. The mother's angry reaction is usually ineffective and only serves to make the child less compliant. As emphasized earlier, children do not care about following rules because they lose their affectionate tie to the parent who is angry or exasperated with them and, in addition, the parent does not follow through and enforce the restrictions or threats made while angry or frustrated.

In addition, environmental stressors such as poverty, unemployment, and illness or psychological problems in caregivers such as alcoholism or substance abuse can weaken the parent-child relationship and put the child at greater risk for behavior disturbances. For example, Egeland et al. (1990) found that maternal depression was positively correlated with an increase in the child's disruptive behavior. Additionally, they found that if stimulation, predictability, and organization in the home were low, and stressors, such as financial difficulty or illness were high, behavior problems were more likely to occur. Conduct disorders are diagnosed for children of all social and racial groups. It is important, however, in designing treatment plans to take into account the child's cultural context and use the resources available there. For example, a drug abusing parent may be unable to provide the nurturance, discipline, and predictability that form the basis for developing secure attachments and empathy for others. If so, a grandparent, aunt or uncle, or some other family member may be willing to step in and provide a more secure and responsible relationship for the child. Or, if the gang is the only substitute for safe relationships, it is necessary to help the adolescent find more appropriate groups to identify with, through sports, band, or church youth groups.

SOCIOCULTURAL FACTORS

The skilled clinician takes all factors of the client's world into consideration when making a diagnostic assessment and planning treatment. Even though some commonalities may exist among clients within certain cultural groups, each client's worldview will be sculpted by a unique combination of influences. The case illustration that follows describes Brian, an African American child. Understanding the cultural factors that may influence the treatment of African American children are discussed next.

Not all African American families are the same, of course, and significant variations occur as a result of family background, economic and social standing, value systems, and the degree of acculturation to mainstream American norms (Allen & Majidi-Ahi, 1989). There are, however, some commonalities that are worth exploring when working with African American children that may help clinicians be more effective.

African American clients are more likely to drop out of counseling than White clients. The higher dropout rate may be attributed to many possible causes. One of these, according to Allen and Majidi-Ahi (1989), is the suspiciousness that many African Americans have toward White counseling and White institutions. This attitude seems natural given their history in America, plagued by over 350 years of slavery followed by nearly 150 years of discrimination. Racism is something that African Americans contend with on a daily basis, and their caution about White institutions can be seen as self-protective and adaptive.

Furthermore, the psychology field itself has been known to demonstrate a bias against African Americans by seeing cultural differences as "cultural deviance." Often, clinical diagnoses are biased by the influence of social class and the fact that African Americans are still overrepresented in lower income levels in the United States. It is not uncommon, for example, for the more severe diagnoses being given to lower class clients. In addition, mental illness is less often diagnosed for those who are affluent. It thus appears that there are discrepancies in the ability to make unbiased diagnoses cross culturally which suggests that diagnoses and interventions are affected by racial oppression and poverty.

Differences in family structure and socialized gender roles could also lead to misdiagnosis of abnormality by counselors who are unaware of cultural variations. Women in the African American community have traditionally worked, which has required more flexibility between the roles of males and females and the reliance on extended family for added support (Hill, 1972). Women are often socialized in a way that encourages assertiveness, while men are encouraged to show emotion and be nurturing (Lewis, 1975). Both of these trends were witnessed in Brian's family. The mother was strong and forceful, while the father demonstrated a capacity for nurturance. They also demonstrated their ability to utilize these alternative gender roles in treatment to help Brian. Lewis (1975) also found that African American families were more likely to share responsibilities and decisions concerning child care. In a study comparing African American and White families in the Midwestern United States (Gillum, Gomez-Marin, & Prineas, 1984), African American families were found to be less likely to express conflict openly, were more achievement oriented, were more likely to have a moral-religious outlook, and asserted stricter control than White families. These also happened to be some of the differences that Mrs. B., Brian's mother, explained about her family's worldview as we worked together to design treatments that would fit them.

Other factors that influence the clinician's experience with African American clients have to do with communication differences. According to Allen and Majidi-Ahi (1989), it is not common for lower-income African American people to nod or say "uh-huh" when they have heard something. They suggest that, without this information, a therapist might consider an African American child who sits quietly while being given direction sullen or uncommunicative, when in reality this is a culturally normal manner of relating. Because of this lack of verbal feedback, the counselor may need to rely more on nonverbal information with these clients. These authors also note that it is normative for African Americans to engage in conversation while engaged in another activity, and that it is not considered necessary to maintain eye contact in the context of the activity. Because of these differences in communication, it is common for misinterpretations and miscommunications to occur if the counselor is unaware of the range of normative responses for any culturally differing group.

Allen and Majidi-Ahi (1989) note further differences that influence the success of treatment for the African American client. For example, many African American clients place more value on interpersonal warmth rather than the technical competence of the clinician. This makes it important that counselors establish rapport and a collaborative alliance with the clients in order to keep them engaged in the counseling process. Moreover, since African American clients often belong to a network of extended family members, counseling interventions can often be more productive when members of that network are included in counseling and attempts are made to improve the family system as a whole. Furthermore, providing social, spiritual, economic, vocational, recreational, personal, and psychological assistance, rather than individual counseling or medication alone, is likely to yield better outcomes. Flexible knowledge of community referrals, along with creativity and sensitivity to individual needs, is critical in helping clients from many nonmainstream cultures.

Thus, it is important that counseling begin with the assessment of the client's unique worldview. One way that clinicians can do this is by asking clients about the ideas, values, and goals that they view as most important to them in their lives. Armed with this information about the client's world, the counselor can help the client brainstorm options for problem solutions that fit the client's personal value system. The counselor can work with the client to clarify the problems and the direction of counseling best suited for that person in that context. The client then has the option of choosing the solutions that best fit his/her lives from a range of possible solutions *collaboratively* discovered and developed by the client and the counselor together.

CASE ILLUSTRATION

Presenting Problem

Brian was a 10-year-old African American child who was brought into counseling by his adoptive mother. The decision to adopt Brian came about one Sunday morning when Pastor A.'s predominantly African American congregation was touched by his plea for more African American families to adopt these unwanted children. In the weeks that followed, several church members organized a formal church project to give some of these unadoptable children permanent homes with members of their congregation.

Mrs. B. and her husband, touched by the pastor's adoption message, and feeling led as Christians to respond to this need, started adoption proceedings. The adoption process was time consuming and complicated, but Mr. and Mrs. B. were tenacious. After a little more than a year, they were given custody of Brian, age 10, and his biological sister, Alisha, age 8. Brian and Alisha were welcomed into a family consisting of Mr. and Mrs. B. and their biological son, Nathan, age 11. The couple were hopeful that they would finally be able to provide these children with the loving home they never had.

The family didn't know much about the background of the children, except that their parents had a history of drug and alcohol abuse. The children had been placed in foster care when Alisha was an infant and Brian was about 2 years old. Neither child remembered their biological mother or father and had lived in a series of foster homes since their removal from their natural parents. Not much was known about the conditions in the previous foster care placements, other than the fact that one set of foster parents with whom Brian and Alisha had lived were currently being prosecuted for sexual molestation of several of their foster children, including Brian and Alisha.

Brian was brought into counseling because he was acting-out seriously since being placed with his newly adoptive family. The primary concern was that Brian had fondled his sister shortly after the children moved in. To Mrs. B.'s knowledge, this had occurred three or four times. However, Brian had also behaved in a sexually inappropriate way with Nathan. Mrs. B. reported that she had caught Brian "doing things" to Nathan but was so offended and embarrassed by the behavior that she was unable to go into detail about the acts. She also stated that Brian was physically confrontational with Nathan much of the time. In addition, Brian had been discovered stealing CDs and other possessions from Nathan's bedroom. He even tried to sell Nathan's bike to another kid down the street. According to Mrs. B., Nathan was a quiet and passive boy and didn't know how to handle Brian's aggressive behavior. She was seriously alarmed by Brian's behavior and how it was making her biological son's life miserable.

Mrs. B. also complained that Brian never complied with her requests. He was also noncompliant at school and engaged in fights on the playground. She noted further that sometimes Brian would be out in the yard just talking to himself and that she was worried that he was "just plain nuts."

Brian had also become identified as the "problem" in the neighborhood. For example, he had been seen throwing rocks at neighbors' windows and at passing cars. He sometimes defecated in the flower bed then, when neighborhood children would come by, he would pick up his own feces and chase them around with it.

At the time Mrs. B. first came in, she wanted to explore with me the hypothesis that Brian might truly be psychotic, and was considering undoing the adoption arrangement. I hoped that Brian wouldn't be returned to the foster care system again, but also felt deeply for Mrs. B. and the overwhelming problems that were toppling her family. I could understand how Mr. and Mrs. B.'s idealized idea about adoption had been shattered. By the time Brian was brought into counseling Mrs. B. was indeed very disillusioned. I could empathize with her feelings of regret regarding their decision to adopt him, and I conveyed this to her. I also acknowledged that they had not been realistically prepared for what to expect or how to handle Brian. I suggested that before giving up on him, we might be able to find ways to help the family make this adjustment. This offer of help, my empathy for Mrs. B. and her family, and a nonjudgmental stance were critical in developing a relationship with her. Once she realized that she had a working partner who was on her side, her tenacity and problem solving emerged. She agreed, for a while at least, to work with me rather than send Brian away immediately.

Client Description

Brian was a good-looking child of average height and weight. He always came neatly groomed and well dressed. He appeared to be racially mixed, with both African American and Euro-American features. Brian presented as a quiet sullen child who maintained an initial aloofness that made sense given the tremendous rejection and lack of stability that characterized his early life. He was polite, but he rarely initiated conversation or play in the early stages of therapy. Although 10, Brian was emotionally immature and I felt that I would be most likely to engage with him in the context of play.

Social Context

The family lived in a predominately White neighborhood. They maintained ties to the African American community through their church, which was outside their area of residence. This same-race contact was extremely important for the family, since they felt that cultural values and practices between their own race and the mainstream majority culture were quite different. The mother verbalized how these differences were very apparent in parenting practices between African American families compared to families of other races. For instance, Mrs. B. made it clear that she believed it was normal for African American mothers to spank their children. I knew from research and experience that, for some groups, corporal punishment was normative. Speaking in a manner that did not challenge her cultural beliefs, I listened to her firm stance on spanking but expressed the hope that we could identify a range of interventions that would help her to begin disciplining Brian more successfully. Given Mrs. B.'s interest in "returning" Brian, I knew I had to help the family learn more effective ways to manage him or Brian would, once again, be without a family.

Initial Session

During the initial session, I saw Brian and his mother separately. I interviewed his mother first in order to get an idea about Brian's background and problems from her perspective. Mrs. B. was a tall, large-framed woman who was slightly overweight. She worked as a teacher's aide in the public schools and always came to session neatly groomed.

Mrs. B. made it clear to me that she and her family felt strongly linked to their cultural identity as African Americans. Because of this, she indicated that she was very skeptical about whether I, a Latino male, might be able to help her and Brian in counseling. She wondered whether I could understand her way of parenting and her cultural values, which she assumed were different from mine. It has been my experience with clients of color that many assume that regardless of race, counselors are members of an institutionally racist occupation and may have difficulty honoring their cultural values. In Mrs. B.'s case, she stated clearly that she was skeptical of mental health institutions' ability to find viable solutions for her or other African American clients. She described her previous counseling experience with a counselor who had insisted that the family try interventions that were incompatible with their value system, such as having family meetings to decide the rules that would exist in the house. These discussions sensitized me to Mrs. B.'s need to be heard, have her viewpoints acknowledged, and have counseling develop in a highly collaborative manner that was congruent with her cultural values. Clearly, we would need a "working alliance," and interventions would need to be presented merely as suggestions with all demand or authoritarian qualities minimized.

In our initial meeting I assured Mrs. B. that even though I am not African American, my goal would be to explore the family's personal values and help them find solutions or options that would fit them personally. I also assured her that it was not my purpose to impose my personal value system upon her and her family. I told her that I was aware that some counselors had specific "cookbook" values about child-rearing, but I realized that often these standard formulas do not fit African American or Latino families. My response must have been reassuring enough because she responded in a positive manner and was engaged enough to proceed with treatment.

The early stages of counseling were difficult. Mrs. B. wanted quick solutions. At the same time, however, she was reluctant to implement the behavior management plan we discussed that started by changing one behavior at a time. She would state, "I don't think you understand, this may work well for White families or Latino families, but it won't work for us." I maintained a supportive stance and would then explain, "I have respect for what you're telling me, let's keep talking about this and see if we can find some common ground that works for both of us." I would then address each of the behavior management techniques I had suggested, explore whether it violated any personal or cultural value, and then proceed by asking if she would be willing to try the intervention for a specified period of time. I assured her that she didn't have to become White or Latino to accept these techniques (e.g., time-out), and that we would modify any aspects that she found offensive so that the changes would fit for her as an individual and as an African American.

In my individual time with Brian, I found him quiet and sullen, but relatively cooperative. When I asked him why his mother had brought him to counseling, he told me that he did not act "good" at home because his mom made him mad. Brian was unable to articulate exactly what she was doing to make him angry. I asked him about the rules in his new home and he reported that he didn't know exactly what the rules were and this was confusing for him. In the weeks to come we would work toward clarifying those expectations in combined sessions with Brian and his mother.

As the session progressed, Brian continued to be quiet and sullen. He seemed suspicious of this new experience he was being thrust into. I tried to make him feel at ease as I explained how the counseling would work. I told Brian that we would be talking and playing together, and I would see if I could help him and his family get along better. I showed him around the playroom, allowing him to see the selection of toys available. As we went through each section of the room, from one toy to another, he would examine each item, quietly manipulate it, then put it back in its place. We made a tour of the room, and I told Brian that if he wanted, we could start playing today. In a somewhat sullen voice, he replied that he would wait until next time. I got a sense that he felt intimidated by this new place. I imagined that I was intimidating too. I am a big man, have a large beard, and given his molestation, it was possible that adult males might induce considerable fear in him. I knew it would be important to be quiet and gentle in counseling with Brian, letting him make the choices about how fast to go in this new arena. I felt that this was especially important given his lack of choices and history of being disempowered as a result of frequent foster placement changes and sexual molestation.

Even though Brian most clearly met the DSM-IV-TR criteria for conduct disorder by his sexual perpetration, physical aggression and cruelty, and petty thievery, I also suspected that depression and anxiety might be underlying issues, perhaps fueling his acting-out behavior. I also considered the potential contribution or interaction of post-traumatic stress disorder, considering its common occurrence in sexual abuse survivors. However, I believed that Brian's caution and fear also stemmed from his problematic experiences with the social welfare system's bureaucracy and his excruciating history of rejection and abuse by adults. I was an adult and I worked for what he might have perceived as one of the institutions that had failed to protect him and care for him. It would be my job in counseling to prove that I was not another exploitative person. Instead, I could offer him interpersonal safety by providing understanding and warmth that was coupled with firm limits, something different from his previous experiences.

CASE CONCEPTUALIZATION

While there were a multitude of issues that needed to be addressed in this case, three points served as organizing principles. In making treatment plans for Brian, I wanted to focus on:

1. issues of rejection and abandonment in Brian's life;
2. the issue of sexual abuse, both its perpetration by Brian as well as his own victimization; and
3. the need to intervene with his adoptive parents to increase both their levels of nurturance and effective discipline.

Addressing Feelings of Rejection and Abandonment

Brian had lived a life in which each day reminded him that he was somehow unlovable, inferior, and worthy of rejection. From his point of view, his natural parents had rejected him because they were unable or unwilling to care for him. Internally, he might have wondered why he had been born into a world with parents who were so unfit and cared so little for him that he was taken from them. Then, by being tossed from one foster family to another, his feelings of rejection and abandonment were intensified. Budding attachments were repeatedly severed, usually without forewarning or explanation, leaving Brian unwilling to risk emotional involvement again. And finally, upon adoption, it seemed that even here he could not gain the approval of his adoptive mother, no matter what he did.

Brian's racial identity may have exacerbated his experience of being unworthy since members of the majority culture sometimes devalue people from his racial background. Taken together, it all seemed so unfair and out of his control. He had been helpless from the beginning, powerless to make any decision that really mattered in his life. The only thing that was clear for Brian was the fact that he had never been loved and wanted, that people treated him as inferior, and that he had endured one form of rejection and victimization after another. These experiences contributed to his shame-based perception of himself as defective. I hypothesized that Brian's acting-out gave him a sense of control and power by providing a "justification" for the rejection he had experienced and the abandonment he anticipated from the new family. Thus his acting-out could be thought of as a defense against his powerlessness in the face of frequent abandonment and sexual victimization. Brian expected the adoption to end in rejection and removal from the home, as always occurred before. He was dangerously close to evoking this outcome in Mrs. B. There is some twisted dignity in turning the tables, however, and being responsible for actively creating the rejection rather than passively suffering the excruciating shame of helplessness as he is forced to just go along with it again.

Brian had come to view the world as an unpredictable place, and all decisions important to his life were out of his control. So Brian seized power in the small ways that he could. In reality, Brian's adoptivemom was controlling and dominating. So he took power and control by ignoring her and not complying with her demands. In other relationships he also took power in destructive ways. For example, he dominated and molested his sister, Alisha, and abused his more passive adoptive brother, Nathan. I suspected that Brian's history of disrupted attachments robbed him of feelings for his victims. That is, he lacked empathy for others. Further, since so many of the events in his life occurred without regard to his needs, he in turn responded to others without regard for their needs, *often inflicting on them the pain he had previously experienced*. In this way, Brian's history of rejection and abandonment was interconnected with the second issue of sexual abuse.

Abuse in Brian's Life

Because of the severe drug and alcohol abuse history of his natural parents, Brian likely experienced a highly insecure attachment with his mother, even though he reportedly lived with her for two years. Whatever attachment or minimal security that may have been formed was disrupted, however, when the children were removed from the mother's custody and put into foster care. Numerous foster care homes followed and, as often occurs, some were benevolent and some were not. Even if the children started to become attached to a foster family, that all-important emotional tie was destroyed by the frequent custody changes. Not only were these relationships brief and disrupted, Brian had been repeatedly molested in one home. Clearly, for Brian, relationships with adults were not safe. This young child had come to know the world as a dangerous and unpredictable place. Based on his life experiences, he had come to the realistic assessment that it was necessary to be distrustful of adults, and guarded about getting emotionally attached to anyone, since it would only end in the sorrow of separation or the humiliation of abuse. He learned that he could not trust or rely on anyone in the world but himself. Even to rely on himself alone was a dangerous position, however, given the fact that he had power to change very little in his world of pain. This predicament lead him to turn the tables and be strong by dominating and inflicting pain on others, rather than being hurt and being seen as shamefully weak. Thus, Brian's abhorrent behavior, which was indeed destructive to others, was a way of dealing with his own pain.

Finkelhor and Browne (1985) write compellingly about the impact of sexual abuse and note that it can result in "traumatic sexualization," a sense of betrayal, feelings of powerlessness, and stigmatization. Brian's history, including his own sexual victimization, had left him feeling powerless. Even more problematic, he believed that the adults who were in charge could not be trusted to help him or were not powerful enough to protect him. He had experienced betrayal first by his biological family and later by the system that was supposed to care for him but had placed him in homes where he had been victimized.

Increasing Parents' Effectiveness and Nurturance

Brian's adoptive parents consisted of a rigid and controlling mother and an adoptive father who took on few parenting responsibilities. Brian thus lacked a warm or affectionate attachment to a parental figure, something necessary for internalizing and following through on rules and expectations. Predictably, he responded to his adoptive mother's attempts to control him by being noncompliant and by acting-out in ways that would distress her (e.g., attacking Nathan or Alisha, or defecating outdoors). In this way, he was not completely under her control nor was he completely powerless. Her expectations of absolute obedience collided with his life experiences of disempowerment, fueling his acting-out. Brian's adoptive father's minimal parenting in the early stages of therapy may have felt to Brian like the unresponsiveness or emotional distance that he experienced in some of his foster care experiences. Thus, Brian in his new home was faced with two parents whom he may have seen as either unresponsive (father) or controlling (mother). Further, as is usually the case with children having conduct disorder, the parents lacked an effective strategy for disciplining Brian and for responding to his emotional needs. Typically, the two issues of discipline and nurturance go hand in hand. I needed to teach his adoptive parents practical skills in which they could (1) set and enforce reasonable rules and (2) emotionally connect with their new son. In turn, I was convinced that helping Brian's adoptive parents understand Brian's plight would lead them to develop more empathy for him and foster their resolve to enforce appropriate limits, which would greatly reduce his acting-out. Coupling warmth with consistent limits was the key here. Brian's ability to respect his stepparents and others was based on their ability to discipline him effectively and respectfully.

Orienting Constructs

Brian had been referred to our clinic because of the sexual abuse he suffered from a previous foster placement and his acting-out behavior. I knew Brian's molestation of his sister, and his other sexual acting-out behavior, was a common occurrence in children who have been molested themselves. This understanding, and my appreciation for the long-term impact of his disrupted attachment history, helped me to understand Brian's problems. Thus, one of my primary goals was to help Brian come to terms with the emotional impact of this abuse on his life. I hoped that eventually he could begin to talk about those taboo experiences and together we could explore how they affected him. I also wanted to explore, in turn, how his own sexual perpetration might impact his own victims. *Only by first developing empathy for himself as a victim (rather than hating himself for being shamefully weak), and then finding empathy for his own victims, would he be safe from hurting others in the future.* I also hoped to help Brian find more appropriate ways to express his outrage and develop his own sense of self-efficacy (i.e., a sense of control and competence).

The other construct that served to focus my work with Brian is attachment theory and "internal working models." I related to Brian as a child who had never had a secure emotional bond. His own internal concept of himself in relationship to others had been formed by his history of repeated trauma and left him with three problematic templates or cognitive schemas for interpersonal relations. First, because Brian lacked a loving relationship in his life, he did not expect or feel he deserved one. Second, because he was abandoned throughout his life, he expected to be rejected and experienced himself as not being love-worthy. To protect himself from being hurt and disappointed again, he was reluctant to make himself vulnerable by risking commitment in his new home. Third, because he had been exploited sexually, he was distrustful of others and experienced himself as powerless and shameful.

These painful developmental experiences shaped Brian's problematic reactions to his new family. Like many others who have been traumatized, he tried to empower himself by doing to others what they had done to him (i.e., shaming others). His sexual molestation of Alisha, attempted molestation of Nathan, and public defecation can be understood in this light. Although his behavior made sense given his history, this disturbing behavior further alienated him from his new adoptive family. In treatment, Brian needed to be given opportunities to try out new ways of relating that did not fit the three old templates. The challenge was to help him grasp how his previous schemas or ways of understanding relationships accurately fit the past but did not fit the present. I hoped that my relationship with Brian could be characterized by warmth and the security that firm limits provides. If he were not able to elicit anger or rejection in me, even if my rules were violated, it would help to redefine what human relationships could provide. In the context of this new kind of relationship, which Brian had not experienced with anyone before, I could help him adopt new ways of behaving that would improve his life, especially his relationship with his new family. *By not allowing him to reconstruct our relationship along the same old familiar and problematic lines, I hoped to utilize our relationship to provide him a new and better solution.* In turn, I also aimed to give his family the tools they needed to provide Brian a better experience at home, one that involved caring relationships where rules were enforced in an atmosphere of warmth and fairness. My hope was that if Brian and his adoptive family began to value each other, the parents would be willing to invest in the great effort that effective parenting demands. If so, Brian would begin to internalize their rules (i.e., take them on as his own and want to abide by them), which would lead to more rewarding family relationships.

TREATMENT PLANS

My treatment plan was organized across the three issues I addressed earlier: (1) Brian's issues of abandonment and rejection; (2) Brian's sexual molestation; and (3) Brian's adoptive parents' parenting skills.

SHORT-TERM TREATMENT GOALS

1. Establish a trusting relationship with Brian that begins to address issues of abandonment and rejection.
2. Openly address molestation issues, including Brian's molestation of his sister and Brian's own sexual molestation.
3. Take steps to stop Brian's molestation of Alisha and begin to work through feelings related to his own victimization.
4. Develop a working alliance or collaboration with the mother and deescalate the level of conflict between Brian and his mother at home.

INTERMEDIATE TREATMENT GOALS

1. Continue to foster trust in my relationship with Brian. Help Brian to clarify what he is willing to do to obtain greater acceptance by his new family: What behaviors are expected? What are the consequences and rewards?
2. Educate the parents about the normal development of 10-year-olds, and common side effects of molestation, foster placement, and adoption.
3. Teach the parents more effective parenting skills and how they could be applied in the home.
4. Explore ways to enhance Brian's social skills. Facilitate appropriate interaction with neighbors, schoolmates, and church members. Find ways to foster cooperation, self-respect, and self-esteem.

LONG-TERM TREATMENT GOALS

1. Through my relationship with Brian provide an emotional bond and the interpersonal safety that permits him to work through issues of rejection and abandonment. Help Brian to develop empathy, self-control, and social skills in all areas of his life.
2. Uncover and work through molestation issues, especially feelings of powerlessness and shame. Help Brian identify and develop interests that would enhance his sense of competence.
3. Develop consistent and appropriate parenting practices in the family. Encourage Brian's father to share parenting responsibilities and take a more active role in Brian's emotional development.

Initial Treatment Plans

As I began treatment, I considered Brian's molestation of Alisha and his own molestation to be central to his current problems. I felt that these issues needed to take priority in treatment. It was important to help Brian find a way to stop the molestation of his sister because I was worried about her and because Brian might be removed from this home, as he had been removed from numerous foster homes in the past. Psychologically, this would have reenacted Brian's experience of being abandoned and fueled his sense of powerlessness. In addition, the probability of being adopted permanently again would be slim. Brian would probably be exposed to further victimization himself and continue victimizing others. Finally, if he were removed from this home, he would lose the only stable relationship in his life, that which he had with his sister, Alisha. Thus, I hoped to help make the molestation stop so that Brian would not lose the best chance he had been given in life thus far. I was also concerned about Alisha and the way in which she had been victimized. This had to be addressed immediately with Brian and, in order to ensure her safety, Alisha needed to continue the counseling she had begun after the molestation by her foster parents was reported.

Since Brian was a child perpetrator and was receiving treatment while still a child, I felt optimistic about his potential for a successful outcome. Like many, I was initially troubled by Brian's deeply disturbing behavior. As I began to spend time with Brian and learn more about him, however, I felt compassion for this child who had endured so much pain that he would, in turn, inflict pain upon others. Further, Brian's lack of a secure attachment and consistent discipline made following rules and having empathy for others meaningless.

In the beginning of treatment, Brian was reticent about playing with the toys in the playroom. It made sense that Brian was hesitant to engage with me—after all, this might represent another relationship he would soon lose. It may also have represented one way for Brian to exert control over yet another situation where his wishes had not been taken into account, a situation he might have felt as "forced" on him. Our first sessions, therefore, were spent talking to each other as I tried to convey my interest in him. I wanted to know as much about him as I could, to try and understand what his world was like. I asked him questions that he responded to in a hostile, defiant way:

THERAPIST: How do you feel, talking to me?

BRIAN: (shrugs with indifference)

THERAPIST: Do you feel like you were forced to come?

BRIAN: What's new about that?

THERAPIST: I know that sometimes adults force children to do things they don't want to do. Sometimes they do it because they care and want to be helpful, but sometimes they do it to be mean and hurtful. I think your mother brought you here because she would like it if you all got along better. I think she wants to be helpful. I know I want to be helpful.

BRIAN: Oh ya? (sarcastically)

THERAPIST: I can't help your family without your help, Brian. Perhaps you and I can have fun together here and also find ways to have fun with your family without anybody being hurt or made to feel bad.

Brian's barely perceptible nod suggested that he heard me but his reluctance to engage made sense given his history. Given my grave concern about Brian's molestation of his sister, I felt the need to address this early:

THERAPIST: Brian, do you know what I mean when I use the term molest?

BRIAN: Yeah, when you touch someone's dick or pussy.

THERAPIST: Your mother tells me that you molested your sister, Alisha. Let's talk about what went on, Brian. How many times did it happen?

BRIAN: I don't know.

THERAPIST: I'm wondering what you might be thinking right now about me bringing this up and talking about what happened with you and Alisha?

BRIAN: (sits without making eye contact and does not answer)

THERAPIST: Do you have any ideas about what Alisha has been feeling toward you since this happened?

BRIAN: (tone is once again sullen and angry) I don't know!

THERAPIST: Do you think it will happen again?

BRIAN: (no response)

THERAPIST: You know, Brian, I'm wondering if something like this might have happened to you?

BRIAN: No!

THERAPIST: Brian, this really is a very hard thing to talk about. Have you ever been able to talk with someone about this—someone who was on your side and who wanted to help you?

BRIAN: Fuck you, man, leave me alone!

THERAPIST: Sounds like there's some big feelings here. Let's do this: I want to say one more thing, and then let's do something you want. I'm thinking that if something like that did happen to you, you may be REALLY angry at the person who did it, and angry at me for bringing it up. How does that sound to you?

At this point, Brian softened and shrugged his shoulders. Sensing that this was as close as I was going to get, I decided to back off. Even though we appeared to reach a dead end with regard to this topic, once Brian entered therapy, molestation of his sister was never reported again. I believe that by making my knowledge about the molestation of his sister explicit (in conjunction with other interventions which will be discussed later), Brian was able to end the molestation. I did on several occasions tell Brian how proud I was that he was not molesting Alisha anymore. We also discussed together ways to express feelings that did not hurt others. Although I asked Brian again if anything similar to his sister's molestation had ever happened to him, his response was a cynical "just leave it alone." I had subsequently steered him toward the anatomically correct dolls, wondering if his play with them would provide a vehicle for talking about his own victimization. He showed me how he had touched his sister and used his finger to penetrate her but once again refused to address his own molestation. I believe the shame of this was more than he could face at this stage in treatment. To establish a "bridge" to

Brian, I began telling him a story about "another boy I used to know who had a problem." I told him that this other boy had been urinated on by a bigger person and made fun of in a public restroom. He was hurt, scared, and embarrassed and did not want to talk about what happened for awhile—until he felt safe and knew that I would help him.

I then shifted back to Brian and assured him that if something like that had ever happened to him, I'd be sad for him and want to help him, just like I was concerned for the other boy I knew. I also let him know that some children who are hurt in that way feel angry and sometimes try to hurt others in the same way they were hurt (Brian became extremely attentive upon hearing this). I said their feelings were understandable but that they usually learned it was better to talk about it to an adult they trust and to try and find other ways to feel good about themselves. I closed by letting him know that if it's not safe and not a good time in our relationship to discuss something like this, he's the one to make that decision. I was aware that trust would need to develop between us before Brian felt safe enough to disclose such a degrading, shame-inducing experience. Molestation was not something an already disempowered boy would divulge to yet another "untrustworthy" adult. I would need to prove to Brian, with my actions rather than my words, that I was an adult of a different sort. Perhaps my most basic treatment goal was to find ways to let Brian know that not all relationships in life would be ones in which he would be the inferior, the powerless, and the loser.

I did let Brian know that if he had ever been molested and wanted to talk about it, I would be available and responsive. Although I felt that talking about the molestation would help Brian, I did not want to force this on him as it would only dynamically replay the force-compliance routine that characterizes victimization. I wanted Brian to feel empowered to choose when to discuss this issue.

Normally I do not request that the parent attend every session but, in this family's case, I thought it would be important because Brian was so unclear about rules and expectations at home. It has been my experience in working with conduct disordered children that family interventions are usually the most powerful, and I try to include parents in the treatment process. Mrs. B. would join us for 30 minutes of our 1½ hour session. This time would be spent clarifying rules and expectations for Brian, and collaborating in the development of behavior management plans. I hoped that this would clarify ways in which Brian might become successful within the home and please his parents, and I also hoped to teach the mother some parenting skills in the process. I wanted to use this time to help both Brian and his mother develop empathy for each other. To achieve this, I looked for opportunities in every session to try and voice each one's point of view in ways that would make it palatable to the other. For example, I would say, "So, mom, you're really saying you want Brian to make his bed before breakfast and not take things out of his brother's room. And you, Brian, are really telling us that you don't know what the rules are. Perhaps we could set up a chart that lists family rules and expectations and put them on the door to your room."

Mrs. B. was very disturbed by Brian's lack of compliance with her requests in the home. I knew that if Brian could improve in this area, both he and his new mother would be much happier. It would also represent a small success in counseling on which we could build. I began by discussing with Mrs. B. what behaviors she would like to see change. Her initial responses had an angry, demanding quality yet were nonspecific or global such as, "I want him to be a good, responsible child." In reality, Brian had no idea what being a "good, responsible child" really meant or entailed behaviorally. Therefore, defining the mother's behavioral expectations more specifically became our mission during the conjoint part of our sessions.

As treatment progressed, we talked about attending to cues in Brian's behavior, learning to recognize when he was headed for misbehavior, and how to intervene early and prevent the behavior from escalating—for example, when Brian began to tease Nathan, to intervene and separate them before he became aggressive. We also talked about using time-outs, in which Mrs. B. (or Nathan or other family members) and Brian could be apart from each other when they were angry, then return and settle the dispute after they had both calmed down. I talked to Mrs. B. about identifying a time-out place (like a chair facing a corner in a quiet part of the house) and giving Brian a timer set with five minutes, with instructions not to leave until the timer went off. Especially in the beginning, it might be necessary for Mrs. B. to stand behind the chair with no verbal interaction except to put her hand on Brian's shoulder if he tried to stand up. Once Brian realized her seriousness about this, there would eventually be less need for her to stand close by during time-outs. I thus attempted to implement behavior modification plans that would teach Mrs. B. more effective ways to control Brian's behavior.

We started out by defining some behaviors for Brian to change. Mrs. B. had difficulty being specific and would say, for example, that she wanted him to listen to everything that she said. I explained that this was too broad, and it would be difficult to figure out whether Brian was really listening or not. We discussed how it would be easier if we chose a behavior that could be witnessed and measured. Mrs. B. made it clear that one of the things that she expected Brian to do each day was to make his bed and clean up his room, which he regularly failed to do. I explained that our new plan would work best if we started out working with just one behavior, and later on we would be able to add more. So, Brian agreed that he would try making his bed every day. I explained that for a new behavior, it's asking too much that Brian be perfect the first week, so we agreed that he could miss making his bed one day out of the week and still get a reward. I asked Brian what kind of a prize would be worth working for. There was a special comic book that Brian loved. He had seen it in the convenience store but had never had any money to buy it. Mrs. B. promised to buy it for him if he complied with their agreement. We drew up a contract that had a definition of the target behavior (i.e., making his bed), the expected frequency (number of times the behavior is required per week, in this case, six out of seven times), and anticipated reward if the contract was fulfilled (the comic book). Brian and his mom both signed the contract. In addition, I gave them a star chart on which Brian could plot his daily achievement by placing shiny metallic stars on the days of the week in which he had performed his target behavior. An excited look came over Brian's face as we discussed his reward, as if he had already earned the treasure.

The following week, Mrs. B. and Brian returned. Brian looked angry. I had informed both of them that the initial period of our conjoint time would be spent checking up on progress and readjusting for the next week's work. During this portion of the session, Mrs. B. immediately complained that Brian had "failed," and said she "knew he could never do what he was told." When I asked how many times he had made his bed, the mother replied that he had made it six out of the seven days, but it had taken much prodding to get him to do it. Because of that, she didn't feel that he should have the magazine. I tried to explain to Mrs. B., in a sensitive manner, that it was important that the rules not be changed after the session. If we wanted Brian to be better at home, it was important that he get what he had earned, otherwise the plan would not work. I also empathized with her feelings of frustration at having to remind him but highlighted the fact that he had indeed successfully met the goals set.

This example represents the difficulty sometimes faced with designing behavioral interventions. I have since learned the importance of asking families what they anticipate the problems might be that would arise with the plan we have designed, and together we brainstorm the potential loopholes. In this instance, I suggested that for the following week, we could add to the contract making the bed before breakfast in the morning and that she needn't remind him. He either did his chore by that time, or he did not. We talked about how all changes to the contract would need to be agreed upon by all of us. Mrs. B. seemed to understand the system better, and she then agreed to give him the magazine after all as acknowledgement of his meeting the contract as originally written. I believed that this became the point in therapy when Brian started to realize that I wanted things to be fair for him in his relationship with his mother. He saw that I might be his advocate and not his enemy, as other adults had been in his history. Confirmation of this fact for Brian, however, was still weeks away. This incident also signaled Mrs. B.'s willingness to listen to reason, and I made overt this assessment as a positive quality to both Brian and Mrs. B. This was the beginning of helping them identify those aspects of their relationship that were positive and worth building upon.

The weeks that followed continued to be difficult. Mrs. B. continued to have difficulty with consistent follow-through. For example, Brian didn't get his reward the following week, even though he met the agreement stipulated in his contract, because he had acted out at school. We again stressed the importance of rewarding appropriate behavior while trying to modify inappropriate behavior. The week after that, Mrs. B. judged some other behavior, instead of the target behavior, in deciding that Brian lacked behavioral control that week. It became clear to me that Mrs. B. had high expectations and difficulty acknowledging the successes. More realistically, I finally had to acknowledge to myself the unwanted reality that she was sabotaging the system and setting Brian up to fail—further fueling his sense of powerlessness which, in turn, led him to act out even further. She complained about the behavior modification process and groaned about our focusing on this little stuff, "when he's such a big problem." I assured her that I understood how overwhelmed she must feel and tried to help her understand why the inconsistency and seemingly arbitrary changes in our contracts could only be counterproductive given Brian's history. For the first few weeks, it was difficult for me to control my own feelings toward her. I felt angry with her and wondered if she was encouraging me to reject her, just as she was rejecting Brian. I also hypothesized that her behavior may have something to do with her own way of seeing the world based on her life experiences. I decided to spend some time with her discussing her own family history so that I could respond to her more empathically. I realized that to some extent she was set in her ways—change was hard for her. I felt, however, that keeping a calm, patient, and nonjudgmental stance with her was critical in keeping her involved with Brian's treatment. I knew that I needed to model for her an ability to remain engaged and responsive, despite her criticism and dissatisfaction with me. I believed that this stance in our relationship was essential in order to enable her to adopt a similar one in her relationship with Brian. In other words, I needed to provide her with the same type of relationship that we were trying to have her provide for Brian.

Thus, I began meeting for a few sessions with Mrs. B. alone. During this time I wanted her to get a sense that I understood how difficult this adoption experience had been for her and her family; and indeed, I believed that this had been the case. She and her husband had hoped to help the children and, in the process, their lives had been unraveled.

I also spent some time getting a sense about who Mrs. B. was before all of this had happened in her life. She was the oldest child from a large family. She had been raised in the inner city when it was a less violent place. Her father had been absent from the household and her mother worked long hours to support the children. The money from a single income, in a family with many children, didn't stretch far enough and the family was economically deprived. Since Mrs. B. was the oldest child in the family, she became the designated parent when the mother was gone. It was a huge responsibility for her as a young girl and forced her to grow up before her time. Mrs. B. seemed older and more worn than her age, and I felt badly that she, like Brian, had a tough life full of unfairness. I also felt badly that what she had hoped would be an act of good will toward these parentless children had turned into something of a nightmare. I thus learned to relate to Mrs. B. out of empathy for her. I saw that her intentions were good despite her increasing frustration with Brian. Beneath her gruff exterior, she was a kind woman. It was to her kind interior, and her own sense of deprivation, that I hoped to appeal in order to help her recognize or appreciate more fully the grim reality of Brian's painful life. I hoped that if she could understand his perspective that she might be able to like him more and be more forgiving of him.

In order to accomplish this, I needed to provide some empathy and caring to Mrs. B. that I hoped she would eventually provide for Brian. Thus, when I saw her sabotaging the behavior modification plans, I responded to her feelings with empathy and would say, "I can see how much he really wants your approval and that it's so hard for you to give it right now. I know you've had so much struggle in your own life and that you didn't get the kind of nurturance he is asking for." This needed to be a tactful bid, so that it wouldn't be heard as critical or judgmental. This was a delicate situation. I wanted Mrs. B. to feel my compassion for her, as if I had an arm of understanding around her, while also expressing my compassion for Brian. I hoped to provide a safe, empathic place for Mrs. B. and use the understanding in our relationship to help her see Brian in a different light: "He's probably looking for a place he can come home to, and I understand that he does it in ways that are hard to deal with. But what he's really doing, underneath, is wanting more of you."

It was my job to help Mrs. B. see that beneath this acting-out, there was a hurting child who had never experienced a secure attachment or responsible discipline. I wanted to convey how children take on parental rules and values when they feel valued by the parent. I also wanted to convey that under Brian's aggressive and defiant exterior was a child who had been deeply wounded by his life experiences. I wanted to convey that responding to the hurt and shame under his disruptive exterior would allow Brian to acknowledge his deep need to be valued. In turn, this would lead to a greater willingness to seek attention in positive ways (i.e., helping at home) rather than by hurting people. With my encouragement, Mr. B. joined us in treatment about the fourth session. Mr. B. was a police officer and had taken some time off work because of a job-related injury. He came to the therapy session dressed informally in a sweatshirt and casual pants. He was a big man, about 6'3", heavily built, and a little overweight.

When Mr. B. came to counseling, I hoped to promote the idea that he and Mrs. B. could function as a team. I found that Mr. B. was more capable of being emotionally available and affirming than Mrs. B. was at this time, and I encouraged her to invite Mr. B.'s participation in working with Brian at home. Mr. B., I learned, had grown up in the suburbs in a family that was working class. There were fewer children in his family of origin compared to Mrs. B.'s; consequently they were more financially stable. Mr. B.'s father had also been absent and, without a role model, Mr. B. had never learned how to be part of an active husband and wife parenting team. He consequently spent lots of time at work and seemed psychologically absent to the family. I had encouraged that he play a more active role in the family by assisting his wife in monitoring Brian and following through on behavior modification plans. This could also relieve Mrs. B. of some of the parenting burden, which she had seemed to take on by herself, just as she had parented her siblings alone in her family of origin.

The father was a large, physically powerful, and gentle man. Though he towered over his wife, she was definitely the one in charge. I thought of Mr. B. as "the lieutenant," taking orders from his wife, "the general." It was interesting to see them interact. Every time he would respond, she would appear to invalidate or contradict him. I came to recognize that this represented her way of interacting and was perhaps a manifestation of her need to maintain control and have her perspective validated. This made sense per her history of having been given responsibility for her siblings, with little validation for how well she had managed. However, even though Mrs. B. seemed to override her husband's opinion about most things, she had respect for his superior understanding of technical issues. This included his understanding of the dynamics involved in the behavior modification contracts. He really understood the purpose of the behavioral interventions and how to implement them. He was very task oriented and would translate to Mrs. B. exactly what she needed to do in order for the behavior modification plans to work. Though I myself had done this in the past few weeks, with very limited success, Mr. B. was able to not only put what Mrs. B. needed to do into words that she better understood, but he was able to keep the program in check during the week. It was instructive for me to observe him and the way in which he was able to get his message across. This reinforced for me *the importance of seeing as many members of a family as possible when working with conduct disordered children and identifying each member's strengths and trying to utilize those strengths.* Mr. B. came for the next six weeks while he was still off work. He was optimistic compared to Mrs. B.'s pessimistic outlook, and Brian made great gains during that period. He was doing well in attaining behavioral goals and receiving the rewards that he had earned. Everyone acknowledged his improvement, except for Mrs. B. who seemed to have cast Brian into a "bad boy" role. Perhaps due to her own adverse life experiences, she was suspicious of success, questioned if it would last, and emphasized the behavior that was still problematic. I acknowledged her concerns but tried to present an additional perspective by noting how much progress we had made despite Brian's horrendous early history.

During this time, Brian and I were continuing to strengthen our relationship. During the first few weeks, Brian was sullen and defiant. He did not want to play, which I viewed as his attempt to exert control over the situation. I tried to align with his need for control by emphasizing that *he* could choose what games to play with. Predictably, Brian then tested me by deliberately breaking several toys. I let him know unambiguously that this behavior was not acceptable but continued to be warm and engaged with him. In this process, I began to disconfirm Brian's view that people would eventually reject him and all he had to do to speed this process was act out. In setting limits, I conveyed to Brian my view that he was worth the effort. This experience seemed to help Brian feel safer or more secure with me and strengthened our relationship.

Over time, I realized that both Brian and I were marking time, dreading the conjoint portion of therapy with Mrs. B. At this point, I chose to take the risk of trying to find a tactful but honest way to share my realization with Brian and asked him if he felt similarly. Surprised that I had spoken so honestly, he agreed and went on to share that he was really quite frightened of his new mother. I attempted to join with him by talking about how powerful and at times demanding she could be. I told him that I thought he had a tough role to play because it seemed so difficult to make her happy. In addition, I wondered aloud that if she was always going to be unhappy and feel that he was a "bad boy," that he may often feel he deserved her anger. Clearly, this socially taboo but reality based appraisal was a powerful thing to say to him. He stared in wonder, as if he couldn't believe his ears and was afraid to speak for fear of breaking the spell. I also shared that while this was a difficult person to deal with, that deep down, I thought that she cared about him and that the task he and I had was to draw that out of her.

As often occurs when the unspeakable is spoken, this forthright exchange changed the nature of our sessions. He began to play with toys in the playroom. No surprise, his favorite activity was playing war. He would go to the sand table and create elaborate scenes with the male army figures. In the first several weeks, the theme was always the same. The "little guys" would be pitted against the "big guys." It was as if Brian could not imagine that the battle could ever be fair. It would be a tremendous battle in which Brian would provide the sounds of the explosions, the humming of the tanks, and the screams of the dying soldiers. The outcome, however, would always be the same, and the little guys would always lose. He was fixed in this relational pattern, and I could see in his metaphor of battle that this was the theme of Brian's life. He too was a little guy, with a history of his own failed battles, and without the hope of ever having enough power to win. Throughout this early stage, my role was that of an observer who relayed what I was seeing both metaphorically and literally.

One day, remarking yet again how much I enjoy playing war, he finally invited me to play. Brian set me the task of representing the big soldiers, and he took the army comprised of smaller soldiers. Over time, the battle scenes generated detailed conversations between Brian and me about battle strategies. I introduced to him the idea that the small characters didn't always have to lose, that they could be more clever, cunning, and planning. They could also be more agile, run faster, and hide better because they were less bulky. We talked about how some really smart military men would be in a position so high that they could get what they wanted purely by negotiation skills, saving many lives. We started to look at, and talk about, all the ways a small guy could develop himself in order to be successful in our mock battle scenes. I hoped to offer options to Brian, as he vicariously replayed over and over again his own position of powerlessness in his life: his past sexual abuse, his history of repeated abandonment, and his current rejection from his new adoptive mother.

I suggested in one session that we mix up the sizes of the soldiers in our armies, with each side having big soldiers and smaller soldiers. At first he was bewildered by this but he was willing to give it a try. Brian began to love playing with the mixed-size armies and he enjoyed the creative strategies that we planned. We would talk about how each type of soldier had his own assets and how the little guys could sometimes be the best if they were smart. Our soldiers began to develop relationships with each other and when one guy got hurt in battle, other fellow soldiers would drag him into a fox hole, call for the medic, and the men would try to care for him in the meantime and hope that he survived. We imagined together what it might be like emotionally to be hurt in battle. I said I really wouldn't want to lose that man, not only because he was a good soldier but because he was also a great buddy. I wanted Brian to understand that all of the men were important, not only as battle objects but as members of the team and as friends to each other. The battle scenes became an important way to build trust in our relationship and to cognitively develop alternative strategies that could translate into Brian's real life. We discussed, for example, instead of throwing feces at neighbors to get their attention, using more socially acceptable behaviors. Over time, Brian was able to generate alternatives, such as inviting kids over to play with his wrestling men, asking them if he could join a game in progress, and pitching in to help a neighbor carry in her groceries.

At home, Brian's original defiance and petty thievery had largely disappeared. However, on one occasion, Brian tried to slip his favorite army character into his pocket. We had established early in counseling the rules of the playroom. They were very simple. Brian could use any toy in the room. However, the toys couldn't be intentionally broken or used to hurt others. They had to stay in the play room and they had to be put away before the end of the session. On this particular occasion, about three months into our sessions, Mrs. B. had been particularly difficult. According to her, Brian was slipping, and she asserted that what I was doing was not working. She found that she needed to come down harder and harder on Brian. Although I questioned her assessment based on my observations and the reports from Brian and Mr. B., I dealt with Mrs. B. relatively passively by asking her to be patient. Following the session, Brian told me he forgot something in the playroom, and we returned to it. At this time, Brian proceeded to pilfer the soldier that had always been considered the leader, the most clever of them all. As he picked up his jacket, I saw Brian put the little plastic soldier into his pocket. I told Brian that he would have to leave the soldier in the playroom because that was the rule, but I could understand why he might like to take him, so that he could continue to have fun with him at home. I said I understood why this soldier was special—he was loved and admired by others, not criticized and rejected as can sometimes happen to soldiers. I wanted Brian to know that I could understand his motivations and the world from his point of view. I also wanted him to understand that it was possible to be with an adult who could impose limits while, at the same time, staying attached in the relationship. It was important for Brian to know that, rather than being judged only by his breach of the rules, that I regarded his acts as being separate from the core of who he was, the core that I saw as valuable in an enduring way. I hoped that my voice conveyed a matter-of-fact tone. I wanted Brian to know that my feelings for him would not change, even while he tested my consistency and availability. Brian needed to know that I could stay emotionally connected to him, even while enforcing limits with him. I watched Brian pull the army guy out of his back pocket and put him back in his place. We finished the session as usual that day, and I told him that I would be looking forward to our next session together. I believed that I had successfully passed his test. I could set firm limits for Brian and, at the same time, be accepting of him as a person. This, I felt, created safety for Brian and allowed us to develop a relationship characterized by trust. Although I believe that a crucial component of this particular behavior was Brian taking a representation of me—a soldier—to help him battle his mother, I knew that I needed to respond to the inappropriateness of stealing. I considered that I would perhaps have to give Brian something concrete (perhaps another soldier) as a representation and reminder that battles could be resolved in a variety of ways.

I also wondered if Brian felt that I had let him down in the conjoint session. Now, not only was he alone once again, but he would have to deal with a larger-than-life mother over the next week. In retrospect, a more effective intervention at the time of the stealing incident would have been to note Brian's "abduction" of the soldier and ask him what made him take him. This would have provided useful information as to whether Brian could yet address his needs directly. If not, it would have provided me an opportunity to discuss the possibility that he experienced the interaction with his mom as an abandonment on my part.

Indeed, in the following session, Mrs. B. was less amenable to suggestions and I found myself working doubly hard. I decided to acknowledge her strengths and validate her efforts as a parent and ask her how she thought we should proceed. This seemed to surprise her, and she began to acknowledge that some of the things we had done had worked. She was then more amenable to continuing the interventions, and I thereafter credited her role and declared how her following through made the real difference in Brian's success.

Developing empathy for others was a major goal of treatment. Brian needed to understand that he was not the only person who was small and picked on, that others who went through painful experiences had feelings similar to his own. I wanted to help change his old problematic responses when these feelings arose. Thus I began teaching Brian more adaptive ways to respond by the way that we would talk about the army characters and their feelings and subjective experiences with war; then I loaned Brian books to read and take home.

The books were a series I had collected that used fantasy characters to demonstrate how it felt to be hurt by bigger, bully characters. The books also explored various creative alternative solutions to obtain more power in situations where one feels powerless. If we read the stories together in session, the activity would have seemed below his level since the books were designed for children younger than Brian, but the reading level was just right for Brian's abilities. So the books became part of his homework assignment. I said, "These books may seem a little easy for you, but the message of the characters is the important part. See if you can understand the lesson that the book teaches and we'll talk about it next week." One of the books, for example, was the story of a small dinosaur who was constantly being physically hurt and humiliated by a huge mean dinosaur (from the book *Tyrone the Horrible* by Hans Wilhelm, New York: Scholastic Inc.). They lived in the same neighborhood and the big bully dinosaur would steal the smaller dinosaur's lunch. He would tease him, punch him, embarrass him, and hurt him physically. The smaller dinosaur had a difficult time getting to sleep at night because he kept thinking about ways he might be able to avoid the bully. The small dinosaur, Boland, thought with his friends about ways in which he could react that might change the situation. He tried every option he could think of. He offered the mean dinosaur ice cream, he tried to ignore him, and he tried to fight back, but all of these options ended in disaster. Finally, the small guy walked by the bully with a sandwich, which was quickly stolen by the big dinosaur. This time, however, the little dinosaur had been clever. He had filled the sandwich with flaming hot peppers that burned his mouth, and the bully never bothered him again. Brian liked these stories because they were like our battle scenes in which the little guys could find ways to prevail through their own creativity and cleverness. We continued to discuss how it felt to be in the losing position and explored various options to become empowered. Brian and I were able to use these books and our play with the army men to explore times when Brian himself had felt powerless and how he might respond in the future when faced with disempowering experiences.

Other than the reading homework, what Brian chose to do in our weekly sessions was usually the same. The only deviation from the battle scenes with the soldiers was Brian bringing in wrestling figures from his World Wrestling Federation (WWF) collection at home, but the theme was always the same. It would always be lifelike human figures fighting each other: there was a lack of creativity. Brian's play was inflexible and unimaginative in the way he compulsively repeated the same conflicts that had been his life experiences. During my time with Brian in therapy, he would never move from confrontational scenes but he showed growth in his ability to articulate the conflict between the soldiers, and the characters gradually became capable of showing emotions and capabilities beyond their potential for aggression. Brian's growth could be witnessed by his transition from the polarization that was observed in the early battle scenes, in which soldiers either were large or small, good or bad, powerful or powerless, or winners versus losers. Later battles were filled with people on both sides who were more real and three dimensional in character. This transition was an indication of growth for Brian. As an observer and participant, I verbalized my observations about how the soldiers had grown and were not all good/bad, powerful/powerless, or winners/losers but sometimes won and sometimes lost, sometimes did bad things but that didn't make *them* bad or unlovable. When possible, I would bring these issues closer to home and talk about whether Brian had ever thought he was bad just because he had *done* something wrong and so forth.

Based on this growth, I returned to the issue of molestation. Broaching the subject again, I asked Brian if he would let me ask him some questions I had about being forced to engage in sexual behavior. I made it clear that the choice was up to Brian, and at this time he chose to not discuss this issue. However, he agreed to let me know if some time felt right in the future. We did make some limited forays into this area before we had to terminate. I had been seeing Brian at a university training clinic and had to leave in June at the end of my school year. Unfortunately, I felt that many issues remained unresolved here. In the limited conversations we had, I worked to help Brian understand that something bad happening to him did not make him a bad person.

Brian's parents learned significantly better ways to cope with his difficult behavior. They learned new skills and gained at least some understanding of what it had been like to live in Brian's world of repeated rejections and abuse. The parents learned slowly how to plan and organize Brian's day to avoid problems—for example, getting him up earlier and having a schedule of activities for before and after school. This list of activities with their deadlines was posted on Brian's bulletin board as well as in the kitchen. The behavior modification plans involved extinguishing undesirable behaviors (e.g., Brian could use foul language no more than once a day to get a star, which was gradually reduced to no more than five times a week and later to three times a week and finally to no times a week) and developing more desirable ones (e.g., making his bed by 7:45 A.M. each morning). This program became more successful as Mr. B., who was more consistent in implementing the program, increased his participation. The interest that Mr. B. had in Brian meant a lot to Brian, since Mr. B. made more efforts to be more affirming of him than had Mrs. B. I encouraged the parents to get Brian involved in some group sports and church activities in order to develop cooperation skills and more age-appropriate social skills. Brian and Nathan both joined Little League, got involved in soccer, and were involved in their church's youth group. In these arenas, they began to share more positive experiences, which was enhanced by Mr. B.'s participation with them.

Revised Treatment Plans

In the initial session, Mrs. B. had stated that Brian would purposely disobey her. As I gathered information from Brian, I began to wonder if cognitive deficits might be causing some of his confusion. Upon further inquiry, I realized that Brian had large lapses of memory and could not even recollect things that should have been important to him. I asked him to keep track of the number of times his mother had to ask him to go to bed the previous night, and this was difficult for him to do. He often couldn't remember our homework assignments for therapy. As I inquired further, it turned out that he couldn't even remember what had happened in past counseling sessions. Furthermore, he couldn't remember fun things he had done in the recent past. This memory dysfunction is a characteristic common in children with conduct disorder. Some neuropsychologists suggest that children who both live in a disorganized/chaotic home, and suffer abuse, often display such memory problems (Kazdin, 1987). I realized that I had to teach Brian some strategies that could help him improve his memory.

I began this work by helping Brian to remember through elaborate rehearsal. We would repeat the rules of the playroom many times during the session, until Brian himself was able to repeat the rules by heart. Additionally we would make lists that helped to remind Brian of important things. This included putting a list of the playroom rules on a chart that we posted on the back of the playroom door. We would also make lists together for the coming week that were designed to help Brian remember homework or other things (e.g., making his bed or taking the trash out) that he planned to do during the week. Part of our weekly session came to involve questioning Brian in order to assess what was important for him that week. I would then write down what he wanted to accomplish in that week on a piece of paper which included each day of the week divided into morning, afternoon, and evening; he would post this in his room when he got home. We would talk about how important it was to check the paper at least three times each day at home (before school, after school, before bed), and I always asked him how much he was able to do from his list during the next therapy session. I often modeled the use of lists in therapy, as we would check off our cleanup list at the end of each session.

We thought up rhymes and funny stories that were associated with things that Brian needed to remember. I told Brian to remember the saying, "They'll get mad, if I don't make my *bed!*" It was important to emphasize that Brian was not bad, if he did not make his bed simply that they would get mad at him. On the contrary, because he was essentially a good boy, he was motivated to keep his parents from thinking which is how he felt when they were mad. Another rhyme we used was, "I must check my *list* or something will be *missed.*" We repeated the words together, exaggerating the rhythm and the rhyme. The rhymes appeared to be helpful in remembering his daily tasks, and we would repeat them as we discussed his counseling homework progress for the last week. We would also chant the rhyme before he left, when we discussed the goals for the week ahead. Brian seemed to enjoy this silliness that we shared together, and it served its purpose by enhancing Brian's ability to remember his daily assignments. It also taught him a skill he could apply in the future. These strategies were also conveyed to the parents and they learned to incorporate them into their parenting with Brian. Mr. B. seemed to enjoy making up rhymes and songs for all the children. Mrs. B. would often shake her head and smile as she described how her husband seemed to be "getting into" the business of reminding the kids of their chores with a little song or poem. I was very pleased that what had been a negative task for Mrs. B. (reminding Brian and the others of their chores) had become an amusing family event.

Balancing Goals

One of the most difficult aspects of balancing goals in this case was my feeling of urgency to address the molestation and perpetration issues with Brian—before a trusting therapeutic relationship had fully developed. I quickly came to like Brian. I felt a deep sadness for the pain that Brian had suffered in his short and intensely difficult life. I also felt great concern over Brian's potential to molest his sister again. If so, she would be deeply hurt and his new family would have a reason to have him removed from the home. After his tumultuous life history, with multiple separations, this would have been the worst yet since it would separate him from his sister—the only lasting relationship in his life. Compelled by my worry for both children, I believe I had pushed too hard initially to get him to talk about his own possible sexual abuse. In retrospect, I wondered if I should have pushed less. I also believe, however, that there was a beneficial effect in discussing the perpetration right from the beginning. It made it clear that I knew what had happened (removing the air of secrecy that almost always shrouds molestation). We had an opportunity to discuss the possibility of it happening again and I was able to open the door to future discussions as our relationship developed. Since the family was fully aware of Brian's potential, we had also discussed ways in which they could better supervise the children in order to prevent Brian from further sexual acting-out. I believe the reason Brian was never caught bothering his sister again was the *full disclosure within the family and the counseling setting,* and not because he had become more cunning in his perpetration. There is something very powerful about naming what has gone unspoken.

The other difficulty was managing Mrs. B. She was challenging for me because she evoked lots of negative countertransference. I found her to be rigid, resistant, and complaining. I used my experience of her to imagine what Brian's experience of her might be, and this helped me to develop even more empathy for Brian. Even though she was difficult, I knew I needed to establish a working relationship with her to be able to keep Brian in treatment. If I alienated her, she would pull him from the treatment as she had done with their first counselor. So, I too had to think of creative solutions in order to bridge this gap I felt between Mrs. B. and myself. I responded to the feelings behind her frustration, I learned about her own history so I could understand her behavior, and I learned from Mr. B. the language and style that she seemed to respond to. Over time, I was able to successfully join with Mrs. B., and this change in our relationship allowed counseling to succeed.

When Mr. B. came to counseling, I promoted the idea that Mr. and Mrs. B. function as a team. I encouraged him to play a more active role in the family by assisting his wife in monitoring Brian and following through on behavior modification plans. Further, since he was an athletic man interested in sports, I broached the idea that he help Brian and Nathan join sporting activities. When Mr. and Mrs. B. worked together on the program, they saw that it worked. This encouraged the father's participation without alienating the mother. Further, given Mrs. B.'s history of parenting her siblings, this process of shared parenting was therapeutic for her. I recommended that she and her husband might benefit by further dividing parenting tasks. So, part of the intervention was to find out what each parent's strengths were and what each could do better, and they were encouraged to operate in that sphere. It happened that mom could do the caretaking in functional areas (i.e., getting the kids to school, fixing lunches), while dad could take care of emotional nurturing (i.e., playing and talking to them more) and discipline.

THERAPEUTIC PROCESS

Relational Reenactments

What I expected Brian to re-create with me in therapy was his role as the "bad boy" who was not going to be wanted and, ultimately, would be sent away. I thought that acting-out would be a major problem in the treatment setting. Although this certainly occurred in the initial part of treatment, it was relatively minimal compared to many children with conduct disorder. Throughout most sessions, however, Brian found some big or small way to test the limits. Because I expected Brian to test me and push my rules, I was prepared to respond promptly but calmly. I went through the same limit setting routine over and over again as Brian broke some playroom rule, tried to steal a toy, played with something "too hard" and broke it, or spoke to me disrespectfully. He clearly found comfort in repeatedly finding that I was firm with him and enforced the rules but continued to like him and take pleasure in our relationship. It was reassuring for Brian to learn that he could not manipulate or control me, and that I did not think he was bad and want to disengage when he was angry or difficult. Although this type of testing behavior continued throughout our relationship, it gradually diminished as he learned to trust our relationship.

I had a sense that Brian had been the loser with adults so many times that he had conceded to being powerless with them unless he acted out. Brian was surprised by the respect that I gave him as we played army, side by side. Our process together was enacting a solution to his conflicts as we would talk about our strategies together as *equals,* rather than I being the directing adult and he being the submissive child. He couldn't believe that I would consider him capable of making good decisions and, because of that, he was initially cautious with me. It took him some time to become less skeptical about my credibility. But, as Brian began to feel more powerful, he saw that I was consistent and fair, and he gradually began to trust me.

I also believed that Brian, like many children with conduct disorder, was also quite depressed at the onset of treatment. As time progressed, he saw that he would not be a victim in our relationship. This freed him to move beyond his ritual of the little men provoking, defying, and fighting the big men for fear of losing to them. He was free to try new plans and think about new ways of conceptualizing the battlefield. These changes may have seemed small in the context of Brian' life but, for him, these were great leaps. The rigidity in his play reflected the repetitive theme of his life, that of powerlessness and victimization. His coping strategy to defend against these shame based feelings was evident in his acting out, especially in his victimization of others. Within our relationship, and with his new family, there was now the possibility for more positive outcomes. In many ways, consistent pain and turmoil had been the only thing he could really count on throughout his life, and he didn't know how to manage being genuinely cared about. Like all children who have suffered such life experiences, he would feel insecure and sabotage himself as the prospect of a better life became possible. Such good news was foreign and unfamiliar to him, and everything he had learned in life confirmed the expectation that this too would soon be taken away from him because he was bad and unlovable. This expectation that all relationships with him would eventually fail induced Brian's caution, testing, and suspicion about his new family life and our relationship. Over time, however, consistent warmth coupled with firm limits lead to increased trust on his part in our relationship. Much more importantly, we were able to generalize some of these characteristics to his new family, and bring about some of the changes that had occurred in our relationship to Brian's relationship with his adoptive parents. Without parallel changes in the family/home setting, positive changes from individual child treatment usually diminish over time rather than continue.

Impediments to Treatment

The biggest impediment to change was Mrs. B. Even though she seemed committed to helping Brian, she continued to be stubborn in her adherence to her own rules, which changed often. She was inconsistent in following through on discipline and often expected things to deteriorate. It was difficult for her to make clear specific requests of the children and even harder for her to deliver fair and consistent consequences. No matter how much I tried to educate her about the power of positive reinforcement, she seemed to cling to the critical and arbitrary control she had grown up with. She scolded, nagged, and degraded Brian until he complied and, when he finally did, it was never good enough. Even though Brian had made significant gains from counseling, Mrs. B. still had a difficult time admitting his progress. Her expectations for future failure made it hard for her to affirm and enjoy current successes. Mr. B., on the other hand, could see that Brian had improved in small ways, and his acknowledgment of Brian's changes empowered Brian to feel more valued in the home and more confident in himself. I tried to maintain periodic phone contact with Mr. B., since he was unable to attend counseling regularly, to keep him involved in Brian's treatment and to keep Brian's door to approval open in the home. I also recommended a parenting group run through the church where Mrs. B. could have feedback from other parents whose cultural values matched hers but who had been able to effectively utilize positive reinforcement. I hoped that this group would also provide emotional and social support for her.

TERMINATION AND SUMMARY THOUGHTS

As the end of my school year and the termination of treatment approached, I had seen Brian about 30 sessions. I felt concerned about the impact that this premature ending was likely to have on Brian. I feared that once again Brian would feel that he was being involuntarily forced away from a relationship that he had begun to trust. In his life of abrupt and artificial endings, the close of our relationship could be profoundly disruptive. About one month before the termination date, I began talking about the ending. I prepared him for this important ending by beginning to summarize where we had come from, how much progress he had made, and where he would go next. We had made major gains in his home life. There had been no more reports of molesting his sister, and the sexual acting-out behavior with Nathan had stopped. He and Nathan still punched each other and fought, but it occurred less frequently now and they also had some positive activities in common (soccer, baseball, church youth group). Brian was getting along better in his classroom and on the playground at school. Brian was more responsive to his mother's requests, even though she still had difficulty acknowledging his improvement. The biggest gain of all, however, was the increased participation of Mr. B. in helping Mrs. B. manage Brian's behavior and his increased involvement in fun activities with all the children. Brian had learned to respect Mr. B. He was a "big guy" who was responsive and consistent. Combining affection and discipline was a twist that Brian had never known. I felt that I had also shown Brian that, at least sometimes, big guys could be caring and firm.

I felt that in our short time together, Brian began to feel like he mattered more to others. Many people in his world were working together to improve his life. He had learned some better ways of handling problems and no longer experienced himself as a powerless victim who could gain control only by victimizing others. Although his mother had improved, I sensed she was going to remain a significant stressor for Brian. Although I did not think it was necessary for Brian to work with a therapist of color, this matching might be helpful for Mrs. B. I gave her the name of a female counselor that I knew to be sensitive to traditional Christian values and, because she was an African American, thought she was more likely to engage Mrs. B. in further treatment for herself and her family.

I also wanted to see Brian increase his social skills and therefore referred him to group therapy with other boys. Without the ability to make friends, Brian was not going to succeed on the playground or in the neighborhood. As previously noted, Mr. B. signed the boys up for sports, and Brian and Nathan were set to play on a team for the next baseball season and were going to soccer practices. I also encouraged church activities that could further help Brian to develop his social skills and build friendships.

Two weeks before the actual termination date, I wanted Brian to directly address the end of treatment with me. I said to Brian, "I think you know what it's like to leave. You've had to leave a lot of places. Do you think it will be difficult?"

Brian replied in a quiet voice, "I don't know." I then asked him, "Do you think it will be sad?" He nodded affirmatively this time. His eyes welled with tears, but he could not articulate his sadness. I told him that our relationship had meant a lot to me, and that I would miss him. He could not speak, but the tears began to stream onto his cheeks, and I saw proof of this bond that had grown between us. It was very difficult for me to terminate with Brian because I knew he faced such a challenging future. For both of us, though, I felt the gifts we had shared would last a long time. As a parting gift, I gave Brian the soldier that he had earlier seemed attached to. In this way, he had a symbol of our relationship and a reminder that there were nonhurtful ways to solve his problems.

Questions for Thought and Discussion

1. Working with conduct disordered children is challenging for most people. What potential behaviors would be the most difficult for you to deal with and why? What personal qualities do you possess that might help or hinder your ability to be effective with these children?

2. Conduct disordered children are often skillful at pushing others away or at making others angry with them. How are you likely to respond to these distancing maneuvers? How would you help these children recognize this interpersonal pattern and learn about its impact?

Suggestions for Further Reading

Kazdin, A. E. (1987). *Conduct disorders in childhood & adolescence.* Newbury Park, CA: Sage. Shows how clinicians can flexibly draw from different theoretical approaches to provide an effective treatment focus. Illuminates how co-morbid disorders such as depression and learning disabilities can be addressed in treating young people with conduct disorder.

Wenar, C., & Kerig, P. (2000). *Developmental psychopathology from infancy to adolescence* (4th ed.). New York: McGraw Hill. (See especially the chapter on "Conduct Disorders and Inadequate Self-Control)". Provides a summary of research on child and adolescent psychopathology, and reviews etiology and treatment approaches.

LINDA: A DEPRESSED THIRD-CULTURE KID CLARIFYING SPIRITUAL VALUES

She rose slowly from her chair as I entered the waiting room, neither resisting nor imitating the self-extending manner of her parents. Her movements were slow and her countenance sad. Her thin frame was covered by a print dress and her straight hair tied with a ribbon. When my eyes turned to her she offered a reluctant handshake. In a moment of silence she spoke in a barely audible voice, "I'm the one my dad called about." She seemed to smile ever so slightly during this split second, then lowered her eyes. They remained downcast as we walked toward my office.

INTRODUCTION

Such was my introduction to Linda, a 16-year-old Caucasian daughter of missionary parents who had returned to the States to get counseling for her. They had become increasingly concerned as reports from her overseas boarding school indicated first subtle, then more substantial changes in her mood and behavior. After consulting with school and mission personnel in East Africa, the decision was made for the family to take an early furlough. Medical testing had ruled out tropical diseases or other physical maladies for her symptoms. Both she and her parents, though resisting it at first, now seemed willing to consider the possibility of depression or some other psychological problem. Thus I began to see Linda on a weekly, outpatient basis.

Characteristics of Depression

Depression is a complex and all-too-common disorder. There is a dramatic rise in depression between the ages of 13 and 15, peaking at ages 17 and 18, and a subsequent decline to adult levels. The Diagnostic and Statistical Manual of the American Psychiatric Association (DSM-IV-TR, 2000) reports that the lifetime risk for major depressive disorder varies from 10% to 25% for women and 5% to 12% for men. It is reported to be twice as common in adolescent and adult females as in adolescent and adult males. We don't really understand all of the factors that contribute to depression or to these commonly reported gender differences. Females may be genetically/hormonally predisposed to suffer more depression than men, or their lives may be more stressful. In contrast, some researchers wonder if men are just less likely to report feeling depressed than women. Further, men may be less likely than women to ask for help and seek treatment if they are depressed. Or, they may be more likely to express their depression through alcohol and substance abuse or other symptoms that lead to different diagnostic labels than women receive for similar problems. Clearly, depression is a complex disorder. Even though we have learned much about it, many basic questions about the causes (etiology) of the different types of depression that occur remain unanswered.

Linda met the DSM-IV-TR criteria for major depression. These criteria include the presence of five or more symptoms during a two-week period: (1) a depressed mood most of the day, nearly every day; (2) markedly diminished interest or pleasure in all, or almost all, activities most of the day, nearly every day; (3) significant weight loss when not dieting or weight gain (a change of more than 5% of body weight in a month); (4) insomnia or hypersomnia nearly every day; (5) psychomotor agitation or retardation nearly every day; (6) fatigue or loss of energy nearly every day; (7) feelings of worthlessness or excessive or inappropriate guilt nearly every day; (8) diminished ability to think or concentrate, or indecisiveness, nearly every day; (9) recurrent thoughts of death, recurrent suicidal ideation, or a suicide attempt or plan for committing suicide.

How do we discriminate between different types of depression or, as counselors say, make a "differential diagnosis"? If Linda had the same symptoms as listed, but to a lesser degree and for a longer period of time (more than two years), she would have received a diagnosis of dysthymic disorder instead of major depression. If she had the same symptoms as listed, *and* had a manic phase of energetic/elated behavior as well, then she would have had a different type of depression known as manic-depressive illness or bipolar disorder.

The symptoms of depression vary by age, though the central feature is a sad or unhappy mood (dysphoria). In addition, depressed people often have feelings of hopelessness, loss of appetite or overeating, sleep disturbance, fatigue, diminished capacity to concentrate, thoughts of death, and especially, feelings of worthlessness and/or guilt. Social and occupational functioning is seriously impaired, such that individuals usually cannot attend school, hold a job, or take care of their children. Sixty to seventy percent of the children and adolescents suffering from depression also have an anxiety disorder (co-morbid—as in two disorders occurring at the same time), which may be generalized (i.e., about many things) or show up as panic attacks or agoraphobia (Cole, Truglio, & Peeke, 1997). Depressed adolescents may also show substance abuse or eating disorders (Hammen & Rudolph, 1996).

For adolescents and children in particular, common symptoms include low self-esteem, withdrawal from others, hypersensitivity to rejection or noninclusion, and a decline in school performance. Anger, agitation, negativism, and irritability, where children and adolescents become oppositional, defiant, or sulky, are common ways in which their sadness is communicated or expressed. Sometimes the negativism may be severe enough to become a conduct problem.

For Linda, prominent features were depressed mood and a sad countenance, loss of interest and pleasure in the things she used to enjoy, fatigue, irritability, and a high degree of anxiety that sometimes seemed close to panic. Further, the depression was clearly affecting her education. As is usually the case, Linda did not understand what originally caused these problems to begin. Sadly but commonly, she believed that she was failing and "bad" because, as hard as she tried, she could not make these hated symptoms go away.

Many issues can trigger or precipitate a depression. Researchers have established a link between insecure attachment and depression in infants, children, and adolescents (Cicchetti & Toth, 1998). As we will see with Linda, children who internalize an image or cognitive schema of themselves as unworthy and others as unloving are more vulnerable to depression. Later in development, for example, depression can be triggered when adolescents feel unwanted by peers, are rejected in romantic relationships, or suffer other interpersonal losses, such as parental divorce or moving away to college. These losses and changes, whether real, perceived, or feared, are usually accompanied by a heavy dose of disappointment. Many times, the loss, fear of loss, or transitions that precipitate the depression have occurred before *and represent a pattern or theme derived from earlier experiences.* Of particular relevance to Linda, the loss of the mother before age 11, whether by death or extended separation, is a vulnerability factor that greatly increases the risk of subsequent depression for most women (Brown, Harris, & BiFulco, 1986). We will see that for Linda, as for others who struggle with this disorder, *two underlying themes often form the basis for depression: feeling unlovable, and believing they are helpless or powerless to change or improve their situation (inefficacy).*

As noted earlier, anger is often a component of depression in young people. Many adolescents, angry about rejection, mistreatment, lack of nurture, and so forth, may direct their anger inward toward themselves (and show sadness) or express themselves more directly (and express irritability and negativism). They often hold the faulty belief that the appropriate expression of anger, frustration, or differences of opinion are unacceptable and they are afraid of being rejected or misunderstood if they communicate more forthrightly or express themselves more authentically. As we will see with Linda, working with her disowned anger was an important part of her treatment.

In addition to these psychosocial aspects of depression, many adolescents also exhibit physiological symptoms (e.g., appetite change, sleep disturbances, fatigue). In the case of someone like Linda, who has spent years living in the tropics under less than ideal public health conditions, it is particularly important to rule out other medical causes. For example, dinghy fever, a tropical disease especially well known to expatriates who live in rural, tropical climates, produces symptoms much like depression.

Sociocultural Context

As I sought to understand Linda and her distress, it was crucial to understand her background and the relationships she had with others. I found it helpful to understand Linda in the context of her identity as a *third-culture kid* or TCK (Useem, 1993). These children, who spend a majority of their developmental years in a culture other than that of their parents, have been found to have discernible differences when compared to their North American-reared counterparts. These differences constitute a cultural feature that is useful to grasp when working with this population.

TCKs include four groups of children: those whose families are in (1) the international business community; (2) the diplomatic corps; (3) overseas military operations; and (4) missionaries. Of the four groups, the families most involved in and deeply integrated into the host culture are missionaries. Traditionally, the children of such parents have come to be known as MKs (for missionary kids) as well as TCKs. Because of their parents' work, it is not unusual for many to attend boarding school for at least a portion, if not most, of their precollege educational careers.

While this is becoming less common, some children begin boarding as early as 7 years of age. Many, however, often live their late childhood and adolescent years in a boarding home at a mission or international boarding school. There are, of course, periodic visits from and with parents, vacations in their parents' home, and regular visits (up to a year's duration) to their parents' home culture (e.g., North America). Although efforts are usually made for significant parental communication with the school, actual practices vary widely among schools, mission organizations, and geographic areas.

Young children growing up in such situations often spend many years immersed in the host culture as well as in the expatriate or mission culture within their country of service. Thus, there is a sense of alienation from their parents' home culture and something of an identification with the host culture. However, they are faced with the dilemma that they can never fully join the host culture as a full-fledged member, and they must make extra efforts to "reenter" the home culture of their parents. Living between two cultures without fully belonging to either, these children essentially develop a culture of their own—thus the term, third-culture kid (Austin, 1983).

Many MKs whose parents are from North America but live overseas are fluent in at least one language other than English. They may also have passable language skills in a less standard language (such as a tribal tongue or regional trade language), depending on parents' work and location. When they are young, they often develop a high degree of comfort with children from the host culture, a pattern that characteristically carries over into comfort and enjoyment of ethnic diversity in adulthood.

As MKs move into later adolescence and young adulthood, they tend to be most comfortable with others who have had extensive cross-cultural experiences, and to be knowledgeable about the world beyond their years. Integration into standard North American adolescent culture is seldom easy, however. Even during times of furlough, American games such as Trivial Pursuit and discussions of the latest musical groups or clothing fads are anathema to them. The lack of world awareness seen in their North American peers sometimes fuels a sense of themselves as "odd" and "unacceptable."

Similar to stateside families who are subject to frequent moves and separations (e.g., ministers, military), MKs have typically experienced many transitions and relocations that increase their vulnerability to depression. As MKs reenter the American culture, painful feelings of grief and loss often emerge from previous unresolved transitions. Add to this the usual developmental issues and struggles of adolescence, and one can readily see some possibilities for depression.

While the majority successfully negotiate such transitions, there are some casualties. For example, the anticipation of a permanent move and the expectation of disbanding a group of high school classmates who will be widely scattered upon graduation may become especially stressful. The lack of parental understanding or peer support during this period can be a factor in depression. Sometimes the adolescent interprets these losses/transitions as reflecting some type of internal deficit or personal failure. Once the class scatters, there is seldom a "hometown" to which one can return. Their identity, then, is based more on affiliation and relationship rather than being grounded in a specific location, even though identification with the country in which they grew up may remain strong. Thus, some of these external anchors of belonging that hold an adolescent's developing sense of self in place can be threatened by these changes. Even imagining this transition/loss can precipitate depression for some. More importantly, *repeated experience of interpersonal losses or leave-takings that have not been dealt with* (i.e., grieved, mourned, or shared with others who understand) *create depression.* Thus, authentic relationships that allow real feelings are especially important to deter depression as MK and other third-culture adolescents negotiate these myriad transitions (Powell, 1989).

Linda is more clearly understood in the context of her own Christian beliefs and values. Her parents' Christian faith, their commitment to live and work overseas, and the environment of service created by these beliefs, are crucial to who Linda is. Many of her values, self-perceptions, and understanding of life were shaped by these beliefs and by her own choice to become a Christian. These areas of her life were also influenced by others, including the interpretation of Christian principles and beliefs made by those surrounding her, and the consistency (or inconsistency) with which these were translated from spoken or written word to behavior.

Finally, her experiences as a teenager experiencing depression include understanding not only her and her family, but the broad context of Christianity in which she lived. Specifically, missionary and boarding school life, growing up in a culture that could never become fully her own, the requirements of juggling and sorting at least two clearly defined cultures (home and host), and the usual developmental issues of being adolescent all played a part in understanding and treating Linda's depression.

CASE ILLUSTRATION

Presenting Problem

Linda's changes in mood and behavior began soon after she arrived for her junior year (eleventh grade) at school the preceding August. By late January they had magnified and precipitated her family's premature return to the States. She had become a fearful, melancholic, and withdrawn young woman—at times childlike and at other times overly mature. These characteristics stood in sharp contrast to the previously active, outgoing, and inquisitive girl described by her parents. She had been a teen who had become increasingly popular among her school friends and had looked forward to her junior year in boarding school. While usually earning A's and B+'s, her grades had slipped, her energy seemed drained, and she had seemingly lost interest in school and almost all pleasurable activities.

Her parents, friends and school/mission officials were aware of and concerned about these changes. Since physical causes were ruled out, many thought that Christmas break at her parents' work location would help. She appeared more secure and a bit happier there and showed some improvement. However, both parents described her as seeming different and were concerned about her. She was reluctant to share with them any of her thoughts or feelings. While able to describe her fear and pain, she was unable to attach it to specific issues or events. She frequently apologized for not doing better.

As we sat in those moments of the first session and I heard of this contrast, I found it hard to imagine that her parents were talking of the person sitting so dejectedly across from me. I felt internally conflicted. There was the unspoken expectation by her parents that I would provide the help that might restore her to this earlier self, yet her own despondency caused me to temporarily question whether I could provide what might be needed. This seemed to stimulate a quasi-conscious exploration of both my own faith and the skills and understanding I would need to help her.

Linda had indeed shown some slight improvement during Christmas break and returned to school seeming partially cheerful. She had left the village with a hope that things would be better, partly because of her own prayers as well as those of her parents. Her father, especially, had spent many hours attempting to encourage her and sharing his work activities with her during the weeks of break. She said she knew her parents loved her and wanted her to be better. She didn't want to disappoint them.

Her return to school, however, was traumatic. She felt she had already caused too much concern on the part of her friends and others at school. This feeling became more acute as she realized she wasn't making it. She felt she was taking space in the boarding home that "someone else deserved more than I." She was late for breakfast the first morning, hardly ate, and was fearful as she walked to classes. She was worried that the houseparents would be upset with her. She had become so upset by noon that one of them had come to the classroom building to take her back to the house. With a lot of attention and encouragement, she succeeded in staying at school two weeks. She then became more serious, started having daily crying spells, felt extremely tired, and began losing weight. Then began the steps that eventually brought her to my office.

She at first seemed relieved to be coming to the United States, but then began realizing the enormity of not seeing her friends again for sometime—maybe never, if she didn't get better. She now felt guilt for taking her parents away from their work. Further, she wondered how this would be explained to those in her parents' home church, and to concerned relatives. Even after her parents left the first session and we were alone, she could add little more about her concerns than had already been noted. Her symptoms had become more pronounced: she was not attending school here, was frightened to leave her house (agoraphobic), and had begun spending long periods alone in her room. She became irritable or anxious at any attempt to get her to consider school or social activities.

Linda seemed caught between three worlds: that of her own painful depression, the creeping realization that she had less a sense of belonging here than she had in the boarding school, and the strong but subtle expectations she held for pleasing her parents and living up to these internalized standards. She seemed eager for help, but helpless in knowing how to receive it.

Client Description

Linda was an attractive, thin-featured 16-year-old with straight, rather long, blondish hair. She referred to herself at one point as a dishwater blonde. She carried herself straightforwardly in spite of her downcast eyes and sluggish movements. Behind her sad countenance, there seemed a connection with me through an occasional glance from her dark brown eyes, perhaps seeking to convey something, and sometimes almost pleading. These glances were seldom longer than a second and were usually followed by withdrawal and aversion. In spite of her obvious pain and the silent pauses, she seemed to attend to my comments or questions and, at some level, to be considering them. It was as if she was watching closely and attempting to read my expectations. At other moments she seemed to be testing me as though she were hopeful. Yet, the feeling of her discouragement and distress was pervasive and expressed itself in passivity.

In the initial phases of that interview she did seem free to make occasional comments even with her parents present. I observed that these seldom revealed feelings or perspectives, however, but only factual details. Her parents seemed gentle and caring in their descriptions of her, and were generally nonintrusive. Linda agreed that she wanted help but didn't know what to do or expect. She and her parents each seemed close to desperation but tried to present themselves as hopeful.

Linda described her present houseparents and some of her friends but could only say, "This year in school was different—it wasn't the same as before," even when asked to describe these differences. Feeling that she might have more to say and desiring to see how she would relate to me alone, I asked her parents to leave for the latter half of the initial interview. The most significant event, in addition to further background information, was a flash of anger when I asked more broadly about the houseparents she had had in her previous years. She seemed particularly distressed when mentioning one in particular.

As noted earlier, Linda's symptom picture met the criteria for major depressive disorder, single episode. However, features of agoraphobia and the possibility of panic disorder were clearly worthy of pursuit. Other than previous experience with MKs, which provided a kind of intuitive context, I was aware that I had little feel for what this depression was about for her. I didn't understand as well as I wanted what the problems really were for Linda now, what had gone wrong for her while growing up that predisposed her to this, and what precipitated the current crisis. There were compelling features to follow up on, such as her early separation from parents, frequent changes of boarding school personnel, the dangers faced by the overseas missionary community, and the seeming attachment to Africans during her early years. Things still seemed so vague, however, and I was left wondering why it was so hard to get to feelings or issues that seemed more substantial.

Social Context

Linda was born in a mission hospital in East Africa, as was her sister ahead of her. The second and last of Ed and Esther's two children, she is nine years her sister's junior. Each had attended the same boarding school. With their age difference, Linda had not spent substantial time with her sister Sally except during vacations at home in the village and during furloughs in the States. However, she reported that Sally had been significant to her in the two years of overlap at school, and she seemed to have a deep, though not intimate, affection for her.

Linda's parents described her as "the sensitive one." She seemed always to identify with the underdog, would shed tears easily when seeing or hearing of someone being mistreated, and seemed to feel things deeply. She often seemed unable to express what she was feeling, however, especially if she considered it a negative feeling such as anger.

Ed and Esther had been educated at a Christian liberal arts college in the midwest. They had become Christians early in life and independently made commitments to serve in overseas missions during a spiritual emphasis week at the college. Not long after they became interested in one another.

Each parent came from midwestern families. Ed had grown up on a farm; Esther in a county seat town in the same state some 100 miles away. Their parental families were intact and most members of their extended families continued to be active in community and church affairs. One of Esther's sisters and her husband had taught for a three-year period at a missionary boarding school in South America. Esther felt especially close to this sister and had shared with her the details of Linda's situation. Ed and Esther, however, had not been free in sharing this information with other family members, nor had they shared much with their stateside church constituency. There seemed to be a quality of avoidance or denial, perhaps shame, in describing to others the reasons for their early return. Linda felt this and was also aware of their attempt to publicly cover their anxiety about her with smiles and platitudes.

Linda's parents seemed to share a deep commitment to one another and to their children. They were respectful in their communication, but two features in their family life emerged with clarity early in our contacts: (1) Anger or disapproval was seldom acknowledged directly; and (2) interpersonal conflicts were downplayed or denied. Esther seemed more willing than Ed to express negative affect (and probably experienced more of it than he). Ed tended to paint a smiling face on nearly any situation.

These characteristics had not gone unnoticed by Linda. During therapy she offered insightful observations about her sister and revealed some insights about what had probably been a period of rebellion for Sally. Further, the parents' expectations of their children were very strong but covert, expressed through subtle disapproval or overly strong approval rather than through direct communication. I sensed this to be true in their expectations of me as well.

Through church affiliation and personal religious conviction, the majority of their extended family members was familiar with Christian missions and believed in their importance. Most, however, had stayed pretty close to home after completing schooling or service in the military. This seemed to provide some stability for Linda during furlough times. Visits to the States sometimes caused her to wonder why she couldn't live and attend school all in one place, like most of her cousins.

The extended family cultures were largely middle class and of conservative/ evangelical religious background. Their behavior and verbalizations were grounded in the basic values of small town friendliness, respect, and helpfulness to others, fortified by their Christian beliefs. Linda's parents seemed to take some pride, especially her mother, in the fact that the families were seen as solid citizens and respected members in their communities. Those same values had operated in Ed and Esther's 27 years of work in Africa.

There was no reported history of mental illness in the family of either parent although one of Esther's aunts had evidently been mentally retarded. In gathering family history, Esther indicated that this had been a shame to the family and seldom had been referred to directly as she was growing up. An uncle of Ed's had his farm repossessed during the Great Depression and Ed seemed to feel a sense of shame in this. An organizing family value seemed to be: "Always be good and look good, and even if things aren't good, try to appear as though they are." I recognized how pivotal and pervasive this value was in their family life, which provided me with the first real "handle" in understanding and treating Linda.

Initial Session

Linda's mild manner and depressed mood made it difficult at first to know where best to try to join with her. Her voice was at times barely audible and her pace of response slow. Yet, in the first few minutes of our meeting, I had seen the hint of a smile and what seemed like glances of anger, suggesting a bit more life and availability of affect than her demeanor indicated. In our first 30 minutes with her parents in the room, she had been given easy opportunity to speak, and they waited patiently for her delayed responses. Linda seemed somehow to take on her mother's anxiety about the situation and at times make it her own. At other times I thought she was repelled by her parents' concern, but instead of communicating this, she seemed to act confused or dejected instead.

In these initial moments, I felt that her parents were quietly assessing my ability to help their daughter. Due to my consultation work with overseas mission organizations (they had been referred by mutual acquaintances), I felt some pressure to provide the very best help possible. In a few minutes, however, I felt less scrutinized by them and realized that my anxiety was due to the exaggerated performance demands I was placing on myself. As I caught myself responding more to my own concern (i.e., countertransference) than to Linda herself, I was able to refocus my attention and feel more effective in joining with her. As I became more present to her, I noticed that Linda seemed to respond by feeling more comfortable and acting a bit stronger with me.

After her parents left the room, Linda moved her chair ever so slightly so as to face me more directly. After a short silence she asked if I had ever been to Africa. The dialogue went something like this:

CL: Have you ever been to Africa?

TH: Yes, I have.

CL: Did you like it?

TH: I thought it was different and beautiful.

CL: (after a pause) I miss being there. (long pause followed by eventual tears) I wish I were there.

TH: Is it better there than here?

CL: Not always. (long pause)

TH: Not always?

CL: No. (long pause) It depends on where you are and who you're with.

TH: M-m-m-m-m

CL: Right now, I'd like to be with Annie, walking through the village watching the children play.

TH: That sounds enjoyable, what's it like?

CL: But I'm not there . . . (followed by a flow of tears and deep sobs) . . . and I don't know if I'll ever get back.

It seemed in that short interchange that Linda had trusted me with something important to her—that she missed Africa and was grieving the possibility that she may never return. (Later in the session I learned that she had been noncommunicative about this to her parents, almost as if to protect them in their decision to bring her to the States.) I chose not to follow up on her affect at that moment, but to wait and see what direction she would take. When she regained her composure, she shifted back to my visit in Africa, asking in more detail about it. I felt this was an important part of building our relationship. We shared several observations about places we had each been to, and she learned that I had at one time actually been on the campus of her boarding school.

As we continued this discussion, I sensed a slight withdrawal and began having second thoughts about disclosing this information. She then asked, "Do you know some of the teachers and staff at (the boarding school)?" When I told her I didn't, she paused for a time, then seemed to relax. I took the risk of acknowledging this by saying, "When I told you I didn't know anyone at (the boarding school), you seemed somehow relieved." She became silent, almost withholding in manner. After some moments, I noted this by saying, "You seem very quiet—almost like you've drawn back a little." After a few seconds she said, "I was afraid you might know Mrs. T." I replied, "No, I don't . . . would that be important to you?" "Yes," she said, "I'm glad you don't know her." Then she was silent.

I broke the silence by shifting to some questions about her symptoms and how they had developed, and attempted in my mind to clarify some hypotheses about her depression. It was difficult to get at any specific event, relationship, or series of events to quite understand it. However, I was beginning to learn more about her. She was very observant and perceptive of others' feelings, seemed to have a vocabulary for expressing what she saw, and was clearly motivated for help. But she seemed to use information from her acute perception to deflect her own feelings, especially if they were anything but positive, and she seemed to defend against them with a level of denial which provided a striking contrast to this strength of perception. As our time expired, we shifted to the practical aspects of making arrangements for further meetings.

As I reflected on the session, I was aware of a certain delight in seeing more energy than I would have suspected from the phone conversation with her father. I was also aware of an inward tension—a pull toward wanting to quickly reduce her seemingly helpless distress. To "take away" this feeling, however, would have given her the message that I could not tolerate her sadness. At the same time I experienced an appreciation for the hint of inward resilience I saw. I later learned that more people had been responding to the side of the tension which seemed to say, "Help me, relieve me of this," rather than the side that said, "I'm resilient, let's find a way out of this." Linda did not need to be rescued from her sadness (which would have emphasized her weakness). Instead, she needed a relationship in which her sadness would be accepted. If I could provide her with such an experience, which she did not have with her family or significant others, I thought her own resilience would emerge.

In the next two sessions I took the dual stance of getting relevant information while attempting to join more with her as a person, both in pain and in her strengths. She affirmed her mother's earlier description that she had been outgoing, friendly, and inquisitive, all of which had changed over the past months. I learned that she had done volunteer literacy work with African children who lived near her school, and that she seemed to identify with Africans, especially those who had been mistreated or seemed sad or discouraged. Linda was able to provide for these children an experience that she herself lacked.

Linda had been popular with her peers, and viewed as a good listener and reliable friend. She seemed to have been on a good track of development. I found myself liking her, even when she showed her depression, agoraphobia, and occasional oppositional stance. These characteristics were more apparent when she talked about God or her Christian faith. When I sought to explore this further, she would often respond with a petulant look, which seemed significant. Over time, I would learn that Linda felt abandoned by God and that this feeling contributed significantly to her depression.

At first, Linda could not identify any particular precipitating event for the depression, and was vague in her description of the internal processes associated with her sadness, fear, and withdrawal. Yet, she seemed bright and had begun giving me glimpses into her anger, strengths, and personal faith. I had on one or two occasions again experienced some fleeting seconds of anxiousness about helping her, as I had in our first session, but I understood how important it was to be with her in both her difficult feelings and her joys. As I began to see more clearly her considerable strengths and understand her sadness, a sense of hope emerged that dispelled my anxiety.

In these sessions she seemed to alternate between having small bursts of energy when talking of something she enjoyed (such as Africa). More often, however, she was prone to appear sad, have some delay in response, and make disparaging comments about herself along with hopeless comments about the future (e.g., "I know I'll never get back to Africa." or "I don't think I'll be able to finish high school"). Since rejection and/or loss and low self-esteem are often at issue in adolescent depression, I began to listen more closely for openings that might lead to a better understanding of these important symptoms. In one session the following exchange took place:

TH: Each time you mention Africa, you seem to brighten up but then become sad.

CL: Oh . . . you don't like it when I'm sad.

This was an important clue to the possibility that she was trying to discover what *my* expectations were, and then trying to meet them. That is, covering her sadness because she held the faulty belief that I—like others in her life—didn't want to see or respond to it. Her statement was also a prompt for me to look closely at how I was responding to her sadness. In the Christian community, there is an unfortunate tendency to see depression as a weakness, something Christians should not be experiencing if they really believe in God's love. Linda was suffering from the effects of such an attitude, and I had to reflect carefully on my own actions to determine if I was unconsciously reinforcing this erroneous belief. As a Christian, I have come to believe that God stands with us in the full range of our feelings.

TH: No, I'm honored that you share those important feelings with me. I see both your sadness and a hint of joy whenever you speak of Africa. I welcome both feelings and would like to hear more about them.

CL: I'm sorry I'm sad . . . it doesn't make it good to be around me. (long silence) A lot of people don't like to be around me.

TH: I want to be around you when you are sad, but maybe you're telling me that a lot of people haven't?

CL: Well, most people. (long silence in which she looked at the floor and began quietly sobbing)

TH: Some particular people?

CL: (long silence) Maybe. (further silence) Well, one person.

TH: One person?

CL: Yes, one person. (pause) Mrs. T.

TH: The person you asked me if I knew?

CL: Yes.

TH: She doesn't want to be around you because you're sad?

CL: Well, not just sad. She thinks I'm not a good Christian.

TH: Not a good Christian?

CL: She accused me of being a volunteer at the literacy program just so I could be with Rob, not because I loved the people who come there. Rob is just a good friend who's really good in literacy work. (pause) And I started crying because what she said hurt and it's not true. Then she said she didn't like being around crybabies . . . she wanted her students to be strong people. (pause) Then she just walked off (long silence and tears)

TH: And then?

CL: I tried to tell Christine, my roommate, but she seemed too busy. I was afraid to tell Mom and Dad because I knew they would worry. (pause) I was really trying to be a good Christian, but . . . (more tears and finally deep sobs)

TH: (after a long pause and some recovery on Linda's part) It really hurt to be thought of as not being a good Christian.

CL: I really tried . . . (more tears)

TH: You really try hard to live out being a Christian . . .

CL: . . . and sometimes nobody seems to notice . . . and I wonder even if God notices . . . (long pause)

At this point it seemed that Linda had begun trusting me enough to reveal one of the events that had hurt her and share the sad feelings that she believed no one wanted to see. I also began to appreciate how important it was for Linda *to protect her parents,* something she thought was part of being a good Christian. She didn't wish for her parents to worry about her being unhappy at school. As the clue had suggested at the beginning of this interchange, she had become quite good at discerning what her parents' (and others') expectations were (i.e., don't be sad) and tried to conform to them. This was partly repeated with me in this session and, at this early point, I was able only to make a small step toward beginning to understand or change it. Others would be taken later.

As we got to know one another, she revealed many instances of hurt at school which she did not convey to her parents (or anyone) for fear of not pleasing them, having her feelings rejected, or being left out. By subtly knowing what people expected and trying to meet these expectations, the chances for rejection were decreased. It was also becoming clear that Linda felt alone, perhaps even abandoned by God, in living out her faith. Sadly, she felt she needed to protect her parents from knowing of this loneliness, which I began to see as one of the origins of her pain. Before this session ended, she had sobbed more and seemed in greater pain. I was tempted to extend the session. Instead, I told her I felt privileged to have been told some of her deeper feelings and believed she was strong for having spoken so clearly about them. I wanted to communicate to her that I could stay with her when she was in pain, and at the same time recognize her strengths. She looked at me somewhat quizzically and then smiled slightly, indicating with nonverbals her readiness to leave.

Reflecting on this session I came again to the notion of being tested, but in a different way. She now seemed to be testing me not so much about my capacity to help but whether I had a need for her not to be sad, as had her father. The deeper test seemed to be whether I could tolerate the pain and sadness she had accumulated over a period of time and that was no longer being denied.

Passing tests often becomes an important therapeutic step. I needed to show her that I could allow her to be sad, unlike her father, and allow her to express the depth of this sadness without fearing that her pain would be denied or discounted, as she expected it to be. A step toward this had been taken as she found, this time, that she could touch the fullness of her own reality by being as sad as she really was.

CASE CONCEPTUALIZATION

Linda's first symptoms appeared when she left the family's village home at the end of the summer and arrived at boarding school. While this generally evoked some anxiety and sadness, this year seemed different. She had a creeping sense of foreboding about her return. She tried to tell herself that her junior year would be the best ever and that when she returned to school everything would be all right.

As she reviewed the latter months of the previous year she began to realize that there had been several disappointments which she had brushed aside, telling herself they were minor and "not to worry about them." Loss of self-esteem is often a contributor to the development of depression, especially in adolescents, and her "storing" these disappointments had begun having its effect. On a couple of occasions she had attempted to mention these disappointments to her parents but felt doing so raised her mother's anxiety so she kept them to herself. The disappointments generally had to do with people not keeping promises they had made to her, and having been overlooked in various school and boarding home activities.

Several clearer hypotheses now presented themselves. Her symptoms escalated when she returned to boarding school. Thus it seemed likely that *repeated attachment disruptions,* which had not been acknowledged or dealt with in any direct way, were taking their cumulative toll. I also hypothesized that the several disappointments from last year that she had disclosed to me—which also revealed that she had many unmet needs—were only a sampling of many others that had occurred over a longer period of time. She had not admitted these fully to herself, nor, given her sensitive nature, had she risked creating interpersonal conflict or being disliked by mentioning them to anyone. Instead, she had attempted to ignore them at one level and, at another, to pray and believed that God would take care of them. When things became worse rather than better, she began to think, first, that she was not "doing things right" and, second, wondered if God was to be trusted with such things.

People, including her parents, seemed to respond to Linda's enthusiasm and optimistic outlook, rather than attempts to express "negative things." Her parents were delighted with these sunny qualities but seemed to be uncomfortable when things were not going well for her. Linda had not felt at liberty to disclose some of her loneliness, disappointments, or fears to her parents but instead tried to handle them in ways she knew they would like: being cheerful and outgoing.

I conjectured that Linda had, at some early point, decided not to cause problems or place any demands on her parents, as her more expressive and assertive sister, Sally, had done. Instead she found ways to prevent disclosing any of her own feelings which might distress them. In this regard, the cheerfulness and outgoingness was an interpersonal coping strategy. *This defense was designed to preserve an attachment and win her parent's approval by meeting their needs at the expense of her own.* This coping strategy had worked so well and become so ingrained, in fact, that she had learned not to share negative feelings, problems, or difficulties with anyone else in her life. As is usually the case with a coping strategy like this, Linda eventually learned to keep them from herself as well. She was no longer being successful, however, as the avoidance of her own affect and her undeveloped capacity to assert her own needs was fueling her depression. It was hard for her to know just how she did feel, what she really wanted, and what she was really like. And all of this confusion and alienation from her own authentic experience was coming to the fore during the "identity" stage of development, so important to adolescence and described with particular emphasis for missionary children by Taylor (1988).

Thus, I hypothesized that Linda was experiencing much more resentment, loneliness, and disappointment than she was aware of. Up to now, it was completely unacceptable for thoughts and feelings like these to be a part of her. If she indeed felt as sad or mad as she really was, she would (in her eyes) be hurting her parents, failing as a Christian, and permanently disrupting her friendships. Several events seemed to be happening all at once to topple her ability to deny or ward off negative feelings:

1. She was disappointed with herself for not being the strong person she believed she should be. She did not wish to cause her parents anguish for sending her to boarding school (as she believed her sister had caused) and wished to demonstrate Christ's sufficiency in caring for her as she sought to follow Him in her Christian walk. When she began to experience some disappointments and distress the preceding year, she felt that she was failing and had become angry at her own weakness. I noted this not only as an important psychological issue but also a spiritual one.

2. She also began experiencing something more accurately described as resentment. She was finding it increasingly hard to leave her parents' home after such a short visit each summer, even though she enjoyed school, her friends, houseparents, and most teachers. At times, her tears in my presence seemed to be those of anger; at other times, they were clearly tears of grief. Understandably, she missed the closeness of her parents and, in anticipating plans for college that would be developing this year, realized that she would be leaving Africa permanently while her parents stayed. She would then have neither Africa nor her parents and she was frightened. I found myself wondering if her open expression of missing Africa and often reflecting on its beauty and meaning for her was a metaphor for the secure attachment she was missing.

Several comments from Linda, as well as observing certain interactions with her parents, helped me clarify that the way she protected her parents was central in causing and maintaining her depression. She did not want to disappoint them, cause them worry or concern, or create for them unnecessary work. She wished to always please them, especially by following their example of Christian commitment.

The tension between these caretaking wishes and her own needs became unmanageable and broke down in symptom development and depression. Though she could not verbalize it to herself or to her parents, at some level she wished to be able to express her hurts and disappointments and receive her parents' soothing comfort. In differing ways, this tension was present with both of her parents. Her father often sought to comfort her, would listen, and share experiences; yet, he seemed not to want to hear specifically about her pain, meeting such attempts with platitudes or gently changing the subject. Her mother seemed more expressive of her own feelings and needs, but this became a role reversal (parentification). Too often, Linda felt these took a twist such that Linda then felt responsible for responding to her mother rather than expressing her own concerns. From both of these relational patterns, a certain "giving up" had resulted. Her internal response was a deep grieving and a depressive hopelessness about ever having someone respond to her feelings and needs.

To illustrate, a break-in occurred at the school during Christmas break of her sophomore year. The bandits had entered several of the dormitories, vandalizing individual rooms as well as other parts of the hall. Personal items belonging to several of the girls had been taken. Not only had she experienced anxiety about her safety following that event, she found she was missing a locket containing a small photo of her parents that they had given her for Christmas during her first year at school. She felt extremely guilty for having left it at school. This appeared to be, again, something Linda adapted to well at the time, but in recent months she had been having dreams where fears for safety, threats of loss, and guilt had been themes. In some respects, she seemed to be blaming herself (internalizing responsibility) for the emotional deprivation she was experiencing. In spite of their deep concern for her, her parents seemed at some level unable to connect with Linda's sensitivity and needs for comfort and security. This event seemed to have highlighted this theme that had repeated in so many different situations and events throughout her development.

Orienting Constructs

Three orienting constructs came to guide my work with Linda. I wanted to (1) respond to her strengths as well as her problems; (2) work within her worldview and utilize Christian beliefs that were relevant for her; and (3) use our relationship to demonstrate that the same faulty expectations and problematic patterns that often occurred with her parents and others did not have to repeat in our relationship or many others.

The constructs of separation and loss, unresolved grief, unmet attachment needs, role reversal and protection of parents, and questions about her acceptability to God all were important in understanding Linda and providing a treatment focus. However, it was also important to acknowledge her strengths: her resiliency, genuine sensitivity to the needs of others, capacity for making friendships, and her sense of identity with her family and with aspects of the African culture.

Her Christian commitment also seemed to be related to each of these and was an important orienting construct. Linda seemed to know, at one level, that her own Christian faith contained the knowledge and wisdom to address each of the issues that tied in with her depression. Yet, at the same time, the feelings of failure to have adequately appropriated this faith in overcoming her problems seemed to exaggerate her sense of guilt and inadequacy and to fuel the depression.

Regarding her Christian theology, Linda did not seem to fully understand the concept of grace or to allow herself to experience it in spite of its importance in her Christian faith. Rather, especially in her present circumstances, she felt unworthy of the acceptance and comfort she desperately wanted and felt she should be blamed and perhaps punished. Thus the concepts of grace, forgiveness, and reconciliation became important orienting points as well. I followed some of the ideas and steps so poignantly described by Smedes (1984).

Linda's denial of her own anger and other negative feelings and belief that they should not be expressed to her parents was so central to her depression that it was clear they *would have to be resolved experientially and relearned in our interaction together*. That is, an important orienting construct would be to provide in our relationship the experience of surfacing and expressing those feelings, and finding that they were accepted, did not disrupt our relationship, or cause me to withdraw. Perhaps I would need to provide some direct and honest expression of feelings and acceptance myself that would, in turn, behaviorally give her permission to experience and express the full range of her own sadness, resentment, and doubts. It was essential for her to experience negative feelings as something that did not in itself disrupt relationships, but could produce greater closeness in some relationships if appropriately expressed. I needed to be on the lookout for such opportunities.

Treatment Plans and Intervention Strategy

I saw Linda's situation as rather complex because it included not only depression, but involved cross-cultural, developmental, and religious issues as well. The first goal was simply to establish an environment and offer a relationship in which Linda would feel comfortable and begin expressing herself. It was especially important for her to freely express her feelings. Linda was much too other-directed. Indeed, even with me, she seemed to be orienting to what she believed my needs were and seemed to be holding back freely or authentically expressing herself.

I found myself wanting to make things better for Linda without her doing the necessary work of self-exploration and risk taking. For example, on several occasions I found phrases of reassurance forming in my mind—but realized expressing these would cut short Linda's opportunity to struggle with the issues being faced. I did not wish to have our relationship so parallel what she had established with her father. With him, she read his expectations, denied her negative feelings, and provided what he wanted in order to have some connection with him—even if it didn't really meet her needs. It felt important that Linda more fully recognize her feelings and needs and not feel that she must protect me from them.

The second goal related to the question of identity. It seemed important to develop a better understanding of Linda's development and the anchors in her identity formation. In one respect Linda saw herself as a child of Africa, yet she was also a child of missionary parents, a Christian, a student in boarding school, and a friend and helper to many. Linda seemed to struggle with these varied identifications and it became important to explore these with her and help her integrate and fully own the strengths in them.

The third goal was to help her clarify her own goals in counseling so a mutually agreed upon contract could be struck. When we initially approached this, her goals were simply, "To get back in school where I belong, to stop being depressed, and to let Mom and Dad get back to what they want to do." As we worked further on these, she was able to be more definitive. The following interchange, which took place in the context of a discussion about how she tended to identify herself, reveals something of this process of developing mutual goals:

CL: Well, I guess being a MK is OK.

TH: OK?

CL: Well, I guess so. I mean, that's what I am and what I've been ever since I was born.

TH: So what's that like?

CL: Well, it's being a daughter of missionary parents . . . (she smiles) . . . someone who is with other MKs and missionaries a lot, and somebody who usually goes to boarding school . . . (long pause) . . . and somebody who gets depressed when they shouldn't.

TH: Oh, gets depressed when she shouldn't? How so?

CL: Well, you're supposed to do things you may not believe in and aren't like you . . . you have to please people or they'll be unhappy with you. And you always have to smile even if you don't feel like it . . . this is depressing . . .

TH: Trying to please people can make you depressed even though you're smiling?

CL: Yes. I don't like to smile when I have to. (long silence and change of body posture to one of sullenness and disengagement)

TH: Did something just happen inside you . . . with your feelings?

CL: Well, maybe.

TH: I noticed you changed the way you were sitting and the way you stopped looking my direction when you talked about being depressed and smiling anyway.

CL: Yeah. (after a long pause) Maybe, maybe something did change . . . well, I guess it did (sitting more alertly now)

TH: Like . . . ?

CL: Like maybe feeling kinda mad.

TH: Mad . . . ?

CL: Maybe. (pause, and with more energy) Yeah, mad.

TH: H-m-m-m

CL: Well, I know there are a lot of reasons I'm depressed. It isn't just being a MK. I don't like myself, other people don't like me, I cause problems for my mom and dad, I take your time, I don't seem any better . . . (she breaks into tears)

TH: (After a pause and some recovery on her part, she looks up at me.) Linda, what you've just said seems very real . . . like you didn't have to be someone you're not.

CL: (seeming even more engaged now) I'm tired of it . . . tired, tired, tired! . . . How was I different?

TH: What you've just said seems to have come from deeper inside you . . . and seems to express some pain and discouragement and anger, all things you really feel. It didn't seem like it was just depression. You seemed to be connected with yourself in a deeper way.

CL: (after a pause) That's what I want, to be connected with myself. I think I used to be, but not anymore.

This interchange, repeated in other big and small ways throughout treatment, was an important therapeutic experience. She had found, for the first time in our relationship, that her deeper feelings of sadness, anger, and disappointment could be expressed without disrupting our relationship. This experience seemed to help her find a sense of connectedness with herself and it laid the foundation for actually making our relationship stronger.

Following this we were able to talk more fully about her wish to feel more securely centered in herself and her own genuine experience. This gave me the opportunity to suggest some issues I believed we needed to explore together in order to reach this goal. In particular, wanting to please and not disappoint her parents;

feeling she was failing as a Christian; and being fearful of separations, sometimes just those of leaving her room or house. Her experience of anger as we sat together was not lost on either of us, however, and we agreed to follow up on it closely. We had begun to set some mutually derived goals and discussed in more detail what therapy might include.

Thus, some further goals became:

- to understand why it was so important to not disappoint her parents and what that meant to her;
- to explore why she felt she was failing as a Christian;
- to examine her fears about separation; and
- to help her discover and express more of her feelings, especially her "not happy" feelings.

She also mentioned the strong desire to return to the school in which she had enrolled here, but we agreed that reaching other internal goals may be necessary first. She seemed to understand that making progress with these related goals were necessary for overcoming her depression. With these shared goals in front of us, I also began thinking of longer-term goals along these lines:

- Help her legitimize her negative feelings, and begin linking these unwanted feelings of anger and disappointment more accurately to the people and situations that evoked them
- Explore more fully her own personal relationship with God, and achieve some increased integration of her faith with her own identity more independently of her parents' faith and wishes (see Fowler, 1981)
- Assist her in making connections between her needs for approval and comfort (e.g., pleasing her parents and submerging her own experiences to the needs of others) and her difficulty in expressing her own feelings and asserting her own needs
- Assist her in seeing the extent to which she was a protector of her parents' feelings and concerns and to begin understanding why and how this had developed

Although I believed we could make significant progress with these goals over a period of months, I was less optimistic about what I could accomplish with her family. Many years of working with adolescents and their families had taught me how much more I could do for Linda if I could successfully engage her parents as partners in the treatment process and help them change too. Her depression, in part, was linked to them and it was important to garner as much support as they could provide for the significant changes Linda and I were embarking upon (Minuchin & Fishman, 1981). However, recalling from our initial sessions both the good intentions they sincerely held for their daughter, and the personal/emotional rigidity they demonstrated, my expectations for parental change were modest.

In order to work successfully with family issues, I knew that I would have to be careful not to *blame* the parents or to identify solely with Linda—I needed to be able to understand and have compassion for both sides. While I believed her parents would find our treatment goals generally acceptable, I also believed it would be challenging for them to help Linda change by changing themselves. Hearing Linda express negative affect, especially if it was anger at them, their work, her school, or the mission, would be painful for them. Could I help her parents expand their worldview in such a way that anger would not be seen as disrespectful or bad and sadness as threatening? Could they tolerate the guilt evoked by learning that Linda was protecting them by reporting only positive feelings and happenings, and never mentioning how painfully she missed her parents while away from them. I often thought about how I could bring up these sensitive issues in our family sessions and talk together safely about them. I did not want to make Ed or Esther feel blamed in any way, but also felt strongly that Linda would stop being ruled by these unspoken and taboo issues if they could just be *named* and made overt—no matter how briefly.

I decided that the family's unwillingness to allow negative feelings, which I considered central to Linda's severe depression, needed to be my first family goal. Linda's parents were feeling increasing stress from keeping the depression a secret from friends and family. Because their handling of this seemed clearly to be affecting Linda, exacerbating her shame and guilt, I felt it necessary to focus on this with them. *Perhaps helping them become somewhat more real and disclosing to friends would, in turn, help them to begin relating more authentically with Linda.* Knowing the tension this might create within the family, but also the profound benefit it could provide Linda, the words of Christ recorded in John 8:32 came to mind as a hope for each of them: "You shall know the truth, and the truth shall make you free."

Therapeutic Process

Over the 15 months of our work together, Linda's progress was at times steady, at times rocky. Early in our contacts I sought psychiatric consultation. Linda began taking the antidepressant Prozac and it diminished her symptoms—allowing her to work more productively in therapy. Medication does not cure a depression, of course, but it helped to decrease some of her symptoms, especially her sleep disturbance, loss of weight, agoraphobia, and inability to activate herself and get up and get going every day.

Almost immediately, Linda's core conflicts began to surface in treatment. She began to experience the intensity of her anger and loss-related grief, and to examine the blocks to their experience and expression that she had felt from her parents and had developed within herself. One core conflict was the need to express these feelings and the fear of rejection and guilt over hurting her parents if she did. Another was the need for nurture and comfort and the anxiety that it would be withheld if she were not happy and nearly perfect. The latter seemed to have been translated even into her relationship with God.

There was no question of the reality of Linda's pain as we delved into the specifics underlying the depression. I sometimes found myself being angry *for* her, especially after some grueling exchanges about her hopelessness, worthlessness, and the losses she hadn't grieved. I knew she had pain and anger she wasn't able to express except in her symptoms (i.e., being depressed). To guard against my own countertransference, I needed to ensure that I didn't feel or express her angry feelings for her, take these unwanted or threatening feelings away from her by trying to fix them, or even take too much responsibility for helping her to express them in our sessions.

After we had met for several months, her seventeenth birthday occurred. She was actually able to celebrate it with some recovered cheerfulness. Her older sister had come home for that weekend. Another missionary family with an adolescent Linda's age also visited and this was a boost for Linda. In the fall, after we had been meeting some six or seven months, she was able to begin school. With some placement exams she was able to start her senior year, although there was still a question of making up some additional requirements during the year.

As these months had passed, she had slowly begun expressing her feelings more clearly, becoming more aware and less frightened of the effect if she admitted them. In one session, as she began getting more in touch with her anger about no one being there as she felt the pain of loss during a particularly difficult transition, an important exchange took place:

CL: I guess I was kind of mad, maybe lonely, too, in not being able to tell anyone. I didn't really know I was mad.

TH: Do you remember more specifically what you felt?

CL: Well, mainly lonesome. I wished I could talk to my dad.

TH: What would have happened if you could?

CL: He would comfort me . . . just by being together. I probably wouldn't tell him I was lonesome . . .
    (At this point she seemed to be deep in thought. When she looked up again her mood had changed from one of quiet but painful reflection to something less acute, almost dull.) I was just thinking of some good times and telling my dad about them. He seemed to like to hear those things, sometimes more than once. (pause) I remember doing a project in science that I really liked. It was about Machu Picchu in Peru, you know, that mysterious city in the Andes where the population seemed to disappear without a reason. Nobody seems to know what happened. Suzie—she was my project partner—and I really worked hard on this. We wrote to the States for some pictures . . . (pause, catches herself) What were we just talking about?

TH: You were telling me about your loneliness and anger. You even seemed to be feeling some of it as we talked.

CL: Did I? H-m-m-m

TH: Something just happened here, I think, that may be important to understand. Could you go back to telling me about your loneliness and anger for a minute?

CL: I don't think so . . . I don't feel it right now.

TH: Do you remember feeling anything else when you started telling me more about it?

CL: No, not especially . . . well, maybe that I shouldn't be telling you about it.

TH: Not telling me . . .

CL: You wouldn't want to hear it . . . even though I knew *you* would, because you've been trying to get me to talk more about it. It's kinda hard to talk about.

TH: With me?

CL: Well, with anyone.

TH: Anyone?

CL: Well, with Dad, I guess. He wouldn't want to hear about those things.

TH: What would he want to hear about?

CL: Good things.

TH: Like you started to tell me after you thought about him, and didn't remember what you had been talking about before?

CL: Yeah . . . Yes . . . Maybe, maybe . . . I think so.

Further discussion helped her discover just how patterned this type of response had become. She had reenacted with me the same pattern she had established with her father. Wishing to talk about something negative, but sensing his desire not to hear that, switching to something positive and submerging the other feelings. Following this, she seemed gradually more free to allow the negative feelings to be put into words. This was a breakthrough: her depression visibly lifted during this period.

A significant amount of time was spent reviewing her past losses with her family and others, and the unresolved hurt and grief she had been carrying. Many pertained to simple oversights she had experienced, more acutely than others perhaps because of her sensitivity to rejection and insecurity about being accepted. Some incidents she remembered were abusive in quality, though she had not to that point construed them as such. Many of her recollections related to the loss of her parents she felt but didn't express as she and her family had made various transitions.

On one occasion she had been confined to her room for several days (except for meals and classes) for not having obtained an excuse for missing chapel. She missed it because she had stopped to help one of the African workers on campus who had fallen and injured herself, but this was somehow overlooked or misunderstood. She had stopped to assist, feeling compassion for the woman and believing as she discussed it later, that it was an expression of her Christian faith.

While she was grounded, a former schoolmate who was a close friend came back for a brief visit, and Linda was not allowed to see her. Though she had felt that this was grossly unfair, she had never reported it to her parents. As we discussed this, her woundedness from the event was poured out in tears, and in time she was able also to acknowledge the outrage she had suppressed for so long. Expressing the depth of feeling over this event seemed to widen the channels for a myriad of other events that she began to recall and discuss.

On several occasions transactions took place between us that resulted in a healing or reparative experience for her. On one such occasion, I came to our session with my left arm in a sling due to a slight injury, experiencing some mild pain. She seemed to take more than usual interest in just how badly I was injured. As I sought to redirect her toward the issues we had been working on, she seemed less involved than in previous sessions. After a couple of unsuccessful attempts to get into much depth with her, this exchange ensued:

CL: Are you sure you're all right?

TH: Yes, it's happened before and should be fine in a few days . . . but my being hurt seems to draw your attention, with the sling and all.

CL: I'm not used to seeing you that way. It's different.

TH: Can you tell me how this makes things seem different?

CL: Well, I want you to be healthy. (laughs) Well, I guess, really, it makes it harder . . . to talk . . . to talk to you.

TH: Talk to me . . . about . . . ?

CL: Oh, I don't know. (pause) Do you want me to get you a drink of water or something?

TH: Thanks, but no. I'm doing fine. I guess I'm just interested in how it's harder for you to talk to me today.

CL: Oh, I don't know. I guess it's just hard to talk about myself when I know you're hurt or in pain.

TH: That's interesting . . . how so?

CL: It just seems . . . just seems, I guess . . . that I ought to be taking care of you somehow. (pause, looks up) Well, you know, I know you're taken care of and everything or you wouldn't be here . . . (trails off)

TH: Yes, my shoulder is being taken care of, but it seems that my injury does have a certain effect on you. Like it draws on you somehow to want to take care of me.

CL: Well, I want to make sure you're OK . . . yeah.

TH: Does that seem to be a familiar feeling for you?

CL: Well, sometimes you make me think of my folks . . . I don't mean you're old or anything . . . and I don't feel good when they're hurt. I want to take care of them.

TH: How do you usually do that?

CL: Oh, I just try to figure out what will help and do it . . . like cleaning the house if I'm in the village, or running errands . . . stuff like that.

TH: So you asked if I'd like to have a glass of water earlier. Things like that?

CL: Yeah, things like that.

TH: But it seemed like you did another thing, too.

CL: What was that?

TH: You didn't want to talk to me about your concerns as you had in the last sessions . . . perhaps didn't want to say anything about the hurts we had been talking about recently.

CL: Huh . . . no, I didn't . . . feel like it today.

TH: I wonder if that's also a familiar thing for you . . .

CL: (pause, seems deep in thought) Yes, yes . . . I didn't want to tell my folks anything that might hurt them. It was just hard to do. I knew they loved me and were concerned for me and that they worked hard. I didn't want . . . I didn't want them to be hurt because I was hurt . . . or to worry . . .

This exchange eventually led in time into a productive discussion of her protectiveness toward her parents. She began to realize that she had negated her own needs out of a sense of not wanting to upset or distress them. She learned that she had subtly taken cues from her father's gentle avoidance of painful or unpleasant things and avoided bringing them up. She also learned that she had been reluctant to mention painful things to her mother because she feared her overreaction to them. Her response to each had been to submerge her own feelings and needs, and she began to see how this had contributed to her depression. As we continued to work on her grieving process, she also realized more fully how her accumulated griefs, which had been avoided or denied in the service of being "happy," had contributed significantly to her depression as well.

Over time, Linda began to wonder about how her coping style related to her faith. She was, in particular, focusing on anger. She became aware that the model provided by her father—never to express it—and that of her mother—to make an exaggerated response to it—had given her little permission to fully experience and express her own. She wondered if it was even right to do so. Given her knowledge of the Bible, I asked her to read the latter part of the fourth chapter of Ephesians and to look especially at the passage in verse 26 about being angry and not sinning ("Be angry and sin not . . ." NASB version). I also asked her to look at the passage in the Gospel of John where Christ throws moneychangers out of the temple. The discussions that followed gave her permission to begin talking about her anger and other negative feelings and soon to begin experiencing and sharing them more fully in a way that she found releasing.

Earlier, I had referred Linda to the Book of Acts (where the Apostle Paul said good-bye to leaders in the church at Ephesus). This passage had been helpful because it provided permission within the context of her Christian beliefs to express herself in the pain of loss and partings. These glimpses into Biblical examples and principles regarding anger also were helpful. Concurrent with these excursions she began keeping a diary, something she had done earlier but given up when the depression had become more profound. Her diary entries became, over a period of time, less questioning and reflective of unresolved pain, and more integrative of her self-understanding, identity, and Christian faith.

In addition to loss and anger, we also incorporated Biblical readings and reflections involving God's acceptance and love for her. We discussed at length the meaning of the commandment to honor her mother and father—how she could follow that and still express her own needs and develop a clearer sense of identity. A significant outcome of this was her eventual decision to risk expressing her anger and other negative feelings even though she feared being misunderstood and not liked for doing so. She had developed the conviction that, in time, doing so would make her healthier and that, perhaps later, her parents would see that and she would honor them by being more capable of a better and fuller relationship with them. An insightful concept, I thought, for someone 17 years old.

An important focus was also on the concepts of grace and forgiveness. Linda could provide a good definition of grace from her Christian education—"the unmerited favor of God." However, her strivings to be always pleasant and happy by avoiding anger and other negative feelings, and to live up to the perfection she believed her Christian faith required, seemed to leave little room for its actual operation.

As Linda became more aware of and began to own negative feelings, she was at first surprised that I still accepted her in spite of them. She gradually began to experience that God might also accept them. As she began to realize that she had little control over whether or not I chose to accept her and her feelings, she also began to acknowledge that she could actually have little control over what God chose to accept. As she began to examine this in light of other Christian beliefs about God, she began to experience less need for controlling things by denying her feelings and being pleasant and perfect. Perhaps God would meet her needs if she would let go of some of her perfectionistic strivings and began looking at what was already being provided for her.

Linda had always been quick to forgive, also as a way of being pleasant and avoiding conflict. As we worked together she began to realize she was paying a high price for this in emotional stress and depression. To do this so automatically meant a further denial of the hurts or other wrongs perpetrated against her. Forgiveness, to be complete, requires that the wronged person weigh fully the effect of the wrong that has been perpetrated. Only then, when denial and avoidance are no longer in play, can the individual truly forgive. In other words, the wronged person has to fully acknowledge the other person's insensitivity. Otherwise, that person's insensitivity is itself not being forgiven. Forgiveness, like acceptance, takes on true meaning when all aspects of the other (good and flawed) are clearly seen and acknowledged. When the "bad" parts are minimized or glossed over, the forgiveness is incomplete or inauthentic. Working through this issue with Linda was enlightening for her. She came to see that the forgiveness and acceptance she received from God encompassed *all* aspects of her being—including positive and negative feelings, kind and unkind deeds. We worked through several examples where she had been hurt or overlooked and examined the consequences of that hurt of wrongdoing in detail. This cast a different light on what she was doing in forgiving others and it allowed her to look at how she experienced the forgiveness of Christ as a basic part of her faith. In time, she became more discerning as she chose to forgive others, and more accepting of the flawed or imperfect parts of herself.

As she continued to make progress, several significant events took place. During Thanksgiving of her senior year, she was able to attend a retreat for MKs in their freshman year of college or in the last two years of high school. She seemed a different person when she returned, exclaiming that there were so many other people there "just like me!" This event greatly enhanced her identity as a MK and TCK, and she began valuing her past experiences in a new way. The speaker had talked about MKs feeling like "ugly ducklings" as they returned to North America and were so frequently misunderstood by peers here. He developed this idea throughout the weekend, using that story to help MKs see that they were really swans, just placed temporarily with ducks. He also talked about the redemptive process which takes place from a Christian view as MKs realize their fuller identities. The richness of their cross-cultural upbringing and even their hurts and loneliness can be redeemed as characteristics that eventually bring them happiness and allow them to develop productive careers. The swan analogy continued to be significant throughout her therapy.

These events and others helped Linda begin thinking more about the grace of God. She felt at one level that she had not deserved nor could even have anticipated these experiences, but they had come to her at the right time. She ultimately came to understand these as acts of grace that she could allow herself to accept as further evidence that God did indeed love her and she had little control over that except in her response. This view, developed over a period of some weeks, allowed her to make a significant change in the way she viewed herself (less guilty, fewer feelings of worthlessness) and helped free her to interact with others much less fearfully. She seemed less anxious and speculated that she probably didn't need to work so hard at being perfect to maintain her faith. She had made significant progress, and soon made mention of our termination.

It came when she told me she had been accepted at the college her parents had attended. Understandably, she mentioned fears about her ability to make this transition, since there had been so many before that had been so problematic and painful. However, this stimulated further discussions about the many other transitions she had made earlier, but was now understanding and resolving. Thus, while the thoughts of college and termination brought temporary fears, they also helped to put in focus the strength of our work, a deeper realization of the gains she had made, and a newly found ability to look with hope toward the future. I affirmed these gains and began helping her integrate the changes she had made with her future plans.

Impediments to Treatment

In retrospect, the largest impediment to treatment was Linda's patterns of turning her anger inward in order to protect her parents (and others) from her negative feelings. These patterns had developed from real experiences in her family and were aggravated through misunderstood expectations of her Christian and missionary subculture. Occasionally, we all met together as a family to review progress or look at a certain issue. In particular, I wanted to work with her father's difficulty in hearing Linda's pain and "not happy" feelings. This invalidation reflected Ed's attempt to compensate for what he felt were his wife Esther's exaggeration of negative feelings and overanxious responses. While this clearly related to his own history, his patterned response to Esther's overreactions had left him almost devoid of the ability to hear feelings of hurt, anger, or despair or to express them himself. In family sessions, I wanted for him to experience my acceptance of the pain or fear that he covered with these patterned responses, in the hope that, in turn, he might be able to offer more of the same to Linda. Some progress was made with this but, sadly, the success was limited with both parents.

As therapy with Linda progressed and she began finding and expressing her anger in my presence, she found her tentative attempts to be more authentic with her parents initially thwarted. In discussing this in one session, I found myself feeling somewhat angry and chose to express it.

CL: I wish it were different . . . I tried to talk to Dad about it but it didn't work.

TH: How didn't it work?

CL: Well, he just didn't seem to want to hear about it. He told me that all these things will work together for good and to try to concentrate on something hopeful. I couldn't concentrate on something hopeful; I just wanted him to understand that I didn't like what had happened (referring to an event of unfairness at school the preceding year).

TH: That you were mad about it?

CL: Yeah, that I thought it was unfair . . . it hurt and I know it made me mad, too.

TH: I'm so sorry that your dad won't listen to you. And that your mother gets overconcerned once you express something that's not gone well for you.

CL: Ohh. (nods "yes")

TH: You want to tell them about it and they either can't listen or get all worked up about it. I'm sorry, and I guess it makes me kind of mad too, it's not what you need.

CL: (after a long pause and a noticeable drawing back) It's OK.

TH: I don't think it is, Linda.

CL: (looks down . . . several moments of silence)

At this point I began worrying that I may have gone too far in expressing my own feelings and had frightened her with the expression of anger itself, especially anger directed at her parents. After a long silence and some thoughts of possible incompetence on my part:

TH: Linda, I notice you've pulled your feet in your chair and curled up, could you tell me what's happened for you?

CL: I'm kinda scared.

TH: Scared?

CL: I don't like it when anybody gets mad.

TH: When I'm mad?

CL: (reluctantly) Yes.

TH: It's hard for you to be angry and hard to be around someone who's angry. I think that's really understandable in light of the experiences you've shared with me. Can you say more about what it's like to be with me right now, knowing that I've just expressed being mad.

CL: Well, it's easier now.

TH: How?

CL: Well, it just is . . . We're talking about it.

This paved the way for some understanding that she could continue becoming more accepting of her own anger and that that could lead to less fear of it in others. As she implied, she was able to see more fully that experiencing it and talking about it in our relationship did not damage the relationship, as she had previously feared, but actually enhanced it. It also led to a discussion about an individual being angry toward someone but that didn't mean rejection of the person. At the conclusion of the following session, having processed this further, we agreed to have her parents in for a session or two to talk about this.

The first of the two sessions we had with them was difficult in that the pattern she had described was acted out within the session. As Linda attempted to tell about the school incident (an approach we had agreed on) her father responded with diverting platitudes, and her mother did indeed became anxious. When we ended that session I felt we had moved too soon on this as Ed, in particular, had seemed especially uncomfortable.

In the next session, however, he had evidently been giving this much thought and even had met with his pastor about it. He began by acknowledging what I had tried to point out, and went into some detail about his own history and how he disliked anger and unpleasantness. He at first defended his position, but later seemed to soften. That all this had been discussed in Linda's presence—that it could be acknowledged and talked about openly and respectfully—was highly significant for her. Being able to make these problems overt and name them, even though some of them didn't really change very much behaviorally, had an immediate and tangible impact on her depression (e.g., at our next individual session, Linda announced that she didn't need to be on Prozac any longer).

In time, Linda was able to see how she had adapted to her father's avoidance of real problems and real feelings, and to her mother's exaggeration or overreaction to these, by not expressing what she needed to express. This pattern had permeated much of her life at home and boarding school—undoing her ability to know and understand her own thoughts, feelings, and reactions. As a result, the basic building blocks for developing her sense of self or identity had been profoundly undermined. Accurate empathy and consistent affirmation in treatment gradually allowed Linda to center in her own experience and trust in the validity of her own perceptions for the first time. Linda's depression came to an end as she was able to find and act on her own authentic voice.

Other treatment impediments, such as the pressure perceived by Linda's parents and family to keep up a good face and to make a show of strength and progress for the Christian community, were also gradually addressed. Of particular importance, we spoke together in our family sessions about Biblical principles regarding honesty and integrity of emotional expression. These became important groundings for Linda and both of her parents. Despite significant limitations on how much they could change, I respected and commended her parents for their courage and the risks they took in engaging with me on these issues that seemed so foreign and dangerous to them.

TERMINATION AND SUMMARY THOUGHTS

Linda's spirits remained stable as the shift toward the termination phase began. Much of her former cheerfulness returned, but now it was more balanced rather than an automatic response pattern. Now that she had a better understanding of how and why she had become depressed, she was experiencing a new appreciation for feelings, even negative ones, and was incorporating new understandings of herself into the ongoing development of her identity.

The decision to terminate was made, in part, by her decision to attend college approximately 200 miles away. Yet, I believe we would have reached termination at approximately the same time without this external factor. The fact that she was back on track with her educational plans was one indication of the success of our work together. We spent several sessions reviewing progress and consolidating the gains she had made. Some mild depression returned which clarified that some areas still needed work, and together we tried to anticipate the situations that were likely to be challenging in the future. We also discussed what college might be like, how it compared with boarding school, and how she could form new friendships that allowed her to express things she previously had difficulty doing. The friendships she had formed during her last year of high school bore witness to her capacity to do this. Two of her friends would be attending the same college; one would be her roommate.

As I look back on our relationship, I am aware of the impact that Linda had on me as we worked together—which I still carry. The barely audible voice I first encountered had changed into one of greater confidence. The downcast eyes began to look up and, later, ahead. She was clearly grasping the future and seemed much more capable of doing things to make it positive. Her thin frame seemed to show more vitality— she had regained the 10 pounds or so she had lost. There was spontaneity that, her parents told me, seemed to be beyond the cheerfulness that they had so valued earlier on. Her clear Christian commitment seemed more mature or internal now—based on her own choices, values, and personal dialogue with God. She was no longer depressed.

Nearly all the mutual goals we had set together were met to one degree or another. Others showed progress but were not met to the extent I might have hoped. Again, as I look back, I do so in admiration of Linda's hard work, of her parents' openness and support, and with gratitude to God for the goals that were accomplished. Like a parent, perhaps, I must admit to wishing that a bit more had been done and, also, that I might have been there to see it all accomplished. But therapy is not the same as parenting, even though it bears some of the same qualities. Like a good parent, the therapist supports the child's developing self and celebrates her increasing self-sufficiency. It was time for Linda to go.

As we terminated, I shared with Linda how much I valued her and her successes in treatment. We talked of many of our experiences together, laughed at some of the times we had miscommunicated, and affirmed that the relationship had been a good one. I was tempted to offer a follow-up session now and then as she made her adjustment to college and came back for an occasional visit. But I thought better of it. She did not raise it as a desire then, nor has she ever contacted me again for another session. I take this as a silent statement that she was really ready to say good-bye and that, this time, the transition was a healthy one for her. As a statement of my own faith, I trust that she is using the things she learned in therapy and is living fully and productively.

Questions for Thought and Discussion

1. Think about any formative spiritual or religious experiences you may have had. Have these affected your development? How have your beliefs changed or remained the same over the years?

2. Feeling responsible for the well-being or happiness of caregivers (e.g., an alcoholic father, a lonely mother) is often the source of anxiety and depression for children. Has this been an issue in your life? If so, how has this made you more empathic to others and/or left you prone to guilt and depression?

Suggestions for Further Reading

Aponte, H. J. & Winter, J. E. (1987). The person and practice of the therapist: Treatment and training. In M. Baldwin & V. Satir (Eds.), *The use of self in therapy.* New York: Haworth Press. This chapter helps counselors look into their own lives and dynamics as well as that of the client, and search out ways of better understanding how the relationship may bring about change.

Faiver C., Ingersoll R., O'Brien E., & McNally, C. (2001). *Explorations in counseling and spirituality.* Pacific Grove: Brooks/Cole. This concise book provides interventions and useful information to help counselors incorporate spirituality into their work with clients, and helps counselors explore their own spirituality.

O'Donnell, K. & O'Donnell, M. (1988). *Helping missionaries grow: Readings in mental health and missions.* Pasadena, CA: William Carey Library. This pithy volume clarifies the relationships, conflicts, and stresses experienced by Christian missionaries working cross culturally.

SELF-ASSESSMENT OF COUNSELOR'S INTERPERSONAL PROCESS SKILLS

In each of the case studies, you will see that the counselors are using the same interpersonal process skills to help their clients. The following questionnaire delineates these process-oriented interventions. Use this self-assessment measure to evaluate your current level of skill in working with each of these dimensions. If you have not seen a client yet, try to imagine how easy or difficult it would be for you to respond in these ways.

1. Counselor makes process comments or finds other ways to discuss misunderstandings and talk openly about potential problems that may be occurring between the client and the counselor.

1	2	3	4	5	6	7
not at all characteristic			characteristic			extremely characteristic

2. Counselor actively tries to understand the client's sociocultural context and how race, religion, and gender have shaped her* subjective worldview.

1	2	3	4	5	6	7
not at all characteristic			characteristic			extremely characteristic

3. Counselor accurately identifies and reflects the central meaning or emotional message in what the client has just relayed.

1	2	3	4	5	6	7
not at all characteristic			characteristic			extremely characteristic

*The female pronoun is used throughout to refer to the client.

4. Counselor helps the client relay her narrative and express her thoughts and feelings.

1	2	3	4	5	6	7
not at all characteristic			characteristic			extremely characteristic

5. Counselor helps the client explore and discuss her personal reactions toward the counselor and what is happening between them in the counseling relationship.

1	2	3	4	5	6	7
not at all characteristic			characteristic			extremely characteristic

6. Counselor has difficulty attending to how the client may be interacting with the counselor in the same problematic ways that she describes doing with others.

1	2	3	4	5	6	7
not at all characteristic			characteristic			extremely characteristic

7. Counselor has difficulty following the client's lead and stays close to the problems and issues that the client reports as relevant or significant in her life right now.

1	2	3	4	5	6	7
not at all characteristic			characteristic			extremely characteristic

8. Counselor explores developmental events as they arise in the conversation naturally, rather than leading the client back to historical connections.

1	2	3	4	5	6	7
not at all characteristic			characteristic			extremely characteristic

9. Counselor helps the client focus inward on her own thoughts, feelings, and reactions.

1	2	3	4	5	6	7
not at all characteristic			characteristic			extremely characteristic

10. Counselor has difficulty inviting the client to express whatever feelings she may be experiencing as they occur in the session.

1	2	3	4	5	6	7
not at all characteristic			characteristic			extremely characteristic

11. Counselor is able to extend herself and actively reach out when necessary to maintain the client's engagement in a collaborative relationship.

1	2	3	4	5	6	7
not at all characteristic			characteristic			extremely characteristic

12. Counselor is nonjudgmental and responds to the client in an accepting and understanding manner.

1	2	3	4	5	6	7
not at all characteristic			characteristic			extremely characteristic

13. Counselor looks for relational patterns that might provide an organizing theme in the client's interpersonal problems.

1	2	3	4	5	6	7
not at all characteristic			characteristic			extremely characteristic

14. Counselor attempts to link recurrent patterns of behavior between the client and others to the current interaction between the client and counselor.

1	2	3	4	5	6	7
not at all characteristic			characteristic			extremely characteristic

15. When the client appears to become defensive or resistant, counselor helps the client explore what the danger or threat is that may have just been evoked.

1	2	3	4	5	6	7
not at all characteristic			characteristic			extremely characteristic

16. Counselor is reluctant to focus the client away from complaining about or describing the problematic behavior of others and toward the client's own personal reactions.

1	2	3	4	5	6	7
not at all characteristic			characteristic			extremely characteristic

17. Counselor responds to the client's global descriptions or generalized statements about themselves and others by seeking further specificity or concrete illustrations.

1	2	3	4	5	6	7
not at all characteristic			characteristic			extremely characteristic

18. Counselor is empathic and tries to understand the personal or unique meanings of the client's experience from the client's subjective point of view.

1	2	3	4	5	6	7
not at all characteristic			characteristic			extremely characteristic

19. Counselor cannot be a "participant/observer" who is simultaneously empathic and objective.

1	2	3	4	5	6	7
not at all characteristic			characteristic			extremely characteristic

20. Counselor is emotionally available and conveys "presence" as the client relays her narratives.

1	2	3	4	5	6	7
not at all characteristic			characteristic			extremely characteristic

21. Counselor creates *immediacy* by sharing her own reactions to what the client has just said or done.

1	2	3	4	5	6	7
not at all characteristic			characteristic			extremely characteristic

22. Counselor encourages the client to be an active, equal partner in understanding the problems and initiating the changes.

1	2	3	4	5	6	7
not at all characteristic			characteristic			extremely characteristic

23. Counselor helps the client discern discrepancies between her typical public presentation (persona) and her own authentic voice and genuine experience.

1	2	3	4	5	6	7
not at all characteristic			characteristic			extremely characteristic

24. Counselor considers unwanted ways that significant others have responded to the client in the past and uses this awareness to provide a new or reparative response to the client.

1	2	3	4	5	6	7
not at all characteristic			characteristic			extremely characteristic

25. Counselor has difficulty seeing how the client's relational patterns could interact with the counselor's own personal issues to impede treatment.

1	2	3	4	5	6	7
not at all characteristic			characteristic			extremely characteristic

26. Counselor helps the client appreciate how her defensive style was originally necessary and adaptive, but is no longer needed in many current relationships.

1	2	3	4	5	6	7
not at all characteristic			characteristic			extremely characteristic

27. Counselor demonstrates the cognitive flexibility and wide emotional range necessary to respond to the client's varying needs.

1	2	3	4	5	6	7
not at all characteristic			characteristic			extremely characteristic

28. Counselor evaluates the effectiveness of her interventions by evaluating the client's positive or negative reactions to them.

1	2	3	4	5	6	7
not at all characteristic			characteristic			extremely characteristic

29. Counselor feels she can be authentic with the client without feeling distanced or ingenuine by the constraints of her role as counselor.

1	2	3	4	5	6	7
not at all characteristic			characteristic			extremely characteristic

30. Counselor is able to balance the two-sided challenge of being forthright and direct with the client while remaining empathic and respectful.

1	2	3	4	5	6	7
not at all characteristic			characteristic			extremely characteristic

SENSITIVITY TO COUNTERTRANSFERENCE PROPENSITIES

This exercise is designed to help you anticipate your own personal reactions to evocative material or feelings that a client might present. Use each of the following statements to assess your potential countertransference propensities. If you have not seen a client yet, try to imagine how you are likely to respond.

1. If a client becomes critical or angry toward me, it is often difficult for me to remain open and nondefensive.

1	2	3	4	5	6	7
not at all characteristic			characteristic			extremely characteristic

2. When my clients leave our session in pain, I often feel as though I have not done enough to help them.

1	2	3	4	5	6	7
not at all characteristic			characteristic			extremely characteristic

3. In overt or covert ways, I tend to move clients away from experiencing or expressing their painful feelings.

1	2	3	4	5	6	7
not at all characteristic			characteristic			extremely characteristic

4. I try to encourage my clients to express negative feelings (e.g., anger, disapproval) they may be having toward me.

| 1 | 2 | 3 | 4 | 5 | 6 | 7 |

not at all characteristic   characteristic   extremely characteristic

5. I am often reluctant to speak forthrightly and address what is going on between the client and me, even though the client is likely to benefit from such directness.

| 1 | 2 | 3 | 4 | 5 | 6 | 7 |

not at all characteristic   characteristic   extremely characteristic

6. I am comfortable setting appropriate limits and boundaries with clients when necessary.

| 1 | 2 | 3 | 4 | 5 | 6 | 7 |

not at all characteristic   characteristic   extremely characteristic

7. I tend to avoid making emotional contact with clients or caring about them because it might lead to a loss of appropriate boundaries or foster dependency.

| 1 | 2 | 3 | 4 | 5 | 6 | 7 |

not at all characteristic   characteristic   extremely characteristic

8. I tend to find myself in subtle control battles with my clients.

| 1 | 2 | 3 | 4 | 5 | 6 | 7 |

not at all characteristic   characteristic   extremely characteristic

9. I am uncomfortable with ambiguity or uncertainty and tend to direct what is going to happen next in my counseling interactions.

| 1 | 2 | 3 | 4 | 5 | 6 | 7 |

not at all characteristic   characteristic   extremely characteristic

10. It is often hard for me to move my clients toward an internal focus where they can explore their own contributions to their problem, even though I know it would be therapeutic.

| 1 | 2 | 3 | 4 | 5 | 6 | 7 |

not at all characteristic   characteristic   extremely characteristic

11. I tend to either talk too much or too little when I feel overly affected by my client's issues.

| 1 | 2 | 3 | 4 | 5 | 6 | 7 |

not at all characteristic   characteristic   extremely characteristic

12. I readily identify with my clients and have difficulty letting go of their problems while outside of the counseling setting.

| 1 | 2 | 3 | 4 | 5 | 6 | 7 |

not at all characteristic   characteristic   extremely characteristic

13. I am comfortable making self-involving statements or process comments about what is occurring between the client and me when I think it would be helpful.

1	2	3	4	5	6	7
not at all characteristic			characteristic			extremely characteristic

14. I have difficulty accepting clients' genuine expressions of warmth or appreciation toward me.

1	2	3	4	5	6	7
not at all characteristic			characteristic			extremely characteristic

15. I often carry out the familial role of caretaker, rescuer, or peacemaker in my professional work as a counselor.

1	2	3	4	5	6	7
not at all characteristic			characteristic			extremely characteristic

16. I tend to minimize interpersonal conflicts that arise between my clients and me.

1	2	3	4	5	6	7
not at all characteristic			characteristic			extremely characteristic

17. It is often hard for me to acknowledge "mistakes" I have made with clients or times when I have misunderstood them.

1	2	3	4	5	6	7
not at all characteristic			characteristic			extremely characteristic

18. I tend to be patient rather than frustrated or irritated with clients who appear to be needy, dependent, or helpless.

1	2	3	4	5	6	7
not at all characteristic			characteristic			extremely characteristic

19. I tend to be quiet during sessions or "hold back" in order to avoid making mistakes.

1	2	3	4	5	6	7
not at all characteristic			characteristic			extremely characteristic

20. I usually remain accepting and engaged with clients who make choices that disagree with my values.

1	2	3	4	5	6	7
not at all characteristic			characteristic			extremely characteristic

21. I tend to become impatient or irritated when clients are slow at making change.

1	2	3	4	5	6	7
not at all characteristic			characteristic			extremely characteristic

22. I am often concerned that my clients will perceive me as unskilled or inadequate.

    1   2   3   4   5   6   7

not at all characteristic   characteristic   extremely characteristic

23. Rather than tolerating ambiguity and seeing what emerges from the client, I often find myself filling silences and easing awkward moments out of my own discomfort.

    1   2   3   4   5   6   7

not at all characteristic   characteristic   extremely characteristic

24. I tend to have trouble distilling my clients' core affective messages or reflecting the deeper meaning in their narratives.

    1   2   3   4   5   6   7

not at all characteristic   characteristic   extremely characteristic

25. It tends to be hard for me to express my disagreements with clients.

    1   2   3   4   5   6   7

not at all characteristic   characteristic   extremely characteristic

26. It is usually too uncomfortable for me to give clients unwanted but honest interpersonal feedback.

    1   2   3   4   5   6   7

not at all characteristic   characteristic   extremely characteristic

27. When clients criticize or disapprove of me, I tend to justify or defend myself rather than fully listen to and explore their concerns.

    1   2   3   4   5   6   7

not at all characteristic   characteristic   extremely characteristic

28. I tend to overqualify my comments or dilute the emotional impact of my interventions to avoid having too much influence or impact on my clients' lives.

    1   2   3   4   5   6   7

not at all characteristic   characteristic   extremely characteristic

29. Even though clients initially may feel sad or mad, I bring up the issue of our impending termination.

    1   2   3   4   5   6   7

not at all characteristic   characteristic   extremely characteristic

30. I often think about ways in which my own personal issues could impact the counseling relationship.

    1   2   3   4   5   6   7

not at all characteristic   characteristic   extremely characteristic

31. Rate the degree to which you believe you are aware of your countertransference propensities.

1	2	3	4	5	6	7

not at all characteristic   characteristic   extremely characteristic

32. I am generally aware of the types of clients that are difficult for me, and with the kinds of problems with which I am most likely to act out my countertransference propensities.

1	2	3	4	5	6	7

not at all characteristic   characteristic   extremely characteristic

After rating yourself on each of these, return to those items for which you have rated yourself as highly characteristic. Discuss with a partner or reflect alone on the questions you found relevant and consider how each of these selected issues could limit your ability to respond effectively to your clients.

REFERENCES

Acosta, F. (1984). Psychotherapy with Mexican-Americans: Clinical & empirical gains. In J. Martinez & R. Mendoza (Eds.), *Chicano psychology* (2nd ed.), (pp. 163–188). New York: Academic Press.

Adler, G. & Buie, D. H. (1979). The psychotherapeutic approach to aloneness in borderline patients. In J. LeBoit & A. Capponi (Eds.), *Advances in psychotherapy of the borderline patient* (pp. 433–448). New York: Jason Aronson.

Ageton, S. (1983). *Sexual assault among adolescents: A national study.* Rockville, MD: National Institute of Mental Health.

Albano, A. M., Chorpita, B. F., & Barlow, D. H. (1996). Childhood anxiety disorders. In E. J. Mash & R. A. Barkley (Eds.), *Child psychopathology* (pp. 196–241). New York: Guilford Press.

Alexander, F., & French, T. (1980). *Psychoanalytic therapy: Principles and application.* Lincoln, Nebraska University of Nebraska Press.

Allen, L., & Majidi-Ahi, S. (1989). African-American children. In J. Taylor Gibbs & L. Nahme Huang (Eds.), *Children of color: Psychological interventions with minority youth* (pp. 148–178). New York: Mc Graw Hill.

Amato, P. R., & Keith, B. (1991b). Parental divorce and the well being of children: A meta analysis. *Psychological Bulletin, 110,* 26–46.

American Psychiatric Association. (1980). *Diagnostic and statistical manual of mental disorders* (3rd ed.). Washington, DC: Author.

American Psychiatric Association. (1987). *Diagnostic and statistical manual of mental disorders* (3rd ed. rev.). Washington, DC: Author.

American Psychiatric Association. (1994). *Diagnostic and statistical manual of mental disorders* (4th ed). Washington, DC: Author.

American Psychiatric Association. (2000). *Diagnostic and statistical manual of mental disorders* (4th ed-TR). Washington, DC: Author.

Anastopoulos, A., Shelton, T., DuPaul, G., & Guevremont, D. (1993). Parent training for attention-deficit hyperactivity disorder: Its impact on parent functioning. *Journal of Abnormal Child Psychology, 21,* 581–596.

Anastopoulos, A. D., & Barkley, R. A. (1989). Biological factors in attention deficit-hyperactivity disorder. *Behavior Therapist, 11,* 47–53.

Anderson, K. E., Lytton, H., & Romney, D. M. (1986). Mothers' interaction with normal and conduct-disordered boys: Who affects whom? *Developmental Psychology, 22,* 604–609.

Andrulonis, P. A. (1991). Disruptive behavior disorders in boys and the borderline personality disorder in men. *Ann. Clin. Psychiat.,* 3(1), 23–26.

Araji, S., & Finkelhor, D. (1986). Abusers: A review of the research. In D. Finkelhor and Associates, *A sourcebook of child sexual abuse* (pp. 89–118). Beverly Hills: Sage Publications.

Arnold, L. E. (1996). Sex differences in ADHD: Conference Summary. *Journal of Abnormal Child Psychology, 24,* 555–567.

Arroya, W., & Cervantes, R. C. (1997). The Mexican-American child. In J. Noshpitz (Ed.), *Handbook of child & adolescent psychiatry* (Vol. 4, pp. 532–543). New York: Wiley.

Atkinson, D. R., Thompson, C. E., & Grant, S. K. (1993). A three dimensional model for counseling racial/ethnic minorities. *The Counseling Psychologist, 21,* 257–277.

Atlas, J. (1995). Association between history of abuse and borderline personality disorder for hospitalized adolescent girls. *Psychological Reports, 77,* 1346.

Attie, I., & Brooks-Gunn, J. (1995). The development of eating regulation across the life span. In D. Cicchetti & D. J. Cohen (Eds.), *Developmental psychopathology, Vol. 2.: Risk, disorder, & adaptation* (pp. 332–368). New York: Wiley.

Austin, C. N. (l983). *Cross-cultural re-entry: An annotated bibliography.* Abilene, TX: Abilene Christian University Press.

Axelson, J. (1999). *Counseling and development in a multicultural society* (3rd ed.). Pacific Grove: Brooks Cole.

Bandura, A. (1997). *Self-efficacy.* New York: Freeman.

Baren, M. (1994). ADHD: Do we finally have it right? *Contemporary Pediatrics, 11,* 96–124.

Barkham, M., & Shapiro, D. (1986). Counselor verbal response modes and experienced empathy. *Journal of Counseling Psychology,* 33(1), 3–10.

Barkley, R. (1998). *Attention deficit hyperactivity disorder: A handbook for diagnosis & treatment* (2nd ed.). New York: Guilford.

Barkley, R. A. (1985). Attention deficit disorders. In P. H. Bornstein & E. A. Kazdin (Eds.), *Handbook of clinical behavior therapy with children.* Homewood, IL: Dorsey Press.

Barkley, R. A. (1996). Attention-deficit/hyperactivity disorder. In E. J. Mash & R. A. Barkley (Eds.), *Child psychopathology* (pp. 63–112). New York: Guilford.

Bart, P. B., & O'Brien, P. H. (1985). *Stopping rape: Successful survival strategies.* Elmsford: Pergamon Press.

Baum, C. G. (1989). Conduct disorders. In T. H. Ollendick & M. Hersen (Eds.), *Handbook of child psychopathology* (2nd ed.). New York: Plenum.

Beck, A. T., & Freeman, A. (1990). *Cognitive therapy of personality disorders.* New York: Guilford Press.

Beck, A. T., Rush, A. J., Shaw, B. F., & Emery, G. (1979). *Cognitive therapy of depression.* New York: Guilford.

Beitchman, J. H., Zucker, K. J., Hood, J. E., DaCosta, G. A., & Akman, D. (1992). A review of the short-term effects of child sexual abuse. *Child Abuse and Neglect, 16,* 537–556.

Berliner, L., & Elliott, D. M. (1996). Sexual abuse of children. In J. Briere, L. Berliner, J. A. Bulkley, C. Jenney, & T. Reid (Eds.), *The APSAC handbook on child maltreatment* (pp. 51–71). Thousand Oaks, CA: Sage.

Bernstein, G. A., Borchardt, C. M., & Perwien, A. R. (1996). Anxiety disorders in children and adolescents: A review of the past 10 years. *Journal of the American Academy of Child and Adolescent Psychiatry, 35,* 1110–1119.

Biederman, J. (1991). Attention deficit hyperactivity disorder (ADHD). *Annals of Clinical Psychiatry, 3,* 9–22.

Biederman, J., Faraone, S., Mick, E., et al. (1995). High risk for attention deficit hyperactivity disorder among children of parents with childhood onset of the disorder: A pilot study. *American Journal of Psychiatry, 152,* 431–435.

Biederman, J., Newcorn, J., & Sprich, S. (1991). Comorbidity of attention deficit hyperactivity disorder with conduct, depressive, anxiety, and other disorders. *American Journal of Psychiatry, 148,* 564–577.

Black, B. (1995). Separation anxiety disorder & panic disorder. In J. March (Ed.), *Anxiety disorders in children & adolescents (pp. 212–234).* New York: Guilford.

Blagg, N., & Yule, W. (1994). School phobia. In T. H. Ollendick, N. J. King, & W. Yule (Eds.), *International handbook of phobia and anxiety disorders in children and adolescents* (pp. 169–186). New York: Plenum.

Blatt, S. J., Sanislow, C. A., Zuroff, D., & Pilkonis, P. (1996). Characteristics of the effective therapist: Further analysis of the data from the NIMH TDCRP. *Journal of Consulting and Clinical Psychology, 64,* 1276–1284.

Bower, S. A., & Bower, G. H. (1976). *Asserting yourself.* Menlo Park: Addison-Wesley.

Bowlby, J. (1973). *Attachment and loss: Vol. 2. Separation: anxiety and anger.* New York: Basic Books.

Bowlby, J. (1988). Developmental psychiatry comes of age. *American Journal of Psychiatry, 145,* 1–10.

Briere, J. (1996). *Therapy for adults molested as children: Beyond survival* (2nd ed.). New York: Springer.

Briere, J., & Zaidi, L. (1989). Sexual abuse histories and sequelae in female psychiatric emergency room patients. *American Journal of Psychiatry, 46*(12), 1602–1606.

Brown, C. W., Harris, T. O., & BiFulco, A. (1986). Longterm effects of early loss of parent. In M. Rutter, C. E. Izaro, & P. B. Read (Eds.), *Depression in young people: Developmental and clinical perspectives* (pp. 251–296). New York: Guilford.

Browne, A., & Finkelhor, D. (1986). Impact of child sexual abuse: A review of the research. *Psychological Bulletin, 99,* 66–77.

Bruch, H. (1973). *Eating disorders: Obesity, anorexia nervosa, and the person within.* New York: Basic Books.

Bruch, H. (1984). Four decades of eating disorders. In D. M. Garner & P. E. Garfinkel (Eds.), *Handbook of psychotherapy for anorexia and bulimia* (pp. 7–18). New York: Guilford.

Buchanan, C., Maccoby, E., & Dornbusch, S. (1992). Adolescents and their families after divorce: Three residential arrangements compared. *Journal of Research on Adolescence, 2,* 261–291.

Buie, D. H. & Adler, G. (1982). The definitive treatment of the borderline patient. *International Journal of Psychoanalytic Psychotherapy,9,* 51–87.

Burgess, A. W., & Holmstrom, L. L. (1974). Against Rape. *The American Journal of Psychiatry, 131,* 981–986.

Busch, B. (1993). Attention deficits: Current concepts, controversies, management, and approaches to classroom instruction. *Annals of Dyslexia, 43,* 5–25.

Calhoun, K., & Atkeson, B. (1991). *Treatment of rape victims: Facilitating social adjustment.* New York: Pergamon Press.

Campbell, S. B. (1990). *Behavior problems in preschool children.* New York: Guilford.

Campbell, S. B. (1991). Longitudinal studies of active and aggressive preschoolers: Individual differences in early behavior and in outcome. In D. Cicchetti & S. L. Toth (Eds.), *Internalizing & externalizing expression of dysfunction: Rochester symposium on developmental psychopathology, 2,* 57–90. Hillsdale, NJ : Erlbaum.

Cantwell, D. P. (1996). Classification of child and and adolescent psychopathology. *Journal of Child Psychology and Psychiatry and Allied Disciplines, 37,* 3–12.

Carlat, D. J., Camargo, C. A., & Herzog, D. B. (1997). Eating disorders in males: A report on 135 patients. *American Journal of Psychiatry, 154,* 1127–1132.

Cashdan, S. (1988). *Object relations therapy.* New York: Norton.

Castro-Martin, T., & Bumpass, L. (1989). Recent trends and differentials in marital disruption. *Demography, 26,* 37–51.

Cervantes, R. C., & Arroyo, W. (1994). DSM-IV: Implications for Hispanic children and adolescents. *Hispanic Journal of Behavioral Sciences, 16,* 8–27.

Cervantes, R. C., Salgado de Snyder, V. N., & Padilla, A. M. (1989). Posttraumatic stress in immigrants from Central America and Mexico. *Hospital & Community Psychiatry,* 615–619.

Chase-Lansdale, P. L., Cherlin, A. L., & Kiernan, K. E. (1995). The long-term effects of parental divorce on the mental health of young adults: A developmental perspective. *Child Development, 66,* 1614–1634.

Cherlin, A. (1992). *Marriage, divorce, remarriage: Social trends in the U.S.* Cambridge, MA: Harvard University Press.

Cherlin, A. J., Furstenberg, F. F., Chase-Lansdale, P. L., Kiernan, K. E., Robins, P. K., Morrison, D. R., & Teitler, J. O. (1991). Longitudinal studies of effects of divorce in children in Great Britain and the United States. *Science, 252,* 1386–1389.

Childress, A. C., Brewerton, T. D., Hodges, E. L., & Jarrell, M. P. (1993). The kids' eating disorders survey (KEDS): A study of middle school students. *Journal of the American Academy of Child & Adolescent Psychology 36,* 395–407

Cicchetti, D., & Garmezy, N. (1993). Prospects and promises in the study of resilience. *Development and Psychopathology, 5,* 497–502.

Cicchetti, D., & Rogosch, F. A. (1997). The role of self-organization in the promotion of resilience in maltreated children. *Development and Psychopathology, 9,* 797–815.

Cicchetti, D., & Toth, S. L. (1998). The development of depression in children and adolescents. *American Psychologist, 53,* 221–241.

Clarke-Stewart, K., & Hayward, C. (1996). Advantages of father custody and contact for the psychological well-being of school-age children. *Journal of Applied Developmental Psychology, 17,* 239–270.

Cole, D. A., Truglio, R., & Peeke, L. (1997). Relation between symptoms of anxiety and depression in children: A multitrait-multimethod-multigroup assessment. *Journal of Consulting and Clinical Psychology, 65,* 110–119.

Cole, P., Zahn-Waxler, C., Fox, N., Usher, B., & Welsh, J. (1996). The individual differences in emotion regulation and behavior problems in preschool children. *Journal of Abnormal Psychology, 105,* 518–529.

Connors, M. E. (1996). Developmental vulnerabilities for eating disorders. In L. Smolk, M. P. Levine, & R. Striegel-Moore (Eds.), *The developmental psychopathology of eating disorders: Implications for research, prevention, and treatment.* Mahwah, NJ: Lawrence Erlbaum.

Cousins, L., & Weiss, G. (1993). Parent training and social skills training for children with attention-deficit hyperactivity disorder: How can they be combined for greater effectiveness? *Canadian Journal of Psychiatry, 38,* 449–457.

Crick, N. R., & Dodge, K. A. (1994). A review and reformulation of social information-processing mechanisms in children's social adjustment. *Psychological Bulletin, 115,* 74–101.

Curry, J., & Murphy, L. (1995). Comorbidity of anxiety disorders. In J. March (Ed.), *Anxiety disorders in children & adolescents* (pp. 301–317). New York: Guilford.

Damon, L., & Card, J. (1992). Incest in young children. In R. Ammerman, & M. Hersen, (Eds.), *Assessment of family violence.* New York: John Wiley & Sons, Inc.

DeJong, A., Hervada, A., & Emmett, G. (1983). Epidemiological variations in childhood sexual abuse. *Child Abuse and Neglect, 7,* 155–162.

Department of Public Safety. (1994). *Analysis of Crime and Police Activity,* City of Eugene, Oregon.

Diaz-Guerrero, R., & Szalay, L. B. (1991). *Understanding Mexicans & Americans: Cultural perspectives in conflict.* New York: Plenum.

Downs, W. (1993). Developmental considerations for the effects of childhood sexual abuse. Special issue: Research on treatment of adults abused in childhood. *Journal of Interpersonal Violence, 8*(3), 331–345.

Duncan, R. D., Saunders, B. E., Kilpatrick, D. G., Rochelle, F., & Resnick, H. S. (1996). Childhood physical assault as a risk factor for PTSD, depression, & substance abuse: Findings from a national survey. *American Journal of Orthopsychiatry, 66,* 437–448.

Egeland, B., Kalloske, M., Gottesman, N., & Erikson, M. E. (1990). Preschool behavior problems: Stability and factors accounting for change. *Journal of Child Psychology & Psychiatry, 31,* 891–909.

Emery, R., & Forehand, R. (1994). Parental divorce and children's well-being: A focus on resilience. In R. J. Haggerty, L. R. Sherrod, N. Garmezy, & M. Rutter (Eds.), *Stress, risk, and resilience in children and adolescents* (pp. 64–99). Cambridge, England: Cambridge University Press.

Engel, L., & Ferguson, T. (1990). *Imaginary crimes: Why we punish ourselves and how to stop it.* Boston: Houghton Mifflin.

Erickson, E. (1959). Identity and the life cycle. *Psychological Issues,* Monograph 1. New York: International Universities.

Erickson, M. F., Sroufe, L. A., & Egeland, B. (1985). The relationship between quality of attachment and behavior problems in preschool in a high risk sample. In I. Bretherton & E. Waters (Eds.), *Growing points in attachment theory and research. Monographs of the Society for Research in Child Development. 50* (Serial No. 209, Nos. 1–2), 147–186.

Everett, F., Proctor, N., & Cartmell, B. (1983) Providing psychological services to American Indian children and families. *Professional Psychology, 14,* 588–603.

Fairburn, C. G., & Beglin, S. J. (1990). Studies of the epidemiology of bulimia nervosa. *American Journal of Psychiatry, 147,* 401–408.

Fergusson, D. M., & Horwood, L. J. (1996). The role of adolescent peer affiliations in the continuity between childhood behavioral adjustment and juvenile offending. *Journal of Abnormal Child Psychology, 24,* 205–221.

Fergusson, D. M., & Horwood, L. J. (1998). Early conduct problems and later life opportunities. *Journal of Child Psychology and Psychiatry, 39,* 1097–1108.

Fine, S. (1997). Attention deficit hyperactivity disorder (ADHD): Selected review of causes, comorbidity & treatment. *International Journal of Psychiatry in Clinical Practice, 1,* 249–259.

Finkelhor, D. (1984). *Child sexual abuse: New theories and research.* New York: Free Press.

Finkelhor, D. (1990). Early and long-term effects of child sexual abuse: An update. *Professional Psychology: Research & Practice,* 21(5), 325–330.

Finkelhor, D. & Associates. (1986). *A sourcebook on child sexual abuse* (pp. 15–59), Beverly Hills: Sage Publications Inc.

Finkelhor, D. & Browne, A. (1985). The traumatic impact of child sexual abuse: A conceptualization. *Journal of Orthopsychiatry,* 55(4), 530–541.

Finkelhor, D., Hotaling, G., Lewis, I., & Smith, C. (1990). Sexual abuse in a national survey of adult men and women: Prevalence, characteristics, and risk factors. *Child Abuse and Neglect, 14,* 19–28.

Fletcher, J., Shaywitz, B., & Shaywitz, S. (1994). Attention as a process and as a disorder. In G. Lyon (Ed.), *Frames of reference for the assessment of learning disabilities.* Baltimore: Paul H. Brooks.

Fonagy, P., Steele, M., Higgitt, A., & Target , M. (1994). The theory and practice of resilience. *Journal of Child Psychology and Psychiatry, 35,* 231–257.

Foreyt, J. P., & Mikhail, C. (1997). Anorexia nervosa and bulimia nervosa. In E. J. Mash & L. G. Terdal (Eds.), *Assessment of childhood disorders* (pp. 683–716). New York: Guilford.

Forgatch, M., Patterson, G., & Ray, J. (1995). Divorce and boys' adjustment problems: Two paths with a single model. In E. M. Hetherington & E. A. Blechman (Eds.), *Stress, coping, and resiliency in children and families* (pp. 67–105). Mahwah, NJ: Erlbaum.

Fowler, J. W. (1981). *Stages of faith: The psychology of human development and the quest for meaning.* San Francisco, CA: Harper & Row.

Frank, J. D., & Frank, J. B. (1991). *Persuasion & healing: A comparative study of psychotherapy (3rd ed.).* Baltimore: Johns Hopkins University Press.

Freeman, A., Pretzer, J., Fleming, B., & Simon, K. (1990). *Clinical applications of cognitive therapy.* New York: Plenum.

Fromm-Reichman, F. (1950). *Principles of intensive psychotherapy.* Chicago: University of Chicago Press.

Fuller, R. (1997). The African American child. In J. D. Noshpitz (Ed.), *Handbook of child and adolescent psychiatry* (Vol. 4, pp. 484–492). New York: Wiley.

Gadow, K. D. (1991). Clinical issues in child and adolescent psychopharmacology. *Journal of Consulting & Clinical Psychology, 59,* 842–852.

Garcia-Coll, C., & Meyer, E. (1993). The sociocultural context of infant development. In C. Zeanatt (Ed.), *Handbook of infant mental health* (pp. 56–69). New York: Guilford Press.

Gardner, R. (1992). Children with separation anxiety disorder. In J. O'Brien, D. Pilowski, & O. Lewis (Eds.), *Psychotherapies with children and adolescents: Adapting the psychodynamic process* (pp. 3–25). Washington, DC: American Psychiatric Press.

Garmezy, N. (1991). Resiliency and vulnerability to adverse developmental outcomes associated with poverty. *American Behavioral Scientist, 34,* 416–430.

Garmezy, N., & Rutter, M. (Eds.). (1988). *Stress, coping, and development in children.* Baltimore: Johns Hopkins Press.

Gelso, C. J., & Carter, J. A. (1994). Components of the psychotherapy relationship: Their interaction & unfolding during treatment. *The Journal of Counseling Psychology, 41(3),* 296–306.

Gerrol, R., & Resick, P. (1998, Nov.). Sex differences in social support and recovery from victimization. *Paper presented at the meeting of the Association for Advancement of Behavior Therapy.* New York: New York.

Gibbs, J., & Huang, L. (1997). *Children of Color: Psychological interventions with minority youth.* San Francisco, CA: Jossey-Bass Publishers.

Gibbs, N. (1991, June 3). When is it rape? *Time* (pp. 48–54).

Gilbert, S., & Thompson, J. K. (1996). Feminist explanations of the development of eating disorders: Common themes, research findings, and methodological issues. *Clinical Psychology, Science and Practice* 3, 183–202.

Gilligan, C. (1982). *In a different voice: Psychological theory & women's development.* Cambridge: Harvard University Press.

Gillum, R., Gomez-Marin, O., & Prineas, R. (1984). Racial differences in personality, behavior, and family environment in Minneapolis school children. *Journal of the National Medical Association, 76,* 1097–1105.

Ginsburg, G. S., & Silverman, W. K. (1996). Phobic and anxiety disorders in Hispanic and Caucasian youth. *Journal of Anxiety Disorders, 10,* 517–528.

Glick, P., & Lin, S. (1986). Recent changes in divorce and remarriage. *Journal of Marriage and the Family, 48,* 737–747.

Goodman, R., & Stevenson, J. (1989). A twin study of hyperactivity-II. The aetiological role of genes, family relationships and perinatal adversity, *Journal of Child Psychology and Psychiatry, 30,* 691–709.

Gorey, K. M., & Leslie, D. R. (1997). The prevalence of child sexual abuse: Integrative review adjustment for potential response & measurement bias. *Child Abuse and Neglect, 21,* 391–398.

Green, A. (1993). Child sexual abuse: Immediate and long-term effects and intervention. *Journal of the American Academy of Child & Adolescent Psychiatry, 32,* 890–902.

Greene, B. A. (1985). Considerations in the treatment of Black patients by White therapists. *Psychotherapy, 22,* 389–393.

Grilo, C. M., Becker, D. F., Fehon, D. C., Walker, M. L., et al. (1996). Gender differences in personality disorders in psychiatrically hospitalized adolescents. *American Journal of Psychiatry, 153*(8), 1089–1091.

Groth, A., & Birnham, H. (1979). *Men who rape: The psychology of the offender.* New York: Plenum Press.

Gunderson, J. G. (1984). *Borderline personality disorders.* Washington, DC: American Psychiatric Press.

Gunderson, J. G. (1996). The borderline patient's intolerance of aloneness: Insecure attachments and therapist availability. *American Journal of Psychiatry, 153*(6), 752–758.

Gunderson, J. G., & Sabo, A. N. (1993). The phenomenonological and conceptual interface between borderline personality disorder and PTSD. *American Journal of Psychiatry, 150,* 19–27.

Gunderson, J. G., & Zanarini, M. C. (1989). Pathogenesis of borderline personality. In A. Tasman, R. E. Hales, & A. J. Francis (Eds.), *Review of psychiatry.* Washington, DC: American Psychiatric Press.

Hagborg, W., & Konigsberg, B. (1991). Multiple perspectives of therapeutic change and the severely emotionally disturbed adolescent. *Psychotherapy, 22,* 389–393.

Hammen, C. & Rudolph, K. D. (1996). Childhood depression. In E. J. Mash & R. A. Barkley (Eds.), *Child psychopathology* (pp. 153–195). New York: Guilford.

Heiman, M. (1992). Annotation: Putting together the puzzle: Validating allegations of child sexual abuse. *Journal of Child Psychology & Psychiatry, 33,* 311–329.

Heras, P., Gomez, M., & Thomas, J. (1992). Cultural considerations in the assessment and treatment of child sexual abuse. *Journal of Child Sexual Abuse, 1,* 119–124.

Herbert, M. (1974). *Emotional problems of development in children.* New York: Academic Press.

Herzog, D. B., Sacks, N. R., Keller, M. B., Lavori, P. W., von Ranson, K. B., & Gray, H. N. (1993). Patterns and predictors of recovery in anorexia nervosa and bulimia nervosa. *Journal of Child Psychology & Psychiatry, 32,* 962–966.

Hetherington, E. M. (1989). Coping with family transitions: Winners, losers, and survivors. *Child Psychology, 60,* 1–14.

Hetherington, E. M. (1993). An overview of the Virginia Longitudinal Study of Divorce and Remarriage with a focus on early adolescence. *Journal of Family Psychology, 7,* 39–56.

Hetherington, E. M. (1998). What matters? What does not? Five perspectives on the association between marital transitions and children's adjustment. *American Psychologist, 53,* 2, 167–184.

Hetherington, E. M., Clingempeel, W., Anderson, E., Deal, J., Stanley-Hagan, M., Hollier, E., & Lindner, M. (1992). Coping with marital transitions: A family systems perspective. *Monographs of the Society for Research in Child Development, 57* (2–3, Serial No. 227).

Hill, R. B. (1972). *The strengths of black families.* New York: Emerson Hall.

Hinshaw, S., Zupan, B., Simmel, C., Nigg, J., & Melnick, S. (1997). Peer status in boys with and without attention-deficit hyperactivity disorder. Predictions from overt and covert anticocial behavior, social isolation, and authoritative parenting beliefs. *Child Development, 68,* 880–896.

Hirshfeld, D. R., Biederman, J., Brody, L., & Faraone, S. V. (1997). Associations between expressed emotion and child behavioral inhibition and psychopathology: A pilot study. *Journal of the American Academy of Child and Adolescent Psychiatry, 36,* 205–213.

Hirshfeld, D. R., Biederman, J., & Rosenbaum, J. F. (1997). Expressed emotion toward children with behavioral inhibition: Associations with maternal anxiety. *Journal of the American Academy of Child and Adolescent Psychiatry, 36,* 910–919.

Ho, M. H. (1992). *Minority children and adolescents in therapy.* Newbury Park, CA: Sage.

Hoch, P., & Polatin, P. (1949). Pseudoneurotic forms of schizophrenia. *Psychiatric Quarterly, 23,* 248–276.

Holaday, M., Leach, M., & Davidson, M. (1994). Multicultural counseling and intrapersonal value conflict: A case study. *Counseling and Values,* 38(2), 136–142.

Hollingshead, A., & Redlich, F. (1958). *Social class and mental illness.* New York: John Wiley.

Holy Bible. (1960). *New American Standard Version (NASB).* LaHabra, CA: The Lockman Foundation.

Horvath, A. O., & Greenberg, L. S. (1994). *The working alliance: Theory, research, & practice.* New York: Wiley.

Horvath, A. O., & Symonds, B. D. (1991). Relation between working alliance & outcome in psychotherapy: A meta-analysis. *The Journal of Counseling Psychology,* 38(2), 139–149.

Ibrahim, F. (1985). Effective cross-cultural counseling and psychotherapy: A framework. *The Counseling Psychologist, 13,* 625–683.

Ibrahim, F. (1991). Contribution of cultural worldview to generic counseling and development. *Journal of Counseling and Development, 70,* 13–19.

Ichikawa, F. V. (1989). Japanese parents' and children's causal beliefs about academic achievement. *Dissertation Abstracts International, 49,* 23–25.

Jacobvitz, D., & Sroufe, L. A. (1987). The early caregiver-child relationship and attention-deficit disorder with hyperactivity in kindergarten: A prospective study. *Child Development, 58,* 1488–1495.

Johnson, C. L. (1991). Treatment of eating-disordered patients with borderline and false-self/narcissistic disorders. In C. L. Johnson (Ed.), *Psychodynamic treatment of anorexia nervosa and bulimia* (pp. 165–193). New York: Guilford.

Johnson, W. G., Tsoh, J. Y., & Varnado, P. J. (1996). Eating disorders: Efficacy of pharmacological and psychological interventions. *Clinical Psychology Review, 16,* 457–478.

Jordan, J. (1991) *Women's growth in connection.* New York: Guilford.

Jordan, J., Kaplan, A., Miller, J., Stiver, I., & Surrey, J. (1991). *Women's growth in connection: Writings from the Stone Center.* New York: Guilford.

Kagan, S. (1977). Social motives and behaviors of Mexican-American and Anglo-American children. In J. L. Martinez Jr. (Ed.), *Chicano psychology* (2nd ed.), (pp. 45–86). New York: Academic Press.

Kahn, M. (1997). *Between therapist and client.* New York: Freeman.

Karen, R. (1994). *Becoming attached.* New York: Warner Books.

Kaufman, A, Divasto, P, Jackson, R, Voorhees, D, & Christy, J. (1980). Male rape victims: Non-institutionalized assault. *American Journal of Psychiatry, 137,* 221–223.

Kazdin, A., Kreamer, H., Kessler, R., Kupfer, D., & Offord, D. (1997). Contributions of risk-factor research to developmental psychopathology. *Clinical Psychology Review, 17,* 375–406.

Kazdin, A. E. (1990). Childhood depression. *Journal of Child Psychology and Psychiatry, 31,* 121–160.

Kazdin, A. E. (1997). Conduct disorder across the life-span. In S. S. Luthar, J. A. Burack, D. Cicchetti, & J. R Weisz. (Eds.) *Developmental psychopathology: Perspectives on adjustment, risk, and disorder* (pp. 248–272). Cambridge: Cambridge University Press.

Kearney, C. A., Eisen, A. R., & Silverman, W. K. (1995). The legend and myth of school phobia. *School Psychology Quarterly, 10,* 65–85.

Keenan, K., Loeber, R., Zhang, Q., Stouthamer-Loeber, M., & Van Kammen, W. (1995). The influence of deviant peers on the development of boys' disruptive and delinquent behavior: A temporal analysis. *Development and Psychopathology, 7,* 715–726.

Keller, M., Lavori, P., Wunder, J., Beardslee, W., Schwartz, C., & Roth, J. (1992). Chronic course of anxiety disorders in children and adolescents. *Journal of the American Academy of Child and Adolescent Psychiatry, 31,* 595–599.

Kendall-Tackett, K., Williams, L., & Finkelhor, D. (1993). Impact of sexual abuse on children: A review and synthesis of recent empirical studies. *Psychological Bulletin, 113,* 164–180.

Kercher, G., & McShane, M. (1984). The prevalence of child sexual abuse victimization in an adult sample of Texas residents. *Child Abuse and Neglect, 8,* 495–501.

Kernberg, O. (1996). A psychoanalytic theory of personality disorders. In J. F. Clarkin & M. F. Lenzenweger (Eds.), *Major theories of personality disorders* (pp. 106–140). New York: Guilford.

Kids' Eating Disorders Survey (KEDS): A study of middle school students. *Journal of the American Academy of Child and Adolescent Psychiatry, 32,* 843–850.

Kiesler, D., & Van Denberg, T. (1993). Therapeutic impact disclosure: The last taboo in psychoanalytic theory and practice. *Clinical Psychology and Psychotherapy,* 1(1), 3–13.

Killen, J. D., Taylor, B., Hayward, C., Haydel, K. F., Wilson, D. M., Hammer, L., Kraemer, H., Blair-Greiner, A., & Strachowski, D. (1996). Weight concerns influence the development of eating disorders: A 4-year prospective study. *Journal of Consulting and Clinical Psychology, 64,* 936–940.

Kilpatrick, D. (1985). Mental health correlates of criminal victimization: A random community survey. *Journal of Consulting and Clinical Psychology, 53,* 866–873.

King, M. E., & Citrenbaum, C. M. (1993). *Existential hypnotherapy.* New York: Wiley.

Klein, R. G., & Mannuzza, S. (1991). Long-term outcome of hyperactive children: A review. *Journal of the American Academy of Child and Adolescent Psychiatry, 30,* 383–387.

Kortlander, E., Kendall, P., & Panichelli-Mindel, S. (1997). Maternal expectations and attributions about coping in anxious children. *Journal of Anxiety Disorders, 11,* 297–315.

Koss, M. P. (1993). Detecting the scope of rape: A review of prevalence research methods. *Journal of Interpersonal Violence, 8,* 198–222.

Kuba, S. A., & Harris, D. J. (May, 1992). *Eating disorders in women of color: The ethnocultural context in the identification and treatment of eating disorders.* Paper presented at the Annual Meeting of the American Orthopsychiatry Association, New York.

Last, C. G., & Francis, G. (1988). School phobia. In B. B. Lahey & A. E. Kazdin, (Eds.), *Advances in clinical child psychology* (Vol. 11, pp. 193–222). New York: Plenum.

Last, C. G., Francis, G., Hersen, M., Kazdin, A. E., & Strauss, C. C. (1987a). Separation anxiety and school phobia: A comparison using DSM-III criteria. *American Journal of Psychiatry, 144,* 653–657.

Last, C. G., Hersen, M., Kazdin, A. E., Francis, G. & Grubb, H. J. (1987b). Psychiatric illness in mothers of anxious children. *American Journal of Psychiatry, 144,* 1580–1583.

Last, C. G., & Strauss, C. C. (1990). School refusal in anxiety-disordered children and adolescents. *Journal of the American Academy of Child and Adolescent Psychiatry, 29,* 31–35.

Last, C. G., Perrin, S., Hersen, M., & Kazdin, A. E. (1992). DSM-III-R anxiety disorders in children: Sociodemographic and clinical characteristics. *Journal of the American Academy of Child and Adolescent Psychiatry, 31,* 1070–1076.

Leslie, L. A. (1992). The role of informal support networks in the adjustment of Central American immigrant families. *Journal of Community Psychology, 20,* 243–256.

Leslie, L. A., & Leitch, M. L. (1989). A demographic profile of recent Central American immigrants: Clinical and service implications. *Hispanic Journal of Behavioral Sciences, 11,* 315–329.

Levy, F., Hay, D., McStephen, M., Wood, C., & Waldman, I. (1997). Attention-deficit hyperactivity disorder: A category or a continuum? Genetic analysis of a large-scale twin study. *Journal of the American Academy of Child and Adolescent Psychiatry, 36,* 737–744.

Lewandowski, L. M., Gebing, T. A., Anthony, J. L., & O'Brien, W. H. (1997). Meta-analysis of cognitive-behavioral treatment studies for bulimia. *Clinical Psychology Review, 17,* 703–718.

Lewis, D. (1975). The Black family: Socialization and sex roles. *Phylon, 36,* 221–237.

Lindholm, J., & Willey, R. (1986). Ethnic differences in child abuse and sexual abuse. *Hispanic Journal of Behavioral Sciences, 8,* 111–125.

Linehan, M. N. (1993). *Cognitive behavioral therapy of borderline personality disorder.* New York: Guilford.

Lish, J. D., Kavoussi, R. J., & Coccaro, E. F. (1996). Aggressiveness. In C. G. Costello (Ed.), *Personality characteristics of the personality disordered.* New York: Wiley.

Lucas, A. R., & Holub, M. I. (1995). The incidence of anorexia nervosa in adolescent residents of Rochester, Minnesota, during a 50-year period. In H. C. Steinhausen (Ed.), *Eating disorders in adolescence: Anorexia and bulimia nervosa.* Berlin: Walter de Gruyter.

Ludolph, P. S., Westen, D., Misle, B., Jackson, A., et al. (1990). The borderline diagnosis in adolescents: Symptoms and developmental history. *American Journal of Psychiatry, 147*(4), 470–476.

Lyon, M. Chatoor, I., Atkins, D., Silber, T., Mosimann, J., & Gray, J. (1997). Testing the hypothesis of the multidimensional model of anorexia nervosa in adolescents. *Adolescence, 32,* 101–111.

Mahler, M., Pine, F. & Bergman, A. (1975). *The Psychological birth of the human infant: Symbiosis and individuation.* New York: Basic Books.

Manassis, K., & Bradley, S. (1994). The development of childhood anxiety disorders: Toward an integrated model. *Journal of Applied Developmental Psychology, 15,* 345–366.

Manassis, K., Bradley, S., Goldberg, S., Hood, J., & Swinson, R. (1994). Attachment in mothers with anxiety disorders and their children. *Journal of the American Academy of Child & Adolescent Psychiatry, 33,* 1106–1113.

Manicavasagar, V., Silore, D., Curtis, J., & Wagner, R. (2000). Continuities of separation anxiety from early life into adulthood. *Journal of Anxiety Disorders, 14,* 1–18.

Martin, C., Cabrol, S., Bouvard, M., Lepine, J., & Mouren-Simeoni, M. (2000). Anxiety & depressive disorders in fathers & mothers of anxious school-refusing children. *Journal of the American Academy of Child & Adolescent Psychiatry, 38,* 916–922.

Martin, E. (1971). Reflections on the early adolescent in school. In J. Kagen & R. Coles (Eds.), *Twelve to sixteen: Early adolescence.* New York: Wiley.

Martin, L. C. (1992). *A life without fear.* Nashville: Rutledge Hill Press.

Marziali, E., & Alexander, L. (1991). The power of the therapeutic relationship. *American Journal of Orthopsychiatry, 61*(3), 383–391.

Mash, E., & Wolfe, D. (1999). *Abnormal child psychology,* Belmont, CA: Wadsworth Publishing Company.

Masi, G., Mucci, M., Favilla, L., Romano, R., & Poli, P. (1999). Symptomatology & comorbidity of generalized anxiety disorder in children & adolescents. *Comprehensive Psychiatry, 40,* 210–215.

Masten, A., & Coatsworth, J. (1998). The development of competence in favorable and unfavorable environments. *American Psychologist, 53,* 205–220.

Masterson, J. (1985). *Treatment of the borderline adolescent: A developmental approach.* New York: Brunner/Mazel.

McArdle, P., O'Brien, G., & Kolvin, I. (1995). Hyperactivity: Prevalence and relationship with conduct disorder. *Journal of Child Psychology & Psychiatry, 36,* 279–303.

McClellan, J., McCurry, C., Ronnei, M., & Adams, J. (1996). Age of onset of sexual abuse: Relationship to sexually inappropriate behaviors. *Journal of the American Academy of Child and Adolescent Psychiatry, 35,* 1375–1383.

McFarlane, K. & Krebs, S. (1986). Techniques for interviewing and evidence gathering. In K. McFarlane & J. Waterman et al. (Eds.), *Sexual Abuse of young children: Evaluation & treatment.* New York: Guilford.

McGlashen, T. H. (1992). The longitudinal profile of borderline personality disorder: Contributions from the Chestnut Lodge Follow-up study. In D. Silver & M. Rosenbluth (Eds.), *Handbook of borderline disorders.* Madison, CT: International Universities Press.

McKinley, V. (1991). Group therapy as a treatment modality of special value for Hispanic patients. *Social Work with Groups, 13,* 255–266.

McLoed, B. (1986). The Oriental Express. *Psychology Today, 20,* 565–570.

Mellin, L. M., Irwin, C. E., & Scully, S. (1992). Prevalence of disordered eating in girls: a survey of middle-class children. *Journal of the American Dietetic Association, 92,* 851–853.

Mennen, F. (1995). The relationship of race/ethnicity to symptoms in childhood sexual abuse. *Child Abuse and Neglect, 1,* 115–124.

Meyer, W. (1993). In defense of long-term treatment: On the vanishing holding environment. *Social Work, 38,* 571–578.

Millon, T. (1987). *Millon Clinical Multiaxial Inventory-ll: Manual for the MCMI-ll* (2nd ed.). Minneapolis, MN: National Computer Systems.

Minuchin, S., & Fishman, H. (1981). *Family therapy techniques.* Cambridge, MA: Harvard University Press.

Minuchin, S., Rosman, B., & Baker, L. (1978). *Psychosomatic families: Anorexia nervosa in context.* Cambridge, MA: Harvard.

Mizes, J. S. (1993). Bulimia nervosa. In A. S. Bellack & M. Hersen (Eds.), *Handbook of behavior therapy in the psychiatric setting.* New York: Plenum.

Modell, A. H. (1971). The origin of certain forms of preoedipal guilt and the implications for a psychoanalytic theory of affects. *International Journal of Psychoanalysis, 52,* 337–346.

Morgan, S. (1989). Clarifying the Federal definition of severely emotionally disturbed. *Journal of Instructional Psychology, 16,* 173–179.

Morgenstern, J., Langerbucher, J., Labouvie, E., & Miller, K. J. (1997). The comorbidity of alcoholism and personality disorders in a clinical population: Prevalence rates and relation to alcohol typology variables. *Journal of Abnormal Psychology, 106*(1), 74–84.

Morrow, K., & Sorell, G. (1989). Factors affecting self-esteem, depression, and negative behaviors in sexually abused female adolescents. *Journal of Marriage & the Family, 51,* 677–686.

Moskovitz, R. A. (1996). *Lost in the mirror: An inside look at borderline personality disorder.* Dallas, TX: Taylor Publishing Company.

Myers, M. (1989). Men sexually assaulted as adolescents and sexually abused as boys. *Archives of Sexual Behavior, 18,* 203–215.

National Crime Victimization Survey. (1995). *U.S. Bureau of Justice Statistics.* Washington, DC: U.S. Department of Justice.

National Research Council. (1993). *Understanding child abuse and neglect.* Washington, DC: National Academy Press.

Neumann, D. A., Houskamp, B. M., Pollock, V. E., & Briere, J. (1996). The long-term sequelae of childhood sexual abuse in women: A meta-analytic review. *Child Maltreatment: Journal of the American Professional Society on the Abuse of Children, 1,* 6–16.

Niederland, W. G. (1981). The survivor guilt syndrome: Further observations and dimensions. *Journal of the American Psychoanalytic Association, 29,* 413–426.

Ollendick, T., Yang, B., King, N., Dong, Q., & Akande, A. (1996). Fears in American, Australian, Chinese, and Nigerian children and adolescents: A cross-cultural study. *Journal of Child Psychology and Psychiatry, 35,* 113–134.

Orbuch, T. L., Veroff, J. & Hunter, A. G., Black couples, White couples. The early years of marriage In E. M. Hetherington (Ed.), *Coping with divorce, single-parenting, and remarriage: A risk and resiliency perspective.* Hillsdale, NJ: Lawrence Erlbaum.

Ouellette, E. (1991). Legal issues in the treatment of children with attention deficit hyperactivity disorder. *Journal of Child Neurology, 6(suppl),* S68–S75.

Padilla, A. M., Cervantes, R. C., Maldonado, M., & Garcia, R. E. (1988). Coping responses to psychosocial stressors among Mexican and Central American Immigrants. *Journal of Community Psychology, 16,* 418–427.

Paris, J. (1991). Personality disorders, parasuicide, and culture. *Transcult. Psychiatr. Res. Rev., 28*(1), 225–239.

Parker, J. G., Rubin, K. H., Price, J. M., & DeRosier, M. E. (1995). Peer relationships, child development, and adjustment: A developmental psychopathology perspective. In D. Cicchetti & D. Cohen (Eds.), *Developmental psychopathology (Vol. 2: Risk, disorder and adaptation).* New York: Wiley.

Pate, J. E., Pumariega, A. J., Hester, C., & Garner, D. M. (1992). Cross-cultural patterns in eating disorders: A review. *Journal of the American Academy of Child & Adolescent Psychiatry, 31,* 802–808.

Patterson, G. R., Reid, J. B., & Dishion, T. J. (1992). *Antisocial boys.* Eugene, Oregon: Castalia.

Pedersen, P. (1991). Multiculturism as a generic approach to counseling. *Journal of Counseling and Development, 70,* 6–11.

Pelham, W. (1993). Pharmacotherapy for children with attention-deficit hyperactivity disorder. *School Psychology Review, 22,* 199–227.

Pelham, W., Wheeler, T., & Chronis, A. (1998). Empirically supported psychosocial treatments for attention deficit hyperactivity disorder. *Journal of Clinical Child Psychology, 27,* 190–205.

Perugi, G., Delitito, J., Soriani, A., Musetti, L., Petracca, A., Nisita, C., Maremmani, I., & Cassano, G. B. (1988). Relationship between panic disorder and separation anxiety with school phobia. *Comprehensive Psychiatry, 29,* 98–107.

Peters, S., Wyatt, G., & Finkelhor, D. (1986). Prevalence. In D. Finkelhor & Associates (Eds.), *A sourcebook on child sexual abuse* (pp. 15–59). Beverly Hills: Sage Inc.

Pike, K. M. (1998). Long-term course of anorexia nervosa: Response, relapse, remission, and recovery. *Clinical Psychology Review, 18,* 447–475.

Pipher, M. (1995). *Reviving Ophelia.* New York: Ballantine.

Plakun, E. M. (1991). Prediction of outcome in borderline personality disorder. *Journal of Personality Disorders, 5*(2), 93–101.

Powell, J. (1989). Personal integration: Blending transition, learning and relationships. In P. Echerd & A. Arathoon (Eds.), *Planning for MK nurture.* Pasadena, CA: William Carey Library.

Rabian, B., & Silverman, W. K. (2000). Anxiety disorders. In M. Hersen & R. T. Ammerman (Eds.), *Advanced abnormal child psychology* (2nd ed.), (pp. 271–289). Mahwah, NJ: Lawrence Erlbaum.

Renken, B., Egeland, B., Marvinney, D., Mangelsdorf, S., & Sroufe, L. A. (1989). Early childhood antecedents of aggression and passive-withdrawal in early elementary school. *Journal of Personality, 57,* 257–281.

Rodin, J., Striegel-Moore, R. H., & Silberstein, L. R. (1990). Vulnerability and resilience in the age of eating disorders: Risk and protective factors for bulimia nervosa. In J. Rolf, A. S. Masten, D. Cicchetti, K. H. Nuechterlein, & S. Weintraub (Eds.), *Risk and protective factors in the development of psychopathology* (pp. 361–383). Cambridge: Cambridge University Press.

Rogers, C. (1951). *Client-centered therapy.* Boston: Houghton-Mifflin.

Root, M. P. P. (1990). Disordered eating in women of color. *Sex Roles, 22,* 525–536.

Russell, D. (1986). *The secret trauma: Incest in the lives of girls & women.* New York: Basic Books.

Rutter, M. (1985). Family and school influence on behavioral development. *Journal of Child Psychology and Psychiatry, 26,* 349–368.

Rutter, M. (1990). Psychosocial resilience and protective mechanisms. In J. Rolf, A. S. Masten, D. Cicchetti, K. H. Neuchterlein, & S. Weintraub (Eds.), *Risk and protective factors in the development of psychopathology* (pp. 181–214). Cambridge: Cambridge University Press.

Rutter, M., & Garmezy, N. (1983). Developmental psychopathology. In P. H. Mussen (Ed.), *Handbook of child psychology (Vol. 4: Socialization, personality & social development),* (pp. 775–911). New York: Wiley.

Schachar, R., & Tannock, R. (1993). Childhood hyperactivity and psychostimulants: A review of extended treatment studies. *Journal of Child & Adolescent Psychopharmacology, 3,* 81–97.

Schaefer, C. E., Johnson, L., & Wherry, J. N. (1982). *Group therapies for children and youth.* San Francisco, CA: Jossey-Bass.

Schafran, L. (1995, August 26). Rape is still underreported. *The New York Times,* p. A19.

Schiffer, M. (1984). *Children's group therapy.* New York: Free Press.

Schwartz, R. C., Barrett, M. J., & Saba, G. (1984). Family therapy for bulimia. In D. M. Garner & P. E. Garfinkel (Eds.), *Handbook of psychotherapy for anorexia nervosa and bulimia* (pp. 280–307). New York: Guilford.

Sexton, T., & Whiston, S. (1994). The status of the counseling relationship: An empirical review, theoretical implications, and research directions. *The Counseling Psychologist, 22*(1), 6–78.

Sexual Assault Support Services. (1993). *Annual Report 1991–1993,* Eugene, Oregon.

Shaffer, D. (1994). Attention deficit hyperactivity disorder in adults. *American Journal of Psychiatry, 151,* 633–638.

Shaw, D. S., Vondra, J. I., Hommerding, K. D., Keenana, K., & Dunn, J. (1994). Chronic family adversity and early child behavior problems: A longitudinal study of low income families. *Journal of Child Psychology and Psychiatry, 35,* 1109–1122.

Shotland, R. L., & Goodstein, L. (1983). Just because she doesn't want to doesn't mean it's rape: An experimentally based causal model of the perception of rape in a dating situation. *Social Psychology Quarterly, 46,* 220–232.

Simons, R. L. (1996). The effect of divorce on adult and child adjustment. In R. L. Simons & Associates (Eds.), *Understanding differences between divorced and intact families: Stress, interaction, and child outcome* (pp. 3–20). Thousand Oaks, CA: Sage.

Smedes, L. B. (l984). *Forgive and forget: Healing the hurts we don't deserve.* San Francisco: Harper and Row.

Snyder, C. R., Ilardi, S., Michael, S. T., & Cheavens, J. (2000). In C. R. Snyder & R. E. Ingram (Eds.), *Handbook of psychological change: Psychotherapy processes & practices for the 21st century.* (pp. 128–150). New York: Wiley.

Soloff, P. H., Lis, J. A., Kelly, T., Corneliys, J., & Ulrich, R. (1994). Risk factors for suicidal behavior in borderline personality disorder. *American Journal of Psychiatry, 151*(9), 1316–1323.

Sperling, M. (1982). *The major neuroses & behavior disorders in children* (pp. 1–41; 127–172). New York: Jason Aronson, Inc.

Spoont, M. R. (1996). Emotional instability. In C. G. Costello (Ed.), *Personality characteristics of the personality disordered.* New York: Wiley.

Steiner-Adair, C. (1991). New maps of development, new models of therapy: The psychology of women and the treatment of eating disorders. In C. L. Johnson (Ed.), *Psychodynamic treatment of anorexia nervosa and bulimia* (pp. 225–244). New York: Guilford.

Stoiber-Callan, K., & Kratochwill, R. (Eds.). *Handbook of group intervention for children and families.* Needham Heights, MA: Allyn and Bacon, Inc.

Stolorow, R., (2000). *Psychoanalytic treatment: An intersubjective approach.* Hillsdale, NJ: The Analytic Press.

Stolorow, R., Brandchafti, G., & Atwood, G. (1995). *The intersubjective perspective.* Northvale, NJ: Jason Aronson.

Stricker, G., & Gold, J. R. (1996). Psychotherapy intergration: An assimilative psychodynamic approach. *Clinical Psychology: Science & Practice, 3,* 47–58.

Strupp, H., & Binder, J. (1984). *Psychotherapy in a new key: A guide to time-limited psychotherapy.* New York: Basic Books.

Strupp, H., & Binder, J. (1988). *Time limited dynamic therapy.* New York: Basic Books.

Sue, D. W., & Sue, D. (1999). *Counseling the culturally different: Theory and practice* (3rd ed.). New York: Wiley.

Sue, S. (1977). Community mental health services to minority groups: Some optimism, some pessimism. *American Psychologist, 32,* 616–624.

Sue, S., & Zane, N. (1987). The role of culture and cultural techniques in psychotherapy: A critique and reformulation. *American Psychologist, 42,* 37–45.

Taussig, H. N., & Litrownik, A. J. (1997). Self & other-directed destructive behaviors: Assessment and relationship to type of abuse. *Child Maltreatment, 2,* 172–182.

Taylor, M. H. (1988). Personality development in the children of missionary parents. *The Japan Christian Quarterly, 42,* 42–47.

Taylor Gibbs, J. (1997). African-American adolescents. In J. Taylor Gibbs & L. Nahme Huang (Eds.), *Children of color: Psychological intervention with minority youth* (pp. 148–178). San Francisco: Jossey-Bass.

Teeter, P. A. (1998). *Intervention for ADHA: Treatment in developmental context.* New York: Guilford.

Teyber, E. (2000). *Interpersonal process in psychotherapy: A relational approach* (4th ed.). Pacific Grove: Brooks/Cole.

Teyber, E. (2001). *Helping children cope with divorce.* San Francisco: Jossey Bass.

Teyber, E., & McClure, F. (2000). Therapist variables. In C. R. Snyder & R. E. Ingram (Eds.), *Handbook of psychological change: Psychotherapy processes & practices for the 21st century.* (pp. 62–87) New York: Wiley.

Tonge, B. (1994). Separation anxiety disorder. In T.H. Ollendick, N. J. King, & W. Yule (Eds.), *International handbook of phobic and anxiety disorders in children and adolescents* (pp. 145–168). New York. Plenum.

Trickett, P.K., & McBride-Chang, C. (1995). The developmental impact of different forms of child abuse & neglect. *Developmental Review, 15,* 311–337.

Trupin, E., Forsyth-Stephens, A., & Low, B. (1991). Service needs of severely disturbed children. *American Journal of Public Health, 81,* 975–980.

Tsui, P., & Schultz, G. L. (1985). Failure to report: When psychotherapeutic engagement fails in the treatment of Asian clients. *American Journal of Orthopsychiatry, 55,* 561–569.

Tyra, P. (1993). Older women: Victims of rape. *Journal of Gerontological Nursing, 19,* 7–12.

Tzeng, O. & Schwarzin, H. (1990). Gender and race differences in child sexual abuse correlates. *International Journal of Intercultural Relations, 14,* 135–161.

United States Commission on Civil Rights. (1992). *Civil rights issues facing Asian Americans in the 1990s,* Washington: DC: U.S. Government Printing Office.

U.S. Bureau of the Census. (1992). Marital status and living arrangements: March, 1992 (No. 468, Tables G & 5, *Current Population Reports,* Series P-20). Washington, DC: U.S. Government Printing Office.

U.S. Bureau of the Census. (1992). Studies in marriage and the family: Married couple families with children. In *Current Population Reports* (Series P-23, No. 162). Washington, DC: U.S. Government Printing Office.

U. S. Department of Health and Human Services, Children's Bureau. (1998). *Child maltreatment 1996: Reports from the states to the national child abuse & neglect data system.* Washington, D. C.: U. S. Government Printing Office.

Useem, R. (1993). Third culture kids: Focus of major study. *Newslinks: The Newspaper of International Schools Services.* Princeton, NJ: International Schools Services.

Vinogradov, S., & Yalom, I. D. (1994). Group therapy. In R. E. Hales, S. C. Yudofsky, & J. A. Talbott (Eds.), *The American Psychiatric Press textbook of psychiatry* (2nd ed.). Washington, DC: American Psychiatric Press.

Vizard, E., Monch. E., & Misch, P. (1995). Child and adolescent sex abuse perpetrators: A review of the research literature. *Journal of Child Psychology and Psychiatry, 36,* 731–756.

Wachtel, P. L. (1991). From eclecticism to synthesis: Toward a more seamless psychotherapeutic integration. *Journal of Psychotherapy Integration, 1,* 43–54.

Warshaw, R. (1988). *I never called it rape: The Ms. Report on recognizing, fighting, and surviving date and acquaintance rape.* New York: Harper & Row.

Waters, E., Posada, G., Crowell, J., & Keng-ling, L. (1993). Is attachment theory ready to contribute to our understanding of disruptive behavior problems? Special issue: Toward a developmental perspective on conduct disorder. *Development and Psychopathology, 5,* 215–224.

Weinberger, J. (1995). Common factors aren't so common: The common factors dilemma. *Clinical Psychology: Science & Practice, 2,* 45–69.

Weiss, J. (1993). *How psychotherapy works.* New York: Guilford.

Wekerle, C., & Wolfe, D. A. (1996). Child maltreatment. In E. J. Mash & R. J. Barkley (Eds.), *Child psychopathology* (pp. 492–537). New York: Guilford.

Wenar, C., & Kerig, P. (2000). *Developmental psychopathology: From infancy through adolescence* (4th ed.). New York: McGraw Hill.

Whalen, C., & Henker, B. (1991). Therapies for hyperactive children: Comparisons, combinations, and compromises. *Journal of Consulting & Clinical Psychology, 59,* 126–137.

Wilens, T., Biederman, J., Spencer, T., & Francis, R. (1994). Comorbidity of attention-deficit hyperactivity and psychoactive substance use disorders. *Hospital & Community Psychiatry, 45,* 421–423.

Williams, L. M. (1994). Recall of childhood trauma: A prospective study of women's memories of child sexual abuse. *Journal of Consulting & Clinical Psychology, 62,* 1167–1176.

Wilson, G. T., Heffernan, K., & Black, C. M. (1996). Eating disorders. In E. J. Mash & R. A. Barkley (Eds.), *Child Psychopathology* (pp. 541–571). New York: Guilford.

Wong, H. Z. (1985). Training for mental health service providers to Southeast Asian refugees: Models, strategies, and curricula. In T. C. Owen (Ed.), *Southeast Asian mental health treatment: Prevention, services, training and research* (pp. 345–390). Washington, DC: National Institute of Mental Health.

Wrenn, C. (1985). Afterword: The culturally encapsulated counselor revisited. In P. Pedersen (Ed.), *Handbook of cross-cultural counseling and therapy* (pp. 323–329). Westport, CT: Greenwood Press.

Wyatt, G. (1985). The sexual abuse of Afro American and White American women in childhood. *Child Abuse and Neglect, 9,* 507–519.

Wyatt, G. (1990). The aftermath of child sexual abuse of African American and White American women: The victim's experience. *Journal of Family Violence, 5,* 61–81.

Wyatt, G., & Peters, S. (1986). Issues in the definition of child sexual abuse in prevalence research. *Child Abuse and Neglect, 10,* 231–240.

Yalom, I. D. (1995). *The theory and practice of group psychotherapy* (4th ed.). New York: Basic Books.

Yates, A. (1989). Current perspectives on the eating disorders: History, psychological, and biological aspects. *Journal of Child and Adolescent Psychiatry, 28,* 813–828.

Yoshioka, R. B., Tashima, N., Ichew, M., & Murase, K. (1981). *Mental health services for Pacific/Asian Americans.* San Francisco: Pacific American Mental Health Project.

Zill, N., Morrison, D., & Coiro, M. (1993). Long-term effects of parental divorce on parent-child relationships, adjustment, and achievement in young adulthood. *Journal of Family Psychology, 7,* 1–13.

Zraly, K., & Swift, D. (1990). *Anorexia, bulimia, and compulsive overeating: A practical guide for counselors and families,* New York: Continuum.

ABOUT THE COUNSELORS

David Chavez

David Chavez received his educational training from Harvard and the University of California, Berkeley. He is currently a Professor at California State University, San Bernardino and practices part time in the Inland Empire of California. He has interests in preventative interventions with children, parents, and families, and in cross-cultural research.

Barbara Graf

Barbara Graf received her educational training from Antioch University, Azusa Pacific University, and the California School of Professional Psychology in Southern California. She is the director of Loyola Law School's on-campus Psychological Counseling program and has a private practice where she works with children, adolescents, and adults.

Faith H. McClure

Faith McClure received her educational training from the University of California, Los Angeles. She teaches at California State University, San Bernardino and provides consultation to organizations serving the mental health needs of children. Her clinical and research work focuses on children, families, and adults, with a particular focus on factors that promote resilience in those who have experienced trauma.

Cassandra N. Nichols

Cassandra Nichols received her educational training from California State University, San Bernardino, and Ball State University. She has worked in the public school system, in private practice with children and their families, and at several university counseling centers. Her research and practice interests include group therapy with ethnically diverse children, gender and achievement, and sibling attachment.

John Powell

John Powell received his educational training from the University of Missouri-Columbia. He teaches, provides psychotherapy, and provides clinical supervision at the Michigan State University Counseling Center. His interest include cross-cultural adaptation and the relationship between Christianity and psychology. He frequently provides psychological consultation to overseas missionary organizations.

M. Dawn Terrell

Dawn Terrell received her educational training from Yale University and Michigan State University. She is a Professor at San Francisco State University, and is the Director of the SFSU Psychology Clinic. Her counseling and research interests include eating disorders, substance abuse, and gender identity development. She specializes in counseling with multiethnic adolescents, and conducting assessments with culturally diverse populations.

Edward Teyber

Edward Teyber received his educational training from Michigan State University. He is a Professor and the Director of the Psychology Clinic at California State University, San Bernardino. His counseling and research has focused on the effects of marital and family relations on child adjustment, and on parenting and post-divorce family relationships. He is interested in supervision and training and maintains a clinical practice.

Sandy Tsuneyoshi

Sandy Tsuneyoshi received her educational training from California State University, San Bernardino and Michigan State University. She has counseled in multiple settings including inpatient VA and college counseling center facilities. She is especially interested in counseling issues faced by Asian Americans.

Nancy L. Wolfe

Nancy Wolfe received her educational training from California State University, San Bernardino. She has worked for Planned Parenthood as a Teen Intervention Counselor and as an HIV Counselor. For several years she was the Director of Outreach for the Inland Empire Native American Community and is currently working for the Department of Social Services.

Anthony Zamudio

Tony Zamudio received his educational training from the University of California, Irvine, California State University, San Bernardino, and the University of California, Los Angeles. He is currently the Director of Behavioral Sciences at the USC/California Medical Center Family Practice Residency Program where he teaches and supervises residents and psychology interns. He also has a private practice where he works with families and children.

INDEX